The Long Postwar Peace

Contending Explanations and Projections

The Long Postwar Peace

Contending Explanations and Projections

Charles W. Kegley, Jr., Editor

Pearce Professor of International Relations
University of South Carolina

HarperCollins*Publishers*

Sponsoring Editor: Lauren Silverman
Project Coordination, Text and Cover Design: Sona Blakeslee,
    Carnes-Lachina Publication Services, Inc.
Production: Michael Weinstein
Compositor: Carnes-Lachina Publication Services, Inc.
Printer and Binder: R. R. Donnelley & Sons, Inc.
Cover Printer: New England Book Components

Library of Congress Cataloging-in-Publication Data

The Long postwar peace : contending explanations and
  projections / Charles W. Kegley, Jr., editor

    p.   cm.

  Includes bibliographical references and index.
  ISBN 0-673-46093-2
  1. World politics—1945-   2. Peace. I. Kegley, Charles W.
D843.L617 1991
327.1'7—dc20   90-42159
                                CIP

  91 92 93 9 8 7 6 5 4 3 2

Contents

Preface

In the dark days immediately following the Second World War, the image of bombs exploding and armies marching was deeply imprinted in the minds of people throughout the world. War, worldwide, had become a way of life — part of what seemed customary, almost routine. Few expected any other condition to materialize or last. War appeared more of a perennial than a transitory condition.

As the years passed after World War II, images of war did not fade to become a distant memory; expectations of its resumption remained strong, punctuated by the ominous shadow cast by nuclear-tipped missiles and symbolized by the incipience of a new global arms race.

But now, nearly five decades later, those grim prophecies remain unfulfilled, and visions of an apocalyptic third world war seem somehow less real or warranted. Among the great powers, not a single instance of war has occurred, and with the passage of each year the probability of its onset appears increasingly remote. The period since 1945 arguably represents the longest period of great-power peace since the birth of the modern world system in 1495, when Charles VIII's march to Naples ended the era of Renaissance diplomacy.

What explains this blessed but largely unanticipated "long peace"? It was my good fortune to have been invited by Rutgers University to serve as the first Moses and Annuta Back Peace Scholar during the spring semester, 1989, and in that role to organize a scholarly conference. This question was selected as its theme, and seventeen invited scholars convened at Rutgers April 28-29, 1989, to explore the sources of this long postwar peace. Their interpretations were presented as the inaugural event of Rutgers' newly established Moses and Annuta Back Endowment for International Peace. The conference proved to be an exciting, seminal intellectual event, and from it emanated the revised papers which comprise the chapters contained in this anthology of original essays.

At a time when mass annihilation remains an ever-present possibility, discovery of the processes through which peace can be maintained is an urgent necessity. The insights provided by the contributors take a big step toward that goal. Although definitive answers about the surest means to prevent war remain elusive, these explorations succeed in illuminating the ways in which various factors sustain peace and exposing the deficiencies of many favored remedies to the problem of global security. From these essays policymakers, peace researchers, and students of international affairs generally can gain greater appreciation of alternative paths to enduring great-power peace, as well as the limits to their utility. These adventuresome scholars have given us new ways of looking at world politics. By presenting a plethora of new questions, they have created a new agenda for future research and theorizing. In bringing the paradoxes and puzzles that envelop the process of prolonged peace into relief, the thought-provoking essays will, it is hoped, stimulate others to join their search for the means to prevent the ultimate apocalypse.

Many people made this book possible, and their contributions are gratefully acknowledged. First, Dr. Paul Leath, Provost, and Dr. Barbara Callaway, Associate Provost of the New Brunswick campus of Rutgers University, are to be thanked for inviting me to conceive a theme for the first sponsored symposium of the Moses and Annuta Back Endowment for International Peace and to direct it. The support of The Rutgers University Foundation for the project made its development possible, enhanced in great measure by the generous donation provided by Mr. Nathaniel Back for the establishment of an endowment for the study of international peace at Rutgers. Grants that I subsequently secured from the John D. and Catherine T. MacArthur Foundation and from Scott, Foresman/Little, Brown Publishers also contributed greatly to the success and exciting intellectual exchange that occurred at the conference. For their support I am also very appreciative.

In addition, the advice and professional staff support provided by Dr. James Turner Johnson, Mrs. Connie Burke, Mrs. Henriette Cohen, and Ms. Joyce A. Potter at Rutgers' Office of International Programs made the entire project not only manageable but pleasurable. The assessments, feedback, and assistance provided by senior graduate students at Rutgers University (Paul S. Bonk, Ananda Bikash Roy, Mehdi Khajenouri, and Scott D. Wolfel) and at the University of South Carolina (Steven W. Hook) also contributed substantially to the process by which papers were revised and the conference was managed. Reviews of manuscripts by two referees — Linda P. Brady of The Georgia Institute of Technology and Neil R. Richardson of the University of Wisconsin — proved supportive and constructive. Furthermore, the confidence placed in this project in response to the prospectus for this book by Bruce Nichols of Scott, Foresman/Little, Brown, and the support which Jeff Lachina and Francis Byrne provided for its editing and production, greatly facilitated conversion of the colloquia papers to finished chapters. And finally (but not exhaustively), the intellectual resources of the dedicated scholars who allotted their valuable time to the endeavor made the project the provocative statement it most certainly is. In sum, this anthology is a collective product, made possible by the contributions of many people sharing in common a commitment to the generation of knowledge and a belief in its capacity to create a better world.

I am indebted to all of them, and very appreciative of the vision, enthusiasm, and professionalism which they brought to this project.

Charles W. Kegley, Jr.
15 July 1989

PART ONE

An Introduction to Peace and War in the Nuclear Era

CHAPTER ONE

Explaining Great-Power Peace: The Sources of Prolonged Postwar Stability

Charles W. Kegley, Jr.

The year 1945 left a world devastated by six years of globalized war and petrified by the dawn of the nuclear age. The end of World War II did not reduce insecurities — it ushered into being a period of chronic crisis, as the age of overkill produced an age of instability. Since then, the threat of mass annihilation has been constant and has colored every aspect of world politics. And yet the postwar era has been an era of prolonged great-power peace. Nearly 50 years of both *Danger and Survival* (Bundy, 1988) have elapsed.

Indeed, the period from 1945 to the present comprises the longest period of great-power peace since the birth of the modern world system. Whereas the prolonged peace in the aftermath of the Congress of Vienna (1815-1848) and the Franco-Prussian War (1871-1914) were also comparable European state systems that managed for extended periods to persist without a major war, these earlier protracted peaces have not endured as long as has the present one.

When put in historical perspective, the durable postwar peace is a truly remarkable achievement. Since 1700, it has been estimated that 101,550,000 people have been killed in 471 wars (Sivard, 1987), and that between 1600 and 1945 "no fewer than 29 conflicts involving at least two major powers ... were waged in Europe" (Record, 1988). Against this history, war seems endemic and peace statistically improbable. The persistence of the long peace since 1945, moreover, portends the possibility of a dramatic break with the previous historical pattern of intermittent but increasingly destructive wars, and the promise of continued great-power peace. On the eve of the 1990s optimism began to soar as guns began to fall silent and a worldwide military cooldown appeared to be occurring. It even became fashionable for the first time in forty years to talk seriously about the termination of the Cold War and the advent of what Secretary of State James Baker termed in November 1989 the "post-postwar era."

What has inhibited armed conflict and made it feasible to talk of *The Conquest of War* (Hollins, Powers, and Sommer, 1989)? Is it possible to identify the causes of this protracted peace? It is the purpose of this anthology to address these epistemologically difficult questions.

To service the goals of peace researchers and students of international affairs, this book's approach differs from that conventionally taken. In their shared interest in identifying the keys to the prevention of war, traditionally scholars have studied the steps to past wars (Vasquez, 1987). But, as a consequence of this preoccupation with *The Causes of Wars* (Howard, 1983), investigation of the factors that promote *Stable Peace* (Boulding, 1978) has been neglected.

To rectify this neglect, it is advantageous to examine the "long peace" — a phrase coined by John Lewis Gaddis (1986) to dramatize the existence since 1945 of the virtual absence of great-power war. Exploration of the global conditions that have facilitated the maintenance of durable great-power peace might illuminate the keys to war's prevention in ways which examination of the causes of war does not permit.

This approach to *Why Peace Breaks Out* (Rock, 1989) might be likened to that taken recently in health care. War — an external threat to nations' survival — is analogous to internal threats to individuals' health and life in that it, too, is a disease. To prevent disease, medical science has found it useful to study healthy people for clues to the source of their health — with the result that vast strides have been taken in preventive treatment. Similarly, might not peace research benefit from investigation of the practices prevalent in systems that succeed in avoiding war?

Reflection about the properties that have made for this prolonged postwar peace prompts consideration of the changes and continuities that have transpired to create an environment hospitable to security. In a sense, therefore, a secondary purpose of this book is examination of the general nature of world politics since 1945 and its probable future.

Across the span of nearly a half century of turbulent change in world politics, one constant stands out: "There have been no wars among the 48 wealthiest countries in all that time" (Mueller, 1988a:5). This continuity against a backdrop of dramatic changes exerts pressure for consideration of a number of unorthodox questions.

Many paradoxes surround peace in the nuclear age. Consider the dramatic changes that have occurred alongside continuous great-power peace. Superpower interactions have oscillated between periods of intense hostility and détente; technological advances have rendered weapons increasingly accurate and destructive, and conventional weapons have expanded exponentially and become widely dispersed; economic growth has created unprecedented prosperity, but the gap between rich and poor has widened; a rigidly tight bipolar system has given way to the emergence of a multipolar distribution of military power; the collapse of colonial empires has trebled the number of independent states in the system; and the expansion of international trade, communications, travel, and migration has brought those units into a tightening web of mutual interdependence. Hence, great-power peace has been sustained under widely different circumstances: both friction and harmony, both the concentration and the dispersion of power, both the monopolization of military capabilities and the proliferation of weapons, both the entanglement of nations in binding alliances and the disintegration of bloc structures, both poverty and affluence, and both systemic autarky and systemic interdependence. Clearly, the maintenance of peace cannot be safely attributed confidently to the influence of any of these changes or continuities alone, for peace has persisted under diverse conditions. The conundrum of peace *is* puzzling. Must it be, however, a peace that surpassth all understanding? Let us describe how this book's contributors have approached the challenge of making this peace intelligible, as well as the obstacles they confronted.

THE SCOPE OF THE INQUIRY

No consensus exists regarding the reasons why the great powers have avoided war since 1945. The contributors were asked to evaluate rival propositions and encouraged to propose new interpretations. But regardless of the goal pursued, because each contributor probed the question of *why* this peace has endured, each necessarily cast his analysis in an explanatory mode. Rather than dealing with the relatively less difficult tasks of description or prediction, the contributors instead concentrated on the extraordinarily challenging task of *explanation.*

When social scientists speak of explaining an event or phenomenon, they usually refer to endeavors to uncover the causes that produce it and the factors that influence its variation. To explain the long postwar peace, therefore, involves reaching judgments about the causes of its preservation. Few intellectual tasks could be more difficult than causal inference, for philosophers of science (e.g., Nagel, 1961) generally maintain that it is much easier to describe and to predict than it is to explain. And yet, if compelling explanations can be constructed that isolate a phenomenon's causes, then a basis is provided for making sound predictions. With respect to our topic, when armed with cogent explanations we will then be better equipped to prognosticate whether the postwar peace is likely to persist. Prediction is explanation in the future tense.

But the discovery of cogent explanations is exacerbated by the fact that the long postwar peace has been produced by the simultaneous operation of many interacting causes. The quest for a deterministic interpretation that rests on a single cause is bound to prove futile, for, as these essays show, none alone adequately accounts for and thereby explains the prolonged peace. Because the long postwar peace is the product of multiple causes, single-factor explanations are insufficient. The temptation to search for a single cause has been successfully resisted by the contributing authors, many of whom have subjected such seemingly plausible theories to analysis in order to reveal their deficiencies.

Given the barriers to study of a condition whose causes are rooted in multiple influences, how might explanatory analysis meaningfully proceed? As an initial "plausibility probe" by a team of experts, the many potentially potent sources and dimensions were broken into parts so that their individual impact in the causal equation could be estimated. That is, each scholar isolated a discrete ingredient or cluster of related forces in the overall panoply of causal factors, and subjected its impact to evaluation while holding constant or "black-boxing" those other factors that undoubtedly interacted synergistically with it to promote stability. Each essay presents an assessment of rival propositions about the potential influence (positive or negative) of a particular group of causal factors. This reliance on *ceteris paribus* reasoning, which for the sake of analysis momentarily assumes all other things are equal, reduces the analytic task by making it manageable. By breaking the problem into pieces, the roles performed by discrete factors (such as nuclear weapons, the superpowers' conduct, arms control, international law, alliances, or the shifting distribution of military power) *can* be treated, and that task is intellectually tractable. But this division places the analyst at a great disadvantage because it precludes his or her opportunity to paint a comprehensive picture of the entire causal chain.

This book, therefore, is collectively a series of reflections about the impact of particular correlates of peace. Each assessment rests, necessarily, on a kind of "conjunctural" analysis, in which the association of one or more factors in conjunction with the long postwar peace is probed. The results are best understood more as exercises in hypothesis generation than in hypothesis confirmation, for many of the causal propositions examined are not readily amenable to definitive verification or falsification. Nonetheless, the insights produced about the impact of each portion or variable provide a basis for ultimately developing a composite theory of the ways the individual pieces may have fit together to sustain peace. This sets the stage for the construction of a general theory about the processes through which peace may be extended.

This is another way of saying that much work remains to be done to fully understand how the *March to Armageddon* (Powaski, 1989) might be averted. Nonetheless, the ideas about the underpinnings of sustained peace advanced here heuristically suggest where more conclusive answers might be found. And although closure has not been achieved, understanding has been substantially enlarged. Moreover, by bringing disagreement to the surface about conclusions (and about methodological principles and epistemological problems), appreciation has been expanded of the variety of contending explanations and the obstacles to discovery that exist. Likewise, the questions raised about the choices among alternate paths to peace illuminate the danger of reliance on reassuringly simple solutions which, on closer inspection, may have grave risks associated with them. A safer and saner world is dependent on discovery of safe and sane prescriptions for the creation of that world, and rejection of conventional wisdoms that are more conventional than wise. By revealing the limits to our knowledge, the contributors' assessments provide a foundation from which we might better evaluate whether frequently proposed solutions to the problem of war in actuality pose less promise than peril.

Let us place the book's essays into an organizational framework by introducing them and the themes they address.

INTERNATIONAL STABILITY IN A TIME OF TURMOIL: REFLECTIONS ON THE ROOTS OF A PROTRACTED BUT PRECARIOUS PEACE

The eventful year of 1945 was an historical "turning point" (Oren, 1984). The mushroom cloud of Hiroshima marked the termination of one system and the advent of a new one (Rosecrance, 1963). The irony of world politics is that this fragile new system has unexpectedly produced what became *The Long Peace* (Gaddis, 1987b).

That seminal book placed great emphasis on the diplomatic relations of the United States and the Soviet Union whose policies toward one another and toward all others arguably have been instrumental to this outcome. Appropriately subtitled "Inquiries into the History of the Cold War," Gaddis' book traced the evolution of an embittered superpower relationship from its hostile beginnings, through détente, and toward the potential ascendance in the Gorbachev era of meaningful accommodation. His analysis framed the theoretical basis for asking "How The Cold War Might End" (Gaddis,1987a), and presaged Gorbachev's and Bush's pledge to move "beyond the Cold War."

In popularizing the existence of an unanticipated development, Gaddis depicted an outcome directly related only to the superpowers and the other great powers congregated at the apex of the global hierarchy. He did not portray, or attempt to paint a picture of, war and peace in the international system writ large. His account did, however, introduce the puzzle and provoke interest in understanding the diverse elements that have constrained the great powers' use of force against one another. In exploring the systemic constraints that enveloped the great powers' activities, Gaddis paved the way for a more comprehensive examination of the wellsprings of postwar stability. It is from that legacy that the inquiries that follow originate.

We begin with the question of the most accurate way of describing the postwar international environment, whose characteristics shape in fundamental ways the probability of war within it (Kegley and McGowan, 1979).

Characterizing the Unquiet Peace of the Postwar Period

When we speak of the long postwar peace, we employ a great misnomer and run the risk of misrepresenting reality, for since 1945 only the great powers have avoided war, and, at that, only against each other. The long postwar peace appears more accurately to have been a "long war" if the entire system and not just great-power interactions are made the object of observation. Since 1945 a stable great-power tier has emerged alongside a highly unstable Third World one, so that from the perspective of most countries *The Coming End of War* (Levi, 1981) is not in sight, whereas *The End of World Order* (Falk, 1983) is. Although we can observe "the complete absence since 1945 of civil war in the developed world" (Mueller, 1988a), the "internationalization of civil wars" (Raymond and Kegley, 1987) through great-power military intervention has made war a defining feature of the developing world, where since 1945 "there have been 127 wars and 21.8 million war-related deaths" (Sivard, 1989:23). The disappearance of large-scale warfare concomitant with the ascendance of small-scale warfare has produced two systems, a stable "central system" and an unstable "peripheral" system.

Consider the evidence of war's persistence since 1945 provided by Herbert K. Tillema (1989:190-195), as summarized in Figure 1.1. These data show a world experiencing great levels of armed conflict and the frequent use of military force, not peace. This is sobering to those who envision the coming "obsolescence of war" (Weltman, 1974).

Recurrent postwar violence amidst great-power peace underscores the need to refrain from hyperbole in characterizing the present system as a peaceful or stable one. Indeed, it punctuates the importance of accurately describing the attributes of the contemporary global system that may make it different from those of other spans of history. The essays in Part I describe the properties of the post–World War II environment and their impact on the stability that has been maintained in it. In focusing on the constraints imposed by international realities, these evaluations share the perspective of other scholars such as Michael Mandelbaum (1988) who stress the international system's influence on interstate interactions. That is, they are cast at the "systemic" or global "level of analysis" (Singer, 1961).

This approach is pursued incisively by John Lewis Gaddis in "Great Illusions, the Long Peace, and the Future of the International System." In it he moves beyond the historical explanations he advanced in *The Long Peace* to review five general explanatory frameworks, or paradigms, at this macro level, which are often referred to to account for the long peace since 1945: (1) a "nuclear peace," (2) bipolarity, (3) hegemonic stability, (4) environmental change, and (5) long cycles. His comparison of these competing theories is provided not so much for the purpose of evaluating their historical accuracy as to evaluate the extent to which

Figure 1.1
Occurrence of War, 1945-1985

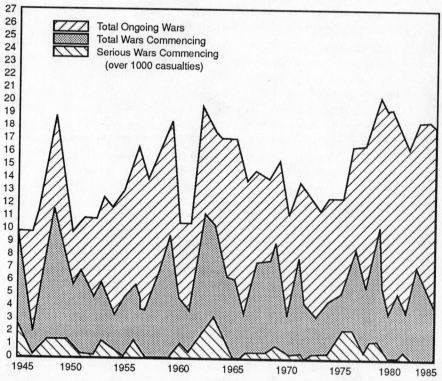

SOURCE: Adapted from data collected by Tillema (1989).

they either reinforce or contradict each other. That exercise, in turn, provides the basis for making predictions about the international system's future. His engaging assessment of theoretical approaches to understanding world politics incorporates a number of intriguing propositions, including a disarming challenge to the common assumption of sustained postwar bipolarity and the hypotheses that the Soviet Union has in effect legitimized U.S. hegemony and that bipolarity reduces the odds of major-power war.

None of these paradigms succeed, in Gaddis' view, in isolating the necessary or sufficient conditions for sustained peace, and each is somewhat incompatible with the others (so that each paradigm undermines the cogency of the others). Nevertheless, they each advance valuable hypotheses as to why "self-deterrence" was practiced by the great powers and make predictions about the likelihood that that peace will endure.

Another interpretation of systemic attributes and their impact on the maintenance of great-power peace is provided by J. David Singer in "Peace in the Global System: Displacement, Interregnum, or Transformation?" Observing changes in global warfare since the Congress of Vienna, and thereby comparing the nuclear to the prenuclear period of 1816-1945, Singer summarizes the changing incidence, magnitude, and level of participation of states in interstate war. He extracts three themes: (1) the displacement or disappearance of war among the industrialized states of the northern hemisphere; (2) the potentially temporary nature of this great-power peace; and (3) whether the historic patterns of warfare might be transformed.

As a complement to the five theoretical foci identified by Gaddis, Singer considers thirteen different possible explanations of the complete absence of war since 1945 between any pair of great powers. But none of these explanations, by themselves, are classified as complete or satisfactory; and the validity of each is seen as dependent upon the ways a large number of intervening factors interact. Nonetheless, they provide a basis for making "contingent forecasts." From them, Singer pessimistically predicts that "the spectre of World War III . . . is by no means behind us." The globally dangerous behavior of elites in both East and West is a source of misunderstanding and conflict, as is the belief that weapons preparations can be used to change others' behavior.

The character of contemporary world politics is examined from still another angle by Michael Brecher and Jonathan Wilkenfeld in "International Crises and Global Instability: The Myth of the 'Long Peace'." Their evidence documents the extent to which the tense postwar era has been *Between War and Peace* (Lebow, 1981) almost continuously. Although the capacity of the great powers to manage crises may through experience have improved (Hermann, 1988), crisis management may be "a dangerous illusion" (Lebow, 1987b) because "the pressures for confrontation" and the "temptations to conflict" may prove irresistible. The disturbing incidence of situations at the brink of war does not inspire confidence that crisis stability will continue or that other states will develop crisis management skills commensurate with their growing war-making capabilities. It is mistaken to dismiss war as an aberration.

Equally disturbingly, Brecher and Wilkenfeld argue that empirical and conceptual flaws are embedded in the "long peace" perspective, including "the remarkable indifference to all interstate relations among the 157 states which are not members of the superpower club," "its 'blind eye' to the 18 interstate and 12 extrasystemic wars from 1945 to 1980 . . . and the 151 international crises from June 1945 to the end of 1985," and "the narrow scope of the Gaddis definition of peace . . . which excludes proxy wars and 'near-miss' direct superpower military hostilities." Brecher and Wilkenfeld find Gaddis' "globalist" orientation misguided because it gives "exclusive attention to the giants, ignoring the pygmies of world politics" and "crisis-generated instability" and thereby fails to recognize the postwar world's chronic instability and far less sanguine prospects for peace. Placed on the research agenda, therefore, are the relationships between world peace, crises, and instability.

To maintain peace, habits of cooperation between rivals are obviously critical. How then are they developed? In "International Structure and the Learning of Cooperation: The Postwar Experience," Manus I. Midlarsky constructs a structural explanation that asks us to visualize the particular structural configuration of the postwar as an information system. In such a hierarchical equilibrium, two forms of redundancy reduce the system's entropy or uncertainty. The first of these — a context-dependent form of a hierarchical equilibrium — serves as a learning device, while the second, a context-free redundancy, acts to reinforce the learning process of the first. No previous international system's structure has possessed these two properties. Collectively, these feedback mechanisms suggest the fundamental importance of psychocultural factors in contributing to the macro-learning on which future peace is predicated. Moreover, his comparison of the postwar structure with an earlier one of a similar type in nineteenth-century central Europe reveals the operation of additional stabilizing elements in the post-1945 system.

As Midlarsky demonstrates, incentives for avoidance of war created by the postwar distribution of power contributed to the growth of habits of cooperation and the development of agreement on tacit rules for a "code of sanity." This progress came through a gradual trial-and-error learning process (George, 1986) from which emerged the rudiments of a "security regime" (Jervis, 1982) in circumstances that positioned the superpowers in rivalry. Its rules suggest that peace depends on the maintenance of boundaries if not barriers between states, and advances important policy principles for the extending of great-power peace. However, Third World conflicts, Midlarsky's model warns, may not benefit from these learning processes, so that far less stability than heretofore experienced might result. Hence, like Brecher and Wilkenfeld, Midlarsky's analysis also points to the possibility that turmoil on the periphery may yet lead to another global catastrophe.

The Impact of the Great Powers' Evolving Relationships

Instead of looking for the sources of the long postwar peace in the attributes of the postwar system, as is the primary point of departure of the essays in Part II, analysis can focus directly on the intentions and practices of the great powers. The essays in Part III probe the question from that perspective.

The competition waged by the United States and the Soviet Union is inspected by Lloyd C. Gardner in "Old Wine in New Bottles: How the Cold War Became the Long Peace." In it he examines American policymakers' perceptions during the Cold War's gestation period between 1945 and 1950 of the best way to preserve world order. This "from the inside, looking out" in contrast to the view "from the outside, looking in" approach to understanding the foundations of peace asks us to contemplate what decision makers do when they make foreign policy decisions (Anderson, 1987) by "opening the black box" and exploring "cognitive processing" in foreign policy decision making (Powell, Purkitt, and Dyson, 1987). It shifts attention from macro processes governing the dynamics of reciprocated interaction between states to policymakers and the tacit rules of the "decision regime" (Kegley, 1987) on which they relied.

Gardner's "thick description" (Geertz, 1973) of the thinking of American policymakers who were *Present at the Creation* (Acheson, 1969) of the Cold War reveals that the concepts usually conceived as core components of their thinking, such as "deterrence" and "polarity," did not figure prominently in their considerations about how to insure stability. Preoccupied with defining the nature of the "communist" threat and developing a strategy to combat it, American leaders thought primarily in geostrategic terms. Their expectation of another general war was very low, but expectation of conflict high. This worldview, Gardner maintains, led the United States to become deeply involved in the internal politics of both European nations and later those of the Third World, and provided the intellectual basis for the Truman Doctrine, NATO, and acceptance of a protracted contest with the Soviet Union for the purpose not of meeting an anticipated military threat so much as to bolster the West psychologically and economically. Each superpower's impulse to enlarge the contest, his arresting, non-conventional thesis implies, globalized the competition by involving others and institutionalized hostility, so as to make the Cold War a *Peace Impossible — War Unlikely* (Nogee and Spanier, 1988) situation. Gardner's account suggests the inherent fragility of relations inspired by fears and questionable premises.

In "Long Cycles, Hegemonic Transitions, and the Long Peace," Jack S. Levy assesses the consequences that might result from the decay of power by the United States and the Soviet Union. Levy brings into focus a message which five centuries of world politics suggest to many theorists: when the hegemonic status of a world leader has been stable, a fragile status quo has materialized; but when the position of world leaders has eroded and power has become dispersed among rival contenders for hegemony, a spasm of instability and carnage characteristically has followed. This outcome is predicted and explained by long cycle theory (e.g., Modelski, 1978; Goldstein, 1988; Thompson, 1988) and hegemonic stability theory (e.g., Gilpin, 1981; Keohane, 1980 and 1989). These theoretical foci center on the question of whether imperial powers imperil or protect peace.

Long cycle and hegemonic stability theory suggest that change in power differentials between states is inevitable, and *Change Without War* (Buchan, 1974) improbable. According to these theories' prognoses, economic and military rivalries amidst the inevitable diffusion of power are destabilizing. Hegemonic decline is dangerous: "It is not altogether clear . . . that a drastic weakening of Soviet power [for example] would add to the chances of peace. As with the Habsburg Empire in 1914, decision makers may be driven into acts of desperation that bring down the entire edifice" (Kennedy, 1988:79). As another observer summarized the conclusions suggested by these theories,

> ... there is every reason to believe that the world of the 1990s will be less predictable and in many ways more unstable than the world of the last several decades. The need, then, is all the greater for a global leader to protect peace and prosperity. .... It is rather basic. So long as there were only two great powers, like two big battleships clumsily but cautiously circling each other, confrontations — or accidents — were easier to avoid. Now, with the global lake more crowded with ships of various sizes, fueled by different ambitions and piloted with differing degrees of navigational skill, the odds of collisions become far greater. (House, 1989:A1)

But this prophecy is meaningful only if the assumptions upon which predictions are made are valid. These theories have a great many limitations, as Levy's lucid critique of their logical coherence and historical validity show. Principal among their deficiencies is their failure to give adequate attention to long-term secular trends, such as the increases in the destructiveness of weapons and warfare. A better and potentially more optimistic outcome may be anticipated, Levy contends, if observers focus less on cycles of hegemony and prosperity and consider the potential capacity of the continuous incremental linear growth of other factors (e.g., world population, economic expansion) to overwhelm these cyclical processes, and, possibly, break the long-term tendency for a general war to erupt periodically. Equally important to Levy is coming to terms with the strategic calculations and psychological influences on decision making in crisis situations when "(1) decision makers perceive that war is inevitable, (2) incremental escalation toward an undesirable outcome becomes a rational act, (3) preemption comes to be seen as a viable option, and (4) psychological dynamics further fuel these rational escalation processes."

The precarious superpower relationship is examined from yet another perspective by Morris J. Blachman and Donald J. Puchala in "When Empires Meet: The 'Long Peace' in Long-Term Perspective." Imaginatively departing from a state-centric conception, they argue that the U.S.-Soviet relationship is not international but interimperial, and that it is reasonable to classify both the United States and the Soviet Union as "empires" whose coexistence can be accounted for by the practices engaged in by previous empires. Historically, imperial powers which have succeeded in establishing empires have tended to be satisfied, status quo states with few incentives for risking the loss of their privileged position by further expansion through direct warfare with other empires. Hence, when empires meet they invariably have become rivals, but rarely combatants.

Looked upon analogously as the most recent period of competition between great empires, the long postwar peace is neither very extraordinary nor especially difficult to explain. Typical behaviors during previous periods of empire rivalries include (1) the avoidance of direct conflict between imperial core states, (2) incessant conflict in geographic regions where empires meet, (3) frequent contests over unincorporated domains, and (4) competition through support of client states' wars. It is also the case that imperial core states characteristically have devoted most of their attention to intra-imperial affairs or dealings with their client states; these dealings have centered on keeping compliant elites in power in peripheral states or otherwise containing deviance and rebellions against core-state suzerainty. Blachman and Puchala show that all of these practices apply to the United States and the Soviet Union over the last four decades, but with the caveat that both intra- and interempire relations have been constantly perceived in Washington and Moscow as continuous aspects of a single global contest for supremacy.

Because "great empires do not fragment very rapidly," Blachman and Puchala predict that intra-empire concerns are likely to continue to preoccupy the United States and Soviet Union while "core-to-core" confrontations become increasingly unlikely. Historically, empires do not collapse in the heat of interempire clashes; rather, as the dizzying pace of change sweeping Eastern Europe and the Soviet Union in 1989 and 1990 suggests, empires tend to deteriorate from internal pressures as stability becomes harder to maintain within each empire's diffused spheres of influence. As a consequence, uneasy coexistence is likely to persist, and a rapid rupture of the postwar superpower peace is not to be expected.

The Influence of Nuclear Weapons: A Nuclear Peace?

Of the many contending explanations of the sources of postwar peace, none enjoys greater support than the belief that modern weapons' annihilating capabilities have prevented their use. As President Eisenhower framed it:

> When we get to the point, as one day we will, that both sides know that in any outbreak of hostilities, regardless of the element of surprise, destruction will be both reciprocal and complete, possibly we will have enough sense to meet at the conference table with the understanding that the era of armament has ended and that the human race must conform its action to this truth or die.

If nuclear weapons are, as Eisenhower maintained, an unusable abomination, then the next logical question becomes whether "Living under the shadow of Hiroshima has engendered caution, which in turn has made for great-power stability and peace" (Kennedy, 1988:77). The essays in Part IV focus on this question.

The conventional view on this theory was expressed by Winston Churchill in 1953 when he speculated that "the annihilating character of [nuclear weapons] may bring an utterly unforeseeable security to mankind. . . . It may be that when the advance of destructive weapons enables everyone to kill anybody else no one will want to kill anyone at all." As he elaborated in 1955, "After a certain point has passed, it may be said, the worse things get the better. . . . Then it may be that we shall, by a process of sublime irony, have reached a stage in this story where safety will be the sturdy child of terror, and survival the twin brother of annihilation."

Ideas have consequences. From this belief has emerged the strategies of the great powers for avoiding war:

> The realization that nuclear weapons have enormously increased the capacity of nations to destroy each other is the cornerstone used to build classical nuclear deterrence theory. With incontrovertible logic, the rising spector of nuclear devastation is linked to the preservation of peace. The very essence of this highly structured argument is that, as the likelihood of virtual extermination increases, the probability that serious disputes will be resolved by nuclear war becomes exceedingly small. The terror created by the threat of nuclear devastation is, therefore, the key to preventing the recurrence of major war. (Kugler, 1984:470)

From this *Deadly Logic* (Green, 1966) derives the conclusion that ". . . any assessment of deterrence will be hard-put not to acknowledge that in a world of widespread nuclear knowledge and at least six nuclear powers, deterrence has been a significant factor in preventing the use of nuclear weapons" (National Conference of Catholic Bishops, 1989:69). But these same proponents also are quick to acknowledge that the policy of nuclear deterrence may not be a stable long-term method for keeping the peace. The question requires a causal inference that resists a definitive answer:

> Deterrence seems to have worked for [over] forty years. Pro-deterrence strategists make too much and the antinuclear critics make too little of the absence of any war between the superpowers for the past four decades. The simple form of the pronuclear argument begs the difficult causal question of ascertaining what would have been the case in the absence of nuclear deterrence, and more important, it also begs the question of why the future should resemble the past. For those who believe that catastrophic failure is inevitable, it is no answer to say simply that deterrence has worked in the past.
>
> At the same time, the argument that deterrence has worked is not without merit. [More than] four decades without war among the great powers is a remarkable period of peace in modern Western history. (The

record is forty-three years between 1871 and 1914.) There is good reason
to believe that nuclear weapons contributed to the prudence that kept
leaders out of war during the past forty years. (Nye, 1989:81-82)

John Vasquez critically examines the issues in this debate in "The
Deterrence Myth: Nuclear Weapons and the Prevention of Nuclear War."
Instead of exploring the unanswerable question of the consequences that
would have resulted if reliance on deterrence had been abandoned, Vasquez focuses on Western policymakers' assumptions about the efficacy of
deterrence and their corollary belief that "MAD is the moral position"
(Kattenburg, 1985). To his mind, nuclear deterrence and mutual assured
destruction are cures in search of a disease, a set of mythical assumptions
comprising little more than folklore. Deterrence through nuclear weapons
and targeting doctrines has not kept the peace and prevented Soviet
aggressive expansionism, Vasquez maintains, because the Soviet Union
never had an appetite for world conquest in the first place. In addition,
the image of the rival blocs eagerly poised to attack each other at the
first sign of weakness is flawed because neither superpower has directly
threatened to attack each other's territory and nuclear weapons were
primarily developed for defensive purposes.

Vasquez shows that the presence of a nuclear deterrent has been
coincidental with several factors that have played a major role in preventing a Soviet-American war. These include the absence of a superpower dispute involving contiguous territory, tolerance of the status quo,
the creation of rules for the competition, effective crisis management,
and successful arms control. It is not nuclear weapons that deter bipolar
war, he concludes, but rather the prospect of total war (even if fought
with conventional arms).

Hence, Vasquez adamantly rejects the prevailing axiom that by
immeasurably increasing the cost of conflict, nuclear arsenals have prevented massive war. He accepts, instead, the reasoning that "It is true
that there has been no world war since 1945, and it is also true that
nuclear weapons have been developed and deployed in part to deter such
a conflict. It does not follow, however, that it is the weapons that have
prevented the war" (Mueller, 1988a:5), or will deter war *After the Cold
War* (Kegley and Schwab, 1991).

Just as the impact of nuclear weapons and deterrence strategies is
highly debatable, so too is the capacity of armaments generally to prevent
war. The postwar peace has unfolded alongside the vertical and horizontal proliferation of weapons, a massive worldwide arms race, and the
global dispersion of military capabilities through the mounting arms
trade. To many, the militarization of the globe has been medicinal, and
the orthodox prescription "if you want peace, prepare for war" is valid —
preparations for war *have* prevented war.

The almost worshipful (Chernus, 1987) faith placed in the possession
of weapons is criticized by Robert C. Johansen in "Do Preparations for

War Increase or Decrease International Security?" Examining the impact of U.S. military preparations, Johansen discerns no evidence for faith in the conventional belief that weapons have contributed to peace. According to Johansen, it would be more accurate to depict deterrence theory as "the ideological lubricant of the arms race" (Thompson, 1982:13) and recognize that arms competition reduces stability and diminishes the actual security of nations. The arms race produced a *security dilemma* (Herz, 1951; Snyder, 1984), and from it has emerged what has been aptly termed *The War Trap* (Bueno de Mesquita, 1981). "From the paradox that defenselessness decreases the probability of attack [comes] the corresponding wisdom that defensive measures only breed more dangerous countermeasures to nullify them" (Wildavsky, 1989:A16). As he argued elsewhere, "It strains credibility to claim that today's security system is substantially less war-prone than ever before. War may be somewhat less rational than ever, but that does not make war significantly less likely — especially when national security managers emphasize that the key to preventing war is to be willing to fight it, and to express that willingness even though to do so appears to be irrational" (Johansen, 1989:72,74,75). Thus, "the mere passage of [nearly five] decades since 1945 without direct combat between major powers provides little assurance of permanent peace" (Johansen, 1989:74).

Inhibiting War: The Uncertain Contribution of Some Alleged Constraints

Vasquez and Johansen effectively illustrate the difficulties of answering the perhaps unanswerable question "Do Nuclear Weapons Matter?" (Hoffmann, 1989). Merely because five decades of peace have coincided with five decades of nuclear arsenals does not establish that the latter caused the former. Correlation is not causation. The linkage is subject to *disproof*, but we cannot prove it. Hence, the relationship of nuclear weapons to postwar peace must be evaluated more carefully if the necessary and sufficient conditions of prolonged peace are to be discerned.

The essays in Part V broaden the inquiry by assessing the impact of still other factors in the causal equation. Illustrative of other approaches are current efforts to free the globe of nuclear weapons, either through technology (for example, the Strategic Defense Initiative) or, more realistically, through disarmament and/or arms control. The latter path is the subject of Joseph Kruzel's assessment. In "Arms Control, Disarmament, and the Stability of the Postwar Era," Kruzel takes a closer look at the widely held but rarely analyzed belief that arms control and disarmament efforts have contributed substantially to postwar stability. Examining arms agreements since 1945, he observes that not a single superpower *disarmament* agreement has yet to be reached; in contrast, the *arms control* dialogue has been more productive. But if the agreements concluded played a role in preserving strategic stability, they did so, Kruzel contends, by ensuring the retaliatory capabilities of the super-powers — arms control has served primarily to preserve, not eliminate, the balance of terror. Arms control thus reinforced the "existential deter-rence" already provided by large arsenals of nuclear weapons rather than initiating a substitute for reliance on those weapons systems. Accordingly, arms control is described by Kruzel as a marginally useful enterprise.

Acknowledging that the risks posed by nuclear arsenals are unac-ceptably risky, for there are simply too many ways in which a nuclear war could start (Carnesale, et al., 1989), Kruzel warns that expecting too much from arms control could undermine deterrence. He also perceives risks in rapidly reducing strategic arsenals through very "deep cuts," which could undermine restraint by tempting one or the other superpower from a perceived sense of advantage or safety to launch a preemptive first strike. Nuclear weapons, he maintains, induce mutual restraint. Then, too, if taken to their logical resting place, drastic nuclear arms reductions could conceivably create conditions conducive to the great powers' return to their pre-Hiroshima propensity to engage in large-scale conventional wars. Such scenarios raise doubts about an approach that might produce the very outcome that it seeks to avoid.

This limitation does not mean that arms control should be avoided. Arms control can perform several stabilizing functions: "One is [contain-ing] the spread of [nuclear] weapons; the other is the vulnerability and flaws of the command-and-control systems on each side" (Newhouse, 1989:19). Hence, arms control, Kruzel would agree, does have a construc-tive role to play. The real issues are about *Next Moves* (Warner and Ochmanek, 1989) — the arms control measures that can best strengthen the fragile foundations of peace in the next decade.

In addition to arms control, another basic military approach to defense is the option of combining capabilities through alliances with others. Because burden sharing is far less expensive than indigenous arms production and self-reliance, alliance formation is one of the most common occurrences in world politics.

But whether alliances facilitate peace or produce war is debatable. Theorists and statesmen disagree because throughout history alliances have performed *both* functions, sometimes inhibiting wars and at other times making their initiation more tempting. At issue is whether the frantic formation of alliances in the "pactomania" postwar era has con-tributed to the system's security, and whether, as alliance structures decay and crumble (Kegley and Raymond, 1989), an era of peace or war will follow.

In "Alliances and the Preservation of the Postwar Peace: Weighing the Contribution," Charles W. Kegley, Jr., and Gregory A. Raymond conclude that the postwar record provides little support for the direct role often ascribed to alliances in fostering extended deterrence. Instead, that impact is perceived to have been indirect and contingent upon the nature of the alliance commitments embraced by the parties to them. In the postwar era some alliances, such as NATO and Rio Pact associated in the 1940s and 1950s with the "Cold War of Position," have provided focal points around which tacit ground rules for the coordination of expectations have developed. These were simple, recognizable, conspicuous, and unambiguous. On the other hand, those nebulous, ephemeral alliances characteristic of the period after the 1960s associated with the "Cold War of Movement" have been counterproductive, entailing commitments that exceeded capabilities and entrapping the superpowers in some Third World conflicts where, arguably, their vital interests were not at stake. Nonetheless, great-power peace has been preserved under both those different types of alliance systems. This suggests that, on balance, alliances have made only a modest contribution to the preservation of the long postwar peace; logically, if both rigid and ad hoc, fluid alliance systems have existed alongside stable great-power relations, then full credit for the absence of great-power war cannot be assigned to the impact of alliance structures, as many enthusiasts (e.g., Abshire, 1988) and policymakers often argue (as President Bush did in May 1989 when he claimed that "containment worked . . . because our alliances were and are strong").

In addition to alliances, still other institutional elements may be included in an inventory of the factors that have played an important role in the preservation of the long postwar peace. Among them, for example, international organizations have undoubtedly been instrumental. Their capacity to mediate and arbitrate interstate disputes and thereby prevent them from escalating to war, while often criticized, is nonetheless impressive (Haas, 1986). Those who assert that the United Nations and other regional collective security organizations have failed because they have not prevented every war from erupting surely are mistaken, for they were never empowered by their creators to perform that mission. Moreover, there is ample evidence that these organizations have resolved many disputes that had the potential to expand to a major war. That is no small contribution.

Also of interest is the potency of legal institutions to moderate the propensity of states to settle disputes by force. That role is also controversial, for many skeptics perceive international law impotent for the control of force (Hoffmann, 1971). The problematic contribution of legal rules and procedures is examined in "International Norms and the Regulation of War" by James Turner Johnson. The problem of how to assess the role of such norms in creating and sustaining the long peace is approached in three steps: (1) identification of the nature and sources of international norms relating to the restraint of war as interpreted by customary and positive jurisprudence; (2) a theoretical and philosophical examination of the relation of international law to underlying normative substructures and the relation of both to behavior; and (3) some insightful judgments about the relative importance of international norms to the maintenance of peace. Acutely aware of the limits of international law's capacity to prevent war, Professor Johnson demonstrates how law nonetheless *is* relevant, and identifies some of the ways in which legal norms along with other factors have promoted international stability since 1945. Concluding that empirical analysis alone cannot answer the question of the influence of norms on the long postwar peace, he shows how normative considerations and shared values comprise critical components of stable international relations.

In many respects, the three essays in this section share an interest in critically evaluating popular approaches to peace. Each factor treated is representative of many others in the same category of potential tranquilizing influences on or paths to global stability. Moreover, they and a congeries of other factors worthy of examination all center on the larger theoretical question crying for greater scholarly evaluation, namely, what influences impact, and in what ways, on the management of interstate rivalries? The essays presented here suggest the need to expand the exploration in order to broaden understanding about peace and its preservation.

The Problematic Future: Projections and Scenarios

A large number of widely divergent images of the prospects for durable peace are plausible. In Part VI, *The Long Postwar Peace* concludes with two projections, the first of which is optimistic, the second pessimistic.

As postwar economic and political linkages have drawn nations into an ever-increasing web of complex interdependencies, many have assumed that these ties might be the glue that could bond states into peaceful relations. However, other observers have appropriately asked if this growing contact might promote, not cooperation, but conflict (Keohane and Nye, 1989). Both consequences from the advent of a world in which everything that occurs anywhere seems to affect the world everywhere are plausible, given "the paradox that interdependence requires a degree of cooperation, yet reliance on others enhances a state's vulnerability to exploitation" (Kegley and Raymond, 1990). Thus, because conflict tends often to be most intense among neighbors and those in frequent interaction, nations brought together may become, not peaceful, but antagonistic. Although some efforts have been made to test the relationship between interdependence and levels of international cooperation and conflict (e.g., Gasiorowski, 1986), these tests have remained inconclusive and opinions about the association between interdependence and peace are divided.

In "Interdependence and the Simultaneity Puzzle: Notes on the Outbreak of Peace," James N. Rosenau explores the problematic contribution of interdependence to the creation and extension of the long postwar peace. To establish a basis for an estimate, the peace accommodations in some six war-torn situations simultaneously occurring in 1988 are examined. This serves as the focus to empirically clarify the theory that expanding global interdependence will reduce the probability of war. Looking at "the outbreak of peace" on the eve of the twentieth century's last decade, Rosenau explores whether the unprecedented high level of peace was associated with expanding interdependence, so that a causal connection may be operative whose inertial force might presage a new era of stable world affairs. The possibility that that transformation might be occurring was strengthened by the fact that in 1989 "for the first time in 31 years . . . no new conflicts started [and] at least eight wars which were going on in 1988 [appeared] to have ended and three more [were] winding down" (Sivard, 1989:23).

Four propositions are offered in support of this encouraging inference. Whereas the analysis of widening peace does not affirm the propositions, neither does it negate them. It instead suggests a number of good reasons for concluding that the continued growth of global interdependence bodes well for further coordination and cooperation, which in turn bodes well for continued military coexistence. Rosenau shows that growing interdependence works quietly but inexorably like a powerful but unseen hand to create pressures for collaboration, benignly making long-term solutions to common problems possible and necessary. A host of problems preclude unilateral approaches and narrow self-interest because they simply are not susceptible to solution by any one nation, and single-country efforts to regain autonomy or use military force to address economic and political challenges under conditions of mutual dependence and vulnerability are suicidal. As the fate of states becomes increasingly interlocked, the incentives for collaboration far outweigh those to be derived from military aggression. Therein may lie the contextual basis for lasting peace about which humanity has dreamed since antiquity.

This cautiously optimistic assessment and projection is questioned by James Lee Ray in "Threats to Protracted Peace: World Politics According to Murphy." As everyone knows, Murphy's Law asserts that anything that can go wrong eventually will. Looking at the clear signs of hope in contemporary global trends, Professor Ray finds ample reason to suspect that Murphy's Law unfortunately will apply to destroy the confidence in that hope for world peace. To him, the current "long peace" is not so unusual; even longer peaceful periods in the past have created optimism that subsequently proved unwarranted. Like previous "ultimate" weapons, nuclear weapons will not guarantee peace, and we can predict with complete certainty (Avenhaus, et al., 1989) that nuclear weapons will sooner or later be used, partly because continual false alarms, accidents, miscalculations, irrationality and misperceptions may easily trigger wars which no one wants. A third world war is probable, but it is improbable that it will result through a conscious choice.

Professor Ray identifies still other reasons for pessimism. For instance, arms control agreements like the INF treaty and a possible START agreement may erode the military stalement on which peace presumably has depended. Similarly, independence between the super-powers, an important source of stability, may be replaced by a more dangerous interdependence. Gorbachev's reforms could fail, making the Soviet Union a desperate and dangerous state, and economic problems in the West could well bring another Great Depression or a collapse of the growing prosperity that has ameliorated political conflict. Civil wars in the developing world provide numerous arenas for future superpower confrontation. And the threat of these conflicts escalating is exacer-bated by the diffusion of more sophisticated military technology (espe-cially ballistic missiles) to the Third World. Thus, for a variety of reasons, the underpinnings of the long peace are so fragile that its durability is doubtful. Murphy's Law need not always be right for things to go wrong.

So we are left with two divergent scenarios to contemplate. One path leads to a more secure world order, brought together by the tightening bonds of interlocked national fates. The other path, well beaten through the ages, leads to another global war through poverty, accident, or the predatory pursuit of power.

However, humankind's destiny is still in its own hands. We have, individually and collectively, the capacity to chart our future and preserve our common civilization and habitat. The future is not preordained. If we can learn from history, we are not doomed to repeat it. As Carl Sagan observes:

> Our talent, while imperfect, to foresee the future consequences of our present actions and to change our course appropriately is a hallmark of the human species, and one of the chief reasons for our success over the past million years. Our future depends entirely on how quickly and how broadly we can refine this talent. We should plan for and cherish our fragile world. . . . It is nowhere ordained that we must remain in bondage. . . . (Sagan, 1989:335)

PART TWO

Characterizing the Unquiet Peace of the Postwar Period

❀
❀

CHAPTER TWO

Great Illusions, the Long Peace, and the Future of the International System[1]

John Lewis Gaddis

"How do you know that you're not going to wind up like Norman Angell?" The question — polite but pointed — came from a graduate student in a seminar I taught at Princeton in the fall of 1987. *The Long Peace* had just come out and I had inflicted it on my students without waiting for the paperback edition, so I had probably asked for something like this. My answer, at the time, was a historian's cop-out: I had written the book as history, not prophecy; even if the post–World War II great-power system were to break up tomorrow, its record of more than four decades without great-power war would more than justify use of the term *long peace* to characterize it.

But having said that, I was not wholly satisfied with it. A long peace on the verge of breaking up would hardly be as robust an explanation of the past as a long peace whose perpetuation seemed likely: by implication my thesis would stand as good history only to the extent that it anticipated at least the immediate future. I had, it appeared, backed into the business of prophecy without having really intended to.

So I thought I should take my student's question more seriously. What assurance did I have that my treatment of the Soviet-American Cold War as a long peace would not repeat the unfortunate fate of Angell's book, *The Great Illusion*, which had demonstrated so eloquently in 1910 that there could never be a protracted great-power war, only to have its argument proven, in 1914, to have been a great mistake? One easy answer was that Angell (1910) had based his assertion on a single assumption about the international system: that as industrialization progresses, nations become less able to afford the risks and costs of all-out war.[2] Clearly, other forces were shaping world affairs at the time: had Angell been more sensitive to these — and to the possibility that they might cancel out the one he had relied on — then his record as a prophet might have been better, if gloomier.

Because I had intended the long-peace thesis as a historical and not a theoretical explanation of the postwar international system, I had not explicitly specified the assumptions that lay behind it; indeed, in a manner characteristic of historians, I had not really attempted to sort them out in my own mind. But if the issue of "robustness" was to be addressed — which is to say, if I was going to establish why the long peace was not going to turn out to be a "great illusion" — then it seemed worth reconsidering the subject in terms of international relations theory with a view to identifying the conceptual foundations upon which it might rest. Solid foundations, after all, imply durability; shaky ones suggest the need to rebuild or, at a minimum, to rethink.

The difficulty, of course, is that there is no universally accepted theory of international relations. Neorealists clash with neo-Marxists, empiricists with deductivists, quantifiers with nonquantifiers, behavioralists with particularists; nor is there even a consensus as to whether the function of theory should be to describe, prescribe, or proscribe.[3] It is all very bewildering for simple historians, who tend not to attach much importance to theoretical refinement in the first place; and yet the only way a historian can say anything meaningful about the future is to project past patterns forward. That requires generalization — theory, if you will — in some form.

One way historians might solve this problem would be to regard themselves as consumers but not necessarily producers of theories.[4] Consumers select merchandise from a wide variety of sources according to their own utilitarian standards; producers specialize by turning out only commodities for which they believe markets exist. No producer, however ambitious, can hope to satisfy all consumer needs; no consumer would feel obliged to purchase only what a single producer makes.

Why, therefore, should historians not take the view that a single international system exists in reality, and that the theorists' conflicting conceptions of it are simply efforts at characterization from varying perspectives and for different purposes? To "buy into" any single theory is to restrict one's ability to explain the wide range of events with which the historian must deal; but to accept each of them uncritically runs the risk of not being able to explain anything at all, since this field so obviously lacks the synthesis that would show how its theories complement — or are even consistent with — one another. The task of the historian, then — like the role of the consumer in the marketplace — may well be to take from the shelf those theories that help us to understand what happened, to reject those that do not, but to do this without producing the unfortunate side effects that come when incompatible theories, like indigestible commodities, are mixed together.[5]

This "consumerist" approach would strengthen the link between history and theory; but it might also provide a new way to assess prospects for international systemic stability in the future. For if one can show that certain theoretical explanations complement or reinforce each other in accounting for specific historical phenomena, that would suggest what the theorists like to call *overdetermination*, which is to say, redundancy in those mechanisms that support and sustain the system in question. Foundations that combine concrete, steel, and brick are likely to be more durable than those consisting exclusively of any one of those materials. But if theories contradict, negate, or otherwise undermine each other, that may be an indicator of potential, if not actual, instability: the analogy would be living in a flimsy house on a slippery slope with poor drainage in an earthquake zone.

In the essay that follows, I have attempted to apply consumerist criteria to see what theory might suggest about the future of the long peace. In doing so, I have sought to ask the following questions:

1. Does the long-peace thesis depend upon an exclusionary or ecumenical theoretical base? "Paradigm pluralism," I acknowledge, is not always a virtue.[6] But any thesis that bases itself upon a single pattern of events and on the exclusion of others risks an opposite deficiency, which is *underdetermination*: that, it would seem, is what happened to Norman Angell. Redundancy, it is said, enhances deterrence — witness the strategic weapons "triad" — why should it not also fortify arguments?

2. If the long-peace thesis does meet this test of paradigm redundancy, does it then avoid yet another danger with an analogue in realm of strategic weaponry: the possibility that intersecting theories, when applied to a specific problem, might cancel each other out? There could be, after all, such a thing as paradigm fratricide:[7] theories derived from different disciplines or from disparate phenomena might well undercut, and even invalidate, the conclusions each might suggest by itself.

With these tests in mind, I will consider five theories that have been advanced to explain the post-1945 international system: (a) nuclear peace; (b) bipolarity; (c) hegemonic stability; (d) "triumphant" liberalism; and (e) long cycles. I will conclude with some speculations about prospects for sustaining the long peace into the future.

A NUCLEAR PEACE

The most widely accepted explanation for the long postwar peace would be, of course, that nuclear weapons deterred those who might otherwise have sought to upset it. Once this quantum jump in destructive capabilities had become available to both the United States and the Soviet Union, the argument runs, neither was willing to risk the use of force to achieve its objectives in the way that nations had routinely done prior to the end of World War II. Nuclear weapons provided a kind of "crystal ball" into which statesmen could look to see the consequences of war before acting to initiate war: as a result prudence, even wisdom, has shaped the conduct of postwar great-power relations to an unprecedented degree (Waltz, 1979; Waltz, 1981; Mandelbaum, 1981; Carnesale, et al., 1983; Craig and George, 1983; Nye, 1987; Jervis, 1989). The record of "atomic diplomacy" — the use of nuclear threats to achieve specific political objectives — may have been unimpressive; the number of nuclear weapons actually built may far exceed what would have been necessary to achieve the crystal ball effect. But, as the most thoughtful historian of the Soviet-American nuclear relationship has recently concluded: "The imperative of avoiding nuclear war imposes great caution on both governments. . . . What each can do to the other, whoever goes first, is more than enough to stay every hand that does not belong to a madman" (Bundy, 1988:592).[8]

These arguments only *suggest* that nuclear deterrence caused the long peace, however; they do not *confirm* that role (George, Farley, and Dallin, 1988:6-7). It is easy to conceive of other stabilizing mechanisms that may have complemented nuclear weapons in sustaining postwar international stability (Gaddis, 1987b:229-32);[9] nor is the presence of nuclear arsenals any guarantee that systemic collapse cannot occur.[10] It is even possible, as John Mueller has argued, that such weapons have had little or nothing to do with the fact that the Cold War has never become hot: that proponents of "nuclear peace" theories have confused the short-term effects of a new weapons technology with a long-term trend toward the obsolescence of great-power war, and have therefore, by concentrating on trees, missed a forest (Mueller, 1989; Mueller, 1988b; Vasquez, herein).

Mueller's argument is an arresting one, and whether one agrees with it or not — I will return later in this essay to his assertions about the obsolescence of war — it ought to make us think about just how we would *know* that nuclear weapons had played any role at all, much less a decisive one, in stabilizing and perpetuating the long postwar peace. History and politics are not physics and chemistry: we have no convenient procedure for rerunning the experiment, shifting the key variable to see what happens. What we can do, though, is to test the "nuclear peace" theory in three ways, one empirical, one counterfactual, and one deductive:

1. The empirical test would be to specify precisely what evidence it would take to falsify the Mueller thesis, and then look for it in the archives. If one could confirm that nuclear weapons had indeed produced effects that went beyond the deterring prospect of yet another conventional great-power war, then one would be safe in assuming at least some role for them in sustaining postwar international stability. Affirmative answers based on archival evidence to the following questions would, I think, produce that confirmation: (a) Did the advent of nuclear weapons demonstrably alter the assumptions of responsible political leaders regarding the feasibility of war in ways for which we cannot otherwise account? (b) Are there instances of actual superpower behavior which only these altered assumptions can explain?[11]

2. But where one is dealing with an unprecedented phenomenon — and the invention of nuclear weapons was certainly that — empirical research cannot easily show that a pattern of events is at work because there is nothing against which to compare it: there is no "control." When theoretical physicists come up against the limits of empirical investigation, however, they regularly resort to "thought experiments"; I see no reason why historians should not do the same. The contemplation of counterfactuals, an exercise obviously not subject to verification in the same manner as traditional archival research, can nonetheless suggest relationships between variables through the simple method of shifting one or more of them and then speculating carefully about the result. Were we to give greater thought to just what constitutes "careful" speculation in this area, counterfactuals might provide a valuable tool that might help us establish the relationship — or lack of it — between nuclear weapons and the long postwar peace.[12]

3. Both factual and counterfactual evidence, in turn, can be applied deductively to test the impact of behavior upon the structure of the international system. Kenneth Waltz has shown that we cannot evaluate the stability of any relationship between nations without taking into account the structure of the system within which they exist; that does not mean, though, that Waltz is a structural determinist. His theory allows for the possibility that the behavior of units within the system can affect the system itself,[13] and it is just such evidence that one would want to look for in determining the impact of nuclear weapons on international systemic stability. But because that condition does not lend itself to precise empirical measurement, one would have to rely here upon deductive reasoning to show a discernible effect, whether in terms of modifying systemic structure or, alternatively, perpetuating it beyond what one would have expected its "normal" life span to be.

This is not the place to attempt a definitive investigation along any of these three lines, although I will have more to say about deduction in the section that follows. The empirical test will require a major research effort lying well beyond the scope of this essay; nor is it clear what conclusions a sustained exercise in responsible counterfactual thinking might produce, because there has as yet been no such effort.[14] Therefore, for the moment, at least, Mueller's argument raises enough questions about nuclear deterrence to suggest that it has not been the critical component of postwar international stability, and that it may even have been, as he has put it, "essentially irrelevant" to that outcome (Mueller, 1988b). The long-peace thesis cannot rely solely upon assumptions about "nuclear peace" to demonstrate robustness; we must broaden theoretical perspectives if we are to avoid great illusions.

BIPOLARITY

A second theory that could be advanced to account for the long peace has to do with the historic shift in the structure of the international system that is said to have occurred at the end of World War II: the replacement of a "multipolar" with a "bipolar" configuration of power. Conventional wisdom had long held "multipolarity" to be a necessary condition for systemic stability, but as Waltz pointed out in 1979, "international conditions have not conformed to the theorists' stipulations." A balance of power, he insisted, required only two things: "that the [international] order be anarchic and that it be populated by units wishing to survive." Not only could a bipolar balance exist; it would even have certain advantages over a multipolar one, in that the responsibility for systems maintenance would be concentrated, not dispersed; defections from alliances would be tolerable, not catastrophic; and the existence of high stakes would encourage responsibility, not risk-taking. Thus, Waltz noted of the United States and the Soviet Union, "two states, isolationist by tradition, untutored in the ways of international politics, and famed for impulsive behavior, soon showed themselves — not always and everywhere, but always in crucial cases — to be wary, alert, cautious, flexible, and forbearing" (Waltz, 1979:121, 173).

But since the world's experience with bipolarity is limited to the years since 1945,[15] and since those years coincide precisely with the existence of nuclear weapons, it is difficult to determine whether bipolarity in and of itself has created stability, or whether that condition has merely reflected the effects of a nuclear standoff. Waltz himself has been less than clear on this point: "The perennial forces of politics are more important than the new military technology," he argued in 1979, but he also acknowledged that "states armed with nuclear weapons may have stronger incentives to avoid war than states armed conventionally" (Waltz, 1979:173-74, 180-81; Waltz, 1986:327-28). By 1981, he had come to the controversial conclusion that "the slow spread of nuclear weapons will promote peace and reinforce international stability" (Waltz, 1981:28), a position that certainly seemed to imply more of a stabilizing role for nuclear deterrence than for structural bipolarity.

One thing at least is apparent: nuclear weapons had nothing to do with the emergence of bipolarity. That condition grew out of the collapse of multipolarity, a development brought about by the Europeans' general imprudence in disregarding Norman Angell in 1914, and by Adolf Hitler's particular imprudence in declaring war on *both* the Soviet Union and the United States in 1941. Even if nuclear weapons had never been invented, a bipolar structure of international relations would almost certainly have emerged in 1945, and would very likely have lasted for some time.

But would it have survived for four and a half decades? The chief index of power at the time bipolarity developed was conventional military strength, and in that respect the United States and the Soviet Union remain, to this day, among the world's strongest states. The instances in which each has actually used conventional forces, though — Vietnam and Afghanistan are the most obvious examples — have revealed unimpressive results: the *usability* of such force simply is not what it once was. Russians and Americans were also known, at the end of World War II, for their respective ideological appeals; that characteristic of bipolarity too has now passed from the scene, at least to the extent that no one today would rate communism as competitive with capitalism when people have the right to choose between them (Brzezinski, 1989; Heilbroner, 1989). Bipolarity never existed in an economic sense: in that realm power has shifted, during the postwar era, from a unipolar to a largely tripolar configuration involving the United States, Western Europe and Japan, but it is one from which the Russians have, until recently, remained almost entirely apart (Gilpin, 1987a; Francis, 1989).

If one lifts nuclear weapons out of the equation and asks whether bipolarity would still exist, one quickly comes up against what may be the single most convincing argument for their stabilizing effect on the international system: it is difficult to think of anything else that could have sustained a bipolar configuration of power — with all of its structural advantages over multipolarity — for so long beyond the time that a non-nuclear bipolarity could reasonably have been expected to last.

It is not easy to specify just how nuclear weapons have done this, although a plausible hypothesis would be that they create a symbolic form of strength; they have, as McGeorge Bundy has suggested, become the psychological indicator of what it is to be — or to continue as — a great power (Bundy, 1988:502-3).[16] They serve, in this way, much the same function that overseas colonies and expensive battleships once did (Van Creveld, 1989:207), or that subsidized national airlines still do. No one knows with any precision just how a colony or a battleship or an airline will enhance a nation's power; indeed, when subjected to cost-benefit analysis, such symbols often produce greater losses than profits. But accounting techniques rarely discourage nations from seeking the prestige that the possession of symbols brings, and it has largely been the prestige of having nuclear weapons that has led statesmen — at least in states that aspire to great-power status — to insist upon obtaining them.[17] One wonders if it is not that prestige, more than anything else, that has maintained the facade of Soviet and American bipolarity long after its reality has faded; that facade has had, in turn, very real effects in shaping structural stability in the postwar world.

One might raise an objection here, though: if nuclear weapons are so important in enhancing prestige, why have more nations not built them, thus bringing us closer than we now are to a Waltzian proliferated world? Some nations have, of course, but without announcing it, a fact that is, in itself, significant: what is it today that makes nuclear capability, for those nations just achieving it, a condition they are unwilling to admit? Why has there been no new acknowledgment of a nuclear arsenal since the Indians' somewhat embarrassed disclosure in 1974? One answer may be that prestige wears thin once one gets to the point of having six or seven nuclear or near-nuclear powers; another could be the stigma attached, in the eyes of many countries, to actually building such weapons in the first place. What that stigma might arise from is not completely clear, but one possibility is that the very structure of postwar bipolarity, sustained as it has been by nuclear deterrence, is now so firmly rooted as to create a presumption against anyone who might do anything to destabilize it. The additional proliferation of nuclear weapons — Waltz's optimism to the contrary notwithstanding — is seen in the world at large as something that would have just that destabilizing effect, and that fact in itself may deter some potential nuclear powers from becoming actual ones.[18]

It is possible, then, that a curious complementarity — even circularity — exists between the "bipolarity" and "nuclear peace" theories: bipolarity could not have lasted in the absence of nuclear weapons; but nuclear weapons do not spread more widely because of the desire to preserve bipolarity. To the extent that the long-peace thesis depends upon the structural prerequisite of bipolarity and upon the behavioral prerequisite of nuclear deterrence, "paradigm redundancy" would appear to exist; the case for either theory in explaining postwar international stability would be much weaker without the other. But alternative theories might also account for this outcome, and it is to these that I now want to turn.

HEGEMONIC STABILITY

"Hegemonic stability" is a third theoretical explanation that could be cited to explain the durability of the postwar international system, but it is one, at first glance, that appears to have little to do with Soviet-American relations. It evolved from an effort to account for what has been, by historical standards, a remarkably liberal world economic order since 1945; the history of the Cold War has seemed almost irrelevant to it. Nevertheless, "hegemonic stability," "nuclear peace," and "bipolarity" theories reinforce each other in interesting ways; there are potentially fruitful, if mostly unexplored, possibilities for integrating them.

The theory of hegemonic stability presupposes a single dominant power committed to maintain — and capable of maintaining — the rules necessary to the functioning of a "liberal" economic order, which is to say, one based on minimizing barriers to trade and investment throughout the world. It assumes an international environment receptive to such an order: if the hegemon is not to become "illiberal," it must achieve legitimacy through consensus, not intimidation. International economies can function in the absence of such a hegemon, but they will not be liberal in character; and as the history of autocracy amply illustrates, hegemons too can exist without being liberal. But if one is to have the kind of world economy that has existed since 1945 — one characterized by unprecedented flows of commodities and capital across international boundaries — then according to the theory there must have been a "hegemon" to make it possible: "hegemony" is a necessary prerequisite for this particular form of systemic stability.[19]

The United States is said to have played the role of hegemon after World War II by taking the initiative in establishing, through the International Monetary Fund and the General Agreement on Tariffs and Trade, a stabilization of currencies and a reduction in trade barriers on an impressive scale. In doing so, it approximated the achievement of Great Britain after the Napoleonic Wars; it had been the failure to sustain such a system after World War I — because neither Britain nor the United States would assume the necessary responsibilities at the time — that hastened the cataclysm of 1939-1945 (Kindleberger, 1973:28). An important question for the future is whether the international economic system can continue to function on a liberal basis as the authority of the United States to impose and enforce the rules gradually erodes — in part, as a consequence of its very success in creating an environment in which prosperous rivals have arisen (Keohane, 1984:243-47; Calleo, 1987).

But "hegemonic stability" theorists have had little to say about the Soviet Union, or even about the Cold War.[20] It is as if our thinking about the post–World War II international system has proceeded along separate but parallel tracks, never intersecting, and yet aimed toward the same objective, which is accounting for the fact that World War III has not occurred. Does it make sense to keep "hegemonic stability" theory in a separate intellectual compartment from "nuclear peace" and "bipolarity"? What happens if the compartmental barriers are removed, and cross-fertilization is allowed to occur?

Much depends, obviously, on whether one is prepared to accept the possibility of dual hegemons. The concept may be difficult to conceive of in the world economy (Kindleberger, 1973:26-28), but it would be hard to think of world politics in terms of anything other than multiple hegemons: there has not been, at least in modern times, a truly "unipolar" system. Certainly Waltz's concept of "bipolar" stability assumes the existence of dual hegemons; indeed functionally it depends on them. But do geopolitical hegemons perform the same stabilizing roles that economic hegemons do? And can they do this at the same time that they compete with each other, as balance-of-power theory suggests they must?

An economic hegemon stabilizes by providing "collective goods" from which all are eager to benefit but for which few — apart from the hegemon — are willing to pay: the examples of tariff non-discrimination, fixed currencies, and even international security come to mind. As this last example suggests, hegemonic stability can have geopolitical as well as economic implications (Gilpin, 1987b:74-75). But what "collective goods" could dual hegemons provide? An obvious possibility is joint "management" of world affairs in such a way as to avoid the disruption of global war, a service from which all nations would benefit but that only super-powers would be in a position to furnish. Significantly, it is precisely management that Waltz cites as the most important operational reflection of postwar Soviet-American bipolarity: despite recurring crises in their own relations, the two superpowers have so ordered their affairs that they have neither stumbled into another war nor allowed others to upset the international system in which they coexist (Waltz, 1979:194-210; Gilpin, 1981:237).

This pattern of dual hegemonic management has functioned at several levels. Even as they piled up vast quantities of nuclear weapons, Russians and Americans also cooperated — through arms control agreements, the discouragement of proliferation, the exchange of technical information, and a general pattern of cautious behavior in moments of crisis — to lower the risk that any one of those weapons, or those of any other nation, might actually be used. Even as they condemned each other's spheres of influence in Europe, the Middle East, Latin America and East Asia, Moscow and Washington made only half-hearted efforts to "roll back" that influence and at times even cooperated quietly to sustain it: rhetoric to the contrary notwithstanding, it is not at all clear that either side was eager to dismantle the Berlin Wall, or to end the division of Germany, or to work for the reunification of Korea. Certainly the United States and the Soviet Union have cooperated to keep crises initiated by third parties from getting out of hand: the history of Arab-Israeli wars since 1948 can hardly be written without taking into account what both superpowers have done to limit them. And that record of cooperative crisis-management is by no means limited to that part of the world: consider Europe itself, where the effect of Soviet and American hegemonic management has been to suppress long-standing national rivalries on both sides of what used to be the "iron curtain" — rivalries that have, more than once in the past, sparked hegemonic wars.[21]

Such dual hegemonic stability by no means stifles change: one need only compare today's membership in the United Nations General Assembly with that of 1945 to see how much change has occurred under Soviet-American management (Gilpin, 1981:237). But the "managers" do maintain a certain structural integrity, much as a dam in a flood-control project would: a great deal of water is allowed to flow through, but only in carefully regulated amounts. The system accommodates change at one level, even as it resists it at another.

What that implies, then, is a cooperative interest in maintaining the system even as competition proceeds within it. Here, too, hegemonic stability theory would appear to reinforce its "nuclear peace" and "bipolar" counterparts in accounting for the long postwar peace. Political economists have shown that cooperation and competition can coexist in the field of international trade: rivalries can be intense, and yet still take place according to hegemonically imposed — but subsequently widely agreed upon — rules. Indeed, such cooperation may survive the demise of the hegemon that established it: regimes can come to serve in the place of a rule-maker, even in what might appear at first glance to be an anarchic international environment (Keohane, 1984:54-55, 62, 88).[22]

Regime theorists are not entirely comfortable applying their model to the field of international security (Jervis, 1983:173-94; Lipson, 1984:12-18); but if regimes can function in the absence of a single hegemon, then it is difficult to see why they could not operate in the presence of two. Certainly recent developments in game theory show how cooperation can evolve among antagonists, even in anarchic situations; historical case studies have confirmed that such patterns are possible, if not inevitable (Axelrod, 1984; Oye, 1986). Even more recently, analyses of postwar Soviet-American relations have begun to draw on regime theory, with promising results (George, Farley, and Dallin, 1988:13-14; Nye, 1987:371-78). To the extent that these developments grow out of the "hegemonic stability" concept, they confirm the relevance of that approach as yet another way of explaining the long peace.

It would be inaccurate, though, to imply that the Soviet and American hegemons have had equal influence in shaping the world since 1945: they have not. The concept of "legitimacy" as a prerequisite for hegemonic stabilization can help us to understand why this asymmetry has existed. Historians are now coming to understand that potential clients *encouraged* the United States to become a hegemon at the end of World War II: they have even begun using the term "empire by invitation" to characterize what happened (Lundestad, 1986; Ikenberry, 1989). The Soviet bid for postwar influence lacked any comparable quality of legitimacy, and so quickly came up against a condition that creates difficulties for hegemons, which is lack of consent. The problem may be more serious in economic than in political/military affairs, but even in the latter field statesmen eventually learn that influence spread by acquiescence tends to cost less than the other variety, a not insignificant consideration.[23]

Why, though, did the American form of hegemony command such widespread support? Here the tendency of hegemonic stability theorists to neglect politics may have caused them to miss something important, for it is difficult to see what could have legitimized an American hegemonic role so quickly and so thoroughly, both in the world at large and — equally important — within a very recently isolationist United States, if not the widely perceived Soviet threat to the postwar balance of power in Europe and Northeast Asia. Could the United States have even become a hegemon without a good deal of inadvertent help from the Russians? The experience of 1919-39, when Americans had the power to play such a role but lacked the motive, suggests just how important a clear and present danger can be in persuading a nation to take on global economic responsibilities. Nor does it seem likely that those responsibilities could have been as successfully executed in the absence of United States guarantees against Soviet aggression: that is what the European architects of a well-known instrument of American hegemony, the North Atlantic Treaty Organization, had in mind when they first proposed it (Calleo, 1987:34-36).[24]

What all of this implies is not only that hegemonic stability theory has something to offer the student of Soviet-American relations; it also suggests an artificiality in efforts to describe the American hegemonic role without considering what the Russians did to bring it about, and how they have unintentionally helped to sustain it. And that, in turn, points to a more controversial conclusion: that if Russians and Americans in fact have come to function as co-hegemons in managing the postwar international system,[25] then perhaps we should recast hegemonic stability theory to take that dual role into account, broadening its purview from political economy to politics in general. Certainly if one makes this modification, there is nothing in hegemonic stability theory that undercuts — and much that reinforces — theories of nuclear peace and bipolarity; their integration might well bring us closer than we are now to a comprehensive explanation for postwar international stability.

"TRIUMPHANT" LIBERALISM

One difficulty with using structural theories such as bipolarity and hegemonic stability to account for the long postwar peace, though, is that there is a static quality to them. They give little attention to the forces that made stability possible in the first place, and even less to those that might sooner or later undermine it. They help us to understand configurations of power across space, but not across time. A Waltzian systemic analysis would see significant change as having occurred once — in 1945 — and would regard the progression of events prior to that time and after it as relatively unimportant. A "hegemonic stability" theorist, by definition, would be more concerned with what holds a system together than with how it came into being or how it might come apart. But international systems are not immortal: they exist in time as well as in space, and that fact suggests the need to be as sensitive to their evolution and prospects as to their structure (Nye, 1988a:249).[26]

The adaptation of structure to environment is, of course, a fundamental characteristic of living organisms: as continents drift and as climates change, new species arise among plants and animals, which is to say, structures evolve. Why should the same not be true of international systems when confronted with long-term alterations in the political, economic, technological, intellectual, or even moral environment? Like the effects of natural selection, these changes would not be apparent overnight; but they might well be detectable over decades, and certainly over centuries. And they might well be dramatic in character: if white moths could become black in response to a specific historical event —

the advent of the industrial revolution in England and its effect in darkening tree trunks — why should not comparably significant but gradual changes in the social and cultural environment affect international systems?[27]

Consider the shift from religious to secular authority that took place in Europe in the 15th and 16th centuries: the modern state system grew out of that environmental change, but structural theorists pay little attention to how that happened, or to the possibility that future transformations might change the system into something else (Cox, 1986:245; Ruggie, 1986:142-43).[28] Or consider what happened to slavery in the 19th century: the institution had been present since the beginning of recorded time, and yet the climate of legitimacy that sustained it eroded so rapidly as to bring about almost universal abolition within a single lifetime (Mueller, 1989:11-12; Ray, 1989).[29] Or consider the implications, for statecraft, of the communications revolution of the late 19th and early 20th centuries: suddenly it became possible to know instantly what was going on all over the world. One could no longer deal with distant events — precisely because they were distant — in a leisurely and disconnected manner (Kern, 1983:65-70).

Neither the individual behavior of nations nor the structure of international systems are sufficient to account for phenomena like these: they show, rather, that moral, economic, and technological conditions evolve quite independently of behavior and structure, but in such a way as to affect both. Even the words "power" and "influence" — so basic to the realist view of international relations — do not necessarily mean the same things in all cultures, at all times. What this suggests is that Russians and Americans might well develop a common interest in sustaining the long postwar peace, so that behavior would reinforce structure,[30] but environmental changes could still then alter both behavior and structure in ways neither level of analysis would by itself predict.

Are there environmental changes of this magnitude at work today? A surprisingly broad consensus is beginning to develop that there is at least one: it involves nothing less than the emergence, however unexpected and however long delayed, of a democratic political order throughout much of the world. "Something very fundamental has happened," Francis Fukuyama has claimed, in the most influential article of 1989: it is "the total exhaustion of viable systemic alternatives to Western liberalism" (Fukuyama, 1989:3).[31]

This "triumph of liberalism"[32] consensus (it is still too early to call it a theory) appears to rest on three related propositions: that war among the great powers has become unthinkable, that international boundaries are increasingly permeable, and that authoritarian regimes based on command economies are no longer viable.[33] Assuming, for the sake of argument, that these trends are indeed underway, I should like to discuss how each of them might affect the theoretical underpinnings, and therefore the probable future, of the long peace.

The Obsolescence of Great-Power War

John Mueller bases his argument about the "essential irrelevance" of nuclear weapons to postwar systemic stability on the proposition that war itself, at least among great powers, has long been on the way to becoming obsolete. Norman Angell was right all along, Mueller suggests, just ahead of his time. World War I convinced those who participated in it that the costs of war had now far exceeded whatever conceivable benefits it could bring; World War II occurred only because of the irrational actions of a single evil genius — Adolf Hitler — and because a largely isolated Japan had not directly suffered from the 1914-1918 experience. After 1945, no great power could contemplate war without the most painful awareness of its costs: that fact in itself would have ensured a long peace, Mueller believes, even if nuclear weapons had never been invented (Mueller, 1989:60-77, 217-19).

This last conclusion is more categorical than many, myself included, would be prepared to accept.[34] But allowing for the deterrent effect of nuclear weapons does not invalidate Mueller's argument that great-power war is becoming obsolete; indeed, the two propositions powerfully reinforce one another. And surely Mueller is onto something important when he argues that we should not assume the indefinite perpetuation of social institutions, however long their history.[35] "Structural realism" is not well equipped to account for the possibility that as technology makes war more devastating, economics and even morality might combine to make it less likely (Mueller, 1989; Ruggie, 1986:148-52; Ray, 1989:438-39). Nor would it easily explain the rise of something we might call, for want of a more precise term, "world opinion," a constraint that has inhibited the use of nuclear weapons in situations where no realistic prospect of retaliation existed (Gaddis, 1987b:104-46), that has undermined colonial empires more effectively than even the most militant revolutionary ever could have, and that has changed the way in which great powers go about collecting their debts: nobody, these days, sends a gunboat to shell a village (Ray, 1989:431-34).

None of this is to say that war itself is passing from the scene: the recently concluded eight-year Iran-Iraq war, after all, came as close to replicating the experience of World War I trench warfare as anything that has occurred since that time. What seems to be happening, rather, is that the world's most powerful nations are increasingly reluctant to get into wars themselves. Four and a half decades have passed since the last all-out great-power war; Korea was the last conflict in which one great power engaged a quasi-great power; and the corrosive experiences of fighting third parties in Vietnam and Afghanistan have now created powerful presumptions against anyone in either Washington or Moscow who would propose repeating even those "limited war" experiences. The result is that the old liberal dream of "perpetual peace," at least among the great powers, now seems a good deal more plausible than it did when Angell prematurely announced its arrival eight decades ago.

What might the "obsolescence of war" imply for the long peace? To claim anything other than "paradigm redundancy" here would be silly: it normally takes great-power wars to end periods of peace, and if such wars are not to take place, then peace should endure. Certainly the assumption that war between the United States and the Soviet Union is ruled out facilitates their joint management of crises elsewhere in the world. One does wonder, though, just what that capacity for management rests on if great powers cannot ever — or at least hardly ever[36] — use force. Can we rely here on what hegemonic stability theory implies about the "image" of power surviving its actual removal from the scene? Can the great powers retain their management function by employing proxies to do their fighting for them? What if those proxies too come to see war as obsolete?

All of this suggests that we would do well to welcome the obsolescence of great-power war but not the erosion of great-power authority: the trick will be to find ways to sustain that authority — and therefore to allow management to continue — without reversing the trend away from war. And that, in turn, will require greater insight than we now have into the nature of great-power authority itself, and the legitimacy that sustains it.

The Permeability of Borders

Classical "realism" came under criticism during the 1970s for neglecting the emergence of transnational phenomena — chiefly economic in character — that were said to be making the world more "interdependent." The argument here was that balance-of-power theory could not account for regional integration: not only had cooperation emerged under conditions of anarchy, but a whole network of relations had developed, quite apart from traditional military alliances and ideological alignments, that was eroding state authority as it had once been understood.[37]

The difficulty with this theory — as with earlier Marxist predictions about states withering away under communism — was that one never quite seemed to arrive at the promised destination. Interdependence grew apace, but with little evidence of a declining role for states in the world at large. Not are there any imminent indications — even in a Europe poised to establish a true common market — that regional institutions are about to make the domestic functions of states obsolete. "The development of regional integration theory," Joseph S. Nye, Jr., has acknowledged, "outstripped the development of regional communities" (Nye, 1988a:239; Holsti, 1989:26-27). One wonders, therefore, whether we have not got our terms wrong; transnational phenomena are real enough, but "interdependence" — with its implied diminution of state sovereignty — may not be the best way to characterize them.

If there is an environmental force at work here, it is probably not so much interdependence as permeability: the declining ability of states — even as they retain their sovereignty — to keep external influences from crossing their borders, or, for that matter, to keep state secrets from flowing the other way. It used to be possible for nations to wall themselves off from alien cultures, technologies, ideologies, and commerce. But no government today can keep its citizens totally isolated from outside influences.[38] Nor is it easy, these days, for governments to keep secrets: the transparency that comes from satellite reconnaissance has made it difficult to conceal, not only deployments of military forces, but even such setbacks as nuclear accidents, forest fires, and mediocre harvests. Nations may not be that much more dependent upon one another than in the past (Waltz, 1979:141, 151, 168-69); but their borders — whatever the direction of the flow of information across them — are surely more permeable than ever before, and are likely to become more so with the passage of time.

It is not just ideas and objects that penetrate, though; for as improbable as this may seem in an age of sophisticated surveillance, it appears to be more and not less difficult than in the past to keep people from crossing borders against the will of governments. Influxes of undocumented aliens have already altered demographic profiles in Western Europe and in the United States; and the international drug crisis provides powerful evidence that modern technology may favor violators of boundaries more than it does those who patrol them. Nor, as the examples of Vietnam and — more recently — East Germany suggest, is coercion very effective any longer in keeping populations from fleeing political repression and economic stagnation in the first place.

The interesting question is what this implies for international systemic stability. Here there is a striking disconnection between what people believe and what history suggests: it has been and remains almost an article of faith among liberals that the more contact that takes place between states and the people who inhabit them, the less the danger of war.[39] But the historical record suggests the opposite: those nations that have most frequently gone to war with one another have been those that had the most contact with one another (Waltz, 1979:138-39; Gaddis, 1987b:234). Since permeability clearly exists and is probably increasing, the possibilities for "paradigm fratricide" — and for a potential indication of systemic instability — would appear to be present: one would want to know at a minimum what basis we have for believing that this historical pattern of familiarity breeding contempt will not sooner or later repeat itself.[40]

Is there evidence that permeability works on balance either to perpetuate or to undermine the long postwar peace? To the extent that one is talking about transparency, the effect is almost certainly stabilizing: with very little public notice, the advent of satellite reconnaissance has almost ruled out the possibility of surprise attack, a prospect that had accompanied, and contributed to the instability of, all previous arms races (McNeill, 1982:371; Gaddis, 1987b:195-214).[41] Traditional concepts of military secrecy have now eroded so far that both sides regularly discuss how to make each side's weapons *visible* to the other; and with no evident sense of irony our own Air Force introduces supposedly *invisible* weapons like the "stealth" bomber to the world with, quite literally, accompanying fanfares (*New York Times*, November 23, 1988).

Satellite reconnaissance succeeds, though, because it is unobtrusive. Other forms of permeability are more noticeable, and, potentially, less stabilizing. Iran's openness to Western influences under the Shah almost certainly played a major role in his overthrow; more recently the Ayatollah Khomeini demonstrated how permeable other borders — our own not excepted — are to the influences of Islamic fundamentalism.[42] Terrorism, of course, presents even more threatening possibilities for exploiting permeability. The rapid Westernization of China that took place within the past decade almost certainly helped bring about the massacre in Tienanmen Square.[43] Nor does it necessarily follow that a Soviet Union open to American cultural, economic, and intellectual influences would enjoy, as a result, a more cordial relationship with the United States: for with permeability comes the capacity to influence internal developments, or to attempt to; the historical record suggests that if temptation follows, relations are almost certain to suffer (Gaddis, 1990:339-41; 1988:311-13).

The phenomenon of permeability is likely to remain with us, because to reverse it one would have to reverse the technology that has made it possible: mass circulation newspapers and periodicals, radio, television, air travel, satellites, tape cassettes, personal computers, and fax machines, together with the tendency of such innovations, once marketed, to decline dramatically in price. Like the obsolescence of war, permeability provides evidence of evolution in the international environment from whose effects the international system is unlikely to remain immune. Such evolution represents progress in the direction of a more liberal world, to be sure; but it by no means accounts for the long postwar peace. And indeed if one flips the question around to ask what, barring nuclear catastrophe, could undermine that peace, environmental influences of this type — even some that appear at first glance to be benign — tend to stand out. Those who seek signs of systemic instability might do well to begin here.

The Failure of Command Economies

World Wars I and II demonstrated, among many other things, that the liberal world order the British attempted to build through hegemonic stability in the 19th century was not up to the authoritarian rigors of the 20th; even American efforts to resurrect it after the defeat of Germany and Japan ran into another form of authoritarian resistance, directed from Moscow and Beijing. Today, though, barriers to the spread of liberalism that fascism and communism imposed appear at last to have fallen (Fukuyama, 1989:3, 9-14); democratic reform may now be close to a universal prerequisite for economic survival in a postindustrial age.

Autocracy was no impediment to industrialization itself; indeed, the existence of command economies in the Soviet Union and China made it possible to force modernization at rapid rates, albeit at great cost. But the extensive utilization of resources under central direction can only carry an economy so far; sooner or later, it must shift to a more efficient but less centralized form of intensive exploitation if it is to remain competitive in a world market from whose effects not even autarkic regimes can wholly insulate themselves (Starr, 1988:6-8). Here arbitrary rule is likely to impede rather than to encourage progress, for as John A. Hall (1987:119-99; 1985:203-9) has argued, without a free flow of information among those responsible for innovation — and without payoffs in the form of an enhanced quality of life — the process of modernization is almost certain to stagnate. Competitiveness requires openness: in an inversion of the classic Marxian dialectic, bourgeois democracy appears to be the path to the next stage of economic development.

One of the most eloquent spokesmen for that argument is, quite unexpectedly, the current head of the Soviet government: Mikhail Gorbachev has repeatedly and explicitly made clear the linkage between democratization and economic revival.[44] The record of China under Deng Xiaoping prior to June, 1989, demonstrated with equal clarity how political liberalization can spur economic development (Harding, 1987:274-77); events since that time have only confirmed the difficulty of trying to continue modernization while reintroducing repression. And the failures of command economies in Eastern Europe produced nothing short of a revolution there during the last half of 1989, with the entire structure of communist rule in Poland, Hungary, East Germany, Bulgaria, Czechoslovakia, and Rumania having collapsed in dramatic succession by the end of the year.

The relationship between democratization and economic growth is by no means exact: prosperity in South Korea, Taiwan, and Singapore did not evolve under the most scrupulous democratic procedures, and states like South Africa, Chile, and Panama under Noriega have been able to keep their economies functioning even in the face of sanctions provoked by the absence of democracy.[45] The United States itself, where democracy flourishes, has hardly been in the vanguard of economic efficiency or technological advance in recent years. Still — and even taking into account recent events in China — we appear to be witnessing a historic shift away from command economies and repressive politics in states that once proudly invoked Marxism-Leninism to justify those practices. The end of that particular ideology, at least as we have historically known it, may well be upon us, and that development in itself could have important implications for the stability of the long postwar peace.

Unfortunately, it is not at all clear what those implications might be. Michael Doyle has suggested, on the basis of convincing historical evidence, that liberal democracies tend not to fight one another (Doyle, 1983a, 1983b), a view that would appear to reinforce Mueller's "obsolescence of war" thesis. But Doyle's argument by no means excludes the possibility of war between liberal and non-liberal states; certainly no one expects the Soviet Union, China, or other Marxist countries now experimenting with the relaxation of economic controls to reach Western standards of democratization anytime soon. And if liberalization should continue to open the way for unrest in Eastern Europe or the Soviet Union, as it now appears to be doing, the need to reassert internal control could quickly erode cooperation at the international level between Moscow and Washington. One rule by which Soviet-American management has functioned during the long peace has been the mutual toleration of spheres of influence (Gaddis, 1987b:239); the relative silence of both the United States and the Soviet Union on the issue of Tibet suggests that a similar principle has long been at work in relations with China as well. But this has meant tolerating the denial of liberties in certain parts of the world: the price of great-power stability has often been repression.

We would appear to have here considerable potential for paradigm fratricide. For if one accepts the thesis that democratization is necessary for further economic progress, one risks challenging the geopolitical status quo upon which the long peace rests. But without economic reform, the Soviet Union is likely to have only the most tenuous claim to the superpower status that bipolarity requires: that claim will rest on the hollow shell of nuclear deterrence, a frail and potentially dangerous support no one would want to see leaned on too heavily. The crackdown on dissent in China has already undermined what had been, over the past decade, a remarkably cordial Sino-American relationship; just how this latest version of a "new" China is to fit into the international configuration of power is as yet quite unclear. Nor is it evident that a post–Cold War Europe could easily accommodate a reunified Germany, despite the fact that liberalization in the East is now bringing about that once improbable event.

This is one area, then, where the postwar international system is not robust, and where Americans would do well to think about where their own interests lie. For in an irony that a great master of irony, Reinhold Niebuhr, would surely have appreciated, the world probably is becoming more like the United States; but it is not at all clear that the United States will like — or indeed ought to like — the results.

LONG CYCLES

But change in international relations is not simply linear in character. Regression as well as advance occurs; Hitlers happen, even in supposedly enlightened centuries. What if the long postwar peace should turn out to be just one phase of a long historical cycle, one destined, sooner or later, to bring us back to the circumstances of global depression and war out of which the current international system emerged? Then all of our speculation about nuclear deterrence, bipolarity, hegemonic stability and liberalism would be largely irrelevant: we would be like penguins stuck on an ice-floe slowly circling the Antarctic, huffing and puffing at each other, occasionally agreeing with one another, while all the time sub-surface currents of which we know nothing are determining whether we drift south and risk cracking up on the rocks, or north and risk melting, or whether we remain in a precarious condition of homeothermal equilibrium.[46]

There is, of course, nothing new about cyclical views of history (Butterfield, 1981:121-26), although their periodic rediscovery does continue to upset those who too easily assume the capacity of individuals and nations to learn from, and therefore, to avoid repeating, the past.[47] Such theories present special problems of verification, given the absence of any clear consensus among long cyclists on just what it is that does repeat and how we might measure it. When one adds the difficulty of dealing with unreliable sources extending over several centuries, together with the temptation of "massaging" data to fit predetermined conclusions, together with the problem of specifying a convincing causal mechanism for such patterns as do emerge, thereby separating them from statistical quirks and haphazard anomalies[48] — when one considers all of this, it is a wonder that analysts of international relations concern themselves with long cycles at all.

They do so, almost certainly, because the very act of generalizing about phenomena implies cyclicity of a sort: if nothing that happened ever resembled anything else that had happened, history would become a random series of events — an unalphabetized telephone book, if you will — devoid of meaning. The very act of interpretation assumes repetition (Gould, 1987:48-49; Joynt and Rescher, 1961:159). Once one grants this point, though, it is difficult to know where to draw the line: cycles exist for periods as brief as the milliseconds required by a single nerve impulse and as long as the 600 million years or so that it takes for supercontinents to form and then break up (Nance, Worsley, and Moody, 1988). The test for the social scientist (who is obliged to operate somewhere between these extremes) should be that of utility: do cyclical explanations tell us anything that we do not already know?

Not surprisingly, the most arduous efforts to find out have focused on the question of war and peace: it is here that long-cycle theory — at least as applied to the study of international relations[49] — is most fully developed. Although there is disagreement about specific details, the theory sees war on a global scale as taking place roughly every 100 to 150 years. These wars result in the emergence of a single hegemon which, although not necessarily the most powerful nation, is the one best positioned to create and to dominate a worldwide system of international relations. The outcome, at first, tends to be a long peace; in time, though, the rise of other states that have chosen to follow the hegemon's example — together with the hegemon's own exhaustion, bureaucratization, and consequent loss of imagination — creates instabilities that lead eventually to global war and to the emergence of a new hegemon, thereby starting the cycle all over again (Gilpin, 1981:9-15; Goldstein, 1988:15-17; Olson, 1982:36-73; Modelski and Morgan, 1985:391-417).[50]

What drives the cycles? Here cycle theorists are in close agreement: all of them single out uneven rates of economic and technological development as the engine propelling the process. It is, Robert Gilpin writes, "the differential or uneven growth of power among states in a system that encourages efforts . . . to change the system" (Gilpin, 1981:93). Paul Kennedy adds that "the rule seems common to *all* national units, whatever their favored political economy, that uneven rates of economic growth [will], sooner or later, lead to shifts in the world's political and military balances" (Kennedy, 1987:436-37). Joshua Goldstein makes the linkage between economic growth and hegemonic war explicit:

> Countries rebuilding from war incorporate a new generation of technology, eventually allowing competition with the hegemonic country. For these reasons, each period of hegemony gradually erodes. Recurring wars, on several long wave upswings, eventually culminate in a new hegemonic war, bringing another restructuring of the core and a new period of hegemony.

Or, to put it more succinctly, "economic growth generates war and is disrupted by it. Great-power war . . . depends on but undermines prosperity" (Goldstein, 1988:282).[51]

What are we to make of long cycles from the standpoint of the long peace? To what extent is such a paradigm consistent with, or antipathetic to, the others that underlie that thesis? Since long-cycle theory projects no new hegemonic war until, at a minimum, the middle of the 21st century, one is tempted to take refuge in a famous Keynesian proposition about being dead in the long run and leave the matter there. For if there really is an unbreakable cycle that runs regularly from peace through prosperity to depression and war, then all that may be left for us is to chronicle its progress, nodding our heads gloomily at each point along the way.

But what if the cycle itself is not immutable? What if the penguins on the ice-floe can hoist a sail, or rig a rudder? Most long-cycle theorists see the process they describe as having originated with the formation of the European state system around 1500 (Modelski and Morgan, 1985:394; Goldstein, 1988:285; Kennedy, 1987:16-30); if that is so, then the cycle has not always existed, and need not always in the future. Even Gilpin, who sees cycles as reflections of "a recurring struggle for wealth and power" present since the beginning of recorded history, does not regard them as inevitable for all time to come: the advent of nuclear weapons, he writes, has "had a profound effect on the conduct of statecraft." Although it is obviously too early to say that the nuclear revolution has made future hegemonic wars impossible, it is significant that this most pessimistic of long cyclists is not prepared to rule out such a development (Gilpin, 1981:7, 213-19).[52]

If in fact nuclear deterrence can reverse long cycles, or at least bring them to a halt, then its relevance to the preservation of peace and stability would be confirmed in the most striking manner. Unfortunately, long-cycle theory provides no conclusive way to test such a proposition short of waiting for the current cycle to complete itself. Similar difficulties arise in trying to establish whether long cycles are consistent with bipolarity, hegemonic stability, and the "triumph of liberalism." The standard of verification in all of these instances will be simple enough: the absence of hegemonic war for two or more centuries. But it is going to take a while to get the necessary evidence on that point.

That assumes, though, that cycles do not vary in frequency or amplitude. They do all the time, of course, in the physical world, and it is worth considering what the implications of such variations might be in the realm of international politics. Paul Kennedy has pointed out, for example, that during the postwar decades "global productive balances have been altering faster than ever before" (Kennedy, 1987:xx). If hegemonic cycles grow out of uneven rates of economic and technological development, and if that development itself is accelerating,[53] then we should expect to see hegemons being hegemons for shorter and shorter periods of time; the next hegemonic war might be nearer than we think.

But cycles can also vary in amplitude: their effects can increase or diminish over time. Shifting environmental conditions such as the obsolescence of great-power war or the liberalization of autocracies could conceivably dampen hegemonic cycles over time, gradually minimizing their effects. If such a development really is taking place, then it, like the phenomenon of acceleration, ought to be detectable within periods we ourselves can manage: we may not have to depend upon great-grandchildren to confirm the validity of long-cycle theory.

The difficulty, of course, would come in deciding just what one would measure if one were seeking to detect changes in the frequency or the amplitude of long cycles. Statistics can document with precision the economic decline of the United States relative to Japan and Western Europe; the Soviet Union — never an economic superpower to begin with — would be revealed as declining even more rapidly.[54] But other statistics would demonstrate how dependent the Japanese, the West Europeans, and certain Middle Eastern states are on the United States for their military security. One could even discern here the outlines of a bargain, by which Washington would provide security indefinitely to nervous allies, while they in turn would indefinitely finance the resulting American budgetary deficit (Gilpin, 1987:331-34, 379). Still other statistics would show that although the number of nuclear weapons in Soviet and American arsenals has continued to increase, threats to use them have diminished steadily since the 1950s, as have nuclear alerts (Betts, 1987:180-81; Bundy, 1988:584-88). But these are all answers in search of questions: until we have specified what kind of evidence it would take to confirm shifts in long-cycle frequency and amplitude, quantitative approaches alone are not likely to get us very far.

We are left, then, to fall back on impressionistic judgments, which may be the best one can hope to accomplish in this field in any event: certainly there is little in long-cycle theory that would provide any reliable basis for prediction on a day-by-day, or even a decade-by-decade, basis. "No two hegemonic conflicts are alike," Gilpin reminds us. "Thus, although a theory of political change can help explain historical develop- ments, . . . it is no substitute for an examination of both the static and dynamic elements responsible for a particular political change" (Gilpin, 1981:49). But this is only to acknowledge the limits of theory itself. For as Waltz has noted: "Theory explains regularities of behavior and leads one to expect that the outcomes produced by interacting units will fall within specified ranges. The behavior of states and of statesmen, however, is indeterminate" (Waltz, 1979:68).

Long-cycle theory provides only a framework, then, within which to think about the long postwar peace. It does not confirm robustness, anymore than it predicts imminent disaster. But it is a useful way of reminding statesmen that the relevant past extends well beyond what they personally have experienced: cyclicity tends to get people's attention in a way that linearity does not. It suggests our relative insignificance against the sweep of time, and is therefore a good antidote to hubris. If one views cycles as subject to modification, they can provide an incentive to focus on long-term as opposed to short-term considerations, on duties as opposed to pleasures.[55] And, taken together with evidence of environ- mental and even behavioral evolution, long cycles can help us to see that history can be two different things at once: just as physicists view light as having the properties of both particles and waves, just as geologists allow for both pattern and particularity, so historians — and social sci- entists as well — should see that linearity and cyclicity are not fratricidal at all, but rather rewardingly complementary (Gould, 1987; Ruggie, 1978:348-406; Rhodes, 1986:131-32; Talbott, 1988:36).

The Future of the International System

The inability to see that point has had a good deal to do with the long-standing (and much complained about) impoverishment of international security studies. The search for predictable regularities — which is to say, for cyclicity we can count on — has had disappointing results: it is as if events have conspired to frustrate those who have sought anything approaching scientific rigor in this field. But an antithetical focus on linearity, for which my own field of diplomatic history is well known, renders generalization anemic, and so removes most possibilities for learning from history in the first place.

If there is ever to be a "grand unification theory" of international relations — and we are nowhere close to that now — it will have to accommodate both cyclicity and linearity. It will need to recognize that some phenomena recur and some do not; but, even more important, it will have to provide ways of distinguishing between them. To paraphrase the famous "serenity prayer" that Reinhold Niebuhr may, or may not, have originated (Fox, 1985:290-91), we will require the vision to generalize where prediction is possible, the humility to refrain from generalization where it is not, and the wisdom to know the difference. But I see little evidence that either the historians or the theorists have thought very much about how to get to that point: the historians, lacking vision, resist linking their work to theory in the first place, while the theorists, lacking humility, claim such sweeping applicability for their generalizations as to make virtually unrecognizable the history upon which they are based.

As a consequence, it has been left to other disciplines, notably the physical, biological, and mathematical sciences, to do the most interesting thinking on how to distinguish recurring from non-recurring phenomena. These so-called "hard" sciences, once supremely confident about their ability to describe and predict, are today moving in the opposite direction: under the influence of "chaos" theory they are learning to allow for randomness, unpredictability, and what the mathematicians call "non-linearity." The implications for the fields of history and international relations theory — neither of them exactly strangers to chaos — could be quite important.

What this new "science of complexity" shows is that although we can predict some things with precision — the motion of the planets around the sun, for example, or the reaction of certain elements when mixed together under the same conditions — there is another large class of phenomena for which prediction will never be possible, for the simple reason that to build a model capable of simulating subjects of this sort, one would have to replicate the subject itself. We can know with great precision how many thousands of years it will take the Voyager II spacecraft to reach the nearest star because, despite the immense size of the system in question, the number of critical variables at work in it lies well within our computational capabilities. But the most sophisticated weather forecaster has only about a 50 percent chance of being right about whether it is going to rain in the next county next week: weather systems may be microscopic by galactic standards, but the number of variables that drives them approaches infinity (Pagels, 1988:226-27).[56]

Simulation is for the scientist what prediction is — or ought to be — for the social scientist: to know what one can simulate is to know what one can reasonably hope to predict. But knowing that means making judgments about what is a manageable number of variables, and it is here that the field of international security studies needs work. We need clearer standards for deciding when that number is low enough to allow simulation, and hence prediction; but we also need to know when to back off, recognizing that we are dealing with so many variables that prediction exceeds our capabilities. The concepts of paradigm redundancy and fratricide can help in making that choice.

For in a field in which no dominant paradigm exists and in which we lack the capability for controlled experiments to develop one, theories are never going to be more than approximations at simulation, and theorists are rarely going to agree about how to do them. That leaves anyone who is interested in prediction little choice but to become a "consumer" in the "marketplace" of theories, taking what seems to work in simulating reality and discarding what does not. And surely we are more likely to be right in assuming continuity for the reality we seek to simulate when different theories predict similar results than we are when a single theory is the sole basis for prediction, or when different theories predict dissimilar results. Overdetermination is a safer basis for anticipating the future than underdetermination; redundancy, for this purpose, is very much preferable to fratricide.

No theory or combination of theories is ever going to provide us with the paradigmatic equivalent of a "crystal ball," in which we can perceive the future with the same clarity we take for granted when we view the past. But theories that successfully explain a system's past do not normally lose their validity as they approach, and even proceed beyond, the present. And because — whether with regard to the past or the future — we are dealing with imperfect approximations of reality in any event, the more diversified the origins and character of the theories that provide our approximations, the more robust the resulting explanations — and predictions — are likely to be.[57]

My own examination of theoretical foundations for the long-peace thesis reveals, on the whole, greater redundancy than fratricide. It therefore provides some basis for confidence that the great-power peace that has already outlasted all others in modern history is reasonably robust, and hence is likely to continue; it also suggests, at a much less cosmic level, my exemption from the unfortunate fate of Norman Angell.

But there is one potentially fratricidal force at work in the current international system; paradoxically, it is the trend most closely associated with what the historic objectives of United States foreign policy are supposed to have been. The impending "triumph" of liberalism, however gratifying that development may be for Americans and however beneficial its immediate consequences for other parts of the world, appears more likely to upset systemic stability than any other tendency now discernible on the horizon. For it is in this area, more than anywhere else, that intersecting theoretical explanations for the long peace seem inconsistent with one another.

This is by no means to predict that liberalism is going to start World War III: the redundant safeguards of nuclear deterrence, bipolarity, and hegemonic management will probably remain in place, and if the long cyclists are correct, we have a while to wait yet before we are due for another great hegemonic conflict.[58] But it is to say that a world of triumphant liberalism is not easy to simulate, and that in turn suggests unpredictability, a condition that has not been conducive to stable superpower relations in the past. One reason the Cold War evolved into a long peace is that Russians and Americans gradually became predictable to each other: the familiarity of adversaries, over time, began to breed not contempt but common interests. A world of unfamiliar adversaries — or even the unlikely possibility of a world in which no evident adversaries exist — would represent a wholly new environment, and that could take some getting used to.

It is here that the behavior of statesmen and not systems will make the critical difference. For in coping with unsimulatable situations, theory — which is only past experience projected forward — is, and should be, of little help: variables overwhelm the capacity for generalization; generalizations, if attempted, are almost certain to mislead. One has little choice under such circumstances but to fall back upon those elusively non-theoretical qualities that we associate with statesmanship — patience, courage, common sense, vision, and humility — qualities whose very resistance to precise definition suggests their adaptability in dealing with the unpredictable.

Human mismanagement retains the capacity to wreck even the most overdetermined of international systems; we are ourselves, through our capacity for blunder, the ultimate fratricidal force. But that is only another way of saying that old-fashioned standards of statecraft, even under the most reassuring conditions of paradigm redundancy and systemic stability, are not likely soon to become obsolete: sustaining the long peace into the 21st century is going to require not only good history and good theory, but good sense (and good luck) as well.

ENDNOTES

1. I wish to thank Karin Wright and Philip Nash for research assistance; the students in my seminars at Ohio University and Princeton University for their patience in discussing many of these issues with me; Emanuel Adler, Erik Hagerman, Chaim Kaufmann, Melvyn Leffler, Ralph Levering, Geir Lundestad, Sean Lynn-Jones, David Nixon, John Ruggie, Steven Van Evera, Fareed Zakaria, as well as Charles Kegley and the other contributors to this volume, for helpful suggestions; and, not least, Erik Yesson of Princeton University, who asked the question.

2. Angell never ruled out the possibility of war itself; his argument was that, once involved in war, modern industrial states would not be able to sustain it. See, on this point, Miller (1986:42, 51).

3. See, on the current state of international relations theory, K. Holsti (1985), Morgan (1981), and Holsti (1989).

4. I am following here a suggestion advanced in Joynt and Rescher (1961: 154).

5. For a defense of utilitarian standards in historical explanation, see Carr (1961:140-41). International relations theorists may object to my characterization of what they produce as "merchandise", or "commodities"; nor are they likely to welcome my suggestion that historians in search of theoretical explanations should "shop around." I will cheerfully apologize to any theorist who has not, at one time or another, "shopped around" in historical accounts for data to support hypotheses.

6. See Holsti (1987:vii-viii, 73-74, 80). As Thomas Kuhn (1970:150) points out, however, the existence of multiple paradigms is often what brings about transitions from one dominant paradigm to another.

7. I am aware of the impropriety involved, strictly speaking, in equating "theories" with "paradigms." However, the terms "paradigm redundancy" and "paradigm fratricide" seem to me preferable to the alternatives, which would be the inelegant "theory redundancy" and "theory fratricide." Convinced that the field of international security studies needs no new infusion of graceless jargon, I have here exercised the historian's prerogative of preferring style to fussiness.

8. Betts (1987) assesses the effectiveness of nuclear threats. For the size of the nuclear arsenal, see Rosenberg (1983).

9. I use the term *stability* in Kenneth Waltz's sense: "A system is stable as long as its structure endures. In self-help systems, a structure endures as long as there is no consequential change in the number of principal units" (Waltz, 1979:135n).

10. Although he accepts the argument that nuclear weapons "have had a profound effect on the conduct of statecraft," Robert Gilpin (1981:215, 218) is careful to note that "[t]he thesis that nuclear weapons have made hegemonic war or a system-changing series of limited wars an impossibility must remain inconclusive."

11. Two recent books (Boyer, 1985; Weart, 1988) strongly suggest a shift in mass consciousness as a result of the development of nuclear weapons. And recent work by Bundy (1988) and Nye (1987) provide considerable empirical evidence for a shift in the attitudes of policymakers as well. Sufficient archival evidence

has long been available to test these propositions for American and British policymakers, although no one has yet done so in a specific attempt to falsify the Mueller thesis. Some information is also becoming available on Soviet and Chinese policies regarding nuclear weapons (Holloway, 1983; Lewis and Xue, 1988).

12. "Much of what passes for nuclear knowledge rests upon elaborate counterfactual argument, abstractions based on assumptions about rational actors, assumptions about the other nation's unknown intentions, and simple intuitions. . . . Obviously, this combination leaves lots of room for spurious knowledge, false learning, and occasional forgetting. . . ." (Nye, 1987:382). True enough, and there may not be much we can do to improve the quality of our assumptions and intuitions. But counterfactual argument is something else again: there is no reason why the same tests of logic that ought to apply to real history cannot be used at least to evaluate the plausibility of counterfactuals, thereby giving us a useful tool for investigating a realm where no one wants factual experience. Bundy (1988) contains impressive examples of what can be done with counterfactuals.

13. "To say that it would be useful to view international politics from the systems level is not to argue that the system determines the attributes and the behavior of states but rather to keep open the theoretically interesting and practically important question of what, in different systems, the proportionate causal weights of unit-level and of systems-level factors might be" (Waltz, 1979:48-49; Waltz, 1986:327-28, 343).

14. Apart, of course, from Bundy (1988). The History, Social Sciences, and International Security Affairs workshop of the American Academy of Arts and Sciences Committee on International Security Studies did hold a session on counterfactual approaches to nuclear history in October, 1989.

15. The most obvious examples of bipolarity — Athens versus Sparta, Rome versus Carthage — were in fact regional rivalries; and although European competition for colonial empire in the 16th through the 19th centuries at times took on the appearance of worldwide bipolarity, it would be difficult to find instances in which the power gradient separating the two predominant states from their nearest rivals was as great as it would be for the United States and the Soviet Union after World War II. See also, on this point, Nye (1988b:585).

16. See also Waltz (1979:185) for a helpful distinction between the "usefulness" and "usability" of force.

17. Gilpin (1981:30-31) provides a good discussion of prestige as a form of power.

18. See, for the complexities involved in deciding *not* to become a nuclear power, Bundy (1988:513-16).

19. This summary of "hegemonic stability" theory is based on Gilpin (1987b:72-73). But see also Keohane and Nye (1977:42-46); and, for a critique of the theory, Keohane (1984:32-39).

20. Gilpin (1981) remains the most sophisticated effort to relate hegemonic stability theory to Cold War history, but that is not the main purpose of the book; nor has his more recent work expanded on the connection.

21. For more on dual hegemonic crisis management, see Gaddis (1987b:238-43).

22. Regime theory is examined in detail in Krasner (1983).

23. Even tyrants, Waltz points out, need cooperation if they are to rule (Waltz, 1979:188-89; see also Gilpin, 1981:16).

24. My own attempt to deal with this issue is in Gaddis, 1987b:61-71). See also, for the propensity of nations to "balance" against threats rather than to "bandwagon" before them, Walt (1987).

25. An interesting problem for historians would be to show just when this pattern of cooperative management began.

26. In his more recent writing, Waltz (1986:327-28) does acknowledge the possibility — and begin to discuss the mechanisms of — further systemic change.

27. I am using the term *environment* here in the sense that Gilpin (1981:53) does: "A state system, like any other political system, exists in a technological, military, and economic environment that both restricts the behavior of its members and provides opportunities for policies of aggrandizement." I would add, though, that moral environments can also affect the behavior of states.

28. A related criticism appears in Wendt (1987:342-44).

29. Something similar happened on a smaller scale, Mueller points out, to dueling. In 1804 it was possible for a sitting vice-president of the United States and a former secretary of the treasury — fearing ridicule if they did not — to agree to settle their differences by firing pistols at one another, with lethal results for Alexander Hamilton. But by the late 19th century, any public figure who proposed resolving a quarrel in this way would have been ridiculed for doing so: social customs had shifted, and a procedure once considered the only way to preserve honor now had come to seem dishonorable, even silly (Mueller, 1989:9-11).

30. Waltz (1979:203) argues, correctly in my view, that they have such an interest now.

31. See also, on the reception of this article, Atlas (1989).

32. I use the term "liberal" here to imply the existence within states of such individual rights as free speech, due process, private property, and elected representation; but also the presence among states of mechanisms for resolving international disputes by means short of war, the threat of war, intervention, or other forms of coercion. For more on the prerequisites for liberalism, see Doyle (1983a:206-13).

33. For more on this consensus, see Huntington (1989).

34. It is not clear to me that the experience of fighting World War II in and of itself would have been sufficient to deter great-power wars in the future. World War I was a more costly conflict for several of the nations involved, but it obviously did not have that effect: even if one attributes the coming of war in 1939 to Hitler's irrationality, it is worth recalling that an entire nation stood behind him, however reluctantly, for six years of bitter fighting; and that despite earlier policies of appeasement, it was the British and the French who declared war on Germany rather than the other way around. Certainly there was little sense at the time among American military planners that World War II would be the last of its kind (Sherry, 1977; Sherry, 1987; Ray, 1989:424-25; Jervis, 1988:80-90).

35. A proposition amply confirmed by the "new" social history (Stone, 1979; Darnton, 1984; Boswell, 1989).

36. One should allow for "pushover" situations like Grenada in 1983 and Panama in 1989.

37. The most influential work in this field was Keohane and Nye (1977); but see also, among many others, Rosenau (1980) and Mansbach and Vasquez (1981). Few if any "neo-liberals" would have gone so far as to claim that the "realist" paradigm was totally outmoded: security was still a concern of states; military

strength did still count for something. But they did assert that the international system no longer functioned solely as a "self-help" arrangement in which each nation was responsible for ensuring its own security; rather, common interests in certain areas had emerged, and that in turn implied the concept of *mutual security*, a phenomenon for which traditional "realism" was ill-equipped to account.

38. As the Chinese discovered when they found themselves confronted, during the June, 1989, student riots, by such unfamiliar phenomena as fax machines, satellite uplinks, and Dan Rather. The rapidity with which communist regimes in East Germany, Bulgaria, Czechoslovakia and Rumania fell late in 1989 only confirms the proposition.

39. For a recent statement of this thesis, see Rosecrance (1986: especially pp. 78-79, 212-13).

40. For a good evaluation of the historical precedents, see Rock (1989: especially pp. 13-15).

41. Satellites do not, of course, reveal enemy intentions. But they can reveal a good deal about the physical deployments that are necessary before one can act on one's intentions.

42. I have in mind here the Salman Rushdie affair, in which the Ayatollah managed, by getting *The Satanic Verses* temporarily removed from bookstore shelves while simultaneously getting it on the best seller lists, to shape the reading habits of several million Americans. For a good account of how Western influences helped set off the Iranian revolution, see Mottahedeh (1985).

43. For one scholar's anticipation of such a backlash, see Harding (1987:134-35, 157, 282).

44. "The broader the scope of the work and the deeper the reform, the greater the need to increase the interest in it and convince millions and millions of people of its necessity. This means that if we have set out for a radical and all-round restructuring, we must also unfold the entire potential of democracy" (Gorbachev, 1987:320). That Gorbachev attributes these thoughts to Lenin, who, we are told, saw "socialism and democracy as indivisible," shows that the Soviet leader is not above bending a little history to make a point.

45. Significantly it was an American invasion, not an economic collapse, that toppled Noriega in December, 1989.

46. I have adapted this image from Pyne (1986: especially chapter one). An irreverent student has pointed out to me that it seems to be easier for historians to think of dependent variables as small animals. He may be right.

47. Witness the remarkable response to Kennedy (1987) during the year that followed its publication.

48. As, for example, presidential "death cycles": every American president elected in a year ending in zero from 1840 through 1960 died in office. The pattern held through seven iterations, but without any causal mechanism to explain it. An yet now, with the retirement of Ronald Reagan, the oldest of all the presidents has broken it. For more on the confusion of correlation with cause, see Fischer (1970:167-69).

49. There is, of course, the whole tangled subject of Kondratieff cycles in economics, from which source much of long-cycle theory originally developed (Goldstein, 1988:25-39). For a good introduction to long-cycle theory in general, see Modelski (1987).

50. Kennedy (1987) also follows this general line of reasoning, although his terminology does not always follow that of the above-mentioned works.

51. Mancur Olson (1982:74-75) provides a slightly different explanation, which focuses on the way "distributional coalitions slow down a society's capacity to adopt new technologies and to reallocate resources in response to changing conditions, and thereby reduce the rate of economic growth." It follows from this, he notes, that "countries whose distributional coalitions have been emasculated or abolished by totalitarian government or foreign occupation should grow relatively quickly after a free and stable legal order is established."

52. It should be pointed out that Gilpin differentiates between "cycles of empire," which precede the modern state system, and the hegemonic cycles that characterize it today (Gilpin, 1981:110-45). See also, on the effect of nuclear weapons on long cycles, Gilpin (1987:351) and Kennedy (1987:537).

53. Although, to my knowledge, no one has worked out a method by which we might measure rates of technological innovation. How would the past forty years compare, for example, with 1870-1910, which saw the development of the telephone, the phonograph, the automobile, electric power, the motion picture, radio, the airplane, and the submarine? Or compare progress in aviation between 1940 and 1965 — where one advanced from the B-17 to manned orbiting satellites — as against 1965 to the present.

54. Such is the conclusion — misunderstood by many of his critics — of Kennedy (1987: especially p. 514).

55. An example of this tendency to focus on a truncated period of observation, and the unwarranted prescription that might be reached, is the habit of leaving the raising of adequate government revenues to the only constituency that cannot complain about this, the unborn.

56. Gleick (1987) is the best general introduction to this field.

57. "Any generalization about the thinking of an age is the more persuasive the greater the conceptual distance between the sources on which it is based" (Kern, 1983:7).

58. Although one cannot rule out altogether the possibility that developments in one area could affect others: it is not too difficult to conceive of a form of "liberalism" that seeks to abolish nuclear deterrence, bipolarity, and hegemonic management.

CHAPTER THREE

Peace in the Global System: Displacement, Interregnum, or Transformation?*

J. David Singer

As we ponder the forty-odd years since the end of World War II, there are reasons to believe that a new era of peace may well be in train. But there are equally good reasons for skepticism in regard to not only the past four decades, but those that lie ahead as well. Perhaps the recent past has been less peaceful than it might appear to observers in the major powers. Perhaps we, like those who basked in the relative harmony of the forty years following the Franco-Prussian War, have been treading the path to a war that lies unexpectedly around the next turning in the road of international history. This chapter will address both of these questions, as well as a third that links the two: what accounts for the absence of central system (i.e., major powers and their industrially developed allies) interstate war since the year that saw not only the leveling of Hiroshima and Nagasaki, but the establishment of the United Nations?

We begin, thus, with the simple empirical question of how much war — and where — since 1945 compared to the prior 130 years, move on to some possible explanations of that distribution, and conclude with some forecasts that rest on these — and prior — "lessons of history." In the opening section, we examine the incidence of different types of war in different regions of the world, and compare the nuclear to the prenuclear period of 1816-1945 in terms of such distributions.

THE INCIDENCE OF DISPUTES AND WAR

Within a few months of the Japanese surrender, the victorious allies found themselves in confrontations with one another over Soviet troops remaining in Iran, allied occupation rights in Berlin, and the general

* The author would like to thank Robert Packer and Ricardo Rodriguez for their assistance in assembling the data and tables, and the contributors to this book for their helpful comments on the earlier draft of this chapter.

meaning of the territorial agreements that had been negotiated at Yalta and Potsdam. While the years that followed have not been particularly harmonious, war has, so far, not occurred.

Cross-Temporal Decline?

Beginning with the frequency of militarized disputes, by which we mean confrontations short of war characterized by the reciprocated threat, deployment, mobilization, or use of force (Gochman and Maoz, 1984), we find an interesting pattern across time. Between 1816 and World War II, there were an average of 14.6 such disputes per decade throughout the interstate system, and from 1946 through 1980, that figure rose to 23.6 per decade. If, however, we control for system size — the number of sovereign territorial states — those figures actually *decline* from 4 per state per decade prior to World War II to 2 per state per decade since. And if we control not for the number of states but the number of *pairs*, the decline appears even more dramatic.

Further, if we then inquire into the probability of such disputes escalating to all-out war, the suggestion of a long peace becomes credible. Between the Napoleonic War and the Second World War, about 15 percent ended in war, contrasted to only 3 percent since then. Restricting our examination to confrontations with one or more major powers on each side, the pre-1939 average of 4.3 per decade rose to 7.7 since then, but while 14 percent escalated to war in the pre-1939 period, it has been close to zero since, with the Chinese and American involvement in the Korean War as the sole exception. And given the question of whether China had really acquired major-power status before that war, one could argue that not a single major-versus-major dispute has escalated to war since V-J Day.

Regional Displacement

But if the experience of the major powers and their allies in the central system has been one of armed rivalry and short-of-war confrontations, the post-1945 period has been far less fortunate for those who live in the peripheral districts. A useful point of entry into that question might be to contrast the cumulative percentages of different indicators of war in the central and peripheral regions over time. Taking the magnitude indicator of international war (interstate plus extrasystemic), half of all the nation-months in Europe had occurred by 1915, three-quarters by 1938, and nine-tenths by 1942, whereas for non-European war the dates were much more recent: 1941, 1963, and 1974. Not quite as soon, and reflecting the rising crescendo in the bloodiness of war, the Europeans passed all of these dismal battle death milestones (50 percent, 75 percent, and 90 percent) between the late 1930s and the second year of World War II, whereas the killing outside of Europe did not reach the 50 percent mark until early in World War II, three-quarters in the years right after that war, and did not experience nine-tenths of its battle deaths between 1816 and 1986 until 1964. And if we use 1946 as our cutting point, and compare the frequency indicators of these three measures of the incidence of international war, the center-versus-periphery *percentage* distribution is as follows:

| | FREQUENCY | | MAGNITUDE | | SEVERITY | |
	Europe	Outside	Europe	Outside	Europe	Outside
1816-1945	97	57	99.99	53	99.95	60
1946-1980	3	43	.01	47	.05	40

Shifting to another indicator — number of nation entries into war — the halfway mark was reached in 1914 for wars anywhere in the system, but 1868 for wars involving at least one major power in Europe compared to 1938 for such wars in the peripheral regions. For minor- versus major-power wars in Europe, half of the nation entries had occurred by 1913, whereas it took until 1932 outside of Europe. Looking at the location of international wars that involved at least one major power, the frequencies and percentage distributions are as follows:

	1816-1945	1946-1980
In Europe	88 (59%)	2 (5%)
Outside Europe	61 (41%)	41 (95%)

Additionally, if we look at the time density of such wars, we find:

	1816-1945	1946-1980
In Europe	one every 1.5 years	one every 17.5 years
Outside Europe	one every 2.1 years	one every 0.85 years

That is, the density of major-power wars occurring in the European system *decreased* by a factor of 12 across the two periods, while those outside *increased* by a factor of 2.5.

Also worth comparing across time are *civil* wars in the two regions of the world, beginning with the observation that since those of 1848-

1849, all but two of the bloodiest (Russia, 1917-1920 and Spain, 1936-1939) have occurred outside of the European system. In contrast to international wars, the impression of a sharp rise in civil wars is correct; the frequency has doubled from 5.3 to 12.6 per decade, but controlling for the number of states in the entire system, the figure shows a modest decline since World War II. But once more, the location of this domestic blood-letting has shifted dramatically from the center to the periphery; with the exception of the Greek case, all of the post-1945 civil wars — until the events of late 1989 in Eastern Europe — have occurred in the peripheral regions of the world.

Even more dramatic is the incidence of "foreign overt military intervention" catalogued by Tillema (1989). In his exhaustive examination of 269 such episodes from the close of World War II through 1985, he finds only the cases of Greece, Turkey, Czechoslovakia, Poland, and Hungary falling within the central system. Furthermore, of the 591 intervening parties, it is true that the major powers, led by Britain and France, account for 25 percent of these armed intrusions, but the remaining 75 percent are accounted for by his "new states" and "other states," almost all of whom are found in the peripheral system.

Finally, Eckhardt (1989) has compiled both civilian and military fatalities from war from 1700 through 1988, and once again the pattern is tragically unambiguous. Between 1816 and 1944, he estimates 7.8 million war-related deaths, of which 48 percent were civilians, with Europe experiencing about 38 percent of the worldwide total. But since 1945, virtually all of the 18.2 million fatalities (of which 64 percent were civilians) were suffered outside the central system. In sum, as Tables 3.1 and 3.2 reveal, the data strongly support the proposition that the locale of — and involvement in — all types of warfare has shifted from the Eurocentered system to the nations at the periphery.

No War in the Central System: How Come?

To summarize, one can hardly speak of a "long peace" since 1945 if the domain is the entire global village (Westing, 1982). As our data show, the level of bloody combat between and within national political entities has not diminished appreciably during this period. It has merely taken a different form and occurred in a different neighborhood. Nevertheless, the absence of any war between major powers in particular, and advanced industrial states in general, is no mean achievement, especially when we consider the intensity and duration of the rivalry between the two superpowers and their military allies. Thus, we turn next to an examination of several plausible explanations, but in rather cursory fashion inasmuch as several of the other chapters in this book take this as their central focus.

TABLE 3.1 International (Interstate and Extrasystemic) Wars (1945-1988) with Participants, Duration, Magnitude, Severity, and Intensity

Name and Number of War	Participant and Code Number	Dates of War and National Dates of Participation	Duration in Months	Magnitude in Nation-Months	Severity in Battle Deaths	Population (×100,000 Pre-war)	Battle Deaths per Nation-Month	Battle Deaths per 10,000 Population
		Interstate (one or more system members on *each* side):						
Palestine 148		05/15/1948-07/18/1948 10/22/1948-01/07/1949	4.7	19.4	8000	312	412.40	2.56
	Iraq 645	05/15/1948-07/18/1948 10/22/1948-10/31/1948		2.5	500	50	200.00	1.00
	Egypt/UAR 651	05/15/1948-07/18/1948 10/22/1948-01/07/1949		4.7	2000	192	425.53	1.04
	Syria 652	05/15/1948-07/18/1948 10/22/1948-10/31/1948		2.5	1000	31	400.00	3.23
	Lebanon 660	05/15/1948-07/18/1948 10/22/1948-10/31/1948		2.5	500	12	200.00	4.17
	Jordan 663	05/15/1948-10/31/1948		2.5	1000	13	400.00	7.69
	Israel 666	05/15/1948-07/18/1948 10/22/1948-01/07/1949		4.7	3000	14	638.30	21.43
Korean 151		06/24/1950-07/27/1953	37.1	514.1	2000000	9588	3890.29	20.86
	North Korea 731	06/24/1950-07/27/1953		37.1	520000	97	14016.17	536.08
	South Korea 732	06/24/1950-07/27/1953		37.1	415000	205	11185.98	202.44
	United States 2	06/27/1950-07/27/1953		37.0	54000	1507	1459.46	3.58
	United Kingdom 200	08/29/1950-07/27/1953		35.0	670	508	19.14	.13
	Philippines 840	09/16/1950-07/27/1953		34.4	90	203	2.62	.04
	Turkey 640	10/18/1950-07/27/1953		33.3	720	209	21.62	.34
	China 710	10/27/1950-07/27/1953		33.1	900000	5468	27190.33	16.46
	Australia 900	12/10/1950-07/27/1953		31.6	281	82	8.89	.34
	Canada 20	12/19/1950-07/27/1953		31.3	310	137	9.90	.23
	France 220	01/01/1951-07/27/1953		30.8	290	430	9.42	.07
	Netherlands 210	01/20/1951-07/27/1953		30.2	110	103	3.64	.11

War	Nation	Code	Dates						
Korean 151 (cont.)	Belgium	211	01/20/1951-07/27/1953		30.2	100	87	3.31	.11
	Greece	350	01/20/1951-07/27/1953		30.2	170	76	5.63	.22
	Thailand	800	01/20/1951-07/27/1953		30.2	110	202	3.64	.05
	Ethiopia	530	05/01/1951-07/27/1953		26.9	120	158	4.46	.08
	Colombia	100	06/06/1951-07/27/1953		25.7	140	116	5.45	.12
Russo-Hungarian 154				0.8	1.6	10000	2101	6250.00	.48
	Hungary	310	10/23/1956-11/14/1956		.8	2500	99	3125.00	2.53
	Russia/USSR	365	10/23/1956-11/14/1956		.8	7500	2002	9375.00	.37
Sinai 157				0.3	1.0	3230	1216	3230.00	.26
	Egypt/UAR	651	10/29/1956-11/06/1956		.3	3000	236	10000.00	1.27
	Israel	666	10/29/1956-11/06/1956		.3	200	18	666.67	1.11
	United Kingdom	200	10/31/1956-11/06/1956		.2	20	516	100.00	.00
	France	220	10/31/1956-11/06/1956		.2	10	446	50.00	.00
Sino-Indian 160				1.1	2.2	1000	11193	454.55	.01
	China	710	10/20/1962-11/22/1962		1.1	500	6701	454.55	.01
	India	750	10/20/1962-11/22/1962		1.1	500	4492	454.55	.01
Vietnamese 163				122.7	729.7	1215992	3421	1666.43	35.54
	United States	2	02/07/1965-01/27/1973		95.6	56000	1942	585.77	2.88
	North Vietnam	816	02/07/1965-04/30/1975		122.7	500000	199	4074.98	251.26
	South Vietnam	817	02/07/1965-04/30/1975		122.7	650000	161	5297.47	403.73
	Australia	900	02/07/1965-12/20/1972		94.4	492	114	5.21	.43
	South Korea	732	05/01/1965-01/28/1973		92.9	5000	284	53.82	1.76
	Philippines	840	10/01/1966-01/28/1973		75.9	1000	327	13.18	.31
	Thailand	800	10/01/1967-01/28/1973		63.9	1000	327	15.65	.31
	Kampuchea	811	03/01/1970-04/17/1975		61.6	2500	67	40.58	3.73
Second Kashmir 166				1.6	3.2	6800	5888	2125.00	.12
	India	750	08/05/1965-09/23/1965		1.6	3000	4749	1875.00	.06
	Pakistan	770	08/05/1965-09/23/1965		1.6	3800	1139	2375.00	.33

(continued)

TABLE 3.1 (continued)

Name and Number of War	Participant and Code Number	Dates of War and National Dates of Participation	Duration in Months	Magnitude in Nation-Months	Severity in Battle Deaths	Population (×100,000 Pre-war)	Battle Deaths per Nation-Month	Battle Deaths per 10,000 Population
Six Day 169		06/05/1967-06/10/1967	0.2	.8	19600	414	24500.00	4.73
Egypt/UAR	651	06/05/1967-06/10/1967		.2	10010	309	50000.00	3.24
Syria	652	06/05/1967-06/10/1967		.2	2500	57	12500.00	4.39
Jordan	663	06/05/1967-06/10/1967		.2	6100	21	30500.00	29.05
Israel	666	06/05/1967-06/10/1967		.2	1000	27	5000.00	3.70
Israeli-Egyptian 172		03/06/1969-08/07/1970	17.3	34.6	5368	354	155.14	1.52
Egypt/UAR	651	03/06/1969-08/07/1970		17.3	5000	325	289.02	1.54
Israel	666	03/06/1969-08/07/1970		17.3	368	29	21.27	1.27
Football 175		07/14/1969-07/18/1969	0.2	.4	1900	44	4750.00	4.32
El Salvador	91	07/14/1969-07/18/1969		.2	1200	19	6000.00	6.32
Honduras	92	07/14/1969-07/18/1969		.2	700	25	3500.00	2.80
Bangladesh 178		12/03/1971-12/17/1971	0.6	1.2	11000	6669	9166.67	.16
India	750	12/03/1971-12/17/1971		.6	8000	5503	13333.33	.15
Pakistan	770	12/03/1971-12/17/1971		.6	3000	1166	5000.00	.26
Yom Kippur 181		10/06/1973-10/24/1973	0.6	3.6	16401	670	4555.83	2.45
Iraq	645	10/06/1973-10/24/1973		.6	278	104	463.33	.27
Egypt/UAR	651	10/06/1973-10/24/1973		.6	5000	357	8333.33	1.40
Syria	652	10/06/1973-10/24/1973		.6	8000	70	13333.33	11.43
Israel	666	10/06/1973-10/24/1973		.6	3000	32	5000.00	9.38
Jordan	663	10/10/1973-10/24/1973		.6	23	25	38.33	.09
Saudi Arabia	670	10/10/1973-10/24/1973		.6	100	82	166.67	.12

Conflict	Code	Country	Dates						
Turco-Cypriot 184			07/20/1974-07/29/1974	0.4	.8	1500	389	1875.00	.39
	352	Cyprus	08/14/1974-08/16/1974 / 07/20/1974-07/29/1974		.4	500	6	1250.00	8.33
	640	Turkey	08/14/1974-08/16/1974 / 07/20/1974-07/29/1974		.4	1000	383	2500.00	.26
Vietnamese-Cambodian (ongoing) 187			05/01/1975-	164.0	328.0	50000	557	152.44	8.98
	811	Kampuchea	05/01/1975-		164.0	20000	81	121.95	24.69
	816	Vietnam	05/01/1975-		164.0	30000	476	182.93	6.30
Ethiopia-Somalia 189			08/01/1977-03/14/1978	7.4	22.2	6000	418	270.27	1.44
	40	Cuba	08/01/1977-03/14/1978		7.4	700	95	94.59	.74
	520	Somalia	08/01/1977-03/14/1978		7.4	3500	33	472.97	10.61
	530	Ethiopia	08/01/1977-03/14/1978		7.4	1800	290	243.24	.62
Ugandan-Tanzanian 190			10/30/1978-04/12/1979	5.5	16.5	3000	314	181.82	1.91
	500	Uganda	10/30/1978-04/12/1979		5.5	1500	125	272.73	1.20
	510	Tanzania	10/30/1978-04/12/1979		5.5	1000	163	181.82	.61
	620	Libya	10/30/1978-04/12/1979		5.5	500	26	90.91	1.92
Sino-Vietnamese 193			02/17/1979-03/10/1979	0.9	1.8	21000	10132	1666.67	.21
	710	China	02/17/1979-03/10/1979		.9	13000	9640	1444.44	.13
	816	Vietnam	02/17/1979-03/10/1979		.9	8000	492	8888.89	1.63
Iran-Iraq 199			09/22/1980-08/20/1988	94.9	189.8	1250000	512	6585.88	244.14
	630	Iran	09/22/1980-08/20/1988		94.9	750000	381	7903.06	196.85
	645	Iraq	09/22/1980-08/20/1988		94.9	500000	131	5268.70	381.68
Falklands 202			03/25/1982-06/20/1982	2.9	5.8	910	855	156.90	.11
	160	Argentina	03/25/1982-06/20/1982		2.9	655	292	225.86	.22
	200	United Kingdom	03/25/1982-06/20/1982		2.9	255	563	87.93	.05

(*continued*)

TABLE 3.1 (continued)

Name and Number of War	Participant and Code Number	Dates of War and National Dates of Participation	Duration in Months	Magnitude in Nation-Months	Severity in Battle Deaths	Population (×100,000 Pre-war)	Battle Deaths per Nation-Month	Battle Deaths per 10,000 Population
Israel-Syria (Lebanon) 205		04/21/1982-09/05/1982	16.5	33.0	1500	133	45.45	1.13
	Syria 652	04/21/1982-09/05/1982		16.5	1000	93	60.61	1.08
	Israel 666	04/21/1982-09/05/1982		16.5	500	40	30.30	1.25
Sino-Vietnamese 208		09/09/1985-02/06/1987	16.9	33.8	4000	11234	118.34	.04
	China 710	09/09/1985-02/06/1987		16.9	1800	10638	106.51	.02
	Vietnam 816	09/09/1985-02/06/1987		16.9	2200	596	130.18	.37

Extrasystemic (one or more system members on *one* side against non-member whose battle deaths remain unknown):

Name and Number of War	Participant and Code Number	Dates of War and National Dates of Participation	Duration in Months	Magnitude in Nation-Months	Severity in Battle Deaths	Population (×100,000 Pre-war)	Battle Deaths per Nation-Month	Battle Deaths per 10,000 Population
Indonesian 418		11/10/1945-10/15/1946	11.2	22.4	1400	570	62.50	.25
	United Kingdom 200	11/10/1945-10/15/1946		11.2	1000	483	89.29	.21
	Netherlands 210	11/10/1945-10/15/1946		11.2	400	87	35.71	.46
Indochinese 421		12/01/1945-06/01/1954	102.0	102.0	95000	419	931.37	22.67
	France 220	12/01/1945-06/01/1954		102.0	95000	419	931.37	22.67
Madagascan 424		03/29/1947-12/01/1948	20.2	20.2	1800	416	89.11	.43
	France 220	03/29/1947-12/01/1948		20.2	1800	416	89.11	.43
First Kashmir 427		10/26/1947-01/01/1949	14.3	14.3	1500	3890	104.90	.04
	India 750	10/26/1947-01/01/1949		14.3	1500	3890	104.90	.04

Hyderbad 430			09/13/1948-09/17/1948	.2	.2	1000	3409	5000.00	.03
	India	750	09/13/1948-09/17/1948		.2	1000	3409	5000.00	.03
Algerian 433			11/01/1954-03/17/1962	88.5	88.5	18000	439	203.39	4.10
	France	220	11/01/1954-03/17/1962		88.5	18000	439	203.39	4.10
Tibetan 436			03/01/1956-03/22/1959	36.7	36.7	40000	6175	1089.92	.65
	China	710	03/01/1956-03/22/1959		36.7	40000	6175	1089.92	.65
Philippine MNLF 439 (ongoing)			01/01/1972-	195.0	195.0	40000	398	205.13	10.05
	Philippines	840	01/01/1972-		195.0	40000	398	205.13	10.05
Ethiopian-Eritrean 442 (ongoing)			01/01/1974-	180.0	180.0	250000	272	1388.89	91.91
	Ethiopia	530	01/01/1974-		180.0	250000	272	1388.89	91.91
East Timor 445			12/07/1975-02/19/1984	98.4	98.4	6000	1360	60.98	.44
	Indonesia	850	12/07/1975-02/19/1984		98.4	6000	1360	60.98	.44
Western Sahara 448			12/11/1975-05/10/1984	101.0	144.8	11500	302	79.42	3.81
	Mauritania	435	12/11/1975-08/05/1979		43.8	2000	131	45.66	1.53
	Morroco	600	12/11/1975-05/10/1984		101.0	9500	171	94.06	5.56
Ogaden 451			07/01/1976-08/01/1977 03/14/1978-08/13/1983	78.0	234.0	18000	410	76.92	4.39
	Cuba	40	07/01/1976-08/01/1977 03/14/1978-08/13/1983		78.0	1500	95	19.23	1.58
	Somalia	520	07/01/1976-08/01/1977 03/14/1978-08/13/1983		78.0	1500	33	19.23	4.55
	Ethiopia	530	07/01/1976-08/01/1977 03/14/1978-08/13/1983		78.0	15000	282	192.31	5.32

TABLE 3.2   Civil Wars (1945-1988) with Participants, Duration, Magnitude, Severity, and Intensity

Name and Number of War	Participant and Code Number	Winner (Intervention, if any)	Dates of War and Dates of Participation	Magnitude in Nation-Months	Severity in Battle Deaths	Population (×1,000 Pre-war)	Battle Deaths per Nation-Month	Battle Deaths per 1,000 Population
Greece* 781		GOV	12/03/1944-02/12/1945 11/15/1946-10/16/1949	38.6	160135	56168	4148.57	2.85
	Greece 350		12/03/1944-02/12/1945 11/15/1946-10/16/1949	37.4	160000	7456	4278.07	21.46
	United Kingdom 200 vs. Communists	(GOV)	12/05/1944-01/11/1945	1.2	135	48712	112.50	.00
China 784		OPP	03/15/1946-04/21/1950	49.2	1000000	455592	20325.20	2.19
	China 710 vs. Communists		03/15/1946-04/21/1950	49.2	1000000	455592	20325.20	2.19
Paraguay 787		GOV	03/07/1947-08/20/1947	5.5	1000	1305	181.82	.77
	Paraguay 150 vs. Leftists		03/07/1947-08/20/1947	5.5	1000	1305	181.82	.77
Yemen Arab Republic 790		OPP	02/17/1948-03/20/1948	1.1	4000	3192	3636.36	1.25
	North Yemen 678 vs. Yahya Family		02/17/1948-03/20/1948	1.1	4000	3192	3636.36	1.25
Costa Rica 793		OPP	03/12/1948-04/17/1948	1.2	2000	756	1666.67	2.65
	Costa Rica 94 vs. National Union Party		03/12/1948-04/17/1948	1.2	2000	756	1666.67	2.65
Colombia 796		GOV	04/09/1948-04/12/1948	.1	1400	10845	14000.00	.13
	Colombia 100 vs. Conservatives		04/09/1948-04/12/1948	.1	1400	10845	14000.00	.13

Burma (ongoing) 799								
Burma vs. rebels	775	ON	09/15/1948-	483.5	46000	18015	95.14	2.55
			09/15/1948-	483.5	46000	18015	95.14	2.55
Colombia 802								
Columbia vs. Liberals	100	GOV	09/15/1949-12/31/1962	159.6	300000	11087	1879.70	27.06
			09/15/1949-12/31/1962	159.6	300000	11087	1879.70	27.06
Indonesia 805								
Indonesia vs. Moluccans	850	GOV	05/31/1950-11/03/1950	5.1	5000	76000	980.39	.07
			05/31/1950-11/03/1950	5.1	5000	76000	980.39	.07
Philippines 808								
Philippines vs. Huks	840	GOV	09/01/1950-07/01/1952	22.0	9000	20316	409.09	.44
			09/01/1950-07/01/1952	22.0	9000	20316	409.09	.44
Bolivia 811								
Bolivia vs. Leftists	145	OPP	04/09/1952-04/11/1952	.1	1500	3070	15000.00	.49
			04/09/1952-04/11/1952	.1	1500	3070	15000.00	.49
Indonesia 814								
Indonesia vs. Leftists	850	GOV	09/20/1953-11/23/1953	2.1	1000	80451	476.19	.01
			09/20/1953-11/23/1953	2.1	1000	80451	476.19	.01
Guatemala 817								
Guatemala vs. Conservatives	90	OPP	06/08/1954-06/30/1954	.8	1000	3159	1250.00	.32
			06/08/1954-06/30/1954	.8	1000	3159	1250.00	.32

(continued)

* indicates internationalized civil war (one or more system members intervening).
+ indicates that GOV or OPP won after the war became interstate.

TABLE 3.2 (continued)

Name and Number of War	Participant and Code Number	Winner (Intervention, if any)	Dates of War and Dates of Participation	Magnitude in Nation-Months	Severity in Battle Deaths	Population (×1,000 Pre-war)	Battle Deaths per Nation-Month	Battle Deaths per 1,000 Population
Argentina 820								
	Argentina vs. Army 160	OPP	06/15/1955-09/19/1955	3.2	3000	18972	937.50	.16
			06/15/1955-09/19/1955	3.2	3000	18972	937.50	.16
Indonesia 823								
	Indonesia vs. Leftists 850	GOV	12/15/1956-12/31/1960	48.6	30000	85654	617.28	.35
			12/15/1956-12/31/1960	48.6	30000	85654	617.28	.35
Lebanon* 826								
	Lebanon 660	GOV	05/09/1958-09/15/1958	6.2	1400	176318	225.81	.01
	United States 2	(GOV)	05/09/1958-09/15/1958	4.2	1400	2082	333.33	.67
	vs. Leftists		07/16/1958-09/15/1958	2.0	0	174236	0.00	0.00
Cuba 829								
	Cuba vs. Castroites 40	OPP	06/15/1958-01/02/1959	6.6	5000	6523	757.58	.77
			06/15/1958-01/02/1959	6.6	5000	6523	757.58	.77
Iraq 832								
	Iraq 645 vs. Shammar Tribe and Pro-western Officers	GOV	03/06/1959-03/10/1959	.2	2000	6952	10000.00	.29
			03/06/1959-03/10/1959	.2	2000	6952	10000.00	.29
South Vietnamese* 835								
	South Vietnam 817	OPP+	01/01/1960-02/06/1965	110.4	302000	197842	2735.51	1.53
	United States 2	(GOV)	01/01/1960-02/06/1965	61.2	300000	14100	4901.96	21.28
	vs. Viet-Cong		01/01/1961-02/06/1965	49.2	2000	183742	40.65	.01

Zaire (Congo, Kinshasa)* 838		GOV	07/04/1960-09/01/1965	64.3	100050	23292	1555.99	4.30
Zaire	490	(GOV)	07/04/1960-09/01/1965	61.9	100000	14139	1615.51	7.07
Belgium	211		07/04/1960-09/01/1960	2.4	50	9153	20.83	.01
vs. Katanga and Leftists			11/07/1964-11/22/1964					
Laos 841		GOV	10/15/1960-07/15/1962	21.0	5000	959	238.10	5.21
Laos vs. Pathet Lao	812		10/15/1960-07/15/1962	21.0	5000	959	238.10	5.21
Kurdish Autonomy 843		GOV	09/16/1961-11/22/1963	26.2	500	7098	19.08	.07
Iraq 645 vs. Kurds			09/16/1961-11/22/1963	26.2	500	7098	19.08	.07
Algeria 844		GOV	07/28/1962-01/15/1963	5.6	1500	10920	267.86	.14
vs. Former Rebel Leaders	615		07/28/1962-01/15/1963	5.6	1500	10920	267.86	.14
Yemen Arab Republic* 847		GOV	11/15/1962-09/03/1969	140.3	101000	31900	719.89	3.17
North Yemen	678	(GOV)	11/15/1962-09/03/1969	81.7	100000	4640	1223.99	21.55
Egypt/UAR vs. Royalists	651		12/15/1962-10/31/1967	58.6	1000	27260	17.06	.04
Laos* 850		OPP	04/19/1963-02/15/1973	315.5	18500	213340	58.64	.09
Laos	812	(GOV)	04/19/1963-02/15/1973	117.9	15000	2510	127.23	5.98
United States vs. Pathet Lao	2		05/15/1964-02/01/1973	104.6	500	191830	4.78	.00
North Vietnam	816	(OPP)	05/15/1965-02/15/1973	93.0	3000	19000	32.26	.16

(continued)

* indicates internationalized civil war (one or more system members intervening).
+ indicates that GOV or OPP won after the war became interstate.

TABLE 3.2 (continued)

Name and Number of War	Participant and Code Number	Winner (Intervention, if any)	Dates of War and Dates of Participation	Magnitude in Nation-Months	Severity in Battle Deaths	Population (×1,000 Pre-war)	Battle Deaths per Nation-Month	Battle Deaths per 1,000 Population
Sudan 853		GOV	10/01/1963-02/28/1972	100.9	250000	12940	2477.70	19.32
Sudan vs. Anya Nya	625		10/01/1963-02/28/1972	100.9	250000	12940	2477.70	19.32
Rwanda 856		GOV	11/15/1963-02/06/1964	2.8	2500	3060	892.86	.82
Rwanda vs. Watusi	517		11/15/1963-02/06/1964	2.8	2500	3060	892.86	.82
Dominican Republic* 859	Dominican Republic 42	GOV	04/25/1965-09/01/1965	8.4	2526	197760	300.71	.01
	United States 2	(GOV)	04/25/1965-09/01/1965	4.1	2500	3520	609.76	.71
	vs. Leftists		04/29/1965-09/01/1965	4.3	26	194240	6.05	.00
Uganda 862	500	GOV	05/23/1966-06/01/1966	0.3	2000	8833	6666.67	.23
Uganda vs. Buganda Tribe			05/23/1966-06/01/1966	.3	2000	8833	6666.67	.23
Guatemala 864	90	GOV	00/00/1967-04/13/1984	208.4	138000	4898	662.19	28.17
Guatemala vs. rebels			00/00/1967-04/13/1984	208.4	138000	4898	662.19	28.17
China 865	710	GOV	01/15/1967-09/01/1968	19.6	50000	733540	2551.02	.07
China vs. Red Guard			01/15/1967-09/01/1968	19.6	50000	733540	2551.02	.07

Country / Participant	Code	GOV/OPP	Dates					
Nigeria	868	GOV	07/06/1967-01/12/1970	30.2	1000000	51120	33112.58	19.56
Nigeria Biafrans	475	GOV	07/06/1967-01/12/1970	30.2	1000000	51120	33112.58	19.56
Kampuchea (Cambodia)*	871	OPP	03/20/1970-03/15/1975	176.6	156000	250950	883.35	.62
Kampuchea South Vietnam	811 817	(GOV)	03/20/1970-03/15/1975	59.6	150000	6700	2516.78	22.39
United States	2	(GOV)	03/27/1970-04/30/1972	25.1	5000	18330	199.20	.27
vs. Khmer Rouge			05/01/1970-01/01/1973	32.0	500	204800	15.63	.00
North Vietnam	816	(OPP)	03/30/1970-03/15/1975	59.9	500	21150	8.35	.02
Jordan*	874	GOV	09/17/1970-09/24/1970	.4	2100	8560	5250.00	.25
vs. Palestinians	663	GOV	09/17/1970-09/24/1970	.3	2000	2310	6666.67	.87
Syria	652	(OPP)	09/20/1970-09/23/1970	.1	100	6250	1000.00	.02
Pakistan	880	OPP+	03/25/1971-12/02/1971	8.3	500000	116589	60240.96	4.29
vs. Bengalis			03/25/1971-12/02/1971	8.3	500000	116589	60240.96	4.29
Sri Lanka	883	GOV	04/06/1971-05/16/1971	1.3	2000	13000	1538.46	.15
vs. Janatha Vimukthi Peramuna	780	GOV	04/06/1971-05/16/1971	1.3	2000	13000	1538.46	.15
Burundi	886	GOV	04/30/1972-05/25/1972	.9	50000	3403	55555.56	14.69
vs. Hutu	516	GOV	04/30/1972-05/25/1972	.9	50000	3403	55555.56	14.69

* indicates internationalized civil war (one or more system members intervening).
+ indicates that GOV or OPP won after the war became interstate.

(continued)

TABLE 3.2 (*continued*)

Name and Number of War	Participant and Code Number	Winner (Intervention, if any)	Dates of War and Dates of Participation	Magnitude in Nation-Months	Severity in Battle Deaths	Population (×1,000 Pre-war)	Battle Deaths per Nation-Month	Battle Deaths per 1,000 Population
Philippines (ongoing) 889		ON	10/01/1972-	195.0	40000	39040	205.13	1.02
	Philippines 840 vs. New People's Army		10/01/1972-	195.0	40000	39040	205.13	1.02
Zimbabwe (Rhodesia) 892		OPP	12/28/1972-12/28/1979	84.0	12000	5512	142.86	2.18
	Zimbabwe 552 vs. Patriotic Front		12/28/1972-12/28/1979	84.0	12000	5512	142.86	2.18
Pakistan 893		GOV	01/23/1973-07/00/1977	53.2	8600	66749	161.65	.13
	Pakistan 770		01/23/1973-07/00/1977	53.2	8600	66749	161.65	.13
Kurdish Autonomy* 894		GOV	03/14/1974-04/03/1975	25.2	5000	43261	198.41	.12
	Iraq 645 vs. Kurds		03/14/1974-04/03/1975	12.6	4500	10765	357.14	.42
	Iran 630	(OPP)	03/14/1974-04/03/1975	12.6	500	32496	39.68	.02
Lebanon (ongoing)* 895		ON	04/13/1975-	396.1	28460	14212	71.85	2.00
	Lebanon 660 vs. Leftists		04/13/1975-	164.6	26200	2589	159.17	10.12
	Israel 666	(GOV)	06/06/1982-	78.8	450	4027	5.71	.11
	Syria 652	(GOV/OPP)	04/09/1976-	152.7	1810	7596	11.85	.24
Angola (ongoing)* 898		ON	11/11/1975-	473.1	341000	41051	720.78	8.31
	Angola 540		11/11/1975-	157.7	336200	6315	2131.90	53.24
	Cuba 40	(GOV)	11/11/1975-	157.7	4000	9290	25.36	.43

(continued)

	Code	Side	Dates					
Angola (cont.)								
vs. UNITA South Africa	560	(OPP)	11/11/1975-	157.7	800	25446	5.07	.03
Afghanistan (ongoing)* 901		ON	06/01/1978-	235.5	1055000	284475	4483.64	3.71
Afghanistan Russia/USSR vs. Moslem Rebels	700 365	(GOV)	06/01/1978- 12/22/1979-	127.0 108.3	1000000 55000	21050 263425	7874.02 507.85	47.51 .21
Iran 904	630	OPP	09/03/1978-02/15/1979	5.4	7500	37900	1388.89	.20
vs. Anti-Shah Coalition		OPP	09/03/1978-02/15/1979	5.4	7500	37900	1388.89	.20
Nicaragua 907		OPP	10/01/1978-07/18/1979	9.5	35000	2340	3684.21	14.96
vs. Sandinistas	93	ON	10/01/1978-07/18/1979	9.5	35000	2340	3684.21	14.96
El Salvador (ongoing) 910		ON	07/01/1979-	114.0	69000	4714	605.26	14.64
El Salvador	92	GOV	07/01/1979-	114.0	69000	4714	605.26	14.64
Chad* 911		GOV	03/22/1980-08/07/1988	261.0	11200	62172	42.91	.18
Chad France vs. Frolinat	483 220	(GOV)	03/22/1980-08/07/1988 08/09/1983-08/07/1988	100.5 60.0	10000 200	4477 54652	99.50 3.33	2.23 —
Libya vs. FMLF	620	(OPP)	03/22/1980-08/07/1988	100.5	1000	3043	9.95	.33
Mozambique (ongoing)* 912		ON	10/21/1979-	220.6	200500	18559	908.88	10.80
Mozambique	541		10/21/1979-	110.3	200000	11629	1813.24	17.20

* indicates internationalized civil war (one or more system members intervening).
+ indicates that GOV or OPP won after the war became interstate.

TABLE 3.2 *(continued)*

Name and Number of War	Participant and Code Number	Winner (Intervention, if any)	Dates of War and Dates of Participation	Magnitude in Nation-Months	Severity in Battle Deaths	Population (×1,000 Pre-war)	Battle Deaths per Nation-Month	Battle Deaths per 1,000 Population
Mozambique (*cont.*)	Zimbabwe vs. Renamo 552	(GOV)	10/21/1979-	110.3	500	6930	4.53	.07
Nicaragua (ongoing) 913	Nicaragua vs. Contras 93	ON	03/18/1982-	81.7	43000	2955	526.32	14.55
			03/18/1982-	81.7	43000	2955	526.32	14.55
Peru (ongoing) 916	Peru vs. Shining Path 135	ON	03/04/1982-	81.9	15000	18226	183.15	.82
			03/04/1982-	81.9	15000	18226	183.15	.82
South Yemen 919	South Yemen vs. rebels 680	GOV	01/13/1986-01/29/1986	.5	12000	—	24000.00	—
			01/13/1986-01/29/1986	.5	12000	—	24000.00	—
Sri Lanka (ongoing) 922	Sri Lanka vs. Tamils 780	ON	07/25/1983-	65.2	8500	15416	130.37	.55
			07/25/1983-	65.2	8500	15416	130.37	.55
Sudan (ongoing) 925	Sudan vs. Sudan People's Liberation Army 625	ON	11/17/1983-	61.5	12000	20362	195.12	.59
			11/17/1983-	61.5	12000	20362	195.12	.59

Uganda 928				90.3	102000	13179	1127.07	7.74
Uganda vs. rebels	500	OPP	10/08/1980–04/24/1988	90.5	102000	13179	1127.07	7.74
Iran 931				10.9	14000	39536	1284.40	.35
Iran vs. rebels	630	GOV	06/06/1981–05/03/1982	10.9	14000	39536	1284.40	.35
Somalia (ongoing) 934				80.4	10000	5085	124.38	1.97
Somalia vs. North Somali rebels	520	ON	04/21/1982-	80.4	10000	5085	124.38	1.97
India (ongoing) 937				58.5	4000	746742	68.38	.01
India vs. Sikh Independence	750	ON	02/14/1984-	58.5	4000	746742	68.38	.01
Colombia 940				56.0	20000	28217	357.14	.71
Colombia vs. rebels	100	GOV	03/15/1984–11/14/1988	56.0	20000	28217	357.14	.71
Burundi 949				.1	5000	—	50000.00	—
Burundi vs. Hutu	516	GOV	08/18/1988–08/22/1988	.1	5000	—	50000.00	—

* indicates internationalized civil war (one or more system members intervening).
+ indicates that GOV or OPP won after the war became interstate.

Uppermost in the minds of most of us in the wealthier neighborhoods of the world community is, of course, the relationship between nuclear weapons and the absence of interstate war in this region. While this may well account for a good part of the variance, some other sets of variables *might* also have been at work, and they are presented here in outline form:

1. Displacement hypotheses:
   a. Regional shift, but system's structure and culture assures *some* "normal" frequency of war.
   b. Majors now use proxy nations to fight for them.
   c. Majors fight against "hostile" regimes or insurgents, all of whom are militarily and industrially inferior.
2. Substitution hypotheses:
   a. Arms race is a safer substitute for war.
   b. Recurrent militarized disputes are safer form of conflict than war.
3. Historical trend hypotheses:
   a. Today's major powers already passed through the war-prone phase, as have earlier majors.
   b. More are nations becoming democratic and/or capitalistic, and these societies are not only less war-like, but rarely fight one another.
   c. Destruction from, and memories of, the two World Wars.
4. Psychocultural hypotheses:
   a. Growth of norm that war is ethically unacceptable.
   b. Decline in nationalism and/or religiosity.
   c. Decline in ideological conviction and commitment.
   d. Decline in public trust in government officials and institutions.
   e. Self-fulfilling belief in improbability of war.
5. Technological (communication and observation) hypotheses:
   a. Monitoring and surveillance offers assurance of rival's military capabilities and deployments, with less fear of surprise attack or sudden discovery of inferiority.
   b. Relative ease, speed, and reliability of summit conversation via hot line, etc., in disputes and crises; lower likelihood of misunderstanding or of subordinates pursuing private strategies.
   c. Television coverage provides rapid and graphic reportage, making public more aware of carnage and able to express immediate opposition to war-like behavior.
   d. Increasing access of elites to the publics of nations in other bloc, vitiating unseen and therefore more threatening enemy.
6. Technological (weaponry) hypotheses:
   a. Nuclear weapons useless for war fighting; too destructive and nondiscriminating.
   b. Even "clean" nuclear weapons will produce long-range radiation across northern hemisphere, affecting all parties.

  c. "Nuclear Winter" and other as-yet-unknown consequences too menacing for all parties.

  d. Even a highly successful first strike, backed up by ABM systems, cannot be sufficiently "disarming" to eliminate unacceptable retaliatory damage.

  e. Danger of conventional war escalating to nuclear use is inhibiting.

  f. "Conventional" technology could produce more devastation than WWII.

  g. Ethical norms vis-a-vis nuclear, biological, and chemical weapons.

  h. High-tech weapons and surveillance systems permit arms control and limitation agreements.

7. Resource self-sufficiency hypotheses:

  a. Both superpowers are virtually self-sufficient in natural resources and food.

  b. Other major powers have adequate access to resources.

8. Economic self-sufficiency hypotheses:

  a. All majors have had adequate access to export markets to date (but may not obtain for long).

  b. All majors have had adequate access to capital and to investment opportunities.

9. Geographical location and contiguity hypotheses:

  a. Superpowers as main rivals have negligible contiguity — usually a necessary condition for war.

  b. Consequently the confrontation of large conventional land forces is via allies in Europe, and not directly opposing.

  c. Given locations, etc., U.S. largely a naval power and Soviet Union largely a land power, and thus less direct threats to one another.

10. System structure hypotheses:

  a. Highly bipolar system with NATO and WTO each deterring the other.

  b. No defections of bloc allies in Europe.

  c. Non-European (e.g., China, Egypt) defections tolerable.

  d. Allies exercise restraining influence.

  e. Spheres of influence well defined and accepted in Europe, if not elsewhere.

  f. Despite weaknesses, UN institutions have helped to inhibit and contain dispute escalation.

11. Domestic constraints hypotheses:

  a. Support for military build-up far from unanimous in United States, Soviet Union, or allies.

  b. Such support often contingent upon promises of prudence.

  c. Conflicting demands on limited funds, trained personnel, etc.

  d. Recognized costs, and failures, of recent military adventures, and consequent hostility to belligerent foreign policy.

   e. Pressing domestic problems, often seen as exacerbated by
      military preparedness and policy belligerence.
12. Interactive hypothesis: None of these factors alone would have
    prevented WWII, but the combined and cumulative effects have
    sufficed to date.
13. Perhaps this *is* the lucky number!

THE PROSPECTS

There are several strategies available for generating predictions
regarding the incidence of some phenomenon of interest in the social
sciences. Leaving aside tea leaves, chicken entrails, and the position of
the stars, there would seem to be three of interest here. The first is simple
extrapolation: observe the trend line or cyclical pattern of the phenomenon over some respectable period of time in the past, and extend that
pattern into the future. A second, and somewhat more reliable method,
is to generate a fair amount of correlational knowledge based on a systematic examination of some relevant past, and then make a forecast
(used here interchangeably with prediction) of a contingent sort. That is,
if war increases with the increase of systemic polarity or capability concentration (it does, but more clearly in the nineteenth century than in
the twentieth), we can predict that *if* such conditions obtain, *then* war
will increase. The third is to predict on the basis of a coherent and
empirically supported theoretical model; also contingent, this type of
forecast not only takes account of the factors that seem to account for
variation in the outcome variable, but also of the changing relationships
among variables that is characteristic of all developing systems (i.e., *all*
biological and social systems and many physical systems).
    While there has been no reproducible test of the relative reliability
of these three strategies, the partial evidence to date suggests that reliability increases as we move from extrapolation to correlation to theory-
based strategies (Singer and Wallace, 1979; Singer and Stoll, 1984). Given
our modest progress in developing one or more dynamic theories for
explaining or predicting the incidence of war, we have no choice here but
to rely heavily on the extrapolational and correlational methods, somewhat enhanced by a theoretical model that may yet grow up to become
a theory in the scientific, codified knowledge, sense of the word. In this
section, then, we essay some predictions on the probable incidence of
international and civil war over the next few decades.
    As suggested by the title of this chapter, my reading of the evidence
leads, at best, to mild pessimism. First, those who live in the peripheral
regions will not only remain peripheral in their access to the needs and
wants of life, but will continue to experience more than their share of
bloody violence. Second, and equally ominous, my sense is that the spectre

of World War III is by no means behind us. These two predictions are, of course, not unrelated, but space limitations preclude more than a summary treatment of the factors that might account for several more decades of recurrent war among and within the states of Africa, Asia, the Middle East, and Latin America.

The Peripheral System

Inasmuch as one of the more plausible catalysts of major-power war is that of international or civil war in the peripheral regions, a cursory overview might be in order here. Beginning with the ominous prospect of a continuing round of civil wars, the most salient factor is that of factional struggle for power within these often newly independent states. Superimposed on the twin conditions of widespread poverty and long-standing ethnic hostilities, there is the frequent problem of leadership that is incompetent, corrupt, and often in the service of a major-power government, "intelligence" agency, or corporate interest group. After the early spurt in development, many of these economies are close to stagnant and burdened with expensive armies and external debt payments. The tinder-box nature of these societies would be bad enough if left alone, but superpower intervention of one sort or another typically makes it worse. In pursuit of export markets (increasingly military), raw materials, cheap labor, profitable investment, and military bases — not to mention expanding the sphere of influence or denying it to the rival power — the Soviets and Americans along with others exacerbate internal conflicts and problems through their usually clumsy and often violent interventions. The 43 civil wars fought in these regions since 1945 are depressing enough, and the fact that 15 became internationalized merely adds to one's sense of pessimism. Further, eight of these foreign military force interventions were on the part of major powers.

The one auspicious fact in this depressing record is that in no cases did major powers become directly involved militarily on both the government *and* the insurgent side. Better yet, in no case was the U.S. on one side and the USSR on the other. In other words, despite the frequent military involvement of the superpowers in these internal struggles, and the fact that much of that involvement took the form of weapons supply or teams of technicians, the superpowers were careful to avoid direct confrontation in the gray areas of the globe.

There are good reasons to expect that while the people living in the poorer sections of the global village can expect several more decades of recurrent bloodshed, this violence is unlikely to generate major-power war. First, there is the historical pattern of relative prudence of the past four decades. Second, when the majors *have* invested heavily in efforts to expand or maintain their spheres of influence via the military instrument, the results have been less than cost-effective. Regimes in these neighborhoods have come and gone, as has their allegiance to one or the other major-power blocs.

And in the two most dramatic cases — Vietnam and Afghanistan — the consequences have been disastrous for the indigenous populations and their neighbors, and brought in their train extraordinary costs for the Americans and the Soviets. For their efforts, the superpowers have expended treasure, generated concern among their allies, exacerbated the existing hostility and suspicion toward them within the Third and Fourth World, severely damaged their own economies, and witnessed considerable domestic opposition and resentment. A decade and a half after its Indo-China intervention, the U.S. is still suffering the political and economic consequences, and as the USSR completes its disengagement from Afghanistan, it must contemplate much of the same for many years into the future. Nor have their political elites and counter-elites — more in the Soviet Union than in the U.S. — failed to notice the maladaptive consequences of these misadventures.

Third, and partly as a result of the above experiences, the Soviet Union and the U.S. find it necessary to invest attention, energy, and resources closer to home as well as at home. Economic dislocation and political disaffection within the two societies (especially the former) will inhibit new efforts to impose their wills beyond their more proximate spheres of influence, and alliance partners will be more vigorous in counseling restraint.

A fourth factor is, of course, the evolution of weapons technology. Despite heavy investment in the hardware and organization for low-intensity warfare, the prospects of military success are not bright. That is, the current and prospective phases in technological evolution make it considerably easier to hold territory than to seize it, and give a marked advantage to those defending home turf vis-a-vis those invading it. To put it more graphically, a relatively small number of ill-trained irregulars are now able — thanks to "user-friendly" technology — to destroy tanks and aircraft of superior firepower and range in the hands of better trained and conventionally superior foreign forces. Nor should we expect that the majors' indigenous allies, be they government or insurgent forces, will fare any better on these battlefields, especially given the likelihood that the invaders will be on the side of a faltering and unpopular regime or what is perceived as a counter-revolutionary force of mercenaries. To borrow from an impressive psychological experiment of several decades ago (Thibaut and Kelley, 1959), the major powers may well enjoy "fate control" in the sense of being able to inflict great destruction, but will rarely enjoy "behavior control" in any effective and continuing sense.

A fifth factor — not to be dismissed — is the normative one. Born and baptized in the nineteenth century, and erratically institutionalized in the twentieth, the principle of national self-determination seems to be growing in legitimacy and acceptance. Just as war in general may be "going out of style," the use of force to deny self-determination — which may not necessarily be humane, competent, or democratic — to any nationality, linguistic, or ethnic group is likely to come under increasing fire and command less and less support worldwide. And to the extent that these norms find increasing expression in formal institutions, legal codification, and juridical interpretation, the inhibitions will be that much more powerful.

In sum, this combination of self-interest and normative constraint can be expected to lead, erratically, incrementally, and quite informally at first, to some version of a "sanity code" among the major powers in general and the superpowers in particular. In light, then, of this set of considerations, one need not be utopian to expect a rapidly diminishing tendency of those all-too-likely civil wars in the poorer districts to suffer direct military intervention. And, if indirect intervention — in the form of weapons, parts, ammunition, technicians, training, and funding for military purposes — were equally proscribed by such a sanity code, both the frequency and the duration and severity of those bloody intrusions could be appreciably diminished.

The Central System

Returning now to the strategic confrontation between the superpowers and their European allies, let me attend here to two basic perspectives. One is to see the past forty years as the first segment of a long and unbroken condition of peace, in which the military standoff and strategic deterrence gradually give way to better coordination, less menacing forms of competition, and perhaps even a modicum of positive cooperation. This scenario, while far from outlandish, usually rests on several optimistic assumptions, two of which seem especially crucial.

One is that the Western powers, primarily the U.S., recognize those realities that the Soviets have recently begun to recognize: 1) the capacity to threaten first use of nuclear weapons exercises more of a provocative than a deterrent effect; and 2) maintaining and deploying war-winning capabilities, "conventional" or otherwise, incurs unacceptably high costs at home and abroad, economically, politically, and psychologically. The second assumption is that treating the other superpower and its allies as opportunistically waiting for the chance to strike a conclusive military blow, which therefore must be militarily deterred, strengthens the position at home of the cold warriors, their sycophants, and the acquiescers, and thus diminishes diplomatic creativity and flexibility abroad.

Despite the convenient folklore, confrontation and rivalry abroad may require an external threat *initially*, but the amplification and perpetuation of that threat is largely a function of domestic political, emotional, and economic interests, and soon becomes relatively impervious to the behavior and capabilities of the source of that original threat. Were the above considerations more fully recognized and responded to, an interesting and promising sequence of considerable portent could be set in motion. Such a scenario is spelled out in detail in "Missiles of October — 1988" (Singer, 1986), but suffice to say here that it examines a mix of self-correcting and self-amplifying feedback processes that culminates in a redistribution of power and legitimacy within the societies of America and Europe, interacting with auspicious changes in the behavior of these states.

A second possibility, however, is that these four decades do not, on closer examination, look much different from those thirteen that went before (1816-1946), and that the configuration of *structural* and *cultural* conditions at both the systemic and the national levels should have led by now to war among the major powers. The most salient difference is the *material* transformation represented by nuclear weapons and long-range delivery vehicles. To take much comfort from the coexistence of peace and these doomsday machines is, according to this perspective, to mistake correlation for causation.

To the extent that we draw optimistic inferences from these peaceful decades in the central system, we need to have considerable confidence in three aspects of nuclear "deterrence." One is that — in addition to believing that without it, "the other side" would have launched its assault long ago — the command and control system is so reliable that none of these weapons will ever be fired. An extension of that faith is that if a few *are* fired, the chain reaction to all-out nuclear war can somehow be contained by judicious self-restraint and shrewd bargaining promptly thereafter. Third, and perhaps most far-fetched, is the confidence that all parties will accept the military and political status quo, learn to "live with the bomb," and eschew any efforts to "modernize" their weapon systems. As suggested — and without accepting the fatalistic statistics of cumulative and ever-increasing probabilities of war — to count on the past and settle for a more or less indefinite nuclear stalemate is to court catastrophe.

The better part of wisdom, given the lessons of history regarding the misplaced faith that has accompanied every major innovation in weapons technology (Bloch, 1898), is to recognize the awesome range of events that could destabilize the precarious stand-off, and thus move promptly toward some radical transformations in the way that we pursue national security.

That such transformations need to be radical is all too evident, and they will require an appreciable shift — *inter alia* — in our collective sense of efficacy and in the distribution of legitimacy in our societies. By the former, I mean the need to attend more closely to what we can and can not influence, and by which instruments, in the global village. On the one hand, the elite view in the West is that the reform movement in the Soviet Union is precarious, and that we must be prepared for the reappearance of a more autocratic and (therefore?) expansionist regime in the Kremlin. That could, of course, please and vindicate the more belligerent factions in the West, encourage a return to more provocative weapon systems and more refractory policies, and increase the likelihood of war.

On the other hand, we systematically underestimate the symmetry of the Soviet-American relationship, appreciating that their behavior affects us greatly, yet largely denying that our behavior affects them as well. This is especially true in the realm of rewards and promises, where we act as if there is little to be done in the direction of strengthening the pro-reform and pro-détente forces; in contrast, when it comes to punishment and threat, American national security elites show a touching faith in their ability to deter and inhibit, if not blackmail, by the ways in which we brandish and flaunt our weapons of mass destruction. Typical was the 1974 comment by Defense Secretary Schlesinger that "occasionally the Russians should read in the press that a counterforce attack may not fall on silos that are empty;" that is, our counterforce launch will already have occurred. In short, some prudently chosen rewards now might well reduce the need for imprudently chosen punishments later.

This sort of reemphasis would likely, in my view, generate some useful reinforcement processes, and not only in the USSR. That is, if our behavior could help to perpetuate these early moves to reduce military capabilities and commitments, combined with an increased attention to economic and political reform, the impact on the East European societies could be beneficial to all but a few in that region. But for the Soviets to continue their tolerance of reforms and greater autonomy in its former dependencies, they need to be consistently assured that such transformation will not be exploited by the West and become a security threat to them. American policies can go a long way toward overcoming that particular obsession in the Kremlin. Further, were this loosening of control to occur, it would almost certainly be contagious, and thus accelerate the already evident tendencies of the NATO allies to exercise greater independence. As I argued shortly after the Cuban crisis when there seemed to be some stirrings toward greater independence in the super-power alliances, such a process should help unfetter the restraints of bipolar diplomacy and open up a much larger repertoire of initiatives and trade-offs (Singer, 1963). This sort of process will, of course, depend on some prior, if modest, redistribution of beliefs and influence in the U.S., and while we do not seem to be there yet, there *are* some promising auguries, and those of us in the international security field might well provide a helpful catalyst at today's critical juncture.

CONCLUSION

By some indicators, war has declined in the international system since 1945, and by others, the changes seem quite marginal. But the big news is that the industrial and postindustrial nations have somehow managed to prepare for war with a dedication seldom seen in history, while nevertheless keeping that apocalyptic horseman at bay. Despite the conventional wisdom, all indicators are that this was less a consequence of intelligent policy than a fortunate concatenation of conditions. So benign a set of circumstances is, however, unlikely to endure for long without some major transformations in major-power behavior, diplomatic norms, and system structure.

Meanwhile, as political elites in the central system struggle with a world that is difficult to comprehend and impossible to control, they not only do too little to move us away from the brink of nuclear catastrophe. They also continue policies that play havoc in the peripheral and poor neighborhoods of the global village. In addition to the addictive and futile efforts to install and maintain friendly regimes, while trying to unseat unfriendly ones, an increasing number of nations — East and West, developed and far-from-developed — engage in one of the more incendiary policies of the post–World War II era: less for strategic than for short-run economic purposes, they accelerate the export of weapon systems to nations whose leadership is largely up for grabs, whose resources need to go elsewhere, and whose political and economic development cannot possibly proceed under such conditions. The strategic weapons, the targeting doctrines, the top personnel, and their far-from-reliable command and control systems remain largely in place; at this writing the Soviet-American hard-wired doomsday machine has barely been touched by arms control and arms reduction negotiations. And while one of the superpowers gives every indication of pragmatic retreat from the deadly pursuit of power, its erstwhile rival continues on the familiar path. Toppling some undesirable regimes, shoring up others, testing exotic new weapons, stockpiling those of earlier vintage (albeit at a diminished pace), launching a specious — and international — war on drugs, and ignoring injustice and incompetence at home, the U.S. may well help to reverse the Soviet withdrawal from the struggle. Thus, without some rather dramatic changes in the outlook and behavior of those who lead — and acquiesce — in the societies of the central system, we can look forward not only to a continuation of the slaughter that marks the past four decades in Asia, Africa, the Middle East, and Latin America, but the possibility that the next roll of the diplomatic dice will trigger the ultimate conflagration.

CHAPTER FOUR

International Crises and Global Instability: The Myth of the "Long Peace"

Michael Brecher
Jonathan Wilkenfeld

CONCEPTUAL CRITIQUE

There are many paths to knowledge about global politics since World War II. Professor Gaddis, the catalyst for this book, has chosen to focus on one important aspect of historical reality, namely, *the absence of war between the superpowers*. The accuracy of this statement is beyond doubt; that is, the United States and the Soviet Union have successfully avoided *direct, full-scale military hostilities* since 1945.

This trait of the superpower relationship led Professor Gaddis to designate the postwar era the *long peace*. The term calls to mind a similar phrase for the period, 1815-1914, the "Hundred Years' Peace," though in truth war was widespread during that century, including wars among the major powers, such as the Crimean, Austro/Prussian, Franco/German, and Russo/Turkish Wars between 1856 and 1878.

Taking the long peace as the central fact of the decades since World War II, he provided a thoughtful explanation of that reality in terms of the bipolar structure of the global system and the behavior of the superpowers. First, bipolarity accurately reflected the distribution of military power in the system as a whole. Moreover, it is a simple structure, easier to sustain than the multipolarity of the inter–World War period. Consequently, alliances have been more stable. Defections from the two blocs have not caused major disruptions. These structural factors were, in his view, supplemented by certain inherent stabilizing features of the U.S.-Soviet relationship: the absence of war between them throughout their history; their economic independence from each other, and "no obvious proclivity on either side [stemming from domestic pressures] to risk war" (Gaddis, 1987b:229).

At the behavioral level, Gaddis credited the leaders of the two super-powers with caution due to several factors: the development of nuclear weapons and an effective nuclear deterrent; the "reconnaissance revolu-tion," which greatly reduced the danger of surprise attack; ideological moderation by both parties; and a mutually recognized set of rules of the superpower game. The upshot has been the longest era of peace in the twentieth century and a period of great-power stability to which only a few are comparable in modern world history.

Others may take issue with the Gaddis explanation of the long peace. Our role is to challenge the validity of the thesis as inconsistent with reality, a malaise shared by all "globalists" who focus exclusive attention on the giants, ignoring the pygmies, of world politics.

We have no quarrel with the assertion that the superpowers have avoided war, directly, between themselves for more than forty years, nor with the assessment that this is a major achievement. Rather, we ques-tion the underlying assumptions that (1) the *absence of war* is synony-mous with *stability*; (2) the absence of war *between the superpowers* is synonymous with *global peace*; (3) the absence of *system transformation through war* is synonymous with *global stability*; and that (4) if that idyllic state in the relations between the two superpowers can be sus-tained, the future of global stability is assured.

There are, in our view, several empirical and conceptual flaws in this "globalist" line of argument. One is the remarkable indifference to all interstate relations among the 147 states which are not members of the superpower club or, even if expanded to include the great powers (as in the title of this book) to all nonmembers of what Singer terms the *central subsystem*. Several research projects are moving beyond the dominant system and great-power foci. These include the work on militarized inter-state disputes (Gochman and Maoz, 1984; Gochman and Leng, 1988), major power–minor power wars (Midlarsky, 1988, and this volume), and international military interventions (Pearson and Baumann, 1988).

A second flaw in the Gaddis thesis is that it turns a blind eye to the 18 interstate and 12 extrasystemic wars from 1945 to 1980 as designated by the Correlates of War Project (Small and Singer, 1982: Appendix A; see also Singer, this volume), and the 251 international crises from June, 1945, to the end of 1985 uncovered by the International Crisis Behavior Project (Brecher, Wilkenfeld, and Moser, 1988: Table II.7, and Brecher and Wilkenfeld, 1989: Appendix). Their pervasiveness is evident in a myriad of international crises over *territory*, only one of the several issues in crises, in almost all regions during the four decades after World War II: in the 1940s, between India and Pakistan over Junagadh and Kashmir (1947-1948, and again over the latter, and the Rann of Kutch, in 1965); in the 1950s, between Italy and Yugoslavia over Trieste (1953), Afghan-istan and Pakistan over Pushtunistan (1955, and again in 1961-1962), Honduras and Nicaragua (1957), Egypt and Sudan (1958); in the 1960s, between Ghana and Togo (1960), China and India over their Himalayan borders (1960-1962), Algeria and Morocco (1963), Guyana and Venezuela over Essiquibo (1968, and again in 1981-1983), Iraq and Iran over the Shatt-al-Arab (1959-1960, again in 1969, and since 1980); in the 1970s, between Zambia and South Africa (1971, 1973), North and South Yemen (1972, 1979), Kuwait and Iraq (1973), Morocco and Spain (1975), Greece and Turkey over Cyprus and the Aegean (1974, 1976), Guatemala and the UK (1977), Ethiopia and Somalia (1977-1978); and in the 1980s, between Angola and South Africa (1980, and almost every year thereafter), Somalia and Ethiopia (1980, 1982), Libya and the United States (1981), Ecuador and Peru (1981), Argentina and the UK over the Falklands/Malvinas (1982), Chad and Nigeria (1983), Thailand and Laos (1984), Botswana and South Africa (1985), and Burkina Faso and Mali (1985-1986).

While the East/West protracted conflict has been spared a full-scale war with both superpowers engaged in direct military operations against each other, subsystem conflicts have experienced a plethora of wars; for example, Arab states and Israel in 1948-1949, 1956, 1967, 1969-1970, 1973, and 1982, and India and Pakistan in 1947-1948, 1965, and 1971. More generally, violence was considerably more visible in the era of the long peace than in the pre–World War II period of the 1920s and 1930s: 49 percent to 39 percent in the triggers to international crises; and 26 percent to 11 percent as the primary technique of crisis management in the two periods (Brecher and Wilkenfeld, 1989:46-47).

The vast majority of these wars and crises may not have posed a threat to the survival of the global system. Yet some, like the Berlin Blockade of 1948-1949 and the Cuban Missile Crisis, certainly did so. And all generated disruption; that is, they were sources of instability in that system.

A third flaw is the narrow scope of the Gaddis definition of peace, even in terms of his own negative criterion, namely, the absence of direct military hostilities between the U.S. and the USSR. This excludes proxy wars, in which the two superpowers were engaged in overt conflict through clients, as with Cuba and the UNITA movement in the prolonged Angolan War from 1975 to 1988, or with the Contras and the Sandinista government in the war over Nicaragua throughout the 1980s. It also excludes wars in which one superpower was a direct participant, and the other was involved through military aid, as in the Korean War from 1950 to 1953 and Afghanistan from 1979 to 1989. And it excludes the important phenomenon of "near-miss" direct superpower military hostilities, in some cases where war was avoided altogether (as with the Berlin Blockade and Cuban Missiles), in others where threats and counterthreats and effective signaling kept the U.S. and the USSR from direct involvement in wars between their clients (as in the Arab-Israeli wars of 1967 and 1973). Taken together, the exclusion of these sources of systemic disruption raises profound skepticism about the adequacy of the Gaddis concept, the long peace. Indeed, at the conclusion of his provocative paper, there is a moment of self-doubt: "We may argue among ourselves as to whether or not we can legitimately call this 'peace': it is not, I daresay, what most of us have in mind when we use that term."

There is another conceptual flaw, with profound implications for the validity of the long-peace thesis: it is the equating of instability with war, and of nonwar between the superpowers with global stability. Elsewhere (Brecher, James, and Wilkenfeld, 1990), we have argued that the literature on conflict is skewed to the presence or absence of war as the sole indicator of international (in)stability; further, that the empirical findings relate to war proneness and intensity, not to the broader concept of system instability; and that many international conflicts do not involve violence yet still pose grave challenges to system stability; for example, the three superpower confrontations over Berlin — the Blockade (1948-1949), the Deadline (1957-1959) and the Wall (1961) — did not escalate to war but they posed challenges to the dominant system of world politics during the Cold War.

We also specified our differences with earlier definitions of *stability* and *instability*, which apply to the Gaddis thesis as well. The key to this condition is the concept of change but not necessarily drastic change, such as system transformation or system breakdown, whether or not brought on by full-scale war. These lie at the extreme of the stability/instability continuum, while change refers to *any* shift from an existing pattern of interaction between two or more actors in the direction of greater conflict or cooperation. The former type of change frequently escalates to crisis and, less often, to war. Whatever the issues in dispute, and whether they are tangible or intangible or of high or low value, crisis generates disruption in an international system, whether global, dominant or subsystem, a process similar to war-generated disruption. Moreover, disruption may affect one or more core components of a system — its power hierarchy, alliance pattern, and rules of the game. In short, crisis, like war, whether or not accompanied by violence, represents change and causes disruption, leading to instability.

Stability was redefined as change within explicit bounds or normal fluctuations (Azar, et al., 1977:196-207). The absence of change indicates pure stability, its presence some degree of instability regardless of the source of change — war, crisis, or some less acute generator of disruption. And even acute conflict may — but need not — lead to system breakdown or transformation. Such an extreme outcome, which would maximize system instability, *is the exclusive focus of the Gaddis analysis*.

Our concern goes beyond the extreme of breakdown or transformation to encompass the fullest expression of global instability. We also contend that there are multiple sources of systemic disruption, both in type of conflict and the number of entities. Thus, broader indicators than war and superpowers are necessary in order to tap a wide range of disruptive interaction among states.

We argue that crisis is a much more comprehensive indicator of conflict and disruption than war, for war is a subset of crisis. (Parenthetically, the ICB set of crises includes all the COW wars from 1945 to 1980 — in fact, from 1929 onward.) Some crises are accompanied by violence, whether minor or serious clashes or full-scale war, while others are not. Yet all crises, like wars, cause disruption in an international system; that is, they are sources of instability. Similarly, some states are direct actors in many international crises (such as the U.S. and USSR in 34 and 10 cases, respectively, from 1945 to 1985), others in only one crisis (such as Ghana in the 1960 Ghana/Togo Border Crisis). During the four decades since World War II, more than 100 states were crisis actors.

An *international crisis* in the peace-war issue area, the indicator of global instability in the analysis to follow, is defined as:

> a situational change characterized by two necessary and sufficient conditions: (1) distortion in the type and/or an increase in the intensity of *disruptive interactions* between two or more adversaries, with an accompanying high probability of *military hostilities* or, during a war, an *adverse change* in the *military balance*; and (2) a *challenge* to the existing structure of an international system posed by the higher-than-normal conflictual interactions.

International crises may occur in prewar, intrawar and postwar settings, for example, entry into World War II in 1939, Dien Bien Phu in 1954 (where the use of nuclear weapons was considered by the U.S.), and Truman Doctrine in 1947, respectively. They do not, however, differ with respect to the generic conditions of a crisis, namely, disruption, destabilization and the military dimension. And it is these disruptive interactions, accompanied by the likelihood of violence, which pose a challenge to system stability.

Instability, in this perspective, has been pervasive in global politics since 1945, in superpower relations and the dominant system, as well as for most states and all subsystems. Only extreme instability, as in World War II, leads to system breakdown and transformation, leading to a new equilibrium. This was expressed by two fundamental changes in the structure of the global system after 1945: from multipolarity to bipolarity; and from an essentially Euro-American club to near-universal participation of nations in world politics through a trebling of the number of states over four decades.

Given these conceptual differences with the Gaddis long-peace thesis, we shall present an analysis of the *pattern of global instability* from 1945 to 1985 as evident in the empirical record of international crises during that period. This, we contend, is a more valid representation of reality than the long peace, though, as will be elaborated later, these are not mutually exclusive. We shall present several "cuts" of the relevant data in order to demonstrate the pervasive instability in world politics since the end of World War II: 1) the 25 most destabilizing military-security crises during the four decades (10 percent of the ICB data set), focusing on the instability which they generated, along with an illustration of how the instability score for each case — and for all crises during that period — was derived; 2) international crises and instability by geographic region, conflict setting, and system level; 3) crisis-generated instability over time, by decade and year-by-year; and 4) superpower crises since mid-1945, that is, international crises in which the U.S. and/or the USSR were crisis actors.

INDICATORS AND METHODS

The instability generated by crises was measured by an Index of Instability that incorporates three dimensions: *turmoil, power status*, and *duration*. Turmoil, a synonym for disruption, is the preeminent indicator of the extent of instability in an international system for any time frame — a day, month, year, decade, or era. Initially a set of ten variables, from onset to outcome and legacy, was used to provide a thorough mapping of crisis turmoil: the gravity of threatened values; breakpoint (trigger); crisis management technique; intensity of violence; number of involved actors; extent/type of major power activity, and its effectiveness in crisis abatement; form of outcome; extent of satisfaction with the crisis outcome, and crisis legacy in terms of subsequent tension level.

A factor analysis was then employed to generate a smaller cluster of indicators of turmoil. Among the three factors — behavior, third-party activity, and threat — the first grouped three variables — crisis management technique, intensity of violence, and breakpoint. Since the first factor accounted for a high proportion of the common variance (41.2 percent), it was selected as the sole indicator of turmoil; and factor scores were generated for the 251 international crises from 1945 to 1985.

The primary *crisis management technique* is coded along a scale from nonviolence to violence: *pacific*, including negotiation, e.g., formal bilateral exchange, mediation by global or regional organization, etc., multiple techniques excluding violence, and nonmilitary pressure, such as withholding economic aid, etc.; *nonviolent military* — both physical acts, such as maneuvers, and verbal acts, as in threat to use violence; and *violence*.

The *intensity of violence* refers to the degree of coercive activity as a crisis management technique in an international crisis: it may be *no violence; minor clashes* involving few or no deaths or injuries; *serious clashes* short of full-scale war, or *war*.

Breakpoint or *trigger* to an international crisis is the specific act, event or situational change that catalyzes a crisis for the earliest crisis actor, that is, perceptions of value threat, time pressure and likely military hostilities. Triggers are grouped into four categories: *nonviolent*, including verbal, political or economic acts and external change; *internal*, that is, a verbal or physical challenge to a regime; *nonviolent military*, such as an alert of forces; and *violent*.

The inclusion of power status in the Index of Instability recognizes that the extent of systemic disruption is a function not only of the type of behavior on the part of crisis actors (e.g., negotiation versus violence), but also reflects their power. Stated differently, crises with superpowers as direct participants generate more instability than crises among small powers. The power of each crisis actor was calculated for the year its crisis began as a composite of six components: GNP; military expenditure; nuclear capability; population; size of territory; and alliance capability. Power status, derived from that calculus, was measured on a four-point scale, from superpower (4), through great power (3), middle power (2), to small power (1).[1]

The duration of an international crisis is measured from the first breakpoint to the last exitpoint, that is, from the trigger for the first actor until crisis termination for the last actor to exit from a crisis. These events signal the beginning and the end of disruptive interaction (turmoil) among the participants. The inclusion of duration for each actor recognizes that systemic disruption will be more (or less) extensive the longer (or shorter) the time from onset to termination for the crisis as a whole.

The overall Index of Instability is represented by the following equation:

[1]
$$I_j = (T_j + 1.775624) \left(\sum_{i=1}^{N} (P_i (\log_{10} (D_i)) + 1) \right)$$

where
I_j = instability generated by crisis "j" ($j = 1,....,251$).
T_j = turmoil associated with crisis "j" (1.775624 is added to the turmoil factor score so there will be no negative values).
P_i = power status of actor "i" in international crisis "j".
D_i = duration in days as a crisis actor for actor "i" in crisis "j".

In short, the instability generated by an international crisis is a function of its turmoil, the power status of the participants, and its duration.[2]

The method used to derive instability scores for each international crisis in the ICB data set will be illustrated by the October–Yom Kippur Crisis of 1973-1974. As shown in Table 4.1, the predominant crisis management technique was multiple including violence, and the intensity of violence was full-scale war. Based on these data, the overall score for turmoil was 2.56. As for power status, the U.S. and the USSR were superpowers; thus P_1 and P_2 each = 4. The three Middle East crisis actors were great powers *in the Middle East system at the time*; thus P_3 (Egypt), P_4 (Israel), and P_5 (Syria) each = 3.

The first breakpoint of that crisis was the evidence of an impending Egyptian-Syrian attack, perceived on October 5 and the trigger to a crisis for Israel. The other four direct participants became crisis actors at different points in time — Syria on October 10, the U.S. on October 12, Egypt on October 18, and the USSR on October 22. Similarly, the actors exited at different points in time. Egypt was the first on January 18, 1974, when its Disengagement Agreement with Israel was signed. The last exits occurred with the signing of the Israel-Syria Disengagement Agreement on May 31, 1974, the termination date for Israel, Syria, the U.S., and the USSR. Thus, the duration for actors in that crisis was as follows: U.S., 232 days D_1; USSR, 222 days D_2; Egypt, 93 days D_3; Israel, 239 days D_4; and Syria, 234 days D_5.

Having derived the values for turmoil, power status and duration, the Index of Instability for the 1973-1974 Middle East Crisis was calculated according to [1].

With the indicators and methods clarified, we turn to the analyses specified above, beginning with the most destabilizing crises.

DATA ANALYSIS

Our data set, as noted, comprises 251 international crises from June, 1945 to the end of 1985. The first erupted from a dispute between Turkey and the USSR over the territories of Kars and Ardahan, located in northeast Turkey bordering on Soviet Armenia; it lasted from June 7, 1945 to April 5, 1946, with the U.S., the USSR, and the UK deeply involved in a prelude to the Cold War. This East/West crisis, which ended with a symbolic unilateral act — a U.S. announcement that the body of the deceased Turkish ambassador in Washington was being returned to Istanbul on the battleship *Missouri* — reemerged with fresh Soviet demands on Turkey, the Turkish Straits Crisis, August 7 to October 26, 1946. The last case in the data set was the Burkina Faso/Mali Border Crisis, from December 20, 1985, to January 18, 1986. Neither superpower was involved in any form. There were serious clashes. The crisis ended with an agreement between the adversaries.

Because of space limitations, Table 4.1 presents the relevant data and the overall instability score for the 25 most destabilizing international crises during the four decades.

What do the composite data on these crises reveal? The minimal *number of* states as *crisis actors* was two, India and Pakistan in both Kashmir crises, and India and China in their border crisis and war.[3] At the other extreme, there were seven crisis actors in War in Angola — Zambia, Zaire, South Africa, Angola, Cuba, the USSR, and the U.S., in the order of their entry into that crisis. There were six actors in the Israel Independence Crisis and in the Prague Spring, with five in several cases, October–Yom Kippur, Korean War II and Shaba II. The most frequent cluster was four actors, in eight of the 25 international crises.

As expected, the primary *crisis management technique* in all of these crises was violence, and most of them exhibited full-scale war. However, less *intense violence* is evident in six crises: serious clashes short of war in Taiwan Straits I, Afghanistan, Congo II, Shaba II, and the Lebanon/Iraq Upheaval, and minor clashes in the Prague Spring. And the crisis *trigger* reveals considerable variation — with a catalyst other than violence in seven cases.

In the October–Yom Kippur Crisis, it was a nonviolent military act, specifically, the movement of Egyptian troops toward the Suez Canal on October 5 and a change from defensive to offensive posture on the part of Syrian forces on the Golan Heights. In four cases, the trigger was political in nature: in Taiwan Straits I, the formation of SEATO in August, 1954, a perceived threat by the PRC; in the Invasion of Cambodia, a demand by Cambodia on March 13, 1970 that all Vietcong and North Vietnam forces be withdrawn within 48 hours; in Chad/Libya IV, a *volte face* by the two principal leaders, Goukouni Oueddei and Hissene Habré, reneging on a March, 1979 France-Nigeria–brokered agreement to enlarge the Provisional State Council, a crisis trigger for Libya; and the publication of Czechoslovakia's "Action Program" on April 9, 1968, triggering crises for East Germany and Poland, the onset of the Prague Spring Crisis. An internal challenge triggered two crises: the formation of a secessionist Revolutionary Council in Stanleyville, the Congo, on August 4, 1964, after rebel forces had occupied the city; and, in the Lebanon/Iraq Upheaval, the murder on May 8, 1958 of a reformist editor of a procommunist Beirut newspaper, a vocal critic of President Chamoun's pro-Western orientation, triggering a crisis for Lebanon. Finally, an external change triggered the Israel Independence Crisis for five Arab states, namely, the formal creation of Israel on May 15, 1948.

The high-instability crises will now be dissected along several other crisis dimensions: value threat; superpower activity and its role in crisis abatement; the relative effectiveness of global organization involvement in these cases; the crisis-conflict link; and the substance and form of outcome.

TABLE 4.1 Most Destabilizing International Crises, 1945–1985

Name of Crisis	Duration: Trigger-Termination	Number of Crisis Actors	Intensity of Violence	Crisis Management Technique	Trigger	Turmoil Score[a]	Power/Duration Score[b]	Instability Score[c]
(1) War in Angola	7/12/75-3/27/76	7	War	Violence	Indirect Violent	2.86	40.64	116.19
(2) October-Yom Kippur War	10/5/73-5/31/74	5	War	Multiple Inc. Violence	Non-Violent Military	2.56	36.51	93.46
(3) Korean War II	10/1/50-7/10/51	5	War	Violence	Violent	2.86	26.95	77.08
(4) War of Attrition II	1/7/70-8/7/70	3	War	Violence	Violent	2.66	22.90	60.91
(5) Taiwan Straits I	8/-/54-4/23/55	3(6)[d]	Serious Clashes	Violence	Political	1.82	31.85	57.97
(6) Afghanistan Invasion	3/15/79-2/28/80	4	Serious Clashes	Violence	Violent	2.54	22.62	57.45
(7) Invasion of Cambodia	3/13/70-7/22/70	4	War	Violence	Political	2.72	19.92	54.18
(8) Bangladesh	3/25/71-12/17/71	3(4)[e]	War	Violence	Violent	2.67	19.53	52.14
(9) Sino-Vietnam War	2/9/78-3/15/79	4(5)[f]	War	Violence	Violent	2.82	17.96	50.65
(10) Vietnam Ports Mining	3/30/72-7/19/72	3	War	Multiple Inc. Violence	Violent	2.90	17.42	50.52
(11) Kashmir II	8/5/65-1/10/66	2(3)[g]	War	Multiple Inc. Violence	Violent	3.05	15.51	47.30
(12) Congo II	8/4/64-12/30/64	4	Serious Clashes	Violence	Internal Challenge	2.20	20.86	45.89
(13) Chad/Libya IV	4/12/79-11/10/79	3	War	Violence	Political	2.94	15.56	45.75
(14) Israel Independence	5/15/48-7/20/49	6	War	Violence	External Change	2.60	17.02	44.25

(15) Kashmir I	10/24/47-1/1/49	2	War	Violence	Indirect Violent	3.24	13.21	42.80
(16) Chad/Libya III	4/15/78-8/29/78	3	War	Violence	Indirect Violent	3.08	13.60	41.89
(17) Korean War I	6/25/50-9/30/50	4	War	Violence	Violent	2.87	14.43	41.41
(18) Dien Bien Phu	3/13/54-7/21/54	3	War	Multiple Inc. Violence	Violent	2.42	16.92	40.95
(19) Lebanon War	6/5/82-5/17/83	3	War	Multiple Inc. Violence	Violent	2.88	14.17	40.81
(20) Basra-Kharg Island	2/21/84-7/11/84	4	War	Violence	Violent	2.70	15.06	40.66
(21) Shaba II	5/11/78-7/30/78	5	Serious Clashes	Violence	Violent	2.38	17.00	40.46
(22) Yemen War I	9/26/62-4/15/63	4	War	Multiple Inc. Violence	Indirect Violent	2.92	13.80	40.30
(23) India/China Border II	9/8/62-1/23/63	3[h]	War	Violence	Violent	2.63	15.22	40.03
(24) Prague Spring	4/9/68-10/18/68	6	Minor Clashes	Multiple Inc. Violence	Political	1.74	22.58	39.29
(25) Lebanon Iraq Upheaval	5/8/58-10/-/58	4	Serious Clashes	Multiple Inc. Violence	Internal Challenge	2.18	17.97	39.17

[a] The "turmoil score" is computed as follows: the score for each international crisis on factor 1 (behavior) plus 1.78 (the lowest negative value for any crisis on factor 1). The latter term ensures that all turmoil scores will be positive.

[b] The "power/duration score" is computed for each crisis as follows: $i=1$ $(P_i(\log_{10}(D_i+1)))$ where P_i = power status of actor i, and D_i = duration in days for each crisis actor.

[c] The "instability score" is computed by multiplying the "turmoil score" by the "power/duration score" for each international crisis.

[d] The USA, PRC, and Taiwan each experienced two foreign policy crises in the Taiwan Straits I international crisis.

[e] Pakistan was an actor in two foreign policy crises in the Bangladesh Crisis, together with Bangladesh and India, hence the number of crisis actors is six.

[f] Vietnam was an actor in two foreign policy crises in the Sino/Vietnam War Crisis, together with Thailand, Cambodia, and the PRC, hence the number of crisis actors is five.

[g] India was an actor in two foreign policy crises in the Kashmir II crisis, together with Pakistan, hence the number of crisis actors is three.

[h] India was an actor in two foreign policy crises in the India/China Border II crisis, together with the PRC, hence the number of crisis actors is three.

As expected, almost all of the most destabilizing crises exhibit a high *value threat*. Thus, influence was the highest value perceived as threatened in 12 of the 25 cases (by France and the U.S. in Dien Bien Phu, the USSR in the Prague Spring, and Israel and Syria in the Lebanon War of 1982-1983). Grave damage was anticipated in four cases (by India in the 1962 border crisis and war with China). And *existence*, the highest value, was perceived to be at stake in six cases (by Israel in the Independence Crisis, and Pakistan in the Bangladesh Crisis).

Active *participation by extraregional powers* in high-instability crises was widespread and intense: in *Asia*, the U.S. militarily and the USSR with military aid in the two Korean War cases, France and, to a lesser extent, the U.S. and the UK in Dien Bien Phu, the U.S. in Taiwan Straits I, Invasion of Cambodia, and Vietnam Ports Mining, and the USSR intensely in Afghanistan, with the U.S. providing military aid to the guerrillas, altogether, in 7 of 12 crises; in the *Middle East*, the U.S. and the UK in the Lebanon/Iraq Upheaval, the USSR in War of Attrition II, both superpowers in the October–Yom Kippur War; and in *Africa*, both superpowers, along with Belgium, in Congo II, the U.S. and the USSR in War in Angola, the U.S. in Shaba II, and France in Chad/Libya III and IV.

In Asia, except for the Korean War cases, USSR involvement in high-instability crises was always confined to the political sphere whenever the U.S. was a crisis actor. However, in the one Asian case with intense USSR involvement, namely, Afghanistan, the U.S. did not back off. The Soviet Union was much more active in Middle East high-instability crises, extending military aid in the Lebanon/Iraq upheaval, direct military support to Egypt in War of Attrition II, and massive military assistance to both Egypt and Syria during the October–Yom Kippur War. In Africa, too, the Soviets were heavily involved militarily, in support of the Stanleyville rebels during Congo II, much more so to the Angola Government, partly through proxy Cuban activity, in War in Angola and again to Angola in Shaba II. However, like the U.S., it remained aloof from the Chad/Libya protracted conflict and specific crises between the two protagonists; both superpowers recognized the primacy of French interests in that region. Finally, only in War in Angola did the Soviets risk direct confrontation with the U.S. Elsewhere they were more prudent.

As for *superpower roles in crisis management*, the U.S. record was found to be more positive. It was the most important factor in winding down three of the high-instability cases (e.g., War of Attrition II), the USSR in none. The U.S. was also an important contributor to abatement in eight cases, the USSR in four (the U.S. in Congo II, the USSR in Kashmir II, and both in the October–Yom Kippur War). And while the U.S. escalated three crises, the USSR escalated seven of them (the U.S. *vis-a-vis* Bangladesh, the Soviet Union in War in Angola).

The *UN role* in these crises was much less consequential. It was not involved in four cases. It did not contribute to crisis abatement in 13 others. And it was never the decisive factor. In four crises it played an important role (a cease-fire agreement in Kashmir I). In two others it escalated the crisis (authorizing the crossing of the Yalu River by U.S.-led UN troops, in Korean War II).

Many of the most destabilizing crises from 1945 to 1985 were linked; that is, they recurred with the same actors. This was true of India and Pakistan in the three South Asian cases — two on Kashmir and one on Bangladesh. Several cases were part of the Indochina conflict — Dien Bien Phu, Invasion of Cambodia, and Vietnam Ports Mining, with the U.S. and Vietnam as adversaries in all of them, though passively in the first. And in Africa the two Chad/Libya crises were part of a lengthy conflict. In fact, all but 6 of the 25 high-instability crises — Lebanon/Iraq Upheaval, India/China Border II, Congo II, Prague Spring, Shaba II, Afghanistan — occurred within a *protracted conflict*.

The overwhelming majority of these crises (21 of 25) terminated with an ambiguous *outcome* for the adversaries, that is, a combination of victory, defeat, stalemate, or compromise other than a strict victory/defeat pairing. Some ended in compromise (for North Vietnam, South Vietnam and the U.S. in the Ports Mining Crisis, for Israel, Syria and the USSR in October–Yom Kippur War). Others ended in stalemate (Iraq and Iran in Basra–Kharg Island). The other four outcomes were definitive (victory for China, defeat for India in their border crisis and war).

A majority of these cases (16 of 25) ended in agreement, formal or informal (a Security Council–sponsored cease-fire between India and Pakistan on January 1, 1949, terminating Kashmir I, and the Soviet-mediated Tashkent Agreement ending Kashmir II on January 10, 1966; the Brazzaville Agreement on July 30, 1978 ending Shaba II). Seven cases terminated through a unilateral act (South Vietnamese forces began to withdraw from Cambodia on July 22, 1970 — Invasion of Cambodia, and the formation of a National Unity Government in Chad on November 10, 1979 — Chad/Libya IV).

Turning to the second analytic "cut" on global instability, the distribution of the most destabilizing crises in *time* and *space* is presented in Table 4.2. These crises increased in frequency since the mid-1950s, from four to seven to eight in the most recent decade. They also exhibit time clusters — four each from 1947-1950 and 1962-1965, five each from 1970-1973 and 1978-1980, all of them in the Third World. The largest concentration occurred in the most recent decade (8 of 25).

Asia was the preeminent crisis *region* during the four decades, accounting for 12 of the 25 cases, followed by the Middle East with seven, and Africa with five. None erupted in the Americas, and only one in Europe, whereas many of the best-known international crises occurred in these two regions — Berlin Blockade, Berlin Deadline, Berlin Wall,

TABLE 4.2 Most Destabilizing International Crises, 1945-1985: Time and Space

	Africa	Americas	Asia	Europe	Middle East
1945-1954			Kashmir I (1947-1948) Korean War I (1950) Korean War II (1950-1951) Dien Bien Phu (1954) Taiwan Straits (1954-1955)		Israel Independence (1948-1949)
1955-1964	Congo II (1964)		India/China Border II (1962-1963)		Lebanon Iraq Upheaval (1958) Yemen War I (1962-1963)
1965-1974			Kashmir II (1965-1966) Invasion of Cambodia (1970) Bangladesh (1971) Vietnam Ports Mining (1972)	Prague Spring (1968)	War of Attrition II (1970) October-Yom Kippur War (1973-1974)
1975-1985	War in Angola (1975-1976) Shaba II (1978) Chad/Libya III (1978) Chad/Libya IV (1979)		Sino/Vietnam War (1978-1979) Afghanistan Invasion (1979-1980)		Lebanon War (1982-1983) Basra–Kharg Island (1984)

and Cuban Missiles, respectively. (The reasons for their lower instability scores will be noted later.)

The preeminence of Asia is reinforced by the fact that it had the highest ratio of high-instability crises to all crises in a region — 12 of 55 cases (21.8 percent). The Middle East followed — 7 of 57 (12.3 percent), then Africa — 5 of 82 (6 percent), Europe — 1 of 26 (3.8 percent), and none for the Americas.

Parenthetically, this distribution differs somewhat from that of the most severe crises. The data for 1945-1979 reveal the following: Middle East — 5 of 17 most severe cases; Asia and Europe — 4 each; Africa — 3, and the Americas — 1. However, severity and instability are not synonymous: *severity* refers to the intensity of a crisis while it is in process; instability refers to the fallout or consequences of a crisis for the international system, that is, its importance.[4]

The regional pattern for high-instability crises is also apparent from the average instability scores for all 251 crises from 1945 to 1985, by region. As evident in Table 4.3, Asia ranked first by far with an average instability score of 23.00, followed by the Middle East and Africa, with Europe and the Americas lagging behind.

The starkest finding, in this context, is the *concentration of destabilizing international crises in the Third World*. Put simply, the end of European colonial empires and the trebling of the number of state actors in the global system were accompanied, *inter alia*, by the spread of high-instability crises beyond the European core to the geopolitical-economic periphery of Asia, Africa, and the Middle East. In terms of crises and

TABLE 4.3 Average Instability Scores for International Crises, 1929-1985: Geography, Conflict, System Level

	Average	Frequency	Percent
Geography			
Africa	12.09	82	33%
Americas	7.34	31	12%
Asia	23.00	55	22%
Europe	9.48	26	10%
Middle East	15.14	57	23%
Conflict			
Nonprotracted Conflict	9.93	112	45%
Protracted Conflict	15.77	101	40%
Long War–Protracted Conflict	23.55	38	15%
System Level			
Subsystem	11.46	189	75%
Mainly Subsystem	28.15	29	12%
Mainly Dominant	23.98	20	8%
Dominant System	10.12	13	5%

conflicts, and of crisis-generated instability, the Third World has assumed the mantle of the core! But this cardinal change is conspicuously absent from the long-peace thesis, as it is from almost all Euro-American "globalist" analyses of trends in world politics since the end of World War II.

As for *conflict setting* (see Table 4.3), crises that occurred during a long war–protracted conflict — for example, the Vietnam War — show the highest average instability score by far, as expected. However, supportive of other ICB findings regarding the crisis–protracted conflict link, the average instability generated by crises within such a conflict is 63 percent higher than those outside that setting.[5]

By contrast, *system level* does not seem to affect the extent of instability: the average fallout from crises occurring within a subsystem is virtually the same as those in the dominant system, though the number of cases differs markedly. And the instability scores for mainly subsystem and mainly dominant system crises are very similar.[6] However, the 20 percent of crises that occur in mixed systems, i.e., mainly subsystem or mainly dominant, exhibit extremely high average instability scores, attesting to the potential dangers for the international community of these cross-system phenomena.

Turning to the third analytic dimension, Table 4.4 examines instability in four time periods. The highest average instability score occurred in 1965-1974, followed by 1945-1954 and 1975-1985. When time and space are combined, the rank order was: Asia in 1945-1954 and 1965-1974, almost identical; Europe in 1965-1974 and Africa (only one case) in 1945-1954, almost equal; Asia in 1975-1985 and the Middle East in 1965-1974, almost identical; and at the other extreme, the Americas in 1945-1954, and Africa in 1965-1974.

TABLE 4.4 Average Instability Scores by Decade and Region

| | REGIONS | | | | | |
DECADES	Africa	Americas	Asia	Europe	Middle East	
1945-1954	23.64 1	3.50 4	29.18 15	6.22 12	11.64 8	16.07 40
1955-1964	11.01 18	6.59 11	13.81 17	9.52 6	13.78 17	11.55 69
1965-1974	3.06 8	6.29 5	29.07 14	24.26 4	20.35 17	18.87 48
1975-1985	13.55 55	9.96 11	20.60 9	4.40 4	12.66 15	13.27 94
	12.09 82	7.34 31	23.00 55	9.48 26	15.14 57	14.32 251

(The upper number in each cell is the average instability score. The lower number is the frequency of cases for the cell.)

Since the primary focus of attention in this book is the long peace between the United States and the Soviet Union, it is especially relevant to examine the record for those cases in which the superpowers were crisis actors. Specifically, did these crises generate high or low instability compared to other international crises after World War II? Four groups of cases are identified for this fourth cut of our analysis: crises in which both the U.S. and the USSR were crisis actors; those in which only the U.S. was a crisis actor; cases in which only the USSR was a crisis actor; and crises in which neither superpower was a direct participant.

Given the structure of world politics since 1945 and the central roles of the superpowers, it seems reasonable to assume that crises with their direct participation would be more destabilizing than those in which they were less active or aloof. The mean instability scores for the four clusters support this expectation:

	Mean Instability Score
Joint U.S./USSR crises	42.77
U.S. alone as a crisis actor	20.88
USSR alone as a crisis actor	18.45
Neither superpower as a crisis actor	11.94

There were 12 post–World War II international crises in which both the U.S. and the USSR were crisis actors. These cases, along with their instability scores, are presented in Table 4.5. The three most destabilizing crises during the period under inquiry are included in this subset, namely, War in Angola, October–Yom Kippur, and Korean War II.

TABLE 4.5 Joint U.S./USSR International Crises, 1945-1985

Crisis Name	Trigger-Termination	Instability Score
Azerbaijan	08/23/45 - 05/09/46	9.91
Berlin Blockade	06/07/48 - 05/12/49	17.73
Korean War II	10/01/50 - 07/10/51	77.09
Suez-Sinai Campaign	10/29/56 - 03/12/57	37.51
Berlin Deadline	12/15/57 - 09/15/59	3.11
Berlin Wall	07/29/61 - 10/17/61	15.00
Cuban Missiles	10/16/62 - 11/20/62	6.90
Congo II	08/04/64 - 12/30/64	45.97
Six Day War	05/17/67 - 06/11/67	32.89
October–Yom Kippur War	10/05/73 - 05/31/74	93.51
War in Angola	07/12/75 - 03/27/76	116.17
Afghanistan Invasion	03/15/79 - 02/28/80	57.39

Seven of the 12 cases exhibit high scores on the instability index. Thus, while the superpowers have not engaged in direct military hostilities against each other through the post–World War II era, they have been crisis actors in a number of intensely destabilizing crises, all characterized by full-scale war among other actors.

Students of the contemporary era in world politics will discern an apparent anomaly in the data, namely, low instability scores for the three Berlin crises and Cuban Missiles, usually referred to as watersheds in East/West relations. Yet this should not occasion surprise.

All four cases are among the 15 *most severe* international crises in the ICB data set for 1945-1985, measured by a composite of six indicators already noted — GNP, size of population, nuclear capability, etc. However, as suggested earlier, severity denotes intensity while a crisis is in motion, instability indicates postcrisis impact. It can be argued, from this perspective, that each of these severe East/West confrontations helped to stabilize the U.S./USSR balance, not the reverse.

The Berlin Blockade — its origin, the crisis proper, and the outcome — was a dramatic expression of the post–World War II partition of Europe, and was recognized as such by the major powers. The Berlin Deadline Crisis, while disruptive and worrisome through 1958 and most of 1959, ended in a stabilizing agreement — to ban all nuclear weapons and missiles from Berlin, to limit Western forces in the city, and to resume negotiations on the future of Germany. And the Berlin Wall Crisis reinforced East/West acceptance of the status quo in the city, in Germany and in Europe as a whole. Indeed, that reality, surviving the three Berlin crises, was to serve as the basis for legitimizing the postwar partition of Europe, in the Helsinki Accords of 1975.

The Cuban Missile Crisis, for all its uncertainty and high risk of catastrophic Armageddon, stabilized superpower and inter-bloc relations as no other event since 1945. From 1963 onward the United States and the Soviet Union learned that coexistence on this planet was a necessity, not a matter of choice. Caution became the norm in their global rivalry for influence, especially in the Third World.

This became starkly clear in the only other international crisis in which nuclear escalation seemed possible, namely, the nuclear alert crisis between the U.S. and the USSR at the height of the October–Yom Kippur War. Competition has been pursued everywhere, in Angola, Afghanistan, Nicaragua, the Middle East, etc. But the stability generated by the Cuban Missile Crisis was ever-present in the minds of American and Soviet decision makers as they confronted crises in which clients threatened to draw them into a potential high-risk confrontation. They invariably drew back from the brink — fortunately. In short, the low instability score for Cuban Missiles conforms to the reality of post-1962 superpower behavior.

The only other low instability score in Table 4.5 can also be explained. The Azerbaijan Crisis, ending with a UN-brokered withdrawal of Soviet troops in May, 1946, was followed by more than three decades of relative

tranquillity in the Persian Gulf, until a combination of Khomeini fundamentalism and the Iran/Iraq War seriously destabilized the Gulf region.
Finally, the instability score for all the other superpower crises was only
slightly less than those included in the high-instability group, notably
Suez-Sinai and Six Day War.

CONCLUSION

The evidence of crisis-generated instability from 1945 to 1985 is
overwhelming. The frequency and intensity of war during that period is
examined by Singer (this volume). Suffice it to recall that 19 of the 25
most destabilizing crises in the ICB data set were triggered by, or culminated in, full-scale war. Moreover, the intensity of violence reached
full-scale war in 50 of the 251 international crises during the four decades.
And the cost of those crises in human and material terms was very high:
an estimated one million dead in the Iran/Iraq War from 1980 to 1988;
hundreds of thousands killed in the Vietnam War; three million refugees
in the Afghanistan War; perhaps double that number of refugees from
East Bengal to India during the Bangladesh Crisis, prior to the third
India-Pakistan war in 1971; and hundreds of thousands killed in African
crises and wars since 1960.

The findings on global instability since the end of World War II are
indisputable. Nevertheless, the pattern of instability presented in this
chapter is not incompatible with Gaddis' long peace: the latter is confined
to the absence of war between the two superpowers, while the former
taps the broader notion of disruption in world politics. Stated differently,
nonwar between the U.S. and the USSR can — and did — coexist with
broad and intense disruption in the global system. In sum, global instability does not require violence in superpower relations; and, conversely,
their stable relationship does not require stability among all pairs or
coalitions of lesser powers in the system.

This is not to concur with the thesis that crises on the periphery,
that is, the Third World, tend to stabilize relations among the major
powers. Once more, an analogy with the "Hundred Years Peace" is apparent, namely, the widespread view that the century of alleged tranquillity
was fueled by the expansion of the European great powers into Asia and
Africa, their acquisition of colonies diverting their energies and thereby
making war among them unnecessary. Both are ventures in speculation
without evidence of a causal link — in either century.

If both the long peace and the pattern of global instability represent
part of the reality of post–World War II global politics, which is more
salient? For those who are preoccupied with cataclysmic disaster, the
need to sustain the long peace must be primary. Yet if the pattern of
global instability resumes and even increases its intensity following the
incipient resolution of many regional conflicts in 1988-1989, it could pose

an uncontrollable challenge to states and societies everywhere. Thus, more attention should be accorded to questions relating to global instability — the reasons for its persistence during more than four decades, the sources of its decline in intensity, the likelihood of its resumption, its potential impact on a long-term stable relationship between the superpowers, and the capacity of the global system to absorb disruption by crises and wars in the twilight years of the twentieth century and the decades beyond. That is an agenda for future research on war and peace, crisis, and instability.

ENDNOTES

1. The method of deriving the power of a crisis actor in a specific case and the categories of power status are explained in Brecher, Wilkenfeld, and Moser (1988:22-23).

2. In Brecher, James, and Wilkenfeld (1990), a somewhat different formulation of an Index of Instability was used:

$$I_j = (T_j) \left[\log_{10} \left(\sum_{i=1}^{N} (P_i(D_i)) + 1 \right) \right]$$

In both formulations of the Index of Instability, components are derived from actor and system levels of analysis. Additional work may be necessary to fine-tune the index with an eye toward reliability and validity.

3. A *crisis actor* is a state whose decision makers perceive a threat to values, time pressure for response, and the likelihood of involvement in military hostilities — the three conditions of a foreign policy crisis; that is, a crisis actor is a state that perceives a crisis for itself. A state that does not so perceive but is involved in an international crisis through one of several kinds of activity — military, semimilitary, economic, or political — is termed an *involved actor*. Thus, states may provide massive military aid to a belligerent but be no more than an involved actor, e.g., the U.S. in the Invasion of Afghanistan Crisis, 1979-1980, whereas the USSR was a crisis actor or direct participant.

4. On severity see Brecher, Wilkenfeld, and Moser (1988: Part IV); and on severity and importance see Brecher and James (1986). The conceptual difference between instability and severity will be alluded to later in analyzing the low instability scores of European crises.

5. See Brecher and Wilkenfeld (1989: Chapters 9-11).

6. "Mainly subsystem" crises are those that are predominantly subsystem in focus, but with a spillover to the dominant system, usually when one or more major powers was a crisis actor, e.g., War in Angola, 1975-1976. Similarly, "mainly dominant system" crises have a predominant focus on the dominant system but with a spillover to one or more subsystems, e.g., the Ussuri River Crisis of 1969 between the USSR and the PRC.

CHAPTER FIVE

International Structure and the Learning of Cooperation: The Postwar Experience

Manus I. Midlarsky

In recent years there has been a thawing of the often frigid relations between the superpowers. The intense Cold War of the immediate postwar period gave way to the limited agreements of the 1950s and 1960s and ultimately to the more comprehensive ones of the 1970s and 1980s. A formal manifestation of this changing relationship was the signing of the INF treaty with its implications for more complete arms control and perhaps even disarmament.

How did all of this come about? How did an ideologically intense bipolar conflict involving several limited wars become transformed into what appears to be a budding cooperative relationship? This chapter examines the consequences of international structure for the learning of cooperation. This exploration will provide insight into the processes associated with the emergent cooperation of the contemporary period. At the same time, certain limits to this cooperative relationship will be suggested along with their associated potentialities for systemic war.

After defining several key terms, this chapter will explore aspects of a hierarchical equilibrium theory of systemic war. The international structure suggested by the theory has had certain consequences which can lead to the learning of cooperation. These consequences will be examined, followed by a comparison between the contemporary international structure and its apparent stability, with an earlier structure of a similar type that existed in nineteenth-century central Europe but which ended in warfare. The contrast between these two outcomes will yield additional insights into the bases of postwar stability.

I define systemic war as one entailing the breakdown of the international system as it existed prior to the outbreak of the war. The scope of the war and the degree of civilian-military participation (leading to a large number of civilian casualties and battle deaths) must be extensive in order to yield a systemic breakdown. Essentially, the length of the war and the widespread bloodshed lead not only to the rise of new great powers and the decline of older ones, but also to later extensive efforts to restructure the system in ways that presumably will prevent the emergence of another widespread conflict of this type (e.g., Westphalia, Vienna, Versailles, or San Francisco).

Hierarchical equilibrium is defined as requiring the presence of (1) two or more alliances (or loosely knit empires) of varying size and composition but clearly including a great power and a number of small powers within each, and (2) a relatively large number of small powers not formally associated with any of the great powers. The great powers at the head of each hierarchy and the hierarchies themselves may or may not be equal in power to each other, as long as the power differentials within each hierarchy are substantial. A good case in point is the emergence of the Soviet-dominated hierarchy at the end of World War II which was demonstrably unequal in power to the West.

Earlier empirical analyses (Midlarsky, 1986; 1988) showed that the hierarchical equilibrium distinguishes periods without systemic war (such as the nineteenth century and the postwar years) from those which led to systemic war (such as 1893-1914 and the interwar period). The following analysis will try to explain both the direct and indirect implications of this theory for the postwar experience.

HIERARCHY

Probably the single most important property of the hierarchical structure is the ability of the great power at its head to make important strategic decisions which do not necessarily cater to the interests of its smaller allies. The greater the power disparity between the hierarchy leader and its smaller allies, the greater the freedom of decision making for the great power.

As A. J. P. Taylor (1971:280) commented on Bismarck's use of alliances as stabilizing factors in nineteenth-century Europe, "He [Bismarck] controlled his allies, he did not cooperate with them. . . . In international affairs, as in domestic politics, Bismarck disliked equals; he sought for satellites."

A power asymmetry of this type among allies is tantamount to what may be called the absence of memory or minimization of memory in alliances. The great power is free to act as it pleases in its relations with other powers without the necessity for responsiveness to its own allies and their traditional foreign policy concerns or "memories." A striking illustration of the absence of alliance memory is found in the Cuban missile crisis of 1962, in which the Cubans were not allowed by the Soviets to influence the course of events, which easily could have included a joint Soviet-Cuban crusade against U.S. "imperialism" in the Caribbean. At each such attempt, the Soviets quickly curtailed these efforts. Thus, the crisis could proceed as a superpower confrontation without any of the past local animosities felt by the Cubans toward the U.S. In contrast, the 1914 summer crisis allowed the historic parochial interests of southeast Europe to exert a truly extraordinary and disproportionate effect on the outbreak of World War I.

Here, the interests of the Austro-Hungarians in the Balkans and especially Serbia were allowed to influence the course of events leading to war between the Dual Alliance and Triple Entente. The main precursor of the 1914 summer crisis was the Bosnian crisis of 1908, which pitted Austria-Hungary against Serbia and Russia, after the annexation of Bosnia-Herzegovina by Austria-Hungary. German support of Austria-Hungary during the crisis effectively led to its termination (Bridge and Bullen, 1980:161-63). Later, the emergence of Serbia in 1913 at twice her initial size prior to the Balkan Wars, coupled with an aggressive and effective pan-Slavic propaganda campaign aimed at the ever-growing Slavic population within the Austro-Hungarian Empire, threatened to result in the disintegration of the Empire, as indeed occurred at the end of World War I. In 1914, Austria-Hungary was seen as the only reliable great-power ally of Germany, and her continued existence in that role (especially in opposition to Russia) was perceived as an essential condition for Germany's effective opposition to the Triple Entente. Thus, Bismarck's earlier maxim of scattering promises "so as not to carry them out" (Taylor, 1971:278) was violated in the extreme by this later German reliance on an essentially weaker ally. The residues of Austria-Hungary's conflicts with Serbia and Russia were allowed to influence the behavior of the coalition leader, or put another way, an alliance memory was operative in 1914 which earlier, during the Bismarckian period, simply had not existed.

An instance of the stabilizing consequences of hierarchy is found in the Suez crisis of 1956. As a result of the very large power disparity between the United States and its allies (Great Britain and France), especially in regard to strategic nuclear weapons, American security dependence on the two NATO allies was relatively small. As a consequence, when the Soviet Union threatened these European powers with a nuclear confrontation after the invasion of Suez, the U.S. could take a fairly impartial view and not support its allies in their venture. The historic foreign policy interests of Great Britain and France in the Middle East and North Africa and the memory of the then fairly recent appeasement of Hitler (often compared to Nasser of Egypt, who had unilaterally nationalized the Suez Canal) were not allowed to influence U.S. policy in the crisis. Had the security dependence on its allies been greater, then the U.S. might have felt obliged to respond to the Soviet threat, with the possible onset of a superpower confrontation.

Independent Small Powers

The existence of the independent small powers as the second stipulation of the hierarchical equilibrium leads to the possibility of positive-sum games or an inducement to cooperate.

There exists a long history of the use of small sovereign states as vehicles of cooperation. The entire settlement at the Congress of Vienna turned on the future of the small countries in relation to the great powers. Poland, which already had been divided as of the late eighteenth century, continued under Russian, Prussian, and Austrian control. A portion of Saxony and of the left bank of the Rhine went to Prussia, and Austria received territories in Italy (Kissinger, 1957:171). The existence and disposition of these smaller entities avoided the breakdown of the Congress of Vienna and a possible widespread war.

The contemporary international system also demonstrates the salutary role of the smaller powers. If one of these powers — say Ethiopia — decided to draw closer to the Eastern bloc, another, Somalia, could approach the West. While the Soviet Union sought to buttress its position in Afghanistan without major hindrance by the U.S., the U.S. could do the same in Central America without serious Soviet opposition. Indonesia could veer from a neutralist, sometime pro-Soviet, position in 1965 to a staunchly pro-Western one, at the same time that the Soviets made serious inroads in Africa. Chile could cease being governed by a Marxist party while South Vietnam moved steadily toward incorporation with communist North Vietnam. None of these were zero-sum conflicts but instead situations that eventuated in a constant-sum or positive-sum game, for each side gained something in the end. More generally, with the rise of new nations in the postwar era, both superpowers sought to gain new adherents, principally in the Middle East, Asia, and Africa. Without the existence of these smaller powers, it is possible that more direct superpower confrontations could have occurred.

Perhaps most striking in the post–World War II era was the beginning of overt cooperation between the two hierarchy leaders in 1955 via the neutralization of Austria. This came well before any arms control agreements or other less tractable forms of agreement which require the cooperation of many significant domestic interests. The agreement about the neutralization of a small power which does not have significant strategic or resource advantage could proceed without the added difficulties of potential domestic opposition. Only later, when successful cooperation had already been experienced in a relatively noncontroversial setting, with gains to both sides found in Austrian neutrality, could more difficult forms of agreement be undertaken. This is but one of the cooperative functions of the existence of neutral small powers.

A final — and perhaps obvious but no less important — consequence of the independent small powers is the dampening of polarization tendencies. The greater the number of such powers, the smaller the likelihood that the system will tend toward a completely polarized condition. The positive-sum game of each side benefiting while not vitiating the neutrality of the remaining powers is equivalent to the absence of systemic polarization. New nations can adhere to any one of the existing coalitions, or there can occur an exchange of allies (e.g., Somalia-Ethiopia) that does not lead to a permanent set of alliances in which virtually all countries are allied with one or another coalition. This positive-sum condition stands in contrast to the zero-sum game, which is an ideal candidate for polarizing tendencies in light of gains for a leading power requiring some losses to an opponent.

International Structure as an Information System

Thus far, we have analyzed the hierarchical equilibrium in terms of its structure and the likely consequences of that structure for important aspects of international conflict. Now we will treat the hierarchical equilibrium in a somewhat different fashion, viewing it as an information system — or, more exactly, as one that has certain likely informational consequences associated with it.

Claude Shannon was the first to use entropy not only as a measure of uncertainty[1] or disorder, but as a measure of information (Shannon and Weaver, 1949). The basic idea is that a certain amount of uncertainty is reduced when information is received; the greater that uncertainty reduction, the greater the information. Although information theory was somewhat derogated in the 1960s for not making startling breakthroughs in the meaning of information, it has more recently been appreciated for its abstract qualities. Precisely because it is abstract and therefore applicable to a variety of settings with vastly different informational meanings, it has been enjoying of late a widespread applicability. One of the more striking applications has occurred in genetics, in which the DNA code has been analyzed successfully using information-theoretic concepts (Gatlin, 1972). Of course, the study of linguistics has been greatly enhanced by the use of information theory (Campbell, 1982).

The particular application here does not differ in certain essentials from those in linguistics or genetics. The basic problem is the same, namely, how to introduce a certain degree of redundancy into the informational structure, for in this fashion entropy or uncertainty is reduced. A high-entropy letter sequence would be the essentially random one of

$$T \; Q \; B \; R \; Z \; P \; I \; L \; E \; A \; C \; U \; S \; . \; . \; .$$

A departure from uncertainty or randomness would consist of some repetitions of each of the letters, as in

$$T \; Q \; Q \; Q \; B \; B \; R \; R \; R \; Z \; Z \; Z \; . \; . \; .$$

The entropy of this letter sequence is much less than that of the preceding one. Put another way, the uncertainty has been reduced by the redundancy of letters in the second sequence. Redundancy in both the learning of language and genetics has been found to be the principal way in which uncertainty is reduced and information transmitted. The redundancy also ensures that the message will be clearly received even in the presence of noise. Word or concept repetition is a principal means of avoiding the distortions due to noise, for even if one or more of these were to be lost in transmission, the redundant words or concepts still would be received.

Hierarchies and Context-Dependent Redundancy

There are essentially two ways in which redundancy can be introduced. The first is context-free while the second is context-dependent. In the former, as the name implies, the redundant letters or concepts simply appear without any warning or indication that they are to be expected. A string of alternate letters in the sequence below would be an illustration of this type. The letters preceding "I" are essentially random.

$$Q I T C I L Q M T I B I B Z P I A I \ldots$$

In the second type of redundancy, we are forewarned by the context in which the letter or concept occurs. A sequence of this type would be

$$A B I Q L A B I R P A B I S \ldots$$

in which the letters "AB" always precede the appearance of "I", in addition to the remaining, essentially random letter sequences. Here we have a context-dependent redundancy. It is not only the repetition of the letter "I" that is the redundant element but the ability to predict that "I" always follows "AB". In other words, context-dependency is the key to the entropy or uncertainty reduction.

Learning processes generally have been facilitated by the context-dependent form of redundancy. It is, after all, the redundancy of language in meaningful ways that imparts information. Until the rules of language that make for creative combinations are thoroughly understood (even unconsciously) late in childhood or early adolescence, the chief method of teaching and learning is context-dependent redundancy. The context-free form also is important for daily communication but not necessarily for the learning process. It is precisely these two forms of redundancy that are reflected by the hierarchical equilibrium structure — the context-dependent form in the hierarchy itself and the context-free type in relation to the independent small powers. These redundancies in turn give rise to entropy or uncertainty reductions in relations between the superpowers.

As a learning scenario, the context-dependency occurs in the hierarchical structure. A particular set of nations, namely, the allied smaller powers, essentially cannot be dealt with in important matters by external powers, apart from the leading power within the hierarchy. Of course, in matters that do not impinge on international security such as cultural exchange or certain trade items, the allied smaller powers can be treated as fairly independent from the hierarchy leader. But in matters of international security, the context-dependency is strong if not unbreakable.

The post–World War II period witnessed just such a learning process driven by the geopolitics of a divided Europe. Each of the superpowers learned that any attacks on the smaller allied powers would be resisted by the superpowers even to the point of possibly initiating a nuclear war. Countries such as Greece and Turkey would be defended by policy instruments such as the Truman Doctrine and even small dependent cities such as Berlin would be defended forcibly. Within communist societies, any dissident movements, as in Hungary or Czechoslovakia, would be crushed, with no serious interferences brooked by external powers.

The neutralization of Austria was in effect the first formal statement that established the perpetual neutrality of a formerly occupied territory and in so doing implied the obverse — that allied smaller countries were virtually in perpetuity tied to the hierarchy leader. One can say that it was this agreement that signaled a milestone in the learning process, for after this event there were few serious efforts to directly undermine the control of the opposing superpower over its allies. From this perspective, one could have predicted after 1955 that the United States would not intervene in the Hungarian revolution or the Czechoslovakian imbroglio. Nor would the Soviets make serious moves to engulf West Berlin, especially after the construction of the Berlin Wall as an affirmation of the obverse side of the Austrian neutrality agreement. Indeed, in an analysis of disputes involving the superpowers between 1946 and 1964 only those specifically involving European powers were found to demonstrate systemic instability; when the dispute set was opened to include countries outside of Europe, systemic stability was demonstrated (Midlarsky, 1986).

The smaller, mostly Third World non-European powers have essentially become the venue of conflict discourse between the superpowers. This is likely because of the context-dependent learning process that occurred throughout the 1950s and 1960s which implied the instability of any serious conflict activity on the European continent. The context-dependent learning process of the post–World War II period was facilitated by the redundancy of paired Soviet-allied small powers or U.S.-allied small-power dyads. The U.S. and Italy or the U.S. and Turkey were, for security matters, essentially seen as one, as were the USSR and Bulgaria or the USSR and Hungary. In this fashion, the external entropy or uncertainty of that period was reduced.

Independent Small Powers and
Context-Free Redundancy

A context-free redundancy has emerged alongside the older context-dependent one and in fact reinforces the older type. This second form of redundancy is found in relations between the superpowers and smaller non-European countries. When conflict between the superpowers is enacted essentially outside the European zone of sensitivity, each of these redundant conflicts conveys the basic message that the superpower ambitions remain outside the European camp. Given the extreme instability that conflict in Europe threatens, the context-free redundancy of conflicts involving smaller powers outside of Europe constitutes a reinforcement of the earlier context-dependent learning process. As time passes, the superpowers increasingly institutionalize in their bureaucracies and other collective memories the importance of conflict avoidance in zones of extreme sensitivity.

To be sure, there are other areas of sensitivity such as Central America for the U.S. or central Asia for the Soviets. As these conflicts appear and intensify, there appears (at least thus far) to be a recognition of the importance of treating these as context-dependent, with a minimal degree of interference by the opposing superpower in these ongoing conflicts. In Vietnam in the 1960s, or Africa more recently, as essentially context-free zones of disputation between the U.S. and USSR, the likelihood of direct military confrontation was minimal and so there could be more energetic involvement by the superpowers without serious fear of the onset of systemic war.

The communication process of context-free redundancy in the hierarchical equilibrium can be symbolized in the following way:

$$A_1A_2A_3A_4A_5 \cdots$$

Each of the subscripts refers to a different extra-European conflict with its own unique properties but having the property called "A" of a non-European location. The occurrence of each context-free "A" without serious threat of systemic war reinforces the absence of conflict in Europe which already has been learned to be context-dependent and therefore extremely dangerous to system stability. It is therefore the combination of the earlier learned context-dependence and later reinforcement of context-free redundancy in the form of few serious challenges to the incursion of one of the superpowers into a non-European location that reduces the entropy or uncertainty of the contemporary international system. Normative implications of this scenario and especially the need to maintain the genuine sovereignty of the smaller non-European countries are treated in Midlarsky (1988: Chapter 11).

Contrast these two forms of entropy reduction with that of the traditional multipolar-balance-of-power system. Here the insurance for system stability is the random formation and termination of alliances with any other major power (Kaplan, 1957; Midlarsky, 1983). In this fashion, ongoing enmities are largely avoided with a consequent reduction in the likelihood and extent of systemic polarization. However, the entropy or uncertainty of such a system, virtually by definition, is very high and even approximates the entropy of the first sequence on page 110. Learning by either of the two forms of redundancy is absent here, for there are no contexts in the form of hierarchies, nor independent small powers which effectively participate in the system. Only the number of major powers serves as an effective limit on the entropy of this system, for with a limited number of such powers some of the alliance sequences must be repeated. But only in this way is redundancy introduced. Any increase in the number of new major powers as in fact occurred toward the end of the nineteenth century would automatically increase the entropy and therefore the uncertainty of the international system.

The system of alliances beginning in 1891 with the Franco-Russian Entente was little better from this perspective. The only form of redundancy was context-dependent in the ongoing alliance (but not hierarchical) and even here, the entropy would be substantial because of the exclusive great-power status of virtually all of the alliance members. There would not be the reduced entropy and therefore increased clarity of communication found in the hierarchically organized structure. The absence of a large number of neutral small powers in this configuration also implies the absence of the redundancy of context-independent communication found in the hierarchical equilibrium.

A hegemonic system, as in the existence of a single empire (e.g., Rome), clearly allows for context-dependent redundancy, but at the same time does not support the existence of context-free redundancy because of the inclination of such empires to include within their boundaries virtually all formerly independent small powers. Thus, of all the international systems that have existed historically, the hierarchical equilibrium which stipulates the necessity for a large number of politically independent small powers is the only one that exhibits both forms of redundancy as reductions of entropy and as vehicles for learning.

There also exists an interesting comparison of this communication process with that of "Tit for Tat" in a prisoner's dilemma game (Axelrod, 1984). In "Tit for Tat," the programmed player cooperates on the first move and reciprocates either cooperation or defection on all succeeding moves. The expectation is that after the first cooperative move, the other player will reciprocate, thus leading to an unending series of cooperations. This sequence can be written as

$$C \; C \; C \; C \; C \; C \; C \ldots$$

This clearly is a zero-entropy process with redundancy of communication having eliminated all uncertainty of communication. Unfortunately, if the first cooperative move is reciprocated by defection, then an unending series of defections could occur as follows:

$$C\ \ D\ \ D\ \ D\ \ D\ \ D\ \ D\ \ D\ \ D\ .\ .\ .$$

This is almost a zero-entropy process, with only the first cooperative move raising the entropy above zero.

Here, the redundancy in both cases clearly is context-dependent, for the entire series of moves is dependent on the initial move and the first response. There is no context-free redundancy as in the hierarchical equilibrium. Moreover, the context here is nearly deterministic in contrast to the more probabilistic nature of the two forms of redundancy in the hierarchical equilibrium. In "Tit for Tat," the outcome is an unending series either of cooperations or of defections. Only a somewhat surprising cooperation after a preceding defection (possible but not likely) could alter the defection sequence. In the hierarchical equilibrium the contextual learning is reinforced by the rather unsurprising and unthreatening context-free redundancy, both of which together yield a stochastic process which does not have to veer either to complete cooperation or to an unending feud that could spell mutual destruction. In some sense, the hierarchical equilibrium hedges our bets on the outcomes; it opts for a whole range of possibilities instead of the essentially binary "Tit for Tat."

Comparison with an Earlier Structure

It will be instructive now to compare the postwar period with an earlier counterpart, for in this process of comparison we may be able to discern elements of stability in the contemporary period that are not immediately apparent. The earlier referent period is that found in central Europe between the Congress of Vienna and the unification of Germany. It was at its root a hierarchical equilibrium in miniature in central Europe. Austria and Prussia, the two great Germanic powers, stood at the center of this political world. Although Austria nominally was at the head of the Confederation (Bund) of German states established under Metternich's tutelage at the Congress of Vienna (Kissinger, 1957:232-38), some of the German states hewed closer to Austria, others to Prussia, with still other German states maintaining a neutral posture. For example, in 1866, when Prussia openly opposed Austria in suggesting the dissolution of the Bund and the election of a special German assembly to draft a new constitution excluding Austria, only 9 of the 15 smaller German states supported Austria. These included Hanover, Saxony, Baden, and Bavaria (Thomson, 1966:286). After the defeat of Austria in the war that same year, several of the former Austrian allies — Baden and Bavaria among them — allied with Prussia (Singer and Small, 1968:268).

As we know, this hierarchical equilibrium in miniature disappeared with the unification of Germany in 1871. The question is: why should this have been the case, and in particular why did this process end in major warfare between the principal actors, Austria and Prussia, and additionally, involve an interested external power — France? Even the obvious answers to this query will shed light on some nonobvious reasons for the postwar stability of the hierarchical equilibrium.

The first reason for war and the disintegration of the central European equilibrium obviously is the common German language and history, or in short, German nationalism of the period. It was the rise of German nationalism and Prussia as its eventual champion that made likely the disappearance of the smaller political entities within a united Germany. And Austria as the champion — not of unification but of confederation under her own tutelage — was to be the likely wartime opponent. Here we have for the first time in modern German history an ideology that would transcend the boundaries of the individual German states. Nationalism as a common fabric of identity would replace the older religion-based divisions emanating from the Reformation and the later entrenching of these religious-political divisions as a consequence of the Thirty Years' War. The principle of *cuius regio, eius religio*, wherein the population of a state was required to be of the same religion as its ruler (Pagés, 1970:39-40) of course contributed immensely to the continued political divisions of that region.

In the language of learning developed earlier, a context-dependency was emphasized by this uniformity of faith within a principality and religious distinctions between it and its Germanic cousins. The memories of the earlier devastation of the Thirty Years' War further reinforced the desire to respect the existing boundaries among the Protestant and Catholic states. The risk of ideographic war was to be avoided lest some new massive destruction were to be visited on this region. But in the mid-nineteenth century, a transcendent ideology, nationalism, whose cultural and linguistic emphases would override the religious differences between Protestant and Catholic, contributed strongly to the undermining of this earlier context-dependency and the eventual end of the hierarchical equilibrium in central Europe.

A second and perhaps no less compelling reason for the onset of war between Austria and Prussia was the presence of painful memories of the historic derogation of Prussia and her rulers by the Imperial Austrians. As early as the time of Frederick the Great of Prussia, we find the onset of war fueled by such memories. As Gerhard Ritter comments on the accession of Frederick to the throne,

From the first day his foreign policy sought to make it quite clear to the world that a new epoch had begun in the history of Prussia, that with Frederick's accession a new and disturbing power had joined the concert of Europe. Frederick was convinced that above all Prussia lacked reputation — the respect due to a state which needed to be feared. He was well aware that Vienna had considered his father as nothing more than a poltroon, whose threats and outbursts of anger need not be taken too seriously. (Ritter, 1970:75)

The War of the Austrian Succession as the first of the major wars of the eighteenth century involving Austria and Prussia on opposing sides began soon after, to be followed by the even more bloody Seven Years' War.

A century later, in Bismarck's time, we find strong echoes of this earlier experience. As Edward Crankshaw (1981:132) remarks: "For ten years now his [Bismarck's] one devouring preoccupation had been the elevation of Prussia to a position of at least equality with Austria. If Austria refused to admit this equality — formalized by Prussian hegemony over all Germany north of the River Main — then she would have to be coerced."

Thus, the memories of earlier Austrian diplomatic ascendancy had deep roots in Prussian statesmanship and clearly contributed to the Prussian drive toward hegemony in Germany and ultimately (perhaps unwittingly?) to German unification.

Contrast these two conditions (transcendent regional ideology and strong hostile memories between major powers) derived from the central European experience with those of the postwar period. First, the transcendent nationalist ideology that enabled Prussia to obtain strong popular and ultimately governmental policies favoring unification by the German principalities has no real counterpart in the contemporary period. Indeed, precisely the opposite circumstance has persisted throughout much of the postwar period. The ideological antagonisms between communist East and capitalist West (put in broad terms) prevented any kind of popular or governmental drive toward integration, much as the earlier context-dependency of differing religions in central Europe prevented widespread warfare in pursuit of a transcendent aim.

If there are two competing units for the loyalty of such smaller entities but ideological barriers emphasizing a context-dependency prevent open access to the rival bloc, then the dangers of zero-sum conflicts are minimized. The likelihood of one power gaining a smaller ally from the opposing bloc under these conditions is substantially smaller than under the contrasting circumstance of easy ideological access via a common sentiment such as nationalism. This latter condition is a zero-sum scenario which can ultimately lead to warfare, as occurred in 1866 and again in 1870. As a result, the ideological barriers of the postwar world may have inadvertently supported the tendency by the superpowers to seek gains in the Third World (context-independent activity), instead of engaging in dangerous zero-sum activity of this type in Europe.

Absence of a common language existing across the East-West gap may also have had the unintended consequence of erecting a barrier to serious efforts at "proselytizing" the other side. The only realistic possibility in this regard was to be found in the two Germanies, but here the immediate residue of World War II and its immense losses may have been strong enough to militate against continued activity of this type. Hence, the Berlin Wall was allowed to be built without serious opposition by the Allies. Had the wall not been built, it is possible that the continued drain on the professional infrastructure of East Germany might have led to a societal collapse. This zero-sum gain to the West obviously was intolerable to the Soviets. Here, perhaps, we see a strong confirmation of the importance of barriers of one kind or another existing between contending blocs. In the absence of linguistic and cultural barriers between the two Germanies, a physical barrier needed to be constructed in order to prevent the kind of zero-sum processes that could have resulted in war, much as occurred in mid- to late-nineteenth-century German-speaking Europe.

Just as the postwar zero-sum process was mitigated by ideological, linguistic, and ultimately even physical barriers, so too were memories of past humiliations or failures largely absent. The United States and the Soviet Union simply did not have the long history of competition and deep resentments that characterized the Austro-Prussian relationship. In place of the century-long history of suspicion, there existed a much shorter period of interstate relations between the U.S. and USSR which had even included a period of successful wartime cooperation in the recent past. Certainly whatever overt hostilities occurred between the two countries were confined to the brief intervention by American forces in Siberia after the Bolshevik Revolution which resulted in very few casualties. Although the intervention period was highlighted in Soviet propaganda, and exaggerated claims were made as to American intentions in the later genuine relief efforts of the American Relief Administration at the end of the Russian Civil War, these nodes of hostility in American-Soviet relations did not at all compare with the level of hostility demonstrated by the Soviets toward the far more active interventionist powers — Britain, France, and Japan (Mazour, 1962:602-19). Thus, the Cold War confrontation of the immediate postwar period simply would not be fueled by memories of past intense conflict to anywhere near the same extent as was found in central Europe of the mid-nineteenth century. In other words, the absence of long-term memories of competition and hostility between the two principal actors, along with the absence of transcendent ideologies, distinguishes the postwar period from the earlier central European structure which disappeared as the result of war.

A Feedback Mechanism

There exists an interesting feedback between the permeability of the barrier between blocs and the continued viability of the bloc structure. If one of the blocs is removed from a world economy dominated by the other for ideological or security reasons, this exclusion may in the end yield extreme internal pressure to coordinate the economy of the excluded bloc with the remainder. The Iron Curtain that isolated Eastern Europe ideologically and politically from the West not only had obvious political consequences for the onset of the Cold War, but also generated severe internal economic stresses within the Eastern bloc and especially within the Soviet Union. Stalin's rejection of computers as somehow inspired by the capitalist world, and perhaps also coincidentally useful as an information processing device to be used internally against the dictator, is only one of the more compelling illustrations of the technical and economic consequences of such extreme isolation. The subsequent imperative requirement to catch up technically with the West in this field was a direct consequence of this barrier, at least as interpreted by Stalin.

More generally, the current efforts at *glasnost* and *perestroika* may be understood as a broader consequence of isolation from the West. In its own emphasis on economic distinctiveness during the pre- and postwar period, the Soviet Union centralized to such an extent that free-market forces subsisted only in the so-called underground economy. Inefficiencies and corruption abounded within a governmental sector that did not have to respond to the competitive demands of a domestic or international free market. The absence of the need to compete directly with Western products clearly allowed the Soviets the luxury, albeit temporary, of letting their productive base become essentially obsolete. Now faced with an economically resurgent Europe (perhaps even more so after 1992) on one side and a Japan whose GNP now exceeds that of the Soviet Union on the other, the Soviet failures have become pronounced. As a consequence, in a rather unexpected feedback, the rigidity of the ideological-security structure has generated serious internal economic difficulties which in turn now require serious modifications of that structure. One interpretation of the current attempted transformations within the Soviet Union and benign tolerance of the recent changes in Eastern Europe is as a belated response to its long exclusion — largely self-imposed — from the world economic system and its ideographic aspects. As a result, the ideological and political exclusionary postwar structure ultimately generated its own dissolution, at least insofar as this process has proceeded thus far.

There also is a danger in all of this which is not terribly different from the central European condition of the mid-nineteenth century. The breakdown of formerly existing barriers can yield the further growth of transnational ideologies that can undermine the political control of domestic elites. East Germany obviously is one case in point. It is no accident that *glasnost* and *perestroika* had experienced a considerable earlier development within the Soviet Union with its relative geographic and linguistic isolation, but had a much cooler reception initially among East European governments with populations which have linguistic and historical affinities with the West, such as East Germany or Czechoslovakia. The nationalism of Germany or the former Czechoslovak historic and economic links with the West could be revived in the absence now of strong ideological barriers, to the detriment of both the local communist governments and intrabloc cohesion. As such, the hierarchical equilibrium that had persisted as an essentially stabilizing influence in the postwar period and had led to both context-dependent and context-independent learning by the superpowers could be and in fact has been undermined.

If faced with a breakaway East Germany or Czechoslovakia that allies militarily and exclusively with the West, the Soviet Union still might react in uncooperative ways that could be inimical to world peace. Paradoxically, context-dependent learning and cooperation and especially the clarity of political accords may depend in part on the maintenance of boundaries, if not barriers (mostly ideographic), between blocs, which in turn have serious economic consequences that require some lowering if not elimination of those barriers. If the economic consequences are too severe, such that internal economic dissolution begins within the Soviet Union, that too is a potentially destabilizing consequence for world peace. Soviet decision makers now may be walking a delicate tightrope between the conflicting demands of context-dependent rulemaking required for future political cooperation with the West (in itself requiring the existence of at least some context-defining boundaries), and domestic economic demands that in turn require a blurring of the boundaries of the context in question.

The Evolution of the International System

The context-dependent learning process of the hierarchical equilibrium along with the reinforcement of the context-free process suggest certain evolutionary possibilities. One of these is the possibility of developing rules beyond those simply of context-dependency. Arguments such as these have been strongly suggested to be the basis of evolutionary development in organisms (Gatlin, 1972). Beyond a certain point in the context-dependent learning process, the organism begins to first understand and then later to generate rules for its future ontogeny. The mere learning of new "vocabularies" is not enough; the organism begins to develop a sense of grammar, a set of rules for combining the letters and words in meaningful forms (Chomsky, 1957). Rather than an ad hoc and fitful response to each new context-dependent move by the opponent, there can exist a set of rules which prescribe (and proscribe) conduct far into the foreseeable future.

Most desirable theoretically among all of these possible rule sets is world government which in perpetuity would generate and administer rules of interstate conduct. The recent failures with this particular form suggest that perhaps the international system in 1919 and again in 1946 had not experienced sufficient context-dependent learning to embark on such an enterprise. SALT I and II are more limited and therefore perhaps more successful rule sets. Yet here we find something of a paradox. Signing SALT I and II, the INF treaty, and now the more recent arms limitations agreements could have the consequence of limiting arms races to the point where the integrity of hierarchies could be affected with an increased probability of systemic war. Given the provisions of these treaties, however, this event is unlikely, as both superpowers have retained the ultimate and relatively exclusive advantage of long-range strategic weapons.

The question remains, however, whether the two blocs indeed have reached a point where learning has been sufficient to allow for substantial rule generation. The signing of SALT II in 1979 and its likely ratification by the Senate suggested an affirmative response to this query. But it was the invasion of Afghanistan by the Soviets which prevented that ratification. This in turn suggests that it is the uneven development of the system, in respect to both learning processes and perceived dangers, that is inimical to potential sophisticated rulemaking. The fear of fundamentalist Islam rising on the Soviet central Asian border may have contributed much to the invasion of Afghanistan. If the Afghan population had somehow participated in processes designed to placate the Soviets (an unlikely and unpalatable event), then the risk of such an invasion probably would have diminished. The absence of such an invasion of Finland in the postwar era suggests the presence of precisely those context-dependent learning processes absent in Afghanistan in 1979. Whether highly sophisticated rules can be generated is of course an open question. Yet the fact that the current hierarchical equilibrium has allowed for such learning to take place via its two forms of redundancy suggests possibilities for the current system which likely were absent from the multipolar system of 1919 and the not-yet-risen bipolar one of 1946. As yet, we do not know whether that learning will be built upon successfully.

CONCLUSION

The question of the evolution of the system is an intriguing one. It may well be that the time is ripe for some additional rulemaking; the learning achieved by both superpowers may have proceeded far enough to facilitate this process. The recent Chernobyl disaster with its implications for transnational concerns may have perversely and inadvertently increased the probability of such processes accelerating. On the other hand, the uneven development of the system may inhibit the rulemaking process as we have seen immediately following the invasion of Afghanistan. A disturbing precedent exists in the resolution of certain basic conflicts (such as the Berlin-Baghdad railway) between the major powers in 1914 and the onset of systemic war immediately thereafter as the result of conflict processes begun in the Balkans outside of the great-power arena itself. The war in Afghanistan alone did not have such destabilizing potential. If such a war had spread in central Asia, or Central America were to become an arena of superpower rivalry on the other hand, it is likely that more extensive and sophisticated rulemaking between the superpowers would be overcome by the consequent uncertainties and international crises.

Tension between the need for increased economic contact with the West and the need to maintain the East European context somewhat intact (at least in regard to foreign policy) also may impose serious burdens on Soviet decision makers. It is likely the nexus among the ongoing context-dependent rulemaking, the need to maintain the political context relatively intact, and the requirement for economic cooperation with the West (also tied to internal restructuring) that will decide the future trajectory of East-West relations for the foreseeable future.

Finally, there are implications of the preceding arguments for other contributions to this volume. Because of space limitations, only the most salient derivatives of the theory and corresponding contributions can be mentioned. The hierarchical equilibrium constitutes an alternative explanation (or paradigm, in John Gaddis' usage) for the long postwar peace, one that does not explicitly rely on nuclear deterrence as its principal modus operandi. To be sure, nuclear weapons play an important role in the theory — but as buttressors of the individual hierarchies, not as deterrence mechanisms. Here, large-scale nuclear stockpiles and delivery systems establish a strong power differential between the hierarchy leader and the smaller allied powers as demanded by the theory. The security dependence of the superpower on the smaller allied powers is minimized. Rogue activities of the allied powers become less probable, and if begun are more likely to be curtailed quickly. Global wars such as World War I and other systemic wars that began in circumstances such as these are less likely under conditions of extreme power differentials within blocs.

Thus, the arguments here generally agree with those of John Vasquez on the relative unimportance of nuclear deterrence per se in supporting the long postwar peace, but for reasons having to do with the maintenance of hierarchy and emergent context-dependent rulemaking and cooperation between the superpowers. The arguments here also agree with Charles Kegley's and Gregory Raymond's emphasis on alliances as preservers of peace and as generators of international norms (reviewed intriguingly by James Johnson), and in particular norms of international cooperation. These norms may have constituted one of the important sources of interdependence that James Rosenau suggests have led to the puzzling but important simultaneous ending of six ongoing interstate conflicts in 1988.

ENDNOTE

1. The entropy, $H(X)$, is defined as

$$H(X) = - \sum_{i=1}^{N} p(x_i) \log_b p(x_i)$$

where $p(x_i)$ is the probability of the ith event among the N possibilities and the logarithm is taken to any arbitrary base "b" greater than one. Intuitively, it can be seen that the entropy is a measure of disorder or uncertainty, for it is equal to zero when only one outcome is certain ($\log_b 1 = 0$) and it is at a maximum ($\log_b N$) when all of the outcomes are equally likely. This of course is a condition of maximum uncertainty. Given the international system as one without central direction, there is a distinct advantage in minimizing the entropy or uncertainty of the prevailing international structure. Additionally, only the entropy has a particular structural uniqueness which is elaborated elsewhere (Ornstein, 1973; Sinai, 1976; Midlarsky, 1984). Maximizing the hierarchical structure clearly has the consequence of minimizing the entropy or uncertainty. The great power at the head of the hierarchy would be more certain as the source of decision making, the stronger the hierarchical structure. Alternatively, the weaker the structure, the less certain the center of decision making.

PART THREE

The Impact of the Great Powers' Evolving Relationships

CHAPTER SIX

Old Wine in New Bottles: How the Cold War Became the Long Peace

Lloyd C. Gardner

War . . . is now a purely internal affair. . . . The object of war is not to make or prevent conquests of territory but to keep the structure of society intact. The very word "war" has become misleading. It would probably be more accurate to say that by becoming continuous, war has ceased to exist.
George Orwell, 1984

. . . Liberal instinct . . . is so dear to historians that they lay it out like a guideline through the unmapped forests of prejudice and self-interest as though this line, and not the forest, is our history.
Paul Scott, A Division of the Spoils

The historian Arthur Schlesinger, Jr. (1967), reminded his readers twenty years ago that "the Cold War in its original form was a presumably mortal antagonism, arising in the wake of the Second World War, between two rigidly hostile blocs. . . . For nearly two somber decades this antagonism dominated the fears of mankind; it may even, on occasion, have come close to blowing up the planet." Every now and then during the Cold War's most tense moments, some policymaker was sure to breathe a sigh of relief that World War III had not happened — yet. There was no assurance in these sighs that war could be avoided. "Better twenty years of Cold War," said one at a conference I attended in 1967, "than twenty minutes of nuclear war." Indeed.

More recently, however, scholars have sought to give a rational answer to "why" it hasn't happened: Why have the superpowers managed to avoid nuclear Armaggedon? Answers are easier to formulate, of course, in this post-Vietnam, post-Afghanistan era of superpower "introspection" than they were at the time Schlesinger speculated on the origins and meaning of the Cold War. To suggest that the era might someday be called the long peace, as John Gaddis now proposes, would have seemed odd in the extreme. But today it has caught on. "The long peace that has enfolded the developed world for so long," writes John Mueller (1989:264), "has been the culminating result of a historic process in which the institution of war has gradually been rejected because of its perceived repulsiveness and futility."

There are few indications here that Mueller and Schlesinger are writing about the same events, let alone the same "historic process." One is reminded of the dictum the British historian E. H. Carr set forth: "Before you study the history study the historian," and "Before you study the historian, study his historical and social environment" (Dukes, 1989:185-6). Where Schlesinger stressed tension and uncertainty, long-peace theorists suggest instead an underlying stability; where rival ideologies once seemed engaged in mortal combat, it now appears the traditional balance of power was the central issue all the time. Is the term *long peace* an anodyne label for the Cold War, we should ask ourselves — a way of describing superpower rivalry in less menacing terms for a contemporary audience?

Mueller very carefully restricts the term to the "developed world," a division that may confuse more than it clarifies about the era. And what of the policymakers themselves? Did they recognize such divisions in their thinking? Long-peace theorists tend to look at the postwar era from the outside, and to search for comparisons, so as to be able to "classify" what they find somewhat in the manner of natural science. This is a most useful endeavor, so long as the view from inside does not get lost among the theoretical wrappings and labels in the academician's workshop. What follows below is an effort to reestablish the delicate balance between theory and specifics, by looking at what policymakers said about the challenges they faced, and what they did to establish their vision in the postwar world.

Dean Acheson (1969), in many ways the most durable, as well as the most subtle, policymaker of the Cold War era, entitled his memoirs *Present at the Creation*; and it is indeed proper to begin a reexamination of our old and new assumptions with his view of the postwar crisis confronting the United States. Except for an eighteen-month period, June, 1947, to January, 1949, Dean Acheson served in high-level positions all through World War II and the formative years of the Cold War. As assistant secretary of state for economic affairs during the war he oversaw postwar planning in that area, then as under secretary of state he advised President Harry S Truman about how to formulate the Truman Doctrine and Marshall Plan for congressional approval. Present at the creation he certainly was, and he stayed close to the corridors of power a long time, long enough to advise Kennedy and Johnson on Europe, as well as an old nemesis, Richard Nixon, on how to get out of Vietnam safely.

A few months after leaving office in 1953, Acheson gathered with several former aides who served with him in the State Department for a "seminar" at Princeton University to discuss the conduct and objectives of American foreign policy during the Truman administration. Acheson led off by recalling "some of the matters that I carried in my head when I went back into the State Department [in 1949]." He then produced a copy of a November, 1939, speech delivered at Yale University. The subject that evening was the imminent danger of American "internment" in the Western Hemisphere. The world outside Yale had changed dramatically in recent months, and Acheson's speech reflected the "internationalist" viewpoint about those changes.

As Acheson spoke, the great debate between "internationalists" and "isolationists" that would last until Pearl Harbor was just beginning. It was really the last great debate in American foreign policy until the Vietnam War. The political battles in the United States in the 1930s might look like mere skirmishes from the capitals of Europe, but to many Americans they were equally fundamental to those going on across the seas.

Even before the New Deal tried "capitalism in one country," Walter Lippmann wrote about the momentous changes worldwide in the way international relations were being conducted. National governments, under the pressure of the Great Depression, were replacing the marketplace as arbiter of both international and intranational economic relations. To meet demands that they take control of economic affairs, national leaders everywhere were acting out new roles. "They will enormously increase the scope of government and greatly intensify the dependence of the individual upon government," he predicted. Questions settled by the marketplace in the nineteenth century would now become the subject of government-to-government arrangements. Older matters between nations and empires — frontiers and balance of power — would no doubt remain primary subjects of diplomacy, yet they too would be reshaped (and intensify) under the impact of the effort to manage the commerce of the world (Lippmann, 1932).

Acheson was a personal witness to the spreading impact of what Lippmann foresaw. He had served briefly in the Treasury Department in the early New Deal, until Franklin Roosevelt's "unorthodox" monetary experiments with gold prices led to his resignation. Traditional "liberalism" had given way to a statist vision propagated in the United States by Roosevelt's Brain Trust. Though there were counterforces even within the New Deal, for example, Cordell Hull's strong defense of world order and traditional economic liberalism, the world Acheson looked out upon in November, 1939, more than fulfilled the darkest possibilities in Lippmann's predictions.

In Europe, the Nazi-Soviet Pact had startled political observers, more so in some ways than the outbreak of war; while across the Pacific in Asia, the Japanese now felt an urgency not only to bring the "China Incident" to a successful conclusion, but to drive south as well to establish their "Co-prosperity Sphere." One former Brain Truster, Adolf Berle, summed up the situation in a phrase that perfectly captured all the aspects of the totalitarian challenge. An Axis victory, he wrote, would isolate America in "the unfortunate position of an old-fashioned general store in a town of hard-bitten chains" (Gardner, 1964:160).

These Russo-German and Japanese bids for world domination, Acheson told the Yale audience, threatened to reverse the course of history. In the nineteenth century, he explained, Great Britain had created a true world market, and, not coincidentally, presided over the greatest expansion of human freedoms in history. The current totalitarian challenge to American freedoms and interests, was not directly territorial, but focused on that crucial link between economics and politics.

Throughout the nineteenth century, he went on, Great Britain had provided the leadership and power necessary to establish the world market, while the example of its "liberal" political institutions guided nations along the right paths toward the realization of human freedom. This was the dual meaning of the *Pax Britannica*. "But we can see that certain important factors in its operation are no longer in existence or functioning as they did. We can see that the credits which were once extended by the financial center in London no longer provide the means for the production of wealth in other countries. We can see that the free-trade areas, which once furnished both a market of vast importance and a commodities exchange, no longer exist. We can see that British naval power no longer can guarantee security of life and investment in distant parts of the earth and a localization of conflict nearer home" (Princeton Seminar, 1953).

A return to the political conditions of the past century was not possible nor completely desirable, but that heritage — and future progress — depended upon defeat of the totalitarian states. "No limitations on our freedom of action which we might be willing to accept," Acheson concluded in reference to the dangers war would pose for democratic societies — the dangers "isolationists" always cited — "would equal those which internment on this continent would impose."

Military defeat of the antidemocratic powers, he warned, would not by itself insure the safety of American institutions. Security required reconnecting the future with the past. There would have to be "a stable international monetary system," and the prevention of new "exclusive or preferential trade arrangements with other areas created by military or financial conquest, agreement, or political connection." Those were, as he said, some of the thoughts that stuck in the back of Acheson's mind as he reentered office at the height of the Cold War.

If Acheson in 1953 or 1949 thought back to 1939, his speech at Yale was filled with bitter commentary on the New Deal experiment with "capitalism in one country." Read in the context of the isolationist-internationalist debate of the pre-Pearl Harbor years, Acheson was thus expressing a fear that New Dealism could turn inwards in the face of the external threat, and become fascism or socialism. As would later be the case at the beginning of the Cold War, policymakers (and soon-to-be policymakers like Acheson) felt it essential to win the intellectual battle at home first.

As Acheson well understood, war expanded the role of government in the private economy even more than the New Deal. If "classical" liberalism was to be restored, therefore, it would have to be on a world-wide scale, by reconstructing the world economy in a way that would be conducive to a diminished role for governments intranationally. A delicate task lay ahead. As it turned out, the Cold War became a means for its achievement. The Marshall Plan, it was often said, was like building a TVA every other week, in terms of direct stimulation to the American economy. But that was not the main point. The Cold War relegitimized capitalism politically after the traumas to its institutional and ideological foundations during the Great Depression years and World War II.

All this happened, however, as a remarkable reversal of expectations. It had been assumed during the war that postwar Russian collaboration in American efforts to rebuild the world was essential to their realization. Only skeptics, it seemed, like George Frost Kennan and a few others, foresaw not simply Russian obduracy, but the impossibility of Soviet understanding of American war aims. When Kennan returned to Moscow in 1944, after a seven-year absence, he set out to disabuse his superiors of the "quaint" notion that Russia could be channeled in the direction of postwar collaboration. Listing men who were little known in the West, but whose voices in Soviet councils ranked highest save for one or two, Kennan wrote:

> These prominent Soviet leaders know little of the outside world. They have no personal knowledge of foreign statesmen. To them, the vast pattern of international life, political and economic, can provide no associations, can hold no significance, except in what they conceive to be its bearing on the problems of Russian security and Russian internal life. . . . God knows what strange images and impressions are created in their minds by what they hear of life beyond Russia's borders. God knows what conclusions they draw from all this, and what recommendations they make on the basis of those conclusions.[1]

Within months of the war's end, Washington felt certain it knew what conclusions Russian leaders drew about the West — and their single-minded devotion to using the postwar turmoil and confusion to advance westwards. But would there have to be another war to stop the "Red Menace"? Kennan would recall later that he wrote the famous "X" article, "The Sources of Soviet Conduct," which gave birth to the term *containment*, not to encourage the idea of war with Russia — despite its military imagery — but to reassure the nation that the challenge could be met without war.

Dean Acheson agreed. The postwar Russian-American confrontation was unlikely to turn "hot" soon, unless Moscow miscalculated American determination to defend its worldwide interests. Despite the presence of the Red Army in Eastern Europe, and the forced "evolution" of the governments behind the "Iron Curtain" into one-party dictatorships, he did not believe the Russians would provoke a war with the United States.

The Russians would not push the world to war, he once told David Lilienthal of the Atomic Energy Commission, "unless they are absolutely out of their minds." Instead, the Politburo would work to extend Soviet power through internal subversion (Lilienthal, 1964:215). The real danger, therefore, was that America might be "interned" or isolated without a hot war, just as it might have been before World War II, if the Japanese had not bombed Pearl Harbor.

At Baylor University on March 6, 1947, one week before he asked Congress to supply $500 million in aid to Greece and Turkey to aid those countries resist "direct or indirect aggression," President Truman warned against the worldwide trend toward state intervention and management of domestic and international trade. Peace, freedom, and world trade were inseparable. Unless the trend toward state control of economic systems was halted, he went on, the United States would come under terrific pressure to emulate those practices. "It is not the American way. It is not the way to peace. . . ." (LaFeber, 1971:150-1).

According to the testimony of Ilya Ehrenberg, the Soviet novelist and journalist, the mood in Truman's Washington (described to him by a friend of FDR who was unhappy with the new president's toughness) did not presage an American-initiated war:

> Truman doesn't have a war in mind. He believes that Communism threatens certain Western European countries and could triumph if the Soviet Union were to recover economically and forge ahead. An implacable American policy and atom bomb tests will force Russia to spend all her strength and her resources on modernizing her armaments. The supporters of the hard line talk about the threat of Soviet tanks, but what they're doing in fact is to declare war on Soviet saucepans. (Dukes, 1989:42)

Whatever Ehrenberg heard from his American friend, and however that got reformulated in his memoirs written back in Moscow's harsh atmosphere, it is clear that by 1947 the decision had been made to rebuild the world economy without concern about Russian participation, and, second, that the United States did not expect to win the Cold War by a military assault on the Soviet Union.

THE WAY TO PEACE

Much to the consternation of American Cold War strategists, in the immediate aftermath of World War II the Soviet Union enjoyed several political advantages. Stalinism was not yet synonymous with repression. The memory of the purges and what information existed about the fate of the Russian peasants under forced collectivization did not yet outweigh the heroic exploits of the Red Army against Nazi Germany and its allies. The schism in European politics, which, in part, still depended on prewar interpretations of the Russian Revolution, had not entirely healed, and in some cases was actually wider than before the war. The war had seen "partisan" movements associated with the left fighting the Nazi occupiers, and "collaborationist" politicians aligned with or passive toward the Germans.

The general political trend to the left, which began with the election of a Labour Government in England in July, 1945, was unsettling, not because American leaders feared Clement Attlee or Ernest Bevin (who turned out to be staunch Cold War allies), but because of the implications both for the conduct of international trade and the complications "socialism" engendered when transferred, say, to a more volatile German context, still under the shadow of the extremist politics of the pre-Hitler years, and now divided between capitalist and communist rulers.

When the "crisis" came in 1947, American policymakers, as we have already noted, did not foresee a Russian military offensive. No, Stalin was simply standing by, waiting for the economic distress in Europe, brought on in part by political mismanagement, to collapse weakened internal structures. He would be there, it was assumed, to pick up the pieces.

How this would develop, and what should be done to counter the Kremlin's plans, was the subject of a thoughtful telegram sent to Washington in late 1947 by Ambassador Walter Bedell Smith. The Soviet Union, he reported, had exploited all the non-Marxist-Leninist opportunities opened to it by World War II, filling the vacuum in Eastern Europe with the Red Army, and was now reverting to its "fundamental policy, the irreconcilability of Socialism and Capitalism. . . ." The principal task, therefore, was to get across to the masses of Western Europe as well as to the rest of the world, the realities of life under the Soviet totalitarian system:

> If the majority of the workers and peasants of Western Europe realize what their plight would be under a Soviet controlled regime they would not be so susceptible to Soviet propaganda claims. They would put their shoulders to the wheel to bring about the economic recovery fostered by the Marshall Plan and the Kremlin inspired "revolutionary situation" would vanish into thin air.[2]

Success could not be assured, however, without first grasping the essential point that this was a global ideological crisis. If firm action was not taken to hold back the Soviet threat, it would not end in Eastern Europe. First there would be a Soviet-controlled Europe. "Following this, inevitably, the territory from the North Cape to Dakar and from the Bering Straits to the Dutch Indies will be painted red on the map, while we remain alone to face a menacing and powerful hegemony."[3]

Smith's assertions underscored two points about the "Containment Doctrine" that had become the basis of American Cold War policy. The first was that it was, as its author George Kennan insisted, not intended as a World War III strategy (though Kennan's advocacy of covert actions in Europe also belies his later insistence that it was purely political (Hixson, 1989:57). And the second was that despite Kennan's initial attempts to limit "containment" to key areas, the policy never worked that way in practice, in part because of overriding concerns about the "bandwagon" effect, as put forth here by Ambassador Smith and many others to come. Even Kennan himself was not unsusceptible to the "bandwagon" effect, as his subsequent career demonstrated (Hixson, 1989:68-71).

It is in this context that the debates over the Truman Doctrine are best understood. When the president asked Congress for $500 million to aid Greece and Turkey on March 12, 1947, a domino thesis was already in formulation. Greece became the first domino in the Cold War, although it is not usually remembered that way. George Kennan, for instance, viewed the Greek situation precisely that way — as distinct from (but not necessarily opposed to) the geopolitical concerns British Empire pol-icymakers had always expressed about protecting trade routes in the Mediterranean.

Kennan remembered it this way:

> People in Western Europe did not, by and large, want Communist con-trol. But this did not mean that they would not trim their sails and even abet its coming if they gained the impression that it was inevitable. This was why the shock of a Communist success in Greece could not be risked. (Kennan, 1967:318)

What met in Greece in those fateful months after the war were preoccupations of the sort Dean Acheson carried with him from the prewar crisis, concerns about the internal political situation in Europe as a whole, and an interpretation of the world situation that automati-cally imposed itself on future events. It fell to Acheson, then under secretary of state, to make the presentation on behalf of the administra-tion to the Senate Foreign Relations Committee in executive session hearings.

Senator H. Alexander Smith proved to be the most persistent ques-tioner about the worldwide implications of the newly announced "Truman Doctrine." Smith wanted to know if the Doctrine meant that the United States would be called upon to "finance resistance" in other places, like South America, where there was known to be "communistic infiltration." "I want to see what the implications are throughout the world."

"If there are situations where we can do something effective," the under secretary responded, "then I think we must certainly do it." Not satisfied, Smith came back a little later with a question about the danger that the United States might be spreading itself too thin if it went beyond "certain strategic areas."

> SECRETARY ACHESON: It is true that there are parts of the world to which we have no access. It would be silly to believe that we can do anything effective in Rumania, Bulgaria or Poland. You cannot do that. That is within the Russian area of physical force. We are excluded from that. There are other places where we can be effective. One of them is Korea, and I think that is another place where the line has been clearly drawn between the Russians and ourselves.
>
> SENATOR SMITH: Then we have come to this place in our policy: We are saying, "You have come this far. Now you have to stop or you are running head on into us." Is that what the President's message means?

Acheson was not ready to go quite so far. Instead, he repeated an earlier answer:

> SECRETARY ACHESON: In these areas where our help can be effective in resisting this penetration.[4]

The first thing to note about this key exchange is that Korea is not claimed to be a strategic point militarily, but one where a line has been drawn and American help "can be effective." If that is to be the determining consideration, then the emerging containment doctrine is not at all like classic balance-of-power theories even on a beginning level. Under such a loosely defined principle, moreover, a Soviet probe becomes almost unavoidable. Instead of the fear that the Russian tier of satellites in Eastern Europe would endanger the next and then the next, Acheson is putting containment on a different basis. And this bothered the members of the Foreign Relations Committee.

It is now necessary to pick up on the questions Senator Smith had been asking, as they were developed by his Democratic colleague, Senator Walter George. Like Smith, George was deeply concerned about the worldwide implications of the Truman Doctrine. "I do not see how the President's speech of yesterday," he told Acheson and the Committee, "can be characterized as a mere plea for assistance to Greece and Turkey. If it were mere economic assistance it would be one thing, and it would be easily done. But he put this nation squarely on the line against certain ideologies."

Senators Arthur Vandenberg and Alexander Wiley, meanwhile, had been saying that their first mail in reaction to the president's speech of March 12, 1947, had been an "overriding question" as to why the United Nations could not "take this thing over." There was a fear that the UN was already defunct. Senator George took up that point as part of his statement about Truman's going on record against "certain ideologies."

SENATOR GEORGE: Now, we might as well face it, . . . once you got into the United Nations there would be more than one nation there fighting us on that issue. Russia would have friends. She undoubtedly would have backing on that issue [Greece and Turkey]. I do not see that there is anything for it except just to face this issue straight, and that is what the President did. It clearly put us on the line. Call it communism, totalitarianism, or whatever you want to call it, it is there. If we are going to stand on that line, so far as this issue is concerned I think your United Nations is simply short circuited and out.[5]

The matter of whether a majority could be mustered in the UN, or, more likely, a veto avoided, was less important than what the senators all understood to be the nature of the conflict with the Soviet Union — an ideological conflict. The UN had been designed to stop troops marching across borders. As George said, "so far as this issue is concerned I think your United Nations is simply short circuited and out." But if the UN had been designed to stop troops marching across borders, the Truman Doctrine appeared to raise the issue of military force to stop troops marching inside borders, i.e., civil wars.

It nagged at Senator George, who worried that Congress was about to take the most important step "we have ever taken in our international relationships" without full consideration of what that meant. "You can say what you please about it, but that is the size of it, and I know it and realize it, and I know very, very well that this is simply the beginning of a program the end of which no man can foresee at the moment."

Senator Smith had reminded him that the consequences of not supporting the administration's lead could be even more serious in both the specific event and for overall policy. George countered that he feared more the "legislative paralysis that I have seen here for quite a long time, that when something that is an accomplished fact is announced, the Congress feels it has to take it and it goes on taking it, and if you do not take it you say, 'Look what position you are putting our country in and what position you are putting all our affairs in.' "[6]

George was not alive to see his prescient forebodings become open rebellion when the Johnson administration argued before the same committee twenty years later that the Gulf of Tonkin resolution was the functional equivalent of a declaration of war. But his final words to his colleagues in the secret debates over the Truman Doctrine had an eerie ring to them when the minutes of the executive session were finally made public in 1973. "I do not think I have to defend myself here," he began:

I carried the burden in large part — Senator Barkley and myself did — of the Lend Lease proposal. I have never had any apologies to make for that. But I could then see the shadows of war lengthening all over the earth, and I thought it was absolutely necessary to move.

This is not that situation. Nobody thinks Russia is going to attack us. Nobody thinks Russia is going to make any war now on anybody. Certainly not. That she will keep up the same aggravating aggressiveness that she has had in the past, and infiltrations and the pressures and war of nerves, I guess few of us doubt, few of us question.

I do not know that we will have to go anywhere else in this world, and I do not say that at the moment. I do not see how we are going to escape going into Manchuria, North China, and Korea and doing things in that area of the world. But at the same time that is another question, and we have got the right to exercise common sense. But I know that when we make a policy of this kind we are irrevocably committing ourselves to a course of action, and there is no way to get out of it next week or next year. You go down to the end of the road.[7]

ENLARGING THE SPHERE

The impact of the Truman Doctrine and the Marshall Plan were expected to be felt everywhere — else there was no use in either. As Melvyn Leffler (1988) has argued, the framers of the Marshall Plan understood that Europe's "dollar gap" problem could not be resolved without restoring the prewar trade patterns between the metropolis and its raw materials–producing areas.

In effect, the United States was expected in the postwar world to accomplish what those statesmen had not been able to do: to hold at bay a powerful challenger in Europe itself, while still protecting old imperial trade routes. "And because this [dollar gap] problem was so intractable," writes Leffler, "American officials focused significant attention on safeguarding European access to Third World markets and natural resources and on preserving triangular patterns of international trade whereby European nations traditionally earned dollars through American purchases of raw materials." And, he concludes,

Far from limiting American attention to Europe, the Marshall Plan, along with other considerations, accentuated American interest in those areas around the globe that appeared to be of paramount commercial and financial importance to Britain, France, western Germany, and other participants in the ERP. (Leffler, 1988:279-306)

New players in the game of empire, the United States and Russia were not like their predecessors, and the outcome was not to be determined in such circumstances and by the same means as it had been in the eighteenth and nineteenth centuries. What made the American policymaker's predicament still worse was that while he had to try to juggle relations with the European metropole and the colonial areas on at least two levels, his Soviet adversary had a single explanation for the way the world worked, and a single remedy for the contradictions of world politics.

And just as the Marshall Plan focused attention on the problem, as Bernard Baruch once put it, that economic recovery would be "hijacked," so what happened in Asia, either to protect natural resources for Europeans, or, increasingly, Japanese trade outlets, Cold War policies led to military confrontations on the frontiers. Orwell's picture of the future was coming closer: "It would probably be more accurate to say that by becoming continuous, war has ceased to exist."

Never loath to claim authorship of any plan or initiative — including the term *Cold War* itself — Bernard Baruch explained in a private letter how he had testified to a Senate committee that it would be useless to have the Marshall Plan if the countries we wished to help could be "hijacked" by Russia. "I suggested that the United States ought to be willing to go to war to defend them in case of aggression." The next day, according to the self-styled adviser to presidents, Secretary of State George C. Marshall telephoned him to say that he wished that he had thought of that phrase, and further that British Foreign Secretary Ernest Bevin had asked if U.S. policy would indeed protect Europe against "hijacking." Marshall had said, "Yes."[8]

In a lengthy report to the Cabinet on November 7, 1947, Marshall had concluded that while the advance of communism had been stemmed, the Russians might soon grow desperate and "they may be driven by the dynamism of their own situation to precipitate civil war in Italy and France this winter." American policy had to be, therefore, to restore a "balance of power in both Europe and Asia" (Millis, 1951:340-42).

Here was still more evidence that American policymakers connected events worldwide, international and intranational, and were prepared to use whatever means deemed "effective" to accomplish their goals, whether by means of covert political action (as in Italy), or proxy war (as in Greece), or by "limited war" (as in Korea).

Foreign Secretary Bevin took up the issue of a balance of power from a different angle at the London Foreign Ministers' Meeting at the end of 1947. Once again it had been made clear that the former allies of World War II could not yet solve the issues between them, especially the fate of Germany. In a farewell discussion with Marshall, his British counterpart said that the key was to recognize that the German problem was not just a "mere quarrel" between various Western nations and the Soviet Union. The fundamental issue was where "power" was going to rest. A "Western democratic system" that would include France, Italy, and the British Dominions would have to be devised. "It would be a sort of spiritual federation of the West."

If such a consolidation were achieved, it would become clear to the Soviet Union without war that "having gone so far they could not advance any further." A few weeks later, Bevin sent Marshall a proposal for allying the "ethical and spiritual forces inherent in . . . Western civilization of which we are the chief protagonists." The rest of Europe could rally around such a force, and would look to us "for political and moral guidance and for assistance in building up a counter attraction to the baleful tenets of communism within their borders and in recreating a healthy society. . . ."[9]

Hard on Bevin's message came the 1948 coup in Czechoslovakia and the Berlin Blockade Crisis. George Kennan feared that NATO was being hurried into being by what he would call a prolonged case of the jitters. What he would have preferred was a commitment to provide military assistance to a small group of nations, "whatever was necessary to bolster their internal morale (which was, after all, the heart of the matter). . . ." (Kennan, 1967:398-9).

The trouble with that solution was that it did not take into account the essential differences between what the Russians could achieve in Eastern Europe via control by the Red Army and the communist parties of the satellites, but also by its manipulation of communist parties in the West. And that was what Bevin was trying to say so circuitously. The external menace was so multifaceted that it required the creation of a "spiritual" counterforce.

Thus observed John J. McCloy, one of the Cold War's "wisemen," twenty years later. The "concept" of the North Atlantic Treaty Organization "was not exclusively or even primarily to deter an impending or threatened Soviet military attack."

> There was a deeper and more underlying motive than the fear of a direct invasion of the West. Western Europe in the immediate postwar period, denuded of military strength following the rapid Allied demobilization, was also economically and politically prostrate. It became clear that it was incapable of reviving itself unassisted, certainly not within an acceptable period of time. In this condition Europe faced the largely undemobilized and massive strength of the Soviet Union. The Soviet Union was imbued with an ideological urge and supported by propaganda forms almost stridently hostile to Western concepts and institutions of representative government or any form of collaboration in the political and economic recovery of Western Europe. It was this contrast between Soviet strength and purpose on the one hand and Western European weakness and lack of concentrated direction on the other which prompted the formation of a Western security system. (McCloy, 1969:22-25)

Both NATO and its Asian half-brother, SEATO, had to do with "nation building," although the term is usually applied only to events in the Third World. Looking back in 1953, Dean Acheson discussed the situation in the Princeton seminar this way:

There was also a very strong belief that economic recovery was closely connected with some sort of progress in the security field. It was felt that economic recovery had progressed through what might be called the primitive economic stages: agriculture had been brought up to a tolerable level, what had been done in industry was what could be done without the investment of any considerable capital. But to go beyond the point where the European countries were in mid-1948 required a greater degree, a greater sense of security before there could be the additional economic development which required their confidence, the return of capital which had taken flight from these countries, new investment in plant through the capital of the countries concerned. These ideas were being very actively propagated both in Europe and the United States. The Vandenberg Resolution [which would confirm Congressional approval of President Truman's offer of support to a European military alliance] is the expression of this whole thought in political life in the United States. (Princeton Seminar, 1953)

When Acheson was pressed on the matter of how NATO specifically would meet the internal communist threat, which was at the heart of views like those above and those of John McCloy, during executive hearings on the treaty, the answer he gave was a hedged one. What would happen, asked Senator Alexander Wiley, if France or Italy, for example, became communist "through the application of, let us call it, ideas. That would not be covered."

SECRETARY ACHESON: A purely ideological offensive would not be covered. If you would have a combination of the use of force with an internal fifth column, of course it would.

SENATOR WILEY: Now we are getting down to where I was going to lead you. An internal fifth column would be force if it were connected with the so-called mother country, Russia.

SECRETARY ACHESON: Well, what I was trying to point out is that what you are likely to get is both the use of external force and the use of internal revolution, as you have in Greece. . . . Whether you would reach the same conclusion if the thing were entirely generated from inside, with external political stimulation, is another question.[10]

Acheson and his aides in the State Department really did not want to think about such events. They were interested in prevention rather than cure. Wiley did extract a concession from the secretary of state that consultations could be requested under the NATO treaty to deal with cases of internal disorder aided and abetted by forces outside the pact, but Acheson did not want to leave the impression that "foreign arms" were a very helpful way to put down a political revolution. "It is not likely to be very effective," he said. "If there is absolutely no external force at all, and merely by external stimulation you foment a revolution, foreign armies coming on the scene are not likely to help it very much."[11]

Inside the Department of State there had been serious debates about what was a helpful way to combat subversion and political revolution. In early 1948, for example, Secretary Marshall had queried the American ambassador in Rome about measures being actively studied for deterring the Soviets from attempting in Italy "fifth column action along [the] Czech model," by strengthening the confidence of noncommunist elements. "Please give us urgently your own estimate whether prompt Italian inclusion in our association with . . . a regional security arrangement would be helpful in Italy."[12]

Efforts to define indirect aggression were finally abandoned, and the treaty language left it up to consultations of the sort Senator Wiley would explore with Acheson in an unsuccessful attempt to reduce the continuing ambiguity surrounding NATO obligations. Acheson's concern with prevention rather than a cure stemmed in part from his belief that in fact the internal and external threats posed by "communism" were actually fairly easy to separate. In a statement to the Senate Foreign Relations Committee, this most subtle of diplomats put the issue this way:

> After the failure of the Foreign Ministers Conference late in 1947, General Marshall talked with the Foreign Ministers of Great Britain and France about the situation which faced the Western World. They believed that it was not possible to establish at that time normal and peaceful and constructive relations with the Soviet Union until there was a much more settled situation in the West. The Soviet Union was drawn into the troubled situation in the West, and that made quiet relations within the rest of the world impossible.[13]

In June, 1948, Marshall had tackled a closely related issue: the question of Scandinavian participation in NATO. George Kennan was strongly opposed. "There was a tendency in the Department of State at that time," he wrote, "particularly among the gentlemen of the Office of European Affairs, to want to extend this alliance as far as possible — to jam it, so to speak, as close as possible to the Soviet borders." Kennan felt that the likely result would be a Soviet reaction against Finnish neutrality (Kennan, 1967:412).

Like his objections to the large alliance and his more modest counterproposals for military aid to Europe, Kennan's views did not persuade Secretary Marshall. They were not sufficiently ideological, it seemed. Marshall was anxious to have all of Scandinavia, including traditionally neutral Sweden, associated with the new alliance. He wrote President Truman to ask that he personally take up the matter with Prince Bertil and members of the Swedish Foreign Office when the president received them in Chicago. Sweden's attempts to persuade Norway and Denmark to stay out of NATO, said Marshall, would very likely weaken the area's resistance to Soviet expansion. He suggested that Truman take a strong line with his visitors: "The issue in the world today is not a matter of choosing between two great-power blocs, as seems to be widely believed in Sweden, but is rather the question of the survival of nations which believe in freedom and democratic processes. Such nations have a common interest, and a neutrality policy which reveals a division among the free nations of the world can only serve to invite aggression."[14]

Under Secretary Robert Lovett told representatives of the future NATO powers a few weeks later that there was a "consensus of opinion that the Soviet Union was a threat and that the efforts to meet it should be directed to the ideological as well as the military threat. The respective countries should be strengthened to resist internal as well as external threats."[15] It followed that Sweden's defection, or its neutrality, by suggesting that the struggle was simply one of big-power rivalry, would weaken the internal defenses of the alliance.

Ideological purity was more easily enforced, of course, in the Communist bloc, where no Scandinavian ambiguities were permitted to cloud the issue. At the Cominform organization meeting in September, 1947, Russian "theorists" had castigated the French and Italian parties for collaborating with the bourgeoisie, and made plain Stalin's desire that communists in those countries should do all they could to obstruct implementation of the Truman Doctrine and the Marshall Plan (Deutscher, 1966:586-87).

It is tempting to argue that NATO and its eastern counterpart, the Warsaw Pact, both played an invaluable role in the reconstruction of Europe, not by protecting member countries against outside attack, but by insuring that each side's ideological offensives were kept under control and did not unduly disrupt internal affairs, and, secondly, by providing an external military danger to blame for all failures.

A few weeks after the NATO treaty was signed, Acheson was in a buoyant mood. In a Congressional hearing, Senator Claude Pepper remarked, "The Atlantic Treaty has given these Western European nations some confidence against a resurgent Germany as well as Russia." "Yes," responded the secretary of state, "it works in all directions."[16]

KOREA AND BEYOND

From NATO experiences, the foundation was laid for attempts at "nation-building" elsewhere in the world. Five days before the North Korean attack on South Korea, Acheson addressed a conference of state governors on the communist danger. The Reds could win Europe and Asia, he warned, without firing a shot. And that would mean isolationism with a vengeance, an imposed isolationism. "He scared hell out of us," reported one governor (Smith, 1972:170-71).

When the Korean War began, moreover, Acheson carefully crafted a statement for President Truman to make to the public explaining the situation, explaining it in the context of the "model" he had described to

Lilienthal. "The attack upon Korea," read the key sentence, "makes it plain beyond all doubt that *communism* has passed beyond subversion to conquer independent nations and will now use armed invasion and war" (Smith, 1972:185-86). The distinction between a "communist" threat and a Russian threat would soon be blurred — had in fact already been so confused, as we saw in the 1947 Greek crisis, sometimes by Acheson himself, and sometimes deliberately.

At the same time, Korea made it possible to accomplish certain tricky issues, such as a beginning on the question of German rearmament, precisely because the issues had become blurred. Russia would not provoke a "general" war, then, but it had the capability of arming its puppets and stimulating little wars. Exactly what tactics the Kremlin would use to achieve its purposes, its "grand design," as Americans sometimes called it, to weaken the West and upset the balance in Europe, policymakers did not know. Acheson frankly admitted his puzzlement. The Korean War might be intended either to demonstrate the impotence of the United States or to entangle the bulk of American power in a far-off theater.

All but forgotten, however, was the secretary's prediction back in 1947 that American aid would be used in places like Korea, where it could be "effective." As American power grew, therefore, the more places where it could be "effective" (supposedly) became more important than whatever was behind Russian/communist attacks. Any losses could be disastrous for American interests.

Historians and political scientists have, by and large, ignored Acheson's standard of effectiveness in favor of the "probe" thesis of the origins of the Korean War and the American response. Thus, John Mueller (1988b:55-79) argues that Korea was a "limited probe" that got dangerously out of hand with American and Chinese involvement. If the United States demonstrated a measured resolve, it was believed at the outset of the Korean War, then the Kremlin would abandon efforts to achieve the grand design — at least immediately — and World War III would be prevented.[17]

In this manner, Korea became the first link, as it were, in an explanatory chain for the Cold War. Strung together, these "probes" formed an outer band around the troublesome ideological problems of the Cold War, holding together an otherwise not always cohesive rationale for both superpowers. If the United States did not respond adequately in this first instance, the probe thesis asserts, or if the Soviets still persisted and war erupted elsewhere, then, as Truman said privately at the time, the conflict would escalate and the superpowers would abandon Korea for a showdown in Europe, "where we can use the bomb" (LaFeber, 1989:489).

But the bomb as ultimate threat made it easier in those instances after Korea to justify interventions — as a kind of assurance that general war was unthinkable, and hence the rise of an Orwellian logic of deterrence. The probe thesis, moreover, reinforced other mainstays of

America's vision of itself in the Cold War era, most especially what British historian Christopher Thorne has called the bicycle spoke version of international affairs. According to that view, relations between the super-powers and the rest of the world resemble nothing so much as a series of individual "spokes" emanating from an inner core directly to a point on the periphery. And finally, the probe thesis, by emphasizing the out-ward thrust of Soviet power, focuses constant attention on a Eurocentric view of the world.

These subsets of the probe thesis have a bounce-back effect. The bicycle spoke version, for example, is a component of the agent theory of revolution. Taken together, these portrayed the Kremlin as the head-quarters of what Ronald Reagan (repeating other presidents if in different words) called the "evil empire," the active agent behind untoward events on the Korean peninsula, and eventually almost everyone on the globe. Alternative explanations of the Korean War, for example, which picture the Russians, like their American opposites, as "outside" participants in a bitter civil war that had already cost thousands of lives, have not yet overthrown the probe thesis and its variants.[18]

Paradoxically, Korea's very remoteness and apparent strategic unim-portance (Acheson, in a famous speech early in 1950 had, following the Joint Chiefs of Staff lead, actually placed the peninsula outside the U.S. defense perimeter) magnified its consequences for future occurrences (probes) and options. This line of reasoning went: If the Russians enjoyed such far-reaching powers so many thousands of miles away from Europe, and were so readily willing to throw away Korean and Chinese lives in their quest for victory in the Cold War's main theater, then clearly the superpowers were engaged in a mortal struggle, whether it escalated to sudden nuclear holocaust or not.

For how else could one explain the unremitting wickedness of the "distant and shadowy figures" (Acheson's phrase) who would hurl masses of Koreans and Chinese against the ramparts of the "Free World" for no other purpose than to further their plans of conquest of the core of Western civilization? Writing to the father of a soldier in Korea who had expressed anger at the pointlessness of fighting the Russians this way, the secretary of state said that such frustration and bitterness were natural:

This agony of spirit, so understandable and right, makes it hard to believe that so monstrous an evil can exist in a world based upon infinite mercy and justice.

But the fact is that it does exist. The fact is that it twists and tortures all our lives. And, I believe, to each of us in this case, as in so many others, the great thing is not what happens to us but how we bear what happens to us. (Bundy, 1952:298-89)

World politics in 1950 had thus assumed a form no less menacing than the pre–Pearl Harbor months, and all the more perilous because the enemy had this now dramatically illustrated ability to overleap national boundaries and work his will through a loose group of agencies that American policymakers could give no better title to than "international communism."

Acheson's task remained simple, however, compared to the gyrations required of John Foster Dulles in order to explain how "international communism" actually worked. Dulles had reasoned a rationale for defending Korea in May, 1950, stressing to President Truman the need to take a stand "at some doubtful point" in order to demonstrate that communism was not the "wave of the future." It had to be in Asia, he went on, because

> Indonesia with its vast natural resources may be lost and the oil of the Middle East will be in jeopardy. None of these places provide holding grounds once the people feel that Communism is the wave of the future and that even we are retreating before it.[19]

Truman decided Korea was the "doubtful point." Walking over to a big globe in his office, he told his staff: "This is the Greece of the Far East. If we are tough enough now, there won't be any next step" (Phillips, 1966:297). John Foster Dulles was somewhat more inclined than Truman and his advisers to treat the Third World independently of the European theater of the Cold War, but the connections had been forged in the 1947 Truman Doctrine.

The Southeast Asia Treaty Organization was still four years off, but the sequence in Europe and Asia, in terms of American responses to the sorts of burdens Dulles was describing, was much the same. In both instances American reconstruction efforts were followed by military pacts. But what were these pacts and doctrines designed to thwart? Asked by Senator Henry Jackson to explain the term "international communism" in 1957 at the time of the administration's request for a delegation of Congressional authority to allow the president to use military force in the Middle East area, the "Eisenhower Doctrine," Secretary of State John Foster Dulles at first demurred. International communism, he explained, was a term well known to Congress, because it used it frequently. Then the following colloquy ensued:

SENATOR JACKSON: We want to know what it means in connection with this legislation.
SECRETARY DULLES: It means the same thing here, Senator, exactly as it meant and means in the Mutual Security Act.

SENATOR JACKSON: What did it mean in the Mutual Security Act?
SECRETARY DULLES: Congress passed the act and I assume knows what it meant.
SENATOR JACKSON: You folks in the executive branch administer it. What does it mean?

Dulles finally had to extricate himself from this unpromising dialogue with an attempt to come to terms with the rationale for American Cold War policy.

SECRETARY DULLES: Well, international communism is a conspiracy composed of a certain number of people, all of whose names I do not know, and many of whom I suppose are secret. They have gotten control of one government after another. They first got control of Russia after the First World War. They have gone on getting control of one country after another until finally they were stopped. But they have not gone out of existence. International communism is still a group which is seeking to control the world, in my opinion. (Gardner, 1974:194)

As Dulles spoke, the world became peopled with "aliens," as if the Cold War science fiction films like "Invasion of the Body Snatchers" portrayed an actual state of affairs. From Central America to Southeast Asia, the unsleeping "conspiracy" operated night and day. One of Acheson's colleagues would write later that the real issue, the balance of power, could not be explained otherwise. "As in 1917, as in 1941," asserted Louis Halle (1967), "it was still not possible to tell the American people what the real issue was." Was that really the case? Even if the issue was the balance of power, it was not the same balance of power as in pre–World War I days. It was a vastly more intricate and delicate equilibrium, indeed a set of balances that included internal politics throughout the industrialized world, that both enlisted and sought to overcome ideology, and that was precariously perched on a narrow band of common interests between the industrialized world and the great raw materials–producing areas, former European colonies and emerging nations.

And indeed, in a way, that is what Walt Rostow has been arguing recently in regard to the war in Vietnam, which, as he sees it, should be termed a victory. The American defense of South Vietnam, according to Rostow, allowed the rest of Southeast Asia to pass from the colonial era to nationhood without being captured by the communists. It provided time and a sense of firmness that matched the forces of communist "strength and purpose" (Rostow, 1988:863-68).

The United States paid a heavy price in Vietnam. And it finally dropped more bombs than in any or all of its previous wars. Calling that debacle (for the Vietnamese, for the United States, for the world) a victory is as strained as calling the post–World War II era either the Cold War or the "long peace." Be that as it may, while it is clear such terms have their uses, we should not allow any label to determine the content of our analyses. We still need to look inside the bottle.

ENDNOTES

1. "Russia — Seven Years Later," September, 1944, Department of State, *Foreign Relations of the United States, 1944* (Washington, 1966), IV, pp. 902-12. (Hereafter, *FRUS*)

2. Smith to the secretary of state, November 5, 1947, *FRUS, 1947*, IV, pp. 606-12.

3. *Ibid.*

4. U.S. Congress, Senate Foreign Relations Committee, Historical Series, *Legislative Origins of the Truman Doctrine: Hearings Held in Executive Session*, 80th Congress, 1st session (Washington, 1973), pp. 17, 22.

5. *Ibid.*, p. 15.

6. *Ibid.*, p. 126.

7. *Ibid.*, p. 198.

8. Baruch to William H. Draper, Jr., July 27, 1962, *The Papers of Bernard M. Baruch*, Mudd Library, Princeton University.

9. This account is based on "British Memorandum of Conversation," undated [ca. December 19, 1947], *FRUS, 1947*, II, pp. 815-22, and, British ambassador to the secretary of state, January 13, 1948, *FRUS, 1948*, III, pp. 3-6.

10. U.S. Senate, *Hearings Held in Executive Session: The Vandenberg Resolution and the North Atlantic Treaty*, 80th Congress, 1st session (Washington, 1973), p. 155.

11. *Ibid.*

12. *FRUS, 1948*, III, pp. 45-46.

13. U.S. Senate, Foreign Relations Committee, *The Vandenberg Resolution and the North Atlantic Treaty, Hearings Held in Executive Session*, 80th Congress, 2nd session (Washington, 1973), p. 86.

14. Memorandum to President Truman, June 3, 1948, *FRUS, 1948*, III, p. 135.

15. Minutes of the First Meeting of the Washington Exploratory Talks on Security, July 6, 1948, *ibid.*, pp. 148-55.

16. U.S. Senate, Committee on Foreign Relations, *Reviews of the World Situation, 1949-1950*, Executive Hearings, 81st Congress, 1st and 2nd sessions (Washington, 1974), p. 13.

17. See, for example, McGeorge Bundy's review, "World Without War, Amen," of John Mueller (1989), *Retreat from Doomsday: The Obsolescence of Major War*, in *Washington Post Book World*, March 12, 1989. Bundy notes with approval Mueller's argument that the Cold War was about Europe, with the Soviets pushing for "marginal advantage in ways that led to Western response and so to Cold War." The "regional wars" like Korea and Vietnam, and the crises in Berlin and Cuba, are "not trivial," but there has been no major war.

18. The civil war origins of the Korean War, the ways in which they interacted, and the confusions of superpower involvement are detailed in Cummings

(1981). The issue here is partly one of emphasis, i.e., it makes a great deal of difference whether Stalin acted in Korea to set up some other move in Europe or the Middle East, as Americans thought then and later, or whether by joining with the United States in the division of Korea in 1945, he established conditions that led to his decision, as George Kennan (1967:395) once put it with a fine eye for such distinctions, "to unleash a civil war in Korea."

19. Memorandum, May 18, 1950, in the *John Foster Dulles Papers*, Mudd Library, Princeton University, Princeton, New Jersey.

CHAPTER SEVEN

Long Cycles, Hegemonic Transitions, and the Long Peace

Jack S. Levy

The half-century period since World War II has been violent in many respects. It has witnessed numerous military conflicts involving small and medium-size states, including interstate wars, wars of national liberation, civil wars and revolutions, other forms of internal violence, and transnational terrorism. It has also witnessed several superpower military interventions in weaker states and a few rather serious international crises between the superpowers (see Singer, and Brecher and Wilkenfeld in this book). But this period has not witnessed a major war between the superpowers. It is the longest period of relative peace among the great powers in the last five centuries of the modern system, and is now often referred to as "the long peace" (Gaddis, 1987). If the record of the past is projected into the postwar period, we certainly would have expected a war between the leading states in the system by now. One calculation suggests that the probability of no war occurring between the handful of leading states in the system (the great powers) during a forty-four-year period (e.g., 1945-1989), given the experience of the past five centuries, is about .005 (Levy, 1989d).[1] Thus the long peace is truly an historical aberration, and this has led to a lively scholarly debate on how we might explain it.

The most common explanations for the long postwar peace refer to the role of nuclear weapons (Mandelbaum, 1981; Waltz, 1981; Gaddis, 1987b and in this book; Nye, 1987; Jervis, 1989); the bipolar structure of the postwar world (Waltz, 1979; Gaddis, 1987b and in this book); the increasing economic interdependence among the advanced industrial states (Keohane and Nye, 1989; Rosecrance, 1986; Rosenau, in this book); the emergence of a U.S.-Soviet security regime, norms of cooperation, and crisis management procedures (George, et al., 1988; George, 1984; Johnson, in this book); changing attitudes toward war and the declining legitimacy of war in the Western world (Knorr, 1966; Mueller, 1989; Ray, 1989; Weart, 1988); and long cycles of hegemonic stability and decline (Keohane, 1980; Gilpin, 1981; Modelski and Morgan, 1985; Thompson, 1988; Goldstein, 1988).[2]

It is this last set of theories that is of interest here. My task is to analyze the extent to which theories of long cycles and of hegemonic stability and decline can explain the long peace between the superpowers, and provide plausible forecasts of the likelihood of a major war in the future. I will not assess the role of other causal factors, for those are analyzed elsewhere in this volume, and for this reason I will not attempt to offer a comprehensive explanation for the long postwar peace. A full explanation requires a more complex analysis involving numerous variables and cast within a larger theory of the causes of peace and war, which goes far beyond the purpose of this study. My aim is to isolate one hypothesized explanation for the long peace and to assess its plausibility.

Explanations of the long peace from a long cycle/hegemonic stability perspective are based on extrapolations from earlier eras for which the theory is presumed to be true, and for this reason part of this study will necessarily involve an analysis of the historical validity of hegemonic and cyclical theories. Because these theories are concerned with the presence or absence of a great-power or hegemonic war involving the leading states in the system, I use the term "long peace" in this sense, while acknowledging that in other respects the postwar era has been far from peaceful.

Before we begin, it is useful to note that there are two particularly important versions of the realist theory of international politics. One is balance-of-power theory, which emphasizes the importance of the anarchic structure of the international system, the security dilemma, the destabilizing effects of dangerous concentrations of military power, and the effectiveness of balancing behavior in preventing hegemony. The central proposition of balance-of-power theory is that if one state grows so strong that it threatens to gain a position of dominance over the international system, other great powers will form a blocking coalition to prevent the expansion of the threatening state, and a hegemonic war will follow. "Hegemonic theories," on the other hand, emphasize hierarchies of power and informal systems of norms and order in a nominally anarchic system. The concentration of power in the hands of a single hegemonic power is stabilizing for the system because the leading state uses its power to manage the system to maintain order. Whereas balance-of-power theory hypothesizes that the threat of hegemony is a sufficient condition for a counter-coalition of other great powers and therefore for a general war, hegemonic theory hypothesizes that hegemony is a sufficient and perhaps necessary condition for the absence of a major war (Levy, 1989b).[3] We will examine several versions of hegemonic theory in this paper.

HEGEMONIC STABILITY THEORY

There are several forms of hegemonic theory, but the one receiving the most attention in the international relations literature as a whole is hegemonic stability theory. The theory, often associated with Gilpin

(1975), Krasner (1976), Keohane and Nye (1989), and Keohane (1980, 1984), attempts to explain stability in one particular kind of international political economy — a liberal one characterized by the free play of international market forces in trade, investment, and finance. A necessary condition for stability is the existence of a single dominant state which is both willing and able to use its power to create and maintain a set of political and economic structures and informal "regimes" that maintain order in the system. This requires that the "hegemon" be the most powerful state politically and the most efficient state economically, that it be committed to a liberal order and have a domestic structure conducive to it, and that other leading economic states share similar interests in a liberal order (Ruggie, 1982:382-84; Gilpin 1981:129-31, 1987:72-73). In the absence of a hegemon to help provide collective goods and manage the system, the system will be conflictual and unstable. Hegemonic stability theorists view the United States as a declining hegemon and fear that with declining American leadership the international political economy will become increasingly unstable. Much of the literature on international regimes is concerned with the question of how to create international institutions and norms which facilitate stability and peaceful change in an era of declining hegemony (Keohane, 1984).[4]

Although it might appear that hegemonic stability theory provides a straightforward explanation for the long peace, that conclusion is misleading. Most versions of hegemonic stability theory define hegemony in terms of dominance in economic production, finance, and/or trade, while the role of military power is generally ignored or deemphasized (Krasner, 1976; Keohane, 1980, 1984).[5] The theory attempts to explain the degree of stability in a liberal political economy rather than the incidence or seriousness of military conflict and war, and for this reason hegemonic stability theory is not a theory of peace and war and cannot explain the long peace.[6]

Hegemonic stability theory implicitly assumes that a stable liberal economy contributes to international peace and that its absence makes war more likely. This was originally proposed by Manchester liberals (Silberner, 1946) and is illustrated by the argument that the decline of economic liberalism resulting from the great depression of 1929-1939 contributed to the origins of World War II (Kindleberger, 1973). But the precise causal linkages between economic stability and international war have not been theoretically specified or historically confirmed. Liberal economic systems have some destabilizing as well as stabilizing features with respect to international security issues (Buzan, 1984), and there has been little empirical work to demonstrate which of these features dominates and under what conditions. Most analysts have concluded that economic structure is less important than military and political factors for decisions regarding war and peace between the great powers (Buzan, 1984; Levy, 1989b), though admittedly much more work needs to be done on both the theoretical and empirical levels.

Thus, although hegemonic stability theory might be able to explain the international economic stability of the first quarter-century of the postwar system and the increasing instability in that system since the early 1970s, the question of the long peace falls outside of the scope of the theory. For an explanation of the long peace we must turn to other versions of hegemonic theory.

ORGANSKI'S POWER TRANSITION THEORY

A. F. K. Organski's (1968: Chapter 14) power transition theory incorporates two ideas that have become central in later theories of hegemonic change and war: (1) the destabilizing effects of changing distributions of military power and potential in the international system, which arise from industrialization and other sources of differential rates of growth, and (2) the stabilizing effects of concentrations of military power in the hands of a single dominant state. Organski views the international system as characterized by one dominant power on top and a handful of weaker great powers below, along with other medium and smaller states and dependencies. Whereas balance-of-power theory focuses on static distributions of military capabilities as a key independent variable, Organski emphasizes the interaction effects between the distribution of capabilities and changes in relative capabilities: a major war is most likely when the military power of a dissatisfied challenger begins to approach that of the leading state in the system. The challenger will usually initiate a war in order to accelerate the power transition and to assure for itself the benefits, privileges, and influence commensurate with its newly acquired military power, though it is conceivable (but rare) that the declining leader will initiate a "preventive war."[7] Organski (1968:376) acknowledges that it is possible in principle for power transitions to be accomplished peacefully, but argues that this rarely happens. He emphasizes instead that "the major wars of recent history have all been wars involving the dominant nation and its allies against a challenger who has recently risen in power thanks to industrialization."

Although Organski does not discuss the implications of his analysis for explaining the long peace or projecting into the future,[8] the implications of his power transition theory are fairly clear. Peace for the first quarter-century of the post-1945 era is explained by American dominance. After that, given the gradual but continued American decline and the rise of the Soviet Union and other states, conditions became increasingly ripe for a hegemonic war. The key question for the purposes of prediction and explanation concerns the definition and measurement of power (and the aggregation of its many dimensions). Were we to accept the conventional wisdom that the Soviet Union began to approach the United States in overall military power (though not in economic power or political influence) somewhere in the 1970s, power transition theory presumably would have predicted that conditions have been ripe for a hegemonic war during the last two decades.[9]

Although some of the concepts and hypotheses in Organski's power transition theory have been very influential, and although his contribution should be more widely acknowledged, subsequent theories of hegemonic transitions and war are more fully developed and give more attention to the implications for the contemporary era and for the future.[10] Let us turn now to some of these more recent theories of hegemonic change and war.

GILPIN'S THEORY OF HEGEMONIC TRANSITION AND WAR

Robert Gilpin (1981) attempts to integrate some notions of hegemonic stability theory into a broader theory of hegemonic expansion, decline, transition, and war. Like Organski, Gilpin incorporates military, political, and economic dimensions into his conception of power. He also recognizes that the hegemonic state is not necessarily liberal in character, and extends his analysis to sovereign state systems in general. He argues that the hegemonic state has the capability and motivation to structure the international political, economic, and cultural systems in a way that serves its own interests — by providing a secure environment for trade and investment, by constructing a stable system of international security which helps avoid destructive wars, and generally by maintaining the status quo and its own position of dominance.

The hegemonic state cannot maintain its dominant position indefinitely, however. Although control over an international system provides an expanded resource base to the dominant power, it is also costly to maintain. These protection costs include expenditures on military forces, the financial support of allies, and the provision of collective goods necessary to maintain an international economy. The maintenance of a lead in military technology becomes increasingly expensive as technology diffuses to potential challengers who do not have to pay the full costs of research and development. Economic wealth also diffuses, in part because the same economic processes that initially favor the hegemon ultimately work to the benefit of others. In addition, prosperity and affluence invariably generate both greater demand for consumer goods and services and the emergence of domestic interests with a stake in the status quo (Olson, 1982), which work to inhibit innovation, reduce productivity, and ultimately to undermine the economic foundations of military power. Gilpin argues that the resources devoted to protection and consumption tend to rise at the expense of productive investment and long-term economic growth. Moreover, the perception of military decline invariably leads to even further diversion of resources from productive investment into the military sector for the purposes of protection, which only accelerates the decline in productivity and long-term military potential (Gilpin, 1981: Chapter 4; Kennedy, 1987).

As a result of the decline of the hegemonic power and the ascension of other great powers, a disequilibrium arises between the actual distribution of power in the system and the existing distribution of political, economic, and cultural benefits of an international system that the hegemon helped to create while at the peak of its power. Historically, the primary means of resolving this disequilibrium is a hegemonic war that brings the distribution of benefits in the system into line with the new distribution of power. The hegemonic war generally results in the defeat of the declining hegemon and the rise of a new hegemonic power, which then uses its power and influence to restructure the system to serve its own interests. This ushers in a new cycle of growth, expansion, decline, hegemonic war, and system change (Gilpin, 1981: Chapter 6).

It is conceivable that such a disequilibrium in the international system could be resolved through peaceful change, and Gilpin makes it clear that the future of mankind depends on finding a substitute for hegemonic war as a mechanism for systemic change in world politics. He argues, however, that historically there are no examples of declining hegemons who willingly conceded their dominant position to a rising challenger to avoid war, and no examples of rising challengers who refrained from insisting on a restructuring of the system in order to accommodate their changing economic and security interests (Gilpin, 1981:208-9; Kennedy, 1987).

Thus, Gilpin's theory of hegemonic war and change in world politics provides an alternative explanation for the long peace. World War II resulted in the defeat of Germany (the rising challenger) and the transfer of the role of leadership from Britain to the United States. It restored equilibrium to the system and enabled the United States as the new hegemonic power to use its power and influence to restructure the new system in a way that maintained order and served its own economic and security interests (through the creation of a liberal international economy based on the Bretton Woods system and a security system based on NATO and a worldwide network of alliances). The absence of a major war is explained by the persistence of American dominance and the basic equilibrium between the distribution of power in the system and the distribution of political, economic, and cultural benefits in the system. Though American economic and military dominance began to erode by the early 1970s (Keohane and Nye, 1977), that decline has not been so rapid as to create conditions conducive to a new hegemonic war.

In terms of Gilpin's theory, however, the contemporary system is moving in a dangerous direction. The decline of the relative economic and military superiority of the United States continues, and Japan, China, the Federal Republic of Germany, and — at least until recently — the Soviet Union, have continued to gain in strength. This has created an increasing disequilibrium between the emerging system of decon-

questions about its ability to explain the long peace or to provide forecasts about the future. Had anything on the scale of the two mid-eighteenth-century wars and particularly the Thirty Years' War occurred in the last four decades, it is unlikely that we would continue to refer to this period as the long peace. It would be little consolation in the future if we were able to avoid a "global war" only to suffer through something comparable to the Thirty Years' War.

The explanatory power of long-cycle theory, with its conception of power primarily in terms of naval power in the global system, can even be questioned in the cases of global wars. The theory defines the decline of systemic leadership based on a monopoly of naval power as a necessary condition for global war. This gives far too much emphasis to the importance of naval power relative to land-based military power and to the global system relative to the European system. The causes of World War I, for example, had less to do with the global system than with the fate of Austria-Hungary as an independent great power (and Germany's only major ally) in the face of internal decay, with Germany's fear of the rising power of Russia and her doubts regarding the ability of the German army to hold its own in a European war by 1917, with systems of rigid alliances and mobilization plans which created incentives for preemption in any crisis, and with the domestic crisis within the German Empire (Albertini, 1980; Ritter, 1970; Fischer, 1961, 1974; Fay, 1928; Joll, 1984; Levy, 1991). If the breakdown of leadership and system management were relevant in the origins of World War I, it had far more to do with the collapse of the Bismarckian system than the decline of Britain's naval power and share of world trade.

This argument can be generalized. The primary cause of the great wars of the past, whether they be general wars or the more restricted class of global wars, has been the perception by most of the great powers that one state was threatening to gain a dominant position in Europe. The great powers have always perceived the most serious threats to their interests as coming from the great land powers of Europe — which could threaten their territorial integrity — rather than from the more wealthy naval and commercial powers. This is why the great European military coalitions have always formed against the most threatening continental power rather than against the leading naval power.[17]

Thus a traditional balance-of-power perspective may offer a more convincing explanation than long-cycle theory of the most significant wars of the past, whether they be general wars or the more restricted class of global wars.[18] This is not to say that with the expansion of the Eurocentric system into a truly global system in the twentieth century a balance-of-power perspective provides an equally compelling explanation for the long peace or projections for the future.[19] But it does suggest that the validity of long-cycle theory's explanation of the long peace or the accuracy of its projections into the future cannot be based on the presumed validity of its explanation of the great wars of the past.[20]

Even if long-cycle theory provided a satisfactory explanation of the major wars of the past, it is not clear that one could extrapolate directly into the future. The development of nuclear weapons and long-range delivery vehicles has produced a quantum jump in the costs of all-out war, which makes any major effort to overthrow an existing international order through the use of military force far less likely than in the past. The declining utility (but not obsolescence) of military force for the great powers, particularly against each other (Knorr, 1966; Mueller, 1989), has been paralleled by the increasing viability of a "trading strategy" as a means of influence in the international system, as evidenced by the growing influence of Western Europe and particularly Japan since 1945 (Rosecrance, 1986).[21] Faced with a new cost-benefit calculus, involving both the enormous costs of nuclear war and the opportunity for increased influence through the expansion of their international trade and finance, states intent on restructuring the global political and economic systems will be less likely to adopt the military expansion route than in the past.[22]

The failure of long-cycle theory to recognize the restraining effects of the balance of terror on the behavior of the superpowers (with respect to each other) reflects a more general problem with most cyclical theories of peace and war: they overemphasize the importance of cyclical trends and minimize the importance of long-term secular trends in warfare. The development of nuclear weapons systems and long-range delivery systems is only the most recent manifestation of a secular decline in the frequency of great-power war over several centuries (Levy, 1982; Mueller, 1989), and it is important that this tendency (or at least the underlying conditions which produce it) be incorporated into any explanation of the long peace.[23]

GOLDSTEIN'S THEORY OF LONG CYCLES

Joshua Goldstein's (1988) theory of long cycles incorporates long waves of economic stagnation and expansion in the world economy, the rise and fall of hegemonic states, and the occurrence of major wars.[24] His method is inductive. He first establishes the existence of long economic waves of fifty-year duration and of comparable cycles of war over the last 500 years, establishes the empirical associations between them, and then constructs a theory to explain these observed empirical patterns. Goldstein's concern is with the broader phenomena of great-power war rather than with the more restricted class of global or general wars.

Building upon the work of others, Goldstein compiles an excellent set of data on a variety of economic indicators over the five-century period since 1495. Contrary to the conventional wisdom of most economists that long waves do not exist, Goldstein finds that long economic waves appear to exist in prices, production, investment (though data are scarce), innovation, and wages, but not in trade. These variables are related sequentially: production is followed by investment and then by innovation, prices, and wages. Using Levy's (1983) war data, Goldstein then finds cycles in the severity of great-power war (measured in terms of battle deaths) but not in the frequency of great-power war. The severity of war is highly correlated with the upswing phase of the long economic cycle: upswings have twenty-five times the average annual battle fatalities that downswings do (seven times more in the period prior to the twentieth century). There is a tendency for production to lead war by a decade and for war to lead prices by one to five years (Goldstein, 1988: Chapters 8-11).[25]

These inductively determined, lagged structural relationships form the basis for a theory integrating long economic waves, cycles of hegemony, and great-power war. The relationship between production and war constitutes the core of the theory. Goldstein argues that increases in production generate an increased need for resources to support the expanding economy, which in turn triggers a competition for scarce resources. War then becomes desirable as a means to secure the needed resources under conditions of scarcity. At the same time, the expanding economy increases the resources available to the military sector, which makes a major war possible. The conduct of a major war destroys this resource base, however, resulting in a decline in production, leading to economic stagnation. This economic downturn then reduces both the need for war and the resources necessary to prosecute it. The reduction in the level of war in turn begins to generate sustained economic growth, which initiates a new 50-year cycle.

Goldstein (1988: Chapter 15) uses his theory and supporting historical evidence as the basis for a discussion of the contemporary period and a projection into the future. He sees the United States as a hegemonic power in gradual decline, but one which is still the strongest state in the system. In contrast to the common argument that hegemonic decline itself brings increased risks of instability and war, Goldstein argues that declining hegemony is dangerous only in conjunction with economic expansion. Though economic expansion in production continued through 1968, the hegemonic position of the United States assured the absence of major war, thus explaining the first three decades of the long peace. The economic and hegemony cycles have reversed, however, and declining American hegemony is now accompanied by stagnation in production and prices and consequently a downswing in major war.

On the basis of an examination of current economic trends, Goldstein's (1988:350-57) model forecasts a revival of world economic expansion somewhere between 1995 and 2020, along with the continued hegemonic decline of the United States. As a result, he projects an increasing risk of great-power war between 2000 and 2030, a period of economic upswing and "weak hegemony." Given the increasing costs of war, Goldstein suggests that war might come toward the end of this period, after a long military buildup and persistent pressure for war.

Goldstein (1988:357-64) illustrates the dynamics of the system with the concept of a two-dimensional "cycle space." The system follows a path determined by the conjunction of the economic cycle and the hegemony cycle, which are out of phase. An analysis of this cycle space suggests that the closest historical precedent for the contemporary period is 1872-1893. Both were long-wave downturns and periods of gradual hegemonic decline, and both were phases of low great-power war activity following costly wars of containment by the hegemonic power in the previous upswing phase period. The earlier period was followed in two decades by World War I, so that the 1914 case and the military buildups leading up to it become an important historical precedent for Goldstein's theory of long cycles.

Goldstein does not suggest, however, that a repetition of the 1914 pattern is inevitable. Although economic surplus will continue to be diverted to war, and changes in relative national power will continue to bring the eventual recurrence of hegemonic war, Goldstein notes the contradictory tendency toward the ever-greater destructiveness of war. He concludes that "great-power war cannot continue to recur indefinitely while wars become exponentially more destructive. Thus power politics has brought about its own obsolescence" (Goldstein, 1988:366).[26]

There are several weaknesses in Goldstein's theory of long cycles that limit its utility for explaining the past and therefore for projecting into the future. One concerns the precise temporal relationship between phases of long economic waves and the outbreak of major wars. The theory specifies that major wars should occur toward the end of a long-wave upswing, when states have acquired the military capabilities to fight a major war and when they need war to secure additional resources necessary to sustain productivity. One immediate counterexample that comes to mind, however, is World War II, which began in the last year of an economic downswing (1939).

Goldstein (1988:242-43) acknowledges that World War II is an anomaly (he dates it in 1940, the first year of the new upswing), but asserts that this is the only anomaly out of ten "peak wars." But World War II is not so anomalous. This is evident from an examination of the initiation dates of the ten general or hegemonic wars (Levy, 1985) of the last five centuries with respect to Goldstein's basic phase dating scheme (1988:246-47).[27] The War of Dutch Independence/Spanish Armada began midway through an economic upswing. The Thirty Years' War began two years before the end of an economic downswing in 1620. Two of the three general wars involving Louis XIV began in the downswing phase (one in the last year). The War of Jenkins' Ear/Austrian Succession began one year into an upswing, and the subsequent Seven Years' War occurred later in that upswing. The French Revolutionary Wars began only two years into the economic upswing. World War I began two years before the end of an upswing, and World War II at the very end of a downswing.

Thus, contrary to Goldstein's hypothesis, four of the ten general wars broke out during the middle or end of an economic downswing, and two more occurred within two years of the beginning of an upswing.[28] Because six of ten general wars began within two years of the transition from the downswing to upswing phase of the economic cycle, however, the vast majority of the fatalities from these wars get lumped into the upswing phase.[29] These patterns help to explain Goldstein's conclusion that the phases of the long economic wave are correlated with the *severity* of great-power war but not with the *outbreak* of great-power war.[30]

These observations raise important theoretical questions relating to the causes of war. Although the severity of war might very well be explained in terms of some factors existing after the outbreak of the war, the causes of war must logically be explained by factors existing temporally prior to the outbreak of war. In fact, there may be a considerable lag between these causal variables and the actual outbreak of war. Decisions for war are often the cumulation of a series of decisions regarding military buildups, alliance formation, and imperial expansion that span several years and in some cases even decades; they are also influenced by internal socioeconomic conditions that develop over many years. The causes of World War II, for example, had deep roots in social, economic, and political developments during the depression of the 1930s, and the fact that five of ten general wars occurred in the middle or end of a downswing suggest that the causes of these wars can also be traced to developments in economic downswings. Thus, the observed temporal relationships between the economic cycle and the outbreak of general wars (and great-power wars as well) are inconsistent with Goldstein's causal theory linking the upswing phase of the economic cycle with periods of severe warfare.

These empirical anomalies are perhaps not that surprising if we consider some conceptual problems in Goldstein's theory. The central relationship in the theory is between production and war, but the causal linkages between these key variables are not very well developed. One of Goldstein's (1988:262-63) explanations for the linkage between production and war is the "lateral pressure" argument: production upswings lead to growth, competition for resources, and the propensity toward major conflicts and wars among core countries (Choucri and North, 1975). This raises a number of questions. Do increases in production always lead to competition for external resources, or can these resources be generated internally? Even if it becomes necessary to secure external resources, under what conditions can this be accomplished through trade (Rosecrance, 1986) or (though less likely) through the mutual exploitation of the periphery by the great powers (Kautsky, 1970), rather than through war? Moreover, what is the linkage between imperial wars to secure resources and severe great-power wars in the system's core? Under what conditions do resource wars or other forms of imperial expansion create cross-cutting cleavages and actually reduce the likelihood of a great-power war, as some balance-of-power theorists argue (Morgenthau, 1967:341-42; Levy and Morgan, 1986) and as several diplomatic historians claim was the case for at least two decades prior to World War I (Thomson, 1966: Chapter 20)?

Goldstein (1988:261-62) gives greater emphasis to a "cost of wars" argument in support of his production-war hypothesis.[31] The biggest wars occur only after a sustained period of economic growth, for states have the capability to fight such wars when and only when "treasuries are full." Although this argument may be true for preindustrial times, particularly when the economic ability to hire mercenaries was a critical factor in decisions for war (Howard, 1976: Chapter 2; Kennedy, 1987: Chapter 2), it is not clear whether this argument is valid for the last three or even four centuries.[32] The key question is not whether or not the capacity to fight big wars increases during an economic expansion, but whether the magnitude of the increase is large enough to make a significant difference relative to preexisting war-fighting capacity. This is particularly problematic after the industrial revolution and the emergence of permanent military establishments in peacetime by the end of the nineteenth century, which provided the great powers with a fairly substantial and continuous capacity for fighting major wars.

In addition, there are other factors that might also generate enormous increases in the capacity to fight large wars. Innovations in military technology are critical, but do not necessarily coincide with the upswing phase of the economic cycle, as illustrated by the development of airpower and of the tank as an offensive weapon prior to World War II. Access to inexpensive credit on global markets is particularly important, as Rasler and Thompson (1983) and Kennedy (1987) have shown, and it is not clear that this is highly correlated with economic upswings. Political and organizational factors are important in the development of an administrative and financial system and in the rationalization of military organizations, as illustrated by Gustavus Adolphus in Sweden, the Great Elector in Prussia, and by Richelieu and Colbert in France in the seventeenth century, and by the development of the German General Staff late in the nineteenth century (Osgood, 1967:48-56; Organski and Kugler, 1980: Chapters 1-2). Sociopolitical factors can also contribute to a significant expansion in the capacity for war-fighting, as evident in the *levee en mass* and the "democratization of war" beginning in Napoleonic times (Osgood, 1967:51-3; Millis, 1956). Goldstein's argument would be more convincing if he could demonstrate that the increases in productivity associated with changes in the economic cycle have been translated into significant increases in the size of military establishments and the destructive power of their weapons systems. The very fact that so many great-power wars have occurred during economic downturns or within two years after the beginning of an upswing casts serious doubt on Goldstein's argument.

The lateral pressure and cost-of-war arguments provide particularly weak theoretical foundations for explaining the long postwar peace and projecting into the future. The increasing importance of the technological component of national military strength in the nuclear age seriously undercuts the lateral pressure argument regarding the link between increases in production and competition between great powers over external resources. In addition, because of the enormous destructive power of the nuclear and conventional weapons systems of the great powers, increases in productivity generated by economic upswings have a negligible impact on the preexisting capacity of the superpowers to fight a major war.[33]

There are also some troubling levels-of-analysis problems in Goldstein's (1988:264) theory. Goldstein's lateral pressure argument is a theory of the motivations for war, and represents a national-level focus relevant to the question of the outbreak of major war. But the empirical analysis focuses on systemic-level patterns in the severity of war, since he finds that there is no relation between economic cycles and the outbreak of major war. Thus, there is a mismatch between Goldstein's lateral pressure theory of motivations for war and his empirical analysis of the severity of major war.

Goldstein's cost-of-war argument refers to the ability to sustain a major war, so that the empirical focus on the severity of war is fully appropriate. But the cost-of-war argument also has important implications for the outbreak of war.[34] The economic prosperity that creates the economic surplus that can support a military buildup and therefore a major war is defined by Goldstein as a systemic-level phenomenon — economic cycles refer not to individual states but to the international system as a whole. The implication is that prosperity benefits all states equally and gives *all* great powers an increased capacity to fight a major war. If that were the case, the opportunity for war (defined loosely as the probability of a victorious war at tolerable cost) would not change for any state as the system moves through phases of the economic cycle. The probability of a major war would be constant over time, and the severity of the wars that do occur would be a function of the phase of the cycle.

This is surely an unsatisfactory model of the outbreak of war, and it is inconsistent with empirical reality. Historically, the probability of major war has not been constant over time, but instead has been declining rather rapidly over the last five centuries, and much of this decline can be traced to the increasing costs of war (Levy, 1982).[35] In addition, the incidence of major war is not the same for each of the great powers, and if we look at years or decades rather than centuries we find that within a pattern of long-term decline the incidence of involvement in major wars for each of the great powers is anything but constant. These patterns cannot be explained by a systemic-level theory, and this leads us to a levels-of-analysis problem in Goldstein's cost-of-war argument.

Theoretically (from a rational choice perspective), the expected outcome of war is determined primarily by the dyadic balance of power between two states in conjunction with expectations regarding the likelihood and impact of the intervention of third states. If we have learned anything from theories of power transitions and long cycles, it is that dyadic power balances change as a result of differential rates of growth among states, and that these are important variables in the processes leading to major wars. Goldstein's theory does not incorporate differential rates of growth of states and their impact on both the distribution of power in the international system and on dyadic power relationships among individual states, and for this reason it cannot explain the cost-benefit calculations leading states to war.

These variables do get some attention in Goldstein's (1988: Chapters 13-15) discussion of hegemonic leadership and transition in the two historical chapters and in the analysis of the contemporary system and its likely future evolution. There is no connection, however, between this historical analysis and the theory linking long waves to war (Chapter 12). Goldstein does not incorporate cycles of hegemony of the more general distribution of power in the system into his causal theory of long economic cycles and war, and this helps to explain the absence of a pattern linking economic cycles and the outbreak of major wars.

Admittedly, Goldstein is more interested in broad systemic-level patterns than in national-level behavior. But his theoretical cost-of-war argument has direct implications for national decisions regarding war and peace, so that the examination of the theoretical plausibility and empirical validity of those consequences is relevant for an evaluation of the theory. In addition, a severe war presumes the initiation of war, so that any explanation of the severity of war must include an explanation of the outbreak of war, along with an explanation of its escalation or expansion (Levy, 1990). The level and rate of change of the distribution of power in the international system as a whole and between individual dyads are important variables in both the outbreak and the expansion of war, and must be included in the analysis.

Although the other theories examined above give more attention to the role of the changing distribution of power in the international system, none really develops the precise causal mechanism leading to the outbreak of a major war. In long-cycle theory global war satisfies an important functional need of the system, and occurs after the ability of the world power to provide leadership and manage the system has deteriorated, but the causes of the local war and how it escalates are not specified. Organski (1968) argues that the rising challenger usually initiates a war while it is still the weaker party in order to accelerate the power transition, but this hypothesis is problematic from the perspective of a cost-benefit framework (Levy, 1985; Thompson, 1988: Chapter 10).[36]

Gilpin's (1981) argument that a rising challenger will attempt to change the international status quo as the expected benefits of changing the system begin to exceed the expected costs of change provides a more useful way to conceptualize the problem, even if Gilpin fails to specify the conditions under which this is likely to occur. But the outbreak of major war is not determined by the actions of the challenger alone, and Gilpin (1981:191) notes but does not analyze the possibility of a "preventive war" by the declining power to destroy or weaken the rising challenger while the opportunity is still available and before the power transition is completed. Organski (1968) mentions this possibility but asserts that it is rare. Let us now examine this idea.

HYPOTHESES ON PREVENTIVE WAR

The theoretical importance of preventive war derives from the central role of changing power differentials between states arising from uneven rates of growth.[37] This is the core of Organski's (1968) power transition theory, theories of hegemonic war and change, and of other realist theories of international relations. The historical importance of preventive war has also been widely recognized. This was the basis of Thucydides' (1954:1-23) argument that "what made the Peloponnesian War inevitable was the growth of Athenian power and the fear which this caused in Sparta." Howard (1983: Chapter 1) argues that this is true for most wars: "The causes of war remain rooted, as much as they were in the pre-industrial age, in perceptions by statesmen of the growth of hostile power and the fears for the restriction, if not the extinction, of their own." A. J. P. Taylor (1971) suggests that "every war between the Great Powers (in the 1848-1914 period) . . . started out as a preventive war. . .," and the importance of the preventive motivation arises repeatedly in studies of World War I.

Declining power does not always lead to preventive war, however, as evidenced by the current decline of the United States, the decline of Britain a century ago, and by other historical cases. This raises the question of the conditions under which changing power differentials lead to war (in general or by the initiation of the declining state in particular) and the conditions under which they do not. Organski asserts that

> war is most apt to occur: if the challenger is of such a size that at its peak it will roughly equal the dominant nation in power; if the rise of the challenger is rapid; if the dominant nation is inflexible in its policies; if there is no tradition of friendship between the dominant nation and the challenger; and if the challenger sets out to replace the existing international order with a competitive order of its own. (Organski, 1968:376)

Others have also attempted to specify the conditions affecting the probability of a major war during periods of changing power differentials.[38] Thompson (1988:224-30) accepts Organski's hypotheses but emphasizes in addition the potential power of the challenger and (secondarily) the nature of the developmental sequence involving economic productivity and political effectiveness. Van Evera (1984:72-76) and Snyder (1984:160-61) both note the importance of the magnitude of the shift in power, the relative advantage of the offense compared to the defense, and the expected probability the adversary will initiate a war in the future. Levy (1987) emphasizes the declining state's expectations regarding the magnitude of the power shift, the probability that the challenger will initiate a war in the future, and the probability of victory with tolerable costs in a preventive war fought now, and (secondarily) the risk-taking propensities of decision makers, the influence of the military in the decision-making process, and the existence of internal political incentives for elites to engage in external scapegoating to bolster their internal political support in a period of decline (Levy, 1989a).[39]

There are other policy options available to a dominant power in decline besides preventive military action. These include economic and technological innovation or industrial revitalization to reverse the underlying sources of decline; the formation of an alliance against the rising challenger; concessions to the rising challenger in order to ensure that a power transition which is perceived to be inevitable is also peaceful; and the reduction of the costs of system leadership through military retrenchment or the reduction of political commitments (Gilpin, 1981:188-94; Levy, 1987). The question of the conditions under which declining power leads to the adoption of one or more of these options rather than preventive military action is an important one and essential for a complete theory of preventive war.

Although there are numerous historical cases which have been labeled as "preventive wars," the causal importance of the preventive motivation relative to other variables in these and other cases has yet to be established through rigorous and systematic empirical research. Moreover, there have been no serious efforts to test any of the above hypotheses regarding the conditions under which a declining state (or even the rising challenger) will initiate a war, so that there is little empirical evidence to validate preventive war hypotheses.[40]

The absence of empirical validation of preventive war hypotheses is compounded by their theoretical limitations. Hypotheses on the preventive motivation for war have not been grounded in any more general theory of international politics, conflict, and change. Changing power is not treated endogenously, so that we cannot explain or predict when changing power differentials will arise. These hypotheses have also failed to incorporate a theory of the strategic interaction or bargaining between the declining state and its rising challenger. This precludes a comprehensive analysis of when power shifts lead to war, to the formation of new alliances to compensate for declining power, or to a negotiated settlement to facilitate a peaceful power transition. Thus, a *theory* of preventive war does not really exist.

Although we have no fully developed theory of preventive war to explain the long peace or to make projections into the future (or to discriminate analytically between the last forty years and the next forty years), and although power differentials between states will undoubtedly continue to change, the preventive motivation for war is much less likely to have a significant influence on the superpowers in the nuclear age than it had on great powers in previous historical eras.[41] This conclusion follows directly from the hypotheses suggested herein.

Although the expected magnitude of the power shift has been historically important, its effects should be attenuated somewhat in the nuclear age. Military superiority is more difficult to translate directly into political influence than in the past (at least for the leading states in the system), so that the political consequences of military decline, while not negligible, will be less than in the past (Jervis, 1989). Another important change concerns perceptions of the inevitability of war. Although the preventive motivation for war has been encouraged in the past by the expectation that a future war with the rising challenger was very likely if not inevitable (Lebow, 1981:254-63), such expectations are much less likely to occur in the nuclear age (Jervis, 1989:153-64). The attitudes of political decision makers regarding war have been changing (Bundy, 1988; Nye, 1987), and perceptions of the consequences of an all-out war and confidence in the stability of mutual deterrence make it much more difficult for self-fulfilling prophecies regarding the inevitability of war between the superpowers to arise. This was one of several important factors, for example, that differentiated the Cuban Missile Crisis from World War I and other international crises. Still another key factor in the past was the perception by the declining leader that it had the ability to fight and win a preventive war with acceptable costs, but the destructiveness of nuclear weapons makes this much less likely in the contemporary period.[42]

Another important factor in the past was the offensive/defensive balance of military technology, and in particular the extent to which it created an incentive for a first strike in any crisis (Jervis, 1978). This would compound the preventive motivation with the preemptive motivation for war (Levy, 1987:90-93). The current strategic balance is quite stable, however, given the sheer numbers of strategic forces, the invulnerability of retaliatory forces under existing technology, and the mutual hostage relationship between the superpowers. It is unlikely that new technological innovations will undermine the invulnerability of retaliatory forces to the point of creating politically significant incentives to strike first, at least for the foreseeable future.

Thus, although we may not understand all of the conditions that contributed to the use of force for preventive reasons in previous historical eras, hypotheses on preventive war themselves suggest that the preventive motivation for war will be far weaker for the nuclear powers of the present and future than for the great powers of the past.

CONCLUSION

We have examined several theories of hegemonic transitions, cycles, and war, including hegemonic stability theory, Organski's power transition theory, Gilpin's theory of hegemonic war and change, Modelski's and Thompson's theory of long cycles of world leadership, and Goldstein's theory of long cycles. These structural theories of major wars focus on long-term economic cycles and patterns of hegemonic ascension and decline over which statesmen have little immediate control. They posit that cycles are an inherent feature of the international system, that they continue to operate in the nuclear era, and that they provide an explanation for the long peace and a basis for projecting into the future.

Hegemonic and cyclical explanations of the long peace are troublesome because the theories of war upon which they are based have only limited explanatory power with respect to major wars of the past. These theories are either insufficiently operational to provide testable predictions (Gilpin), too narrowly focused on seapower to explain either major land-based wars or global wars (Modelski and Thompson), or characterized by too large a gap between the observed empirical patterns and the theoretical linkages that are hypothesized in order to account for them (Goldstein). Moreover, none of the theories provides a convincing explanation of the causal mechanisms through which a major war might occur or escalate from a local war. Each posits what are essentially necessary conditions for the outbreak of major war, but none pays much attention to the conditions and processes that might trigger a major war in an era of decline.[43] They emphasize the underlying causes of war but downplay the importance of immediate causes. Stated differently, they focus on conditions of general stability but ignore the sources of crisis stability.

The lack of attention to the most immediate causal mechanisms leading to war becomes particularly problematic in the nuclear era. The destructiveness of nuclear weapons in conjunction with long-range delivery vehicles undermines the capacity of even the strongest states to defend their populations (Schelling, 1966), and the resulting balance of terror makes it more and more difficult to conceive of situations in which the expected benefits of an all-out war exceed its expected costs. This does not mean that nuclear war is impossible, but it forces us to give greater attention to the question of why decision makers might make choices that could lead to massive and unprecedented levels of destruction for their own societies as well as those of their adversaries. Most contemporary analysts believe that such choices, though unlikely, are most likely to be made in situations of crisis; they reject the plausibility of a "bolt from the blue." This directs our attention to the conditions for crisis stability and instability. These cannot be fully analyzed here, but because this perspective is not emphasized elsewhere in this volume, a brief discussion is in order.

Two of the most plausible sequences that might lead to a superpower war involve preemption and loss of control, generally after a process of escalation (Jervis, 1989; Lebow, 1987b; Levy, 1989b). Statesmen who prefer almost anything — including making significant political concessions — to all-out war might still rationally initiate war if they were to perceive that war was inevitable (Jervis, 1989: Chapter 5) and that the failure to preempt would result not in peace but in an adversary's first strike. This accounts for the dangerous dynamics following from the reciprocal fear of surprise attack (Schelling, 1960). Political leaders might also act deliberately to exploit their adversary's fear of war, and in so doing might move the conflict to the point that further escalation toward an undesirable outcome is perceived to be rational,[44] or to the point that they lose control over events (Lebow, 1987b: Chapter 3). Given the destructiveness of nuclear weapons, these scenarios are much more likely to come at the end of an escalation process than at its beginning, and could conceivably lead to war through preemption.

Because of their structural orientation, hegemonic/cyclical theories do not attempt to deal with these processes of escalation, preemption, or loss of control. But these processes have become increasingly important as the quantum jump in the costs of major war eliminates other plausible paths to war, and in their absence it is difficult to explain the final chain of events leading to all-out nuclear war between the superpowers.

My argument is that our understanding of the long peace and the likelihood of its persisting into the future has less to do with cycles of hegemony and prosperity than with the strategic, domestic, political, and psychological conditions under which decision makers come to perceive that (1) war is inevitable, (2) incremental escalation toward an undesirable outcome is rational, and (3) preemption is a viable option, and where (4) psychological dynamics further fuel these rational escalation processes. The exploration of these conditions and processes is an essential task for future research on the sources of the long peace and its prospects for the future.

ENDNOTES

This research has been supported by a Social Science Research Council/MacArthur Foundation Fellowship in International Security and by the University of Minnesota. The views expressed here do not necessarily represent those of the supporting institutions. The author is grateful for many helpful comments and criticisms on earlier versions of this study from Joshua Goldstein, William R. Thompson, and George Modelski, and from Donald Puchala, James Ray, and other participants at the conference on "The Long Postwar Peace" at Rutgers University, April 28-29, 1989.

1. This calculation is based on the application of a Poisson probability model to Levy's (1983) war data. The analysis is very sensitive to certain analytic assumptions and to the question of precisely what it is that is defined not to have occurred since 1945. If the missing event is a general or hegemonic war involving all the leading powers in the system, of which there have been ten during the past five centuries (Levy, 1985), the probability changes to .41 (though the blurring of the distinction between great-power war and hegemonic war in the nuclear age complicates this analysis). Thus, while the absence of a *great-power war* involving any two great powers since 1945 is exceedingly rare by historical standards, the absence of a *hegemonic war* is not particularly surprising.

2. Other explanations for the long peace include long-term historical trends in warfare predating the nuclear age (Mueller, 1989; Levy, 1982); the stabilizing effect of alliances (Kegley and Raymond, 1990); and the role of arms control (Kruzel, 1990). For a good analysis of many of the leading theories see Gaddis (in this book), and for analyses which minimize the role of nuclear weapons see Mueller (1988b), Vasquez (in this book), Kugler (1984), and Morgan and Ray (1989).

There are two other factors which have been tremendously important for the long peace but which have not been given adequate attention in the literature. One is the weakening of the traditional linkage between economic and military power and the fact that the leading military rivalry and the leading economic rivalries are not congruent (at least for the last two decades). The dynamics of the Cold War would have been considerably different had the Soviet Union been the major economic competitor of the United States as well as its leading military challenger. A second factor is the historically unprecedented role of the United States in reconstructing the domestic political and economic structures of Japan and the Federal Republic of Germany in a way that created a set of shared incentives within the Western alliance regarding economic and military issues (Katzenstein, 1978). Theories of interdependence, regimes, and alliances incorporate these shared values but usually treat them exogenously, and fail to explain the role of the United States as hegemonic power in facilitating their emergence. My thanks to Peter Katzenstein for bringing this point to my attention.

3. Because balance-of-power theory and hegemonic theories are based on different analytical assumptions regarding the basis of power, the geographical scope of the system, and the nature of hegemony (Levy, 1985), it does not necessarily follow from the above discussion that these theories are mutually incompatible. They may simply provide different answers to different questions and therefore constitute "incommensurable paradigms" (Kuhn, 1962), but this is a question requiring further research.

4. Because the domain of hegemonic stability theory is limited to those relatively rare instances where political dominance, economic efficiency, and liberal ideology coincide, it is not a general theory of international political economy. It has been applied only to the two periods of British and American leadership in the last two centuries, which is a serious limitation of the theory. For a more general critique of the theory see Keohane (1984: Chapter 3). One study of the last five centuries disputes the hypothesis that free trade is associated with hegemony, and finds instead that it is likely to occur in periods of hegemonic decline (Frederick, 1987).

5. Keohane (1984:39-41), for example, argues that "the hegemonic power need not be militarily dominant world-wide."

6. In his chapter in this book, Gaddis also recognizes that hegemonic stability theory has limited relevance for the Cold War or the long peace, though in the end he is more willing than I am to consider some of the theory's geopolitical implications.

7. We will return to this point in a subsequent section on preventive war.

8. This question is addressed in a recent piece by Kugler and Organski (1989:185-90).

9. Organski and Kugler (1980) use the somewhat questionable gross national product indicator of national power in their empirical test of the theory, and by this measure American dominance, and hence international stability, is still secure.

10. Organski (1968) does not give adequate attention, for example, to the meaning of power, the relationship between politics and economics, the nature of hegemony and how it is maintained, or to the concept of hegemonic war. In addition, the Organski and Kugler (1980: Chapter 1) test of power transition theory is seriously flawed. Two of the four cases upon which it is based — the Franco-Prussian War and the Russo-Japanese War (the others being the two World Wars) — are not of sufficient importance to be classified as hegemonic wars and probably do not even satisfy the more narrow Organski-Kugler definition of a "major war." For more thorough critiques of power transition theory, see Bueno de Mesquita (1980:376-80), Thompson (1988: Chapter 10), and Levy (1985:353-54).

11. One limitation of this and other theories of hegemonic transition is that they fail to specify *which* of several potential challengers to the dominant position of the hegemon will resort to force to achieve its objectives.

12. The pacifying effect of nuclear weapons probably has more to do with the mutual fear of the consequences of nuclear war induced in both adversaries than with the deterrent effect of strategic superiority in specific situations (Jervis, 1989; Bundy, 1988; Organski and Kugler, 1980: Chapter 4; Betts, 1987).

13. Another problem with regard to testing the theory concerns the definition and identification of hegemonic wars (Levy, 1985). We will return to this point in our discussion of long-cycle theory.

14. For a brief discussion of the related question of whether hegemonic war is a necessary or sufficient condition for systemic transformation, see Levy (1990).

15. The continental challenger loses because it fails to augment its land-based military power with the naval strength necessary to defeat the world power's coalition; because it mounts its challenge prematurely, while the world power is still too strong; and because it underestimates the seriousness of its threat to the global position of the world power and thus fails to anticipate the expansion of the war (Thompson, 1988).

16. The exclusion of these cases also suggests that an element of circularity has been introduced into the definition and analysis of global war. If global war is defined in terms of its systemic consequences, then the critical question of the consequences of global war is defined away and cannot be investigated empirically. This raises the question of whether the excluded wars do not fit the long cycle because they are not global wars, whether they are not included as global wars because they do not fit the cycle, or whether they are empirical anomalies

in a cyclical theory of global war (Levy, 1985:359-60). For a response to this criticism, see Thompson and Rasler (1988:339-43).

17. Consider the alliance of England, the Netherlands, and France against the expansionist ambitions of Philip II of Spain late in the sixteenth century; of France, Sweden, the Netherlands, and England against the Spanish and Austrian Habsburgs in the Thirty Years' War; of England, the Netherlands, Austria, and Sweden against Louis XIV of France in the War of the League of Augsburg and (except Sweden) in the War of the Spanish Succession in the late seventeenth century; of Austria, Prussia, Russia, and Britain against France in the French Revolutionary and Napoleonic Wars; and of all of the allied powers against Germany (and Austria-Hungary) in World War I and again (with Japan) in World War II. The coalitions in the two general wars of the mid-eighteenth century and in the Dutch War of Louis XIV were more evenly balanced, which reflected the absence of the perception of a single threat of hegemony on the European continent. This suggests that the widespread perception of an immediate threat of European hegemony approaches a sufficient condition for general war but is not a necessary condition. Note that my argument regarding the seriousness of land-based threats is consistent with Walt's (1987:21-26) emphasis on balancing against threats rather than against power, and on the importance of geographic proximity as a primary source of threat.

18. I readily concede that, in terms of its theoretical structure, balance-of-power theory is not as fully developed as long-cycle theory, and that therefore it cannot at this time be fully tested. One important task for future research is the construction of a theory of general/hegemonic war based on balance-of-power assumptions, and the testing of the theory against the historical evidence.

19. A traditional balance-of-power explanation of the long peace would focus on the role of strategic deterrence, the stability of the postwar alliance system, the effectiveness of U.S. containment of the Soviet Union (the primary threat to the continental balance of power), and the absence of direct and tangible conflicts of interest between the two superpowers.

20. That is, the argument that a Eurocentric balance-of-power perspective is inferior to a globalist perspective for understanding the contemporary world does not lead logically to the conclusion that a balance-of-power perspective is inferior for the purposes of understanding the major wars of previous centuries.

21. Although the importance of trade relative to military strength as an instrument of influence has undoubtedly increased in the postwar period, Rosecrance (1986) underestimates the importance of "trading strategies" in earlier centuries.

22. The current Soviet efforts to reconstruct its internal economic and political system in an attempt to enhance its competitiveness, and its willingness to accept a significant reduction of direct political and military influence over its East European allies, is significant in this regard.

23. Modelski and Thompson would probably attribute the declining frequency of great-power war to some form of historical learning curve.

24. The following discussion builds on Levy (1989c).

25. In a more recent paper Goldstein (1989) uses a vector autoregression model to test the causal dynamics among these economic and war variables for the 1750-1935 period.

26. Goldstein is ambiguous as to whether the obsolescence of power politics has already occurred, or whether it will take another hegemonic war to bring that about.

27. General wars constitute a reasonable basis for analysis because they are undoubtedly the most serious wars of the modern system, and include over 85 percent of the battle fatalities of all interstate wars involving the great powers over that period (Levy, 1983:88-91).

28. The fact that six of the ten general wars occur within three years of a phase change suggests the potential sensitivity of Goldstein's analysis to his phase datings, for small errors in measurement could result in a significant change in his findings. Goldstein conducts his analyses in several different ways to minimize this problem, though some questions remain (Thompson, 1988:188-95).

29. Because of Goldstein's (1988:246) datings of the beginnings of the Thirty Years' War, War of the League of Augsburg, and World War II, all of the fatalities from these wars are put into the upswing phase of the cycle. In addition, for some reason very few of the World War I casualties are put into the downswing period beginning in 1917.

30. I am following Goldstein (1988:247) here and using the standard economic phase periods listed in his book. These phase periods are the basis for Goldstein's findings of a strong tendency for the severity of war to peak at the end of the upswing phase of the economic cycle, and for his acknowledgment of World War II as an "anomaly" (Goldstein, 1988:242-43; 1989). But things in fact are more complex. These standard phases are *price* phases. The central theoretical relationship in Goldstein's model is between *production* and war, and Goldstein finds that production leads price by ten to fifteen years. Thus it would be useful to examine the timing of war in terms of the production cycle (p. 216), recognizing that the production data are less reliable than price data and that the absence of production data prior to the early eighteenth century restricts the historical scope of our analysis.

In terms of the production cycle, we find that World War II is not the anomaly that Goldstein claims, for it occurs in the middle of a production upswing phase (1925-1965). The timing of other general wars presents a mixed picture for Goldstein's theory. The War of Jenkins' Ear/Austrian Succession occurs in the middle of an upswing phase of the production cycle (1732-1746), but the Seven Years' War (which, more important for Goldstein's theory, involved nearly three times the fatalities) occurs a third of the way into the subsequent downswing. The French Revolutionary Wars occur as predicted at the tail end of a production upswing, but the Napoleonic Wars break out in the downswing phase, and nearly seventy-five percent of the fatalities from this combined general war occur in the downswing phase. Finally, World War I (and all of its fatalities) occurs halfway through a production downswing (1902-1924). This pattern of the incidence of general wars and the distribution of their fatalities over the economic production cycle does not provide much support for Goldstein's theory. It would be interesting to see what happens to Goldstein's strong correlation between all great-power wars and the economic cycle if the economic indicator is based on the production cycle rather than the price cycle.

31. Goldstein (1988:288) also mentions (but does not emphasize) a psychological link between economic growth and major wars: economic growth generates a "gung-ho" social mood, which increases the propensity for war.

32. Goldstein (1988:261-62) concedes that "the cost-of-wars argument is especially applicable to preindustrial times."

33. Technological innovations which affect the offensive/defensive balance of military technology, and particularly the vulnerability of strategic retaliatory forces and hence incentives to strike first, affect crisis stability and may be important, but there is no reason to expect that these are correlated with the production cycle.

34. These implications cannot be ignored, for the empirical validity of the logical implications of a theory are an important measure of the validity of the theory itself.

35. At the same time, the revolutions in industrial, nuclear, and communications technologies have diminished the relative importance of territory as an element of national power, at least for the great powers, so that the diminishing value of territorial conquest has contributed further to the declining frequency of war (Knorr, 1966).

36. This hypothesis has been refuted by subsequent empirical analysis (Organski and Kugler, 1980).

37. This section builds on a discussion in Levy (1987).

38. Whereas Organski (1968) frames the question in terms of the conditions under which power transitions are most likely to lead to war, it is important to recognize that rapidly narrowing power differentials may be destabilizing even if they do not lead to a power transition (Levy, 1987; Wayman, 1989).

39. Hypotheses on preventive war are not restricted to the leading states in the system, but may also apply to other states in decline relative to particular adversaries.

40. For recent quantitative empirical tests of the relationship between power shifts and war, see Houweling and Siccama (1988), Wayman (1989), and Kim and Morrow (1990).

41. The effects of regional power shifts on the likelihood of secondary states initiating war for preventive reasons should not be significantly different in the nuclear age than in the past, for none of the conditions for preventive war against an adversary is greatly affected by the possession of nuclear weapons by third states.

42. The costs of preventive war are further increased, at least for the advanced industrial democracies, by the diplomatic and domestic political consequences of the growing popular belief that war is an illegitimate instrument of policy except for the defense of interests that are most directly and immediately threatened (Kegley and Wittkopf, 1989:471; Knorr, 1966; Mueller, 1989).

43. Gilpin provides a framework for analysis, but does not go on to test it against the historical evidence. Hypotheses regarding the preventive motivation for war posit a more specific causal mechanism.

44. Rational escalation toward a mutually undesirable outcome has been modeled by the "dollar auction" (O'Neill, 1986).

CHAPTER EIGHT

When Empires Meet: The Long Peace in Long-Term Perspective

Morris J. Blachman
Donald J. Puchala

When Charles Dickens composed his ever-popular novelette *A Christmas Carol*, he assured his readers at the very outset that "Marley was dead." If the fact of Marley's demise were not understood and accepted from the beginning, the rest of Dickens' moving story could have no impact. Dickens' little work about ghosts and history is a fairy tale. Ours about empires and history is not. Let us nonetheless begin in Dickensian fashion by assuring our readers that the United States and the Soviet Union are *empires*. They look like empires and behave like empires, and they should therefore be studied as empires. If these propositions are not understood and accepted from the start, then our analysis will have little meaning.

The nearly five-decade "long peace" in major-power relations since World War II must be appreciated. Alternatives to superpower peace in the nuclear age are dreadful beyond contemplation. Yet in broad and analytically appropriate historical perspective, our long peace may be neither extraordinary in its occurrence or duration, nor particularly difficult to fathom. To take the long peace of our time as somehow historically exceptional is to assume, perhaps unwittingly, that postwar international relations should have evolved in ways characteristic of traditional *European* nation-state international relations where major-power warfare, via mass military border-crossing and direct assault, was almost incessant. For more than a millennium of European history, peace was only the short period of recovery after the last war and preparation for the next. Obviously, what we have seen in Soviet-American relations since 1945 has not been a continuation of traditional European nation-state international relations.[1] Instead, it is a return to, or at least an analog of, a more deeply seated, universal, and older pattern of international relations characteristic of the uneasy coexistence of great empires. Much of the history of international relations is in fact the story of the rivalries of great empires such as the Babylonian and the Egyptian, or the Roman and the Persian, the Han and the Hsiung-nu, the Byzantine and the Arab, or the Ottoman and the Habsburg. From this perspective, Soviet-American relations in the twentieth century — though conditioned by modern technologies, institutions, and ideologies — are not altogether exceptional.

Empire as a Concept

Because of the connotations associated with "imperialism" in the rhetorics of contemporary East/West and North/South politics, empires are customarily looked upon today as illegitimate forms of political organization, indeed even "evil" forms. All varieties of behavior associated with establishing, maintaining, and extending them, as well as identification of those who engage in such behavior, have come to be associated with political villainy. Contrariwise, behavior directed toward undoing empires, and the perpetrators of such, have come to be associated with political progress. Of course, empires and imperialism have not always been derogatorily regarded, but the times when the symbolism of empire connoted glory, order, justice, and even goodness are long past (Koebner, 1965:61). For political reasons these days, it has been most opportune for imperial statesmen to deny the existence of their own empires, while attributing the villainies of imperialism to their international rivals and adversaries.

Imploring Americans to recognize the reality of their empire, noted political commentator Walter Lippmann wrote in 1927,

> All the world thinks of the United States today as an empire, except the people of the United States. We shrink from the word "empire," and insist that it should not be used to describe the dominion we exercise. . . . We feel that there ought to be some other name for the civilizing work which we do so reluctantly in these backward countries. We do not feel our-selves to be imperialists as we understand that word . . . We have learned to think of empires as troublesome and as immoral, and to admit that we have an empire still seems to most Americans like admitting that they have gone out into a wicked world and there lost their political chastity. (Leiken and Rubin, 1987:81-83)

What is unfortunate in all of this is that the notion of "empire" has been so politicized in our time that it has been stripped of much of its usefulness as an analytical concept. Yet there is no good substitute for the concept "empire," and there is no way to get around the fact that the international politics of the last forty years have been dominated by the internal and external affairs of two very extensive and preponderantly powerful empires, the United States of America and the Union of Soviet Socialist Republics (Spanier, 1988:158-67). George Liska is one of the very few non-Marxist Western scholars who has made effective analytical use of the concept of empire, and he is also one of the very few American scholars who has disregarded the taboo against labeling the United States an empire. Liska's gumption yielded considerable insight. For him, as for us in this chapter, an empire

> is a state exceeding other states in size, scope, salience and sense of task. In size of territory and material resources, an imperial state is substantially larger than the mean or norm prevailing in the existing system. The scope of its interests and involvements is coterminous with the boundaries of the system itself, rather than with a narrower security zone or habitat; the involvement is implemented directly, or indirectly through client states. The salience of an imperial state consists in the fact that no other state can ignore it and that all other states — consciously or half-consciously, gladly or reluctantly — assess their position role, and prospects more in relation to it than to closer neighbors or to local conflicts. Finally, the sense of task which distinguishes the imperial state is typically that of creating and then maintaining, a world order the conditions and principles of which would harmonize the particular interests of the imperial state with the interests of the commonweal. (Liska, 1967:9-10)

For clarity we need only add to Liska's definition of empire that a *state* is a governing organization, distinguishable from the society it governs, and that no personification of the state is necessary (Watkins, 1934:48-49). States "perceive," "sense," "intend," and "pursue" via the persons and personalities of those who direct them. Empires are the *core states* of imperial systems, composed of such cores plus client states that are either directly or indirectly governed by them. *Governing* in an imperial system means controlling from the core in such a manner that subordinate states are continually pressured, directly or indirectly, to support the preferences of the core state. Governing in imperial systems need not imply subjugating, though subjugation is sometimes involved. In historic eras when great empires were the principal actors in international relations, there were two primary modes of international relations: intra-imperial relations between core states and their client states, and interimperial relations between the core states.

By the standards of size, scope, salience, and sense of task that Liska's definition establishes, the U.S. and USSR qualify as empires in the second half of the twentieth century. As they reached their prime in the two decades after 1945, they were continental in size and accordingly endowed in natural resources, very large in population, economically advanced, and readily capable of maintaining order within the societies they controlled as well as of projecting rather awesome power beyond their borders. Their interests had become avowedly global; they have pursued them in virtually every country on every continent. Nor could their interests, if they chose to be interested, ever be ignored, whatever the substantive context. Each has aspired to create a global environment supportive of its interests and values by seeking directly or indirectly to determine the composition of other states' governing elites, or by otherwise constraining others' political decision making in ways that constantly produced outcomes acceptable to the core.

That each of these superpowers evolved a "sense of task," and remains committed to the global vision symbolized in its political ideology, has a great deal to do with the prevailing rivalry between them. Christer Jönsson's study of the impact of ideology on U.S. and Soviet foreign policy makes the point well:

> . . . the onset of the cold war revealed and crystalized the similarities of the two "social myths" at the same time as it blinded the two sides to these similarities.
>
> For the United States and the Soviet Union alike, the enemies thus identified were not really states, but "conspiracies disguised as states."
>
> Both sides thus found themselves fighting "isms" rather than nations and inferring the intentions of the adversary not so much from what they *did* as from what they *were* (imperialists/communists).
>
> The mutual identification of an ideological enemy . . . [helped unleash] the missionary zeal of both foreign policy ideologies. Having long articulated what they were fighting *for*, both now had a clearer vision of what they were fighting "against." . . . The enemy . . . revealed concretely the face of "sin." (Jönsson, 1982:103-4)

Two Twentieth-Century Empires

At the height of its imperium, let us say in 1960 or perhaps shortly before the Cuban Revolution, the United States was the core state of an imperial system that included all of North America, all of Central America, almost all of South America, the western alliance states of Europe, plus Iran, Japan, South Korea, the Republic of China on Taiwan, the Philippines, Israel, a scattering of Pacific islands, and a cluster of Caribbean islands. This global empire had taken more than two centuries to build. The core state, which stretches across North America from the Atlantic Ocean to the Pacific, began — as every American high school student is taught — with a strip of territory along the Atlantic coast of central North America together with some initially unenforceable claims to lands west of the Appalachian Mountains. But even at the beginning, George Washington envisaged that "there will assuredly come a day, when this country will have some weight in the scale of Empires," and some among his contemporaries forecast that "we cannot but anticipate the period, as not far distant, when the American Empire will comprehend millions of souls, west of the Mississippi" (Van Alstyne, 1974:69). Alexander Hamilton is known to have had designs on the Caribbean, and Thomas Jefferson confided to James Monroe in 1801 that it is impossible not to look forward to distant times, when our rapid multiplication will expand it [the United States] beyond those limits, and cover the whole northern if not the southern continent, with people speaking the same language, governed in similar forms, and by similar laws. (Van Alstyne, 1974:87)

Via diplomacy and conquest, the United States pursued its "manifest destiny" through the nineteenth century, and politically assembled, piece by piece, the continental core state of its eventual global empire. Meanwhile, the ascendancy of the central government over the provincial governments, which had far-reaching implications for the accretion of state power, was firmly established between 1861 and 1865.

At the turn of the twentieth century, the United States flirted with colonialism, actually acquired a few overseas possessions, but ultimately found such European-styled imperial arrangements to be rather cumbersome and distasteful. For the most part, the American overseas empire was constructed and maintained through indirect governance: countries and peoples were brought under American dominion via Washington's abilities to keep obliging local elites in ascendance and friendly governments constantly in power. This was accomplished by economically subsidizing friends abroad, educating succeeding foreign elite generations at American institutions, guaranteeing governments' internal security and peoples' external security, arming pro-American forces and factions, and occasionally intervening covertly or overtly to prop up friendly governments or remove dubious ones. The most frequent results of such American practices were predictable flows of supportive policies from beholden governments.

During the first half of the twentieth century, American suzerainty encompassed the Western Hemisphere and the Pacific possessions. After the Second World War it was extended to Western Europe and to the several other anticommunist outposts of the U.S. alliance system. American economic and military assistance continued to keep friendly governments in power in the post–World War II era, but the United States also maintained its ascendance by legitimizing it through moral leadership. Challenge from within the empire was improbable as long as Washington could be perceived as promoting or protecting broadly appealing values.

"Washington was the center of the system," Susan Strange observed in an insightful 1983 essay,

a kind of keep in the baronial capital of capitalism, from which radiated military, monetary, commercial and technological as well as purely political channels carrying the values of American polity, economy, and society down through the hierarchy of allies and friends, classes and cultural cousins, out to the ends of the earth. The new kind of global empire, under the protection of American nuclear power, did not need territorial expansion. It could be achieved by a combination of military alliances and a world economy opened to trade, investment and information. (Strange, 1983:340)

At the pinnacle of its ascendance, let us say just before the Sino-Soviet schism in 1961, the Russian continental empire stretched longitudinally from the western frontier of the German Democratic Republic to the Pacific Ocean. It encompassed most of the Eurasian land mass, including the Baltic states, truncated Germany, Poland, Czechoslovakia, Hungary, Romania, Bulgaria, and Albania in the west, and Mainland China, Mongolia, North Korea, and North Vietnam in the East. Extracontinentally, Soviet suzerainty extended to Cuba, and possibly to South Yemen, Angola, and Ethiopia as well, though the degree of Moscow's control in these latter countries is difficult to ascertain. The contemporary Soviet Empire is, of course, the successor to the Russian Empire of the Tsars, and while the revolution of 1917 etched significant discontinuities into Russian social and economic history, it hardly affected the course of Russian empire building.

The beginning of this course was, in the words of Vernadsky, an "insignificant *ostrog* [block-house] built in the first half of the twelfth century, on an insignificant river by an insignificant princeling [which] became, in the course of time, the pivot of an empire extending into two, and even three continents" (Vernadsky, 1953:390). This twelfth-century minor fortification was destined to become the city of Moscow, and its hinterland, the Duchy of Muscovy, was to become the core of an ever-expanding Slav empire originally peopled by a Nordic tribe designated as *Rus*. Ivan the Great, who ruled Muscovy from 1462 to 1505, is widely credited with consolidating the first centralized Russian state in what is today the Moscow area in the northwestern part of the present-day Soviet Union. Ivan and his immediate successors extended Russia outward by absorbing weaker neighboring Slav principalities and by confronting the more powerful forces of medieval Lithuania, Poland, and Sweden. Later, Ivan the Terrible, circa 1584, pushed east and southeast to the northern shores of the Caspian Sea, finally breaking the power of the Mongols of the Golden Horde, who had since the thirteenth century occupied regions in what are today the Ukraine and Soviet Central Asia. Interaction with the Mongols, Kochan and Abraham observe, "provided future Russian rulers with a model: a state with universalist aspirations, subordinating everything to efficiency in matters of military administration and relying on a class of serving men bound to serve their khan with absolute obedience" (Kochan and Abraham, 1983:24).

After the Russians, expanding eastward, crossed the Urals into Siberia in the 1580s, it took them only another century to annex the vast expanse of central Asia. By the end of the reign of Peter I in 1725, Tsarist hegemony extended to the Pacific Ocean. Meanwhile Russian successes in the Great Northern War between 1706 and 1718 added territory in the Baltic region at Sweden's expense, and later, the three partitions of Poland during the reign of Catherine the Great added to the Russian empire in the west. The Tsars of the nineteenth century focused most of their expansionistic attentions southward and pushed, between 1801 and 1881, through Georgia, Kazakhstan, Turkistan, and Azerbaijan to the northern frontiers of Persia and Afghanistan. The last decades of the nineteenth century found the Tsars consolidating and extending their domain along their Pacific coast.

The Treaty of Brest-Litvosk in 1918 extricated Russia, now reconstituted as the Soviet Union, from World War I, but it cost the Russians dearly in terms of territory in the Baltic region, in the west and in the Black Sea area. However, most of this territory was reconquered by the Red Army by the end of the revolutionary wars in the early 1920s. Estonia, Latvia, and Lithuania were reannexed to the Soviet Union as a result of the Molotov-Ribbentrop Pact of August, 1939; some Finnish territories were annexed to the USSR as a result of the Russo-Finnish Wars of 1940 and 1944; and most of Eastern Europe occupied by the Soviet Union in 1945 became thereafter the new western cordon of the Soviet Empire. With the success of its revolution in 1949, the Chinese Communist Party initially accepted the tutelage of the Soviet Union and thus became a part of the latter's imperial system. Most of the communist parties in power elsewhere in the world did likewise.

Since the Russian empire is largely territorially contiguous, the Tsarist and Soviet governments have opted mainly for direct rule via annexation to the core state and administrative subordination to Moscow. The territories and peoples added to the empire after World War II were, however, governed less directly through the maintenance in power of local communist parties whose leaders have been beholden to Moscow. Rather generous Soviet economic and military assistance has helped client communist governments to control societies in the subordinate states. In several countries in Eastern Europe, communist parties' political monopolies have also been buttressed by large contingents of permanently stationed Red Army troops. Legitimacy has never been a major contributing element in Moscow's indirect rule over client states, though the degree to which legitimacy abetted the government in the core state should not be underestimated.

INTRA- AND INTERIMPERIAL RELATIONS

Our point in going to some length to demonstrate that the United States and the Soviet Union are empires is to open the way to explaining that they have been behaving in the post–World War II era as great empires have typically behaved in the past. We say typically because we are looking at the broad patterning of relations between great empires. As in any historical analogy there are features of the phenomena being compared which are similar and some which are different. As the differences become more prominent and the similarities recede, the utility of the comparison wanes. On the other hand, where the similarities persist over long historical stretches, they can be of great value to assist in our understanding.

If we choose as our historical analogs the celebrated rivalries between the Romans and Parthians (170 B.C.-224 A.D.), and the Romans/Byzantines and the Sasanian Persians (224-642), the Byzantines and Arabs (632-1100), the Ottomans and the Austrians (1539-1914), and the Ottomans and the Russians (1686-1917), we can begin to construct a rough model of international relations under conditions of imperial rivalry. For one thing, simply looking at the dates suggests that historical imperial rivalries continued over long stretches of time, centuries usually. As great imperial rivals were typically powerful, durable, and capable of repeated regeneration from within, contests between them tended to be very long and often inconclusive. They were trials of slow attrition that led less often to victory or supremacy and more often to mutual exhaustión or inability to cope with challenges from newly rising, more vigorous rivals.

Second, warfare between the great imperial rivals was continuous, but it was typically geographically confined to regions of interimperial intersection, i.e., to the marches, where rival armies literally marched back and forth for centuries. While continuous, warfare in the marches was also typically indecisive. By the same token, core state–to–core state onslaughts were rare, capital cities were seldom attacked and taken, and total triumphs or knockout blows were seldom registered. Interestingly, while the inconclusive skirmishing in the marches continued, people living in respective core states and capital cities might have easily perceived themselves in the midst of periods of long peace. But conditions undoubtedly must have appeared very different to the unfortunate souls inhabiting the borderlands. Among the historic cases listed above, only Constantinople succumbed at rival hands. The main reasons for the continuous warfare were successive political rulers' quests for glory, military leaders' need for employment and economic rewards anticipated from plunder and territorial acquisition. Religious zeal sometimes also played a part. As time went on in many cases revanchism, revenge and repayment for defeats and indignities suffered in earlier rounds became important motives for launching succeeding ones. In this way, the constant conflicts came in effect to feed upon themselves. The primary reason that the interimperial wars were usually inconclusive, as well as the reason core states and capital cities could seldom be assaulted, was that the rival empires tended to be closely balanced in their military capabilities (or sometimes in their military inabilities). Thus, they engaged for the most part in centuries-long efforts at wearing one another down. Of course, geography and technology were important factors as well.

In every instance of great imperial rivalry, intra-imperial affairs attracted far greater core state attention than interimperial affairs.

Because of their vastness and internal self-sufficiency, their military invulnerability and the commonly vast physical and ideocultural distances that separate core state from core state, great empires have tended to mutually isolate themselves. Beyond skirmishing along their borders they have typically had little to do with one another and little interest in one another's societies or internal affairs. "The distance that usually separates empires," Liska observed, "is not only geographical but also psychological. It commonly resides in mutual ignorance, including misassessment of power and objectives. Ignorance and misassessment increase with cultural or ideological differences" (Liska, 1967:12).[2] By contrast, core states are typically and constantly involved in securing, consolidating, and deepening their governance within their imperial systems and fixing their hierarchical relations with intra-imperial clients. Threats to the efficacy or continuation of core state governance occur frequently, as some parties, somewhere in the empires, for some reason are almost always in revolt. As empires decline, internal disintegration tends to become ever more problematic and eventually becomes the almost total preoccupation of core state governments, commanding thus their attentions and sapping their resources.

IMPERIAL CONFLICT AND AMERICAN-SOVIET RELATIONS

Each of the essays in this volume seeks to explain or add to our understanding of why the United States and the Soviet Union have not entered into direct military conflict in the four and one half decades since the Second World War. As is typical of great historical interimperial rivalries, conflict between the United States and the Soviet Union has been almost continuous in the post–World War II era. It has often been violent. But it has only rarely been direct, i.e., core state versus core state. In the contest between these two contemporary imperial systems, each core state has used its own military forces as well as those of client states to do continuing battle with what it has seen as agents or manifestations of its rival empire. Historically speaking, such indirect conflict is rather typical of the international relations of great empires. Most frequently these battles have been empire-maintaining exercises conducted principally within the geographic borders of one of the empires and fought between the core state and rebellious elements in a client state. Preoccupations with such intra-empire problems are also historically common, as are repeated revolts at imperial peripheries. Otherwise, contemporary interimperial contests have been fought in portions of the globe not fully incorporated into one of the two systems, i.e., in the interimperial marches, where each of the empires has aspired either to expand or to check its rival's expansion. As the constant and rather inconclusive skirmishing has gone on, the interimperial balance of power has kept the core states reasonably immune from mutual external assault or penetration.

THE BEGINNINGS OF INTERIMPERIAL RIVALRY

When we left the United States and the Soviet Union earlier in this discussion, the two had already emerged as twentieth-century empires. But their mutually preoccupying rivalry most realistically dates from the early post–World War II era. "There probably never was any real possibility," Cold War historian Ernest May writes, "that the post-1945 relationship could be anything but hostility verging on conflict" (May, 1984:209). From Truman to Bush and from Stalin to Gorbachev, the leaders in each of the two core states managed to see in each other the major threat to their ability to flourish, if not just to survive. As early as Potsdam, Truman had decided that the Russians had to be confronted with "an iron fist and strong language" (Messer, 1986:123). He and his inner circle of advisors had determined by the autumn of 1946 that the Soviet Union was an expansionist power bent on conquest. Dwight Eisenhower likewise saw the world imperiled by the "monolithic mass of Communist imperialism" (Immerman, 1982:15). To the authors of NSC-68, the USSR was "the inheritor of Russian imperialism" (Sanders, 1983:33). It needed to be contained.

The view from the Kremlin was no less severe. For Stalin, the enemy in and after the Second World War was not just the Nazis. The enormous losses suffered by the Soviets during the war, along with the historic distrust of the anti-Communist European and American powers generated substantial concern for preserving the security and territorial integrity of the USSR. "When Stalin insisted upon having only 'friendly' governments on Russia's borders, he declared his refusal even to risk reestablishment of the prewar *cordon sanitaire* of noncommunist, anti-Soviet regimes" (Messer, 1986:109). "Since World War II," Dimitri Simes underlines, "the relationship with the United States has continually been among the central considerations of Soviet foreign policy. America . . . became for the Soviet Union a source of constant fear, a constraint on further geopolitical advances" (Simes, 1984:291).

Thus, each of the two empires came to see the other as a distinct threat to its system, and each came to believe that it had to act forcefully to counter efforts by the other to subvert or otherwise detach peripheral states from its imperial system. To fail to do so would be to show weakness, and that, in turn, would likely carry over into unraveling the fabric of imperial control maintained by the respective cores. "As we ourselves demonstrate power, confidence and a sense of moral and political direction," the authors of NSC-68 affirmed, so those same qualities will be evoked in Western Europe. In such a situation, we may also anticipate a general improvement in the political tone in Latin America, Asia, and Africa. . . . In the absence of affirmative decision on our part, the rest of the free world is almost certain to become demoralized . . . they can become a positive increment to Soviet power. (Sanders, 1983:25)

That Soviet concerns were similar is evidenced in Nikita Khruschev's "For New Victories of the World Communist Movement," where the Russian leader pointed out that

There exists in the world today, not just one country of workers and peasants, but a whole system of socialist countries. It is our duty to safeguard peace and ensure the peaceful development of this grand creation. The struggle against imperialism can succeed only if its [i.e., capitalist imperialism's] aggressive actions are firmly resisted. Scolding will not halt the imperialist adventurers. There is only one way in which they will be curbed: steady strengthening of the economic, political and military power of the socialist countries. (Westerfield, 1959:86-87)

Answering exactly why the United States and the Soviet Union emerged as imperial rivals after the Second World War is akin to explaining why Romans and Persians were adversaries in the Second Century A.D., or why Arabs and Byzantines were rivals or Austrians and Turks, or perhaps any of the other great antagonists of history. Explanations range from Raymond Aron's (1967) notion of *la fatalité des positions*, meaning that proximate great powers are somehow historically determined to be rivals, to George Liska's (1967:14) more persuasive observation that a great-power rivalry tends often to be driven by fear based on mutual cultural ignorance. There is in most cases of interimperial rivalry evidence of extensive "mirror-imaging" where statesmen project their own aggressive intentions onto rivals and thus escalate destructive spirals of mutual suspicion. Nor, of course, is it extraordinary for the political leaders of major powers actually to harbor, and conveniently act upon, externally expansionistic intentions. All of these elements, and undoubtedly many others, have been ingredients in Soviet-American rivalry as well.

INTRA-IMPERIAL CONFLICT IN THE POST–WORLD WAR II ERA

While the American and Soviet geostrategic preoccupations have been with their global rivalry, their more practical political-military occupations have been with problems occurring *within* their respective imperial systems. A goodly proportion of the conflicts that have involved the superpowers since the early 1950s have had to do with what would traditionally be called "putting down rebellions in the outlying provinces of the empire." The patterns in most of the cases are similar, and they recur with remarkable regularity: (1) elements within a client state rise up against local elites that are beholden to the core state; (2) the possible success of the rebels raises the possibility that the client state might be separated from the empire; and (3) forces and/or military supplies from the core state are dispatched to suppress the rebellion, thereby maintaining or restoring imperially loyal local elites.

What has been rather remarkable in American and Soviet exercises in putting down rebellions in the outlying provinces is that substantial numbers of the respective core state elites have repeatedly managed to convince themselves that the rebellions within their respective imperial systems have been caused by the provocations and machinations of their rivals. In fact, there is very little evidence to suggest that most of the intra-imperial uprisings were directly fomented by imperial rivals, though there is no denying that many, once initiated, were abetted from the outside. To the extent that the respective elites have actually believed that their intra-imperial problems were caused by rival provocateurs, they have denied themselves the capacity to understand more fundamental causes of the uprisings against them. In any event, combating perceived or proclaimed penetration and subversion from the outside has been the standard justification offered by the respective core state elites to explain their inevitable moves to suppress rebellions.

Client states are not merely passive actors in this process. Often it is elites in those client states who solicit intervention from the core. The conventional wisdom in Latin America for years was that all the elites had to do was invoke the threat of communism and they could get whatever assistance they desired from the U.S. The strategy worked well and often led the U.S. to become embroiled, by providing military weaponry, equipment, uniforms, training and advisers, in supporting client elites in their efforts to suppress "leftist rebels." Even in the case of the U.S. invasion of Grenada in October, 1983, the client states played an important role. Dominica, with a population of about 75,000, led the way as its Prime Minister, Mary Eugenia Charles, petitioned the U.S. on behalf of the Eastern Caribbean States to intervene to save Grenada from barbarism and communism. Their entreaty served both to stimulate the decision to invade and to legitimize it.

There is no question but that pressures for the suppression of empire-threatening rebellions also flowed in two directions in the Soviet cases. Clearly there were those among the local elites in the Soviet client states who stood to lose a great deal from the fragmentation of the Soviet empire, and they were understandably active in encouraging Soviet interventions against their own countrymen, whom they were quick to brand "counter-revolutionaries," "antiparty agitators" and "non-Marxist deviationists." In Hungary in 1956, for example, at the very first signs of unrest, Mr. Gero, the First Secretary of the Hungarian Communist Party, called for Soviet and Warsaw Pact intervention to restore order. Likewise in the Czechoslovakian situation in 1968 the party's "hardliners" saw their political futures more closely tied to the CPSU than to their "liberal" colleagues in Prague, and certainly made Moscow aware of this.

MAINTAINING THE UNITED STATES EMPIRE

Guatemala

Following a successful revolution in October, 1944, Guatemala embarked on a ten-year period of reform. The country did away with many of the vestiges of the earlier dictatorship and achieved a democratic opening. Colonel Jacobo Arbenz Guzman, who assumed the presidency from Juan Jose Arevalo in a peaceful transition in 1951, was intent on furthering reform in Guatemala by redistributing uncultivated lands to peasants after duly compensating owners. This land reform effort aroused the opposition of the U.S.-owned United Fruit Company, which owned over 40 percent of the arable land in Guatemala but cultivated only 5 percent. United Fruit then sought the support of the United States government for the overthrow of the Arbenz regime. Meanwhile, Arbenz had legalized the Communist Party in Guatemala and invited some of its members into his government. The functioning of the Arbenz government thus began to be perceived in Washington as a challenge to the anti-communist fidelity expected of client elites within the United States imperial system (Immerman, 1982).

Guatemala looked to be in rebellion within the empire, and Secretary of State John Foster Dulles was determined to pursue a "clear-cut . . . policy . . . against the intervention of international communism in the hemisphere," and "to take effective measures, individually and collectively, to combat it" (Trudeau and Schoultz, 1986:50). If the articulations of Dulles and other American officials at the time are reliable guides, there is little doubt that Washington (1) saw Arbenz and his policies as unacceptable deviations from appropriate client state elite behavior and (2) interpreted the Guatemalan situation as instigated and abetted by the Soviet Union.[3] Arbenz, of course, was subsequently overthrown as a result of the United States Central Intelligence Agency's now well-known "Operation Success," the reforms were rolled back, and Guatemala entered what were to be three decades of repressive and authoritarian rule (Immerman, 1982; Trudeau and Schoultz, 1986).[4]

The Dominican Republic

With the assassination of Rafael Trujillo in 1961, thirty years of dictatorship were brought to a close. Despite a period of considerable turmoil, the Dominicans managed to elect a President whose tenure in office was cut short by a military coup in 1963. Then in April, 1965, a rebellion broke out. The rebels sought the overthrow of the military regime and the restoration of the deposed president.

Response from the U.S. was swift, overt, and military. President Johnson explained on May 2 why he had ordered some 25,000 American troops into the Dominican Republic:

> Communist leaders, many of them trained in Cuba, seeing a chance to increase disorder, to gain a foothold, joined the revolution. They took increasing control. . . . [The revolution] was taken over . . . and placed into the hands of a band of Communist conspirators. (Franck and Weisband, 1971:79)[5]

Challenge to the empire was not acceptable. "Our goal," he said, "is to prevent another Communist state in this hemisphere." As if to forewarn against any future such attempts, he proclaimed the Johnson Doctrine: "American nations cannot, must not, and will not permit the establishment of another Communist government in the Western Hemisphere" (Franck and Weisband, 1971:79).[6]

Central America

Apparently quiescent in the early 1970s, Central America seemed to erupt at the end of the decade. First came the overthrow of Anastasio Somoza in Nicaragua in July, 1979, and then, three months later, General Carlos Humberto Romero in neighboring El Salvador was toppled. Meanwhile, violence and insurgency continued to bubble up in Guatemala. In the subsequent decade the United States scrambled to hold the line against what it saw as the threat of communist intrusion and the possible loss of not one but two more Cubas.

In Nicaragua, where the incoming Reagan administration found itself confronting a Marxist party in power, the effort was to force the Sandinistas out; and in El Salvador, where the insurgents were a growing force, the strategy was to beef up the local military and defeat the guerrillas on the battlefield.

Despite the efforts of Mexico, Venezuela, Colombia and Panama — joined later by Argentina, Brazil, Peru, and Uruguay — to persuade the U.S. that the "battle" being enjoined in Central America was a "North-South" and not an "East-West" one, the U.S. persisted in the view so well articulated by the National Bipartisan Commission on Central America (Blachman, LeoGrande and Sharpe, 1986):

> The Soviet-Cuban thrust to make Central America part of their geostrategic challenge is what has turned the struggle in Central America into a security and political problem for the United States and for the hemisphere.

The use of Nicaragua as a base for Soviet and Cuban efforts to penetrate the rest of the Central American isthmus, with El Salvador the target of first opportunity, gives the conflict there a major strategic dimension. The direct involvement of aggressive external forces makes it a challenge quite specifically to the security interests of the United States. This is a challenge to which the United States must respond. (Kissinger, 1984:12, 126-27)

Other Cases

The toppling of Mohammad Mossedeque in Iran in 1953, the "economic destabilization" of Chile from 1970 to the overthrow of Salvador Allende in 1973, the invasion of Grenada in October, 1983, support for the Contras in Nicaragua and other exertions against the Sandanista government, as well as prolific military and economic aid to client elites under siege from leftist insurgents have similarly all been empire-maintaining exercises conducted by Washington. As we may glean from the history of empires, someone somewhere within the empire is almost always seen to be in rebellion against the imperial system and its orthodox client elites. The integrity of the empire requires that such rebellions be put down. It is not unusual that the demand for action against such rebellious actions comes from within the client states, at times pushing the core to a more rigid position than it might otherwise have taken.

In the first two decades after the Second World War, the United States was reasonably successful in its empire-maintaining efforts. Fidel Castro's successful anti-imperial rebellion, Cuba's move from the U.S. imperial system into the Soviet system, and the subsequent Bay of Pigs fiasco, combined to produce the only really dramatic early U.S. failure.

Maintaining the Soviet Empire

Eastern Germany

Although direct Soviet control over Eastern Germany, technically speaking, was ended in October, 1949, a large Red Army force remained in the German Democratic Republic and the Communist Party leaders of the GDR remained strictly beholden to Moscow. Rioting broke out in East Berlin in the summer of 1953, ostensibly over the issue of increased work norms imposed by the GDR government on construction workers. This protest escalated into demands to dissolve the East German Parliament and calls for free elections. In short order, the uprising begun in East Berlin spread to several other East German cities, and Soviet troops and tanks rolled in to put down the riots with considerable force.

Notably, the origins of the protest stemmed from Germans' dismay with working conditions in the GDR and their frustration with political repression under the communist regime. The episode was fundamentally a rebellion against the state and Marxist-Leninist ideological orthodoxy, i.e., an intra-imperial revolt. But, it was publicly interpreted and perhaps even privately understood as a provocation from the United States. As *Pravda* explained, "the increase in norms was the only pretext for foreign provocateurs from among the number of foreign agents who have settled in East Berlin" (*New York Times*, June 18, 1953).

Hungary

In the wake of de-Stalinization, pressures for changes built up in some East European countries. Shortly after protesters hit the streets in Hungary in 1956, Russian tanks rolled in; opposition escalated into armed conflict, and fighting broke out throughout the country. Response to the rebellion was rapid and it was soon crushed. Blame was laid at the doorstep of the U.S. and other "reactionary" forces:

> It is known that the forces of reaction within the country were acting in close contact with the international reaction, and immediately after the armed putsch was started they were receiving effective aid from the West. . . . According to official information of the Hungarian Government, . . . airplanes arrived from Austria . . . ; they brought a considerable amount of munitions in boxes marked with the Red Cross and persons who acted as the organizers of the counter-revolutionary putsch. (*Izvestia*, cited in Franck and Weisband, 1971:59)

Such Western attempts to undermine the Soviet empire were, in their view, not new. As they claimed the following year in an official publication, *The Truth About Hungary*,

> energetic preparations for overthrowing the people's democratic system in Hungary and in other East European countries, have been conducted in the United States of America . . . for many years. (Franck and Weisband, 1971:59)

Khruschev sought to dispel any doubts concerning the seriousness of Soviet resolve to counter such rebellions in the future when he spoke at Tatabanya, Hungary in 1958:

> If provocateurs or enemies of the workers attempt a "putsch" or counter-revolution in any Socialist country, then I tell them here and now that all the Socialist countries and the armed forces of the Soviet Union will be ready at all times to give the provocateurs the answer they deserve. (*Keesing's*, June 14-21, 1958:16237)

Czechoslovakia

Once again attempts to liberalize were viewed as a challenge to Soviet hegemony. Following months of discussions, negotiations, and warnings, the flowering of Spring in Prague was brought to an abrupt and violent halt, as Russian and Warsaw Pact troops moved swiftly and massively into the country in 1968. Ambassador Malik argued at the United Nations that the Czechoslovakian affair had been instigated from outside and that Soviet reaction had been appropriate and necessary:

> The Soviet Union has irrefutable data that events in Czechoslovakia can be traced outside that country. There is a dangerous conspiracy of the forces of internal and external reaction to restore the order which had been brought down by the popular revolution. (Franck and Weisband, 1971:107)

Malik continued: "Instructions and directives from abroad" went to anticommunist Czechoslovakians who played "the role of imperialist agents in that country." This was all part of an effort by the U.S.

> to undermine and sap the socialist system . . . and create a breach in the Socialist community. The imperialist circles of the United States, by political and ideological means involving secret, clandestine and subversive measures, stubbornly continue trying to tear apart the socialist community, to break its unity and weaken its ability to confront direct aggression. (Franck and Weisband, 1971:107-8)

Afghanistan

The Soviet Union has historically been vitally concerned with its security in its border areas. Afghanistan's geographic proximity put it squarely in the Soviets' "backyard." When it appeared that the Afghani regime, friendly to the Soviets, was likely to be overthrown and a fundamentalist Islamic one was the likely replacement, they were greatly concerned. They feared the impact such a fundamentalist regime on the border might have on ethnic Moslem populations inside the Soviet Union. They were also worried that the new regime might shift their loyalties away from them and toward the West.

In a preemptive action, the Soviets launched a massive invasion in December, 1979, which, despite their technical superiority, got them bogged down in a decade-long, very costly military quagmire. President Brezhnev explained the Soviet action on the front page of *Pravda*. "Crude interference" from the outside, "tens of thousands of insurgents, armed and trained abroad, whole armed units . . ." he claimed, had been sent to Afghanistan. "In effect," he continued, "imperialism, together with its accomplices, launched an undeclared war against revolutionary Afghanistan." He pointed out that the Soviets had warned that they would not abandon the Afghans in their time of need, and "as is well known, we stand by what we say." He explained:

> The unceasing armed intervention, the well advanced plot by external forces of reaction, created a real threat that Afghanistan would lose its independence and be turned into an imperialist military bridgehead on our country's southern border. ... we could not but respond to the request of the Government of friendly Afghanistan. To have acted otherwise would have meant leaving Afghanistan a prey to imperialism. ... To have acted otherwise would have meant to watch passively the origination on our southern border of a centre of serious danger to the security of the Soviet state. (*Keesing's*, May 9, 1980:30236)

Skirmishing in the Interimperial Marches

While the United States and Soviet Union have no common borders save for the sea frontier in the remote region of the Bering Straits, their respective imperial systems nonetheless adjoin at the numerous points where respective client states come together. These points and these countries therefore are the marches of the empires, and like the borderlands of proximate historic empires, they have been contested. However, the contests, while costly in human lives and material resources, have not significantly altered the interimperial territorial status quo. Soviet attempts immediately after World War II to expand its Eastern European domain to include Greece were thwarted by the United States. After three years and more than a half-million military and civilian casualties, the Korean War was fought to a stalemate in 1953. The battles for the Taiwan Straits between 1954 and 1957 similarly generated a standoff. The United States, after a costly empire-defending experience, was ejected from Vietnam in 1972, thereby slightly altering the interimperial territorial status quo. On the other hand, the Soviet Union, after a comparably expensive failure at imperial expansion, was forced out of Afghanistan in 1989. If the civil conflict in Angola is actually a case of interimperial skirmishing in contested borderlands, the conflict here too appears to have generated impasse.

Core State-versus-Core State Encounters

Direct confrontations between the United States and the Soviet Union have been rare in the post–World War II era, thus lending the appearance of a period of "long peace." As noted earlier, such core state–to–core state confrontations have also been rare historically, mainly because they were perceived as costly, unwinnable because of balanced power, and logistically difficult to manage. It has always been more convenient, moreover, to fight, rampage, and ravage in other peoples' countries in the borderlands away from imperial cores.

Direct confrontations between imperial powers do from time to time occur. In the American-Soviet relationship, the first true interempire conflict occurred in 1948 when the Soviet Union closed off land and water access to the city of West Berlin through East Germany. Despite its very tense moments, this conflict never escalated past the threshold of large-scale violence.

The second and far more serious conflict between the two powers revolved around the placement of Soviet offensive missiles in Cuba in 1962. The U.S. eventually declared a quarantine of the island and said it would stop and search Soviet ships headed there, setting the stage for direct confrontation. But the two powers, seeking to avoid direct conflict, especially to avert escalating to a nuclear exchange, resorted to traditional diplomacy to resolve the crisis.

WHEN EMPIRES MEET: SOME CONCLUSIONS

How useful is it to model the long peace as a phase of interimperial international relations? Our broad sweep through the history of international relations and our staccato survey of post–World War II Soviet-American relations can only be suggestive. But the suggestions they evoke are rather intriguing:

1. The imperial model of United States–Soviet relations would suggest (a) that core states will avoid direct center-to-center clashes, (b) that interimperial conflict in borderlands and other contested peripheral areas will be continuous, and (c) that intra-empire relations, core state to client state, will consume most of the efforts, if not also most of the attention of the core states.

2. The emergence of the United States and the Soviet Union as imperial powers, their behavior toward clients within their respective imperial systems, their behavior regarding peripheral and unincorporated states and their behavior toward each other are all reminiscent of recurrent patterns associated with the great empires and great imperial rivalries of the past. The imperial model is therefore quite informative. The avoidance of direct clashes between imperial core states, or what we describe in Soviet-American relations as the long peace, has strong historical precedent[7] and a sound logic in historical and contemporary balance-of-power thinking. The historical record and contemporary diplomacy clearly affirm that imperial statesmen engage in such balance-of-power thinking. Yet constant conflict at points of interimperial intersection is also a mode of both historical behavior and contemporary

Soviet-American relations. Empire-maintaining behavior, "the putting down of revolts in the provinces," or otherwise keeping loyal elites in power in client states has always been for core states a preoccupying aspect of their international relations. So too, has such empire-maintaining behavior been a practical preoccupation of the United States and the Soviet Union in the post–World War II era.

3. An important aspect of the Soviet-American relationship has been an integrated perception, mutually harbored by governing elites in both core states, of an all-encompassing global contest. The contending leadership of the United States and the Soviet Union have tended to interpret all aspects of their international relations, intra-imperial as well as inter-imperial, as phases of a single pervasive struggle. Balancing nuclear power at the strategic level, fighting small wars along the peripheries of the imperial systems, and combating rebellions within client states have all been perceived as connected. In the same way, imperial rivals have consistently been perceived as the instigators and provocateurs of whatever manner of troubles or obstacles core states have confronted in various modes of intra- and interimperial relations. The "mirror imaging" has been remarkable. It could very well be that such "integrated perceptions of all-encompassing contest" were also common in historical imperial rivalries. However, we have only scant evidence of this because historical scholarship has not directly explored this question.

4. Without entering directly into the discussion about why the United States and the Soviet Union are presently declining from the pinnacles of imperial ascendance, both core states in recent years have been encountering increasing difficulties in their intra-imperial relations. Not only does neither core state any longer appear able to expand its imperial domain, but the respective imperial systems have been diminishing in size and the authority of the core states in peripheral areas has been waning. The withdrawal of Soviet military forces from Afghanistan in 1989, political upheavals in Eastern Europe, and secessionist activities in the Baltic areas of the Soviet Union, the Caucasus, and elsewhere have dramatically signaled the weakening of the Russian empire. Less momentously, though still indicatively, the United States' inabilities to control events in Nicaragua and El Salvador, Washington's need to occupy Panama militarily in order to depose a defiant, petty dictator, and ebbing respect for the U.S. will and authority in Western Europe and Japan all suggest considerable fraying about the edges of the American empire. Historically speaking, there is nothing extraordinary about what is happening to the American and Soviet empires. As noted earlier, empires typically do not "fall"; they rather fragment as client states become able to claim and enforce increasing autonomy.

5. The study of historical empires suggests at least two scenarios for the future of the Soviet and American empires. They are both projections of decline because both the United States and the Soviet Union have passed the peaks of their power. First, there is the pattern of slow decline and eventual descent into historical, though not necessarily physical, oblivion. Here, one might consider the fates of western Rome, Byzantium, Venice, imperial Spain, or Manchu China. Decline is halting, fragmentation is piecemeal, intermittent partial reinvigoration is common, and traditional rivalries are kept alive, though not very vigorously pursued, because they serve the internal political or psychological needs of ruling elites. Meanwhile, new centers of power emerge and new interimperial contests become the axes of international relations.

Alternatively, imperial decline might be precipitous, as with Austria-Hungary, the Ottoman Empire or the Western European colonial empires assembled in the last decades of the nineteenth century. When this more rapid decline happens, former imperial core states become modest, middle powers. The international system expands haphazardly to include numerous new states emerged from the old empires, and constructing a new international order out of small-power pluralism becomes the challenge to diplomacy and the key to stability. Historically, diplomacy frequently fell short of meeting such challenges and rather dangerous eras of increased international anarchy were the results.

Because of the extreme turbulence within the Soviet empire and contagion effects this may have within the American empire, or even within the U.S. core state itself, it is impossible to know in 1990 whether the future courses of the superpowers' respective imperial decline will be slow or precipitous. We agree with Paul Kennedy (1987:488-535) that the two empires are in decline and that economic exhaustion impelled by excessive military spending has been catalyzing the fall. The imperial model suggests that "rebellions in the provinces" are going to become more frequent and increasingly successful as processes of imperial fragmentation accelerate.

6. What then can we expect of the future for these two empires, given what we have learned from the past? Historically speaking, every empire has eventually fallen from its position as the hegemonic power, yet the nature of decline in dominance has varied across time and space. Decline need not spell disaster, though that too has sometimes been the case. Among the factors especially important in affecting the decline of empires have been the quality and vision of leadership. What then do we make of the kinds of choices likely to be selected by the two current empires? The events of 1989 and early 1990 provide a clue to assessing the likely trajectories.

In the case of the Soviet Union, its empire has truly come apart from within. A crucial variable has been the impact of President Gorbachev and his supporters. The introduction of *glasnost* and *perestroika* opened political space inside the core as well as within the periphery. In both, the population leapt at the opportunity, rushing in not only to fill that space, but to open it up even further. This has especially been the case in Eastern Europe, where the Soviet empire had been maintained not only through leaders selected by and sanctioned from the Soviet Union, but by the physical presence — and, as we pointed out earlier, the use — of the Soviet military.

The Soviet empire came about through the forced imposition of control in the aftermath of the Second World War. These peripheral populations had an earlier history of nationhood and, to varying degrees, had enjoyed some semblance of sovereignty in the world state system. Soviet hegemony gave them a target to fire at. The reaction throughout Eastern Europe in tossing out the communist parties and communist party leadership has meant the removal of a leadership and organizational stratum, imposed from abroad, and which in its forty years of control had been unable to convince the people that it deserved to stay in power. The surge of nationalism in the periphery combined with the Soviet core leadership's preoccupation with internal problems might seem to be enough to explain why the Soviets made no effort to contain or control events in Eastern Europe, but that explanation would be inadequate. Added to it must be the sense of vision among the Soviet leadership. The former might be sufficient to explain why the Soviets would be *unable* to continue to impose their will, but it is not sufficient to explain why they were also *unwilling* to attempt to do so. Indeed, the openness of *glasnost* and *perestroika* not only permitted these events, but possibly encouraged them.

This all suggests that the future will be one in which the peripheral units of the Soviet empire will further assert their individuality and the empire will continue to disintegrate. Just as the decisions which led to this pattern of breakup were not historically inevitable, neither will the future direction of relations between and among the empire units be forced into any particular mode. New leadership in the Soviet Union could attempt to reassert control, even relying on the use of brute force. However, such a scenario is unlikely due to the enormous cost that would be incurred — in human and economic resources — in conducting military operations in those areas and in addressing the tension within the core itself.

For the U.S. empire, the pattern of decline has been somewhat different. The imposition of control by the U.S. was mostly accomplished by more indirect means. The leadership of many countries in the periphery of the U.S. empire are not as readily identified as U.S. surrogates (as were those Soviet surrogates in Eastern Europe) and although U.S. military support has been used to quell disturbances, with the exception of the Panama Canal Zone there is no significant presence of troops in any of the nations in the hemisphere. The conditions in the peripheral areas of the two empires differ, and those differences help account for the variation in the kinds of efforts that are mounted to achieve separation or distance from the respective cores.

However, there is also a significant difference in the style and vision of the leadership of the two empires. While Gorbachev has stimulated openness and restructuring, the Reagan and Bush administrations have focused on consolidating power and actually discouraging the rise of alternative systems within the confines of the traditional U.S. sphere of influence. In the American empire, movements for social change and the redress of grievances have been opposed (sometimes with the use of force, directly or indirectly, as in the cases of Central America and Panama) and attempts have been made to smother them. The near future of such efforts may prove counterproductive. Rather than arresting the erosion/crumbling of the empire, they may accelerate it. As the leadership at the core, in the American case, stands in the way of changes that may loosen control over the periphery, it is likely to generate a stronger negative reaction from the periphery against the core.

The good news brought about by the dawning of the nineties is that the relative decline of empire can occur without having the core engage in devastatingly self-destructive behavior, as is demonstrated by the Soviet Union's current policy actions. The bad news is that the U.S. appears to respond to its relative decline in hegemony by resisting changes in ways that reaffirm the more common pattern of empires which were unable to change gracefully. The consequences of this lesson unlearned could be great for both the American core and its periphery. The key question is: Will U.S. policymakers recognize their capacity to change the pattern and adopt constructive and functional policies to readjust to the dramatic changes that have occurred within as well as between and among the units of the empire during the past four decades?

Endnotes

We would like to thank the other authors of this volume for their considered and helpful comments on the original draft of this chapter.

1. It is also rather commonplace to use the conflict between Rome and Carthage in the period of the Punic Wars (264-146 B.C.) as an analog for the modern-day American-Soviet rivalry, i.e., another bipolarity of sorts. Or, sometimes the rivalry between ancient Athens and Sparta that generated the Peloponnesian War (431-404 B.C.) is recalled. Unfortunately both of these historical episodes are frequently used to teach inaccurate lessons. For one thing, most historic imperial rivalries have not ended as did the rivalry between Rome and Carthage, with the total physical annihilation of the vanquished by the victor. Many have in fact ended in the manner of Athens and Sparta, with the utter exhaustion of both contenders. However, the conventional image of the outcome of the Peloponnesian War is that Sparta won the conflict and the "totalitarian" power thus vanquished the "democratic" one. It would be more accurate if we simply recalled that both powers lost.

2. This point was borne out in Robert Nichols' study of U.S. and USSR perceptions of the military balance. He found that "nations base their policies on their perceptions of [the U.S./USSR military] balance rather than on the *objective data*" (Nichols, 1978:11).

3. Guatemala was the first major post–World War II "challenge" to U.S. hegemony in the hemisphere. Not only did the U.S. intervene with a CIA operation, but it worked to use the regional organization of American states to endorse

its general position of anticommunism. This was accomplished with relative ease as the Tenth Inter-American conference in Caracas adopted the "Declaration of Solidarity for the Preservation of the Political Integrity of the American States Against International Communist Intervention," stating "that international communism by its antidemocratic nature and its interventionist tendency is incompatible with the concept of American freedom. . . ." Therefore, "the activities of the international communist movement" constitute "intervention in American affairs" (Franck and Weisband, 1971:51).

The U.S. Senate, in a resolution passed on June 25, 1954, stated that the U.S. had

> strong evidence of intervention by the international Communist movement in the state of Guatemala, whereby government institutions have been infiltrated by Communist agents, weapons of war have been secretly shipped into that country, and the **pattern of Communist conquest has become manifest.** [emphasis added]

The claim that a "pattern of Communist conquest" was "manifest" is especially significant since, as Franck and Weisband (1971:52) point out, "no overt change in Guatemalan government had occurred since 1944 and no foreign bases of troops had been located there."

4. In the eyes of the U.S. policymakers, overthrowing the Arbenz government was not sufficient to protect hegemony. At the onset of "Operation Success," Arbenz had gone to the United Nations Security Council for assistance. To keep control over the situation, the U.S. opposed Guatemala's efforts there. This "was precisely the kind of problem which . . . should be dealt with on an urgent basis by an appropriate agency of the Organization of American States," U.S. Ambassador Lodge told the UN. He then proceeded with the veiled threat that

> if the United Nations Security Council does not respect the right of the Organization of American States to achieve a pacific settlement of the dispute between Guatemala and its neighbors, the result will be a catastrophe of such dimensions as will gravely impair the future effectiveness . . . of the United Nations. (Franck and Weisband, 1971:53-54)

5. The evidence never supported these claims made by President Johnson. George Lister, a foreign service officer, was assigned to assess the impact of the communists. He found that though there were communists involved, they seemed to be small in number, well known to the other "revolutionaries," and relatively insignificant in terms of their power (Personal interview with Mr. Lister). His findings have been corroborated by subsequent academic research.

6. Foreign policymakers believed the Dominican intervention demonstrated the importance of swift and forceful action to contain or roll back communist incursion. A June 5, 1967, issue of *Foreign Policy Briefs* stated the lesson as follows:

> . . . when we confronted the Communists promptly and vigorously in our own hemisphere, as in the Dominican crisis, they were halted; when we failed to recognize and confront them, as in Cuba, the tumor took root and grew. (Lowenthal, 1971:107)

7. Obviously, many of the conditions that prevailed during other imperial rivalries have changed. Distances that rendered serious conflict between the core states impractical or even impossible centuries back are now bridged with little difficulty. Technological achievements over the past 22 centuries have dramatically altered the nature of geographic reach and military capability. These are shifts that would seem to make intercore state warfare more likely. At the same time, the development of a capability to annihilate one another would seem to counterbalance those other changes. The impact of nuclear technology is discussed elsewhere in this volume; see especially the chapters by Gaddis, Johansen, Kruzel, Raymond and Kegley, and Vasquez. Despite those very substantial, even revolutionary, changes, the pattern of avoidance of direct armed conflict between the two core states has persisted across time and space.

PART FOUR

The Influence of Nuclear Weapons: A Nuclear Peace?

CHAPTER NINE

The Deterrence Myth: Nuclear Weapons and the Prevention of Nuclear War

John A. Vasquez

The United States and the Soviet Union have now avoided nuclear war for nearly 50 years. For all the horror and risk that has been attendant on the nuclear age, it is hard to believe that we have survived almost a half-century of what many have called nuclear madness. Yet we are still alive. Why has the ultimate weapon been used in war only twice since its invention?

MUTUAL ASSURED DESTRUCTION

The conventional wisdom is that these weapons are so destructive that they make war irrational. Building on the Clausewitzian conception that war is merely the continuation of politics by other means, early formulators of the deterrence doctrine like Bernard Brodie (1946) saw atomic weapons as ending the role war *sometimes* played in diplomacy as a rational and as an efficient (if brutal) means to an end. Since there could be no victor, all-out nuclear war was seen as irrational. Eventually, there emerged out of this insight the notion of *Mutual Assured Destruction* (MAD) — the proposition that nuclear war could be prevented if both sides were able to destroy the other after absorbing an initial attack (George and Smoke, 1974:49). Although technically MAD was a condition both superpowers found themselves in and not a premeditated policy, it did mean that neither the Soviet Union nor the United States could be expected to win a nuclear war as long as each had a second-strike capability. The United States could deter a direct all-out attack upon itself by showing the Soviet Union that it would still have sufficient nuclear forces to destroy the Soviet Union after such an attack was launched.[1] Herman Kahn (1960:126-138) called this Type I deterrence, and more recently it has been referred to by many as *basic deterrence* (Betts, 1987:10).

Since the American military viewed the United States as vulnerable to attack only through the use of nuclear weapons (Gaddis, 1987b:24-25), Type I deterrence and its logic became the cornerstone of American defense policy. In order to be secure, the U.S. would have to be vigilant to insure that its second-strike capability would not be doubted. Early on, this meant that a portion of the Strategic Air Command would always be in the air. Later, this evolved into TRIAD — the deployment of nuclear weapons on the land (missiles in silos), the sea (submarines), and the air (bombers and now cruise missiles) — so that if one delivery system were knocked out or became out of date, two others would remain. Concerns about second-strike capability helped fuel research and development that would make America first with any technological breakthrough that might upset the delicate nuclear balance of terror. Fear that the other side might be tempted to attain a first-strike capability that would threaten one's own second-strike capability, as well as the realization that defense systems, like the ABM, were costly and fruitless, helped set the stage for arms control talks. These talks helped institutionalize MAD as a condition that would be accepted by the United States and guide its policy for the building and deployment of strategic weapons.

DETERRENCE AS MYTH

When the United States began to deviate publicly from MAD, first with Jimmy Carter's Presidential Directive 59 and then more danger-ously with Reagan advisors talking about trying to win a nuclear war (Smoke, 1984:220-24), MAD seemed less dangerous and risky. With attacks on MAD by such diverse political actors as Ronald Reagan and the American Catholic bishops (National Conference of Catholic Bishops, 1983), some serious-minded and realistic liberals began emphasizing the virtues of nuclear deterrence and the need to learn to live with nuclear weapons (e.g., The Harvard Nuclear Study Group, 1983:253-55). Various policy experts and pundits began pointing out that the absence of nuclear war in the past forty years or so was due to nuclear deterrence (Carnesale, Nye, and Allison 1985:244-45; Broder, 1983). They argued that one of the purposes of nuclear deterrence was to avoid nuclear war (The Harvard Nuclear Study Group, 1983:91, 135, 139), and this meant, despite criti-cisms from the Catholic bishops, that American nuclear deterrence was based on a moral intention (The Harvard Nuclear Study Group, 1983:246-48). It was within this political context that the deterrence myth was born. The argument was now being propagated that nuclear deterrence had prevented nuclear war between the United States and the USSR, and, despite its critics (on the right and the left), it was a necessary evil that would have to be relied upon for some time, since it was the only known way to assure survival in a complex world (The Harvard Nuclear

Study Group, 1983:249, 253-55; Carnesale, Nye, and Allison, 1985:244-46).

Myths are most dangerous when we are unaware that they are myths, when we confuse them with facts. This is generally true in everyday life; it is especially true in foreign policy, where so little is understood about the causes of war, and what *is* understood has little impact on policy. In such a situation, repeated opinion becomes fact. Myth poses as knowledge.[2]

John Lewis Gaddis (1987: Chapter 8) has provided a valuable service by raising for serious inquiry the question of why the post-1945 period has not seen a direct war between the U.S. and the USSR. Although he sees nuclear weapons playing a role, it is hardly the central role that many have given it. Of equal or greater significance is the role of rules that have emerged as the relationship between the two states has unfolded. Just how important has nuclear deterrence been in avoiding nuclear war? Will it continue to work? Is it applicable to other nuclear rivalries? Is it humanity's best hope for avoiding nuclear holocaust? These are the major questions that will be addressed in this chapter, with most emphasis on the first, since how it is answered will shape the answers to the remainder.

There is little evidence to support the claim that nuclear deterrence has prevented nuclear war or that it could do so in the future, if severely tested. The widespread and firmly held conviction that deterrence has worked is a myth for which there is little rational basis of support. To support this thesis, I shall begin by looking at logical problems with the claim that deterrence has prevented nuclear war and then move on to the relevant empirical evidence. Finally, I will conclude with an evaluation of the policy in terms of its future prospect for avoiding nuclear war.

The major logical problem with the deterrence claim is that it is based almost entirely on a faulty causal inference. Just because the United States has had a deterrence policy since the 1950s and there has been no nuclear war does not mean that the policy actually prevented nuclear war. It is like the story of the boy in Brooklyn who runs out of his house every day at 3:30 waving his arms wildly. A neighbor asks, "Why do you run down the street like that at the same time every day?" The little boy replies, "To keep the elephants away." "But there are no elephants in Brooklyn," asserts the neighbor. "See, it works!" declares the little boy.

We can laugh at the little boy, because we know that there are no elephants in Brooklyn, and if there were, they could not be kept away by a little boy running down one street at exactly the same hour every day. But when we do not understand something and have a great fear of it, if people with authority and experience say "this will prevent it," we want to believe them.

When all is said and done, the empirical evidence presented in favor of deterrence may simply be a coincidence. Of course, it may *not* be a coincidence. The point is — we do not *know*. Nor is it going to be easy to find out, because we are trying to explain why something did not happen, and that calls for a considerable amount of knowledge — both factual and theoretical. At best, the deterrence claim is an unsubstantiated assumption that must be carefully scrutinized instead of being accepted as a lesson to be passed from one generation of policymakers to the next. More important, this unsubstantiated assumption is serving as the basis for making decisions that, if incorrect, could result in the end of Western civilization.

Putting aside for the moment the question of other factors that might have prevented war, we can scrutinize the deterrence assumption in the same manner that we might evaluate the action of the boy who kept away the elephants. We can start by asking if there are any elephants present, i.e., was there a threat of nuclear war that the United States successfully deterred? Next, did the U.S. consciously use the deterrence policy to prevent nuclear war? Finally, are the actions that were taken, i.e., the practices of deterrence, the kinds of actions that would prevent war?

The question of whether the Soviet Union has ever considered launching a direct attack upon the United States is a question that has been, at least in public, scrupulously avoided. Yet it is a fundamental question. For if Soviet leaders never had any intention of attacking the United States, then they hardly can be said to have been deterred. Ultimately, the opening up of government files in both countries will help answer this question. As for now, we must surmise the answer as best we can given available information.

To do that systematically, it is important to distinguish between *general* deterrence and *immediate* deterrence, as Patrick Morgan (1983:30, 33-46) does. General deterrence refers to the attempt to prevent an adversary from attacking at any time during an ongoing long-term relationship; immediate deterrence refers to preventing an attack in a specific situation, as in a crisis. One of the problems with inferring the success of general deterrence in the absence of attack is the inability to distinguish those periods where an attack is unlikely from those where it might be highly probable.

General deterrence against a constant nonspecific threat cannot be evaluated, because the threat is so vague that there is no way of determining whether the threat really exists. For this reason, the effectiveness of deterrence should only be assessed in the presence of a situation that portends the danger of war. Such an approach rightly assumes that, during the history of the Cold War, the threat posed by various Soviet leaders has varied and that only a threat that clearly exists can be taken as a test of deterrence policy. Otherwise, successes may be claimed which are the result not of deterrence, but simply of the inertia of the other side.

Typically, the notion of a general threat is deduced from the overall capability of one's adversary. While such an inference may be legitimate in contingency planning, it is not a legitimate procedure for scientific analysis. In contingency planning, one is willing to entertain a variety of hypotheticals, regardless of their probability, as a way of providing insurance against surprise. Such a procedure is not acceptable when one is trying to ascertain the truth, as in a court of law or in the scientific testing of a hypothesis. One cannot assume a threat from capability, because one cannot logically infer objectives from capability. Wealthy individuals or strong states often have the capability to do something, but do not choose to do so, either because they might not have such an objective or they might not want to spend their resources in that manner (see Dahl, 1970:28-29 for a discussion of this basic misunderstanding about power). There must be actual evidence that such objectives exist before one can conclude that the opponent has been deterred from these objectives (George and Smoke, 1974:516). It is clear that the Soviet Union has not attacked the United States. The question is why.

Looking over Soviet-American relations year by year, it is reasonable to conclude that the Soviet Union did not threaten nuclear war against the U.S. any time before 1957 because its arsenal and delivery system were insufficient to the task.[3] Only with the launching of Sputnik was it clear that the USSR had the potential to strike hard at the landbase of the United States. From 1958 through 1962, the U.S. and the USSR were involved in a number of dangerous crises, some of which brought the two states close to war. In the two cases that raised the specter of nuclear war, the 1961 Berlin crisis and the Cuban missile crisis, it was the U.S. and not the Soviet Union that resorted to a threat of nuclear war (George and Smoke, 1974:432-34, 444; Betts, 1987:92-96, 98, 102-6, 117-20).[4] Since then, things have been relatively calm, with the exception of Nixon's 1973 nuclear alert, which again found the U.S. resorting to nuclear threat rather than the other way around (and with hindsight, it appears to have been a premature and unnecessary alarm; see Betts, 1987:123-29).

This cursory review suggests two conclusions. First, the Soviet Union does not appear to have directly threatened nuclear war (Betts, 1987:6-7). If this is the case, then American deterrence has not really been tested. Some might concede this point, but go on to argue that the Soviet Union has not threatened nuclear war because of U.S. nuclear capability, i.e., that deterrence has worked. Clearly, the latter is not known and remains, at best, an untested assumption. Indeed, from what we know about Soviet behavior, the USSR has not been shy about pushing its claims on issues that have been of high salience to it from Berlin to Cuba to Vietnam to Afghanistan. The record offers no concrete evidence that the USSR has threatened nuclear war, and therefore it cannot be validly inferred that the U.S. has deterred such a threat. To do so would be to base the evidence of deterrence on nonevents, which obviously can fail to occur for a variety of reasons. Furthermore, it seems just as plausible, indeed more so, to infer the absence of a Soviet nuclear threat from the fact that such a threat may not have been needed to pursue Soviet foreign policy objectives.

Critics of the position being advanced here might suggest that the major purpose of nuclear deterrence was not to prevent the USSR from launching an attack on the U.S., but from sweeping across Europe with conventional arms. Defense of Western Europe through nuclear deterrence was, of course, a major aim of the United States, but to argue that this was the only aim of the United States is to ignore the evidence that the U.S. has maintained a policy of basic (Type I) deterrence as well as extended deterrence (The Harvard Nuclear Study Group, 1983:135). At the same time, such a criticism would concede the point that deterrence never was used by the United States to prevent nuclear war.[5]

Second, the U.S. has felt free, on at least two occasions, to threaten nuclear war when the Soviet Union appeared to have a second-strike capability. This means that the U.S. has not been deterred by the Soviet Union's Type I deterrence. This provides empirical evidence that Type I deterrence can fail to prevent serious threats of nuclear war. This conclusion should not come as a surprise to anyone familiar with the deterrence literature, since long ago Herman Kahn (1960:140) pointed out that if Type I deterrence worked, Type II deterrence (against a severe Soviet provocation in Western Europe) could not logically be expected to work (Betts, 1987:10-11, 108-10). Indeed, much of Schelling's (1966) reputation rests on his "solution" to this problem, namely his argument that such threats could be made credible if the opponent were convinced of one's irrationality (see also Kilgour and Zagare, 1989; Zagare, 1989). This solution, however, is paradoxical and should have raised questions about the logical viability of deterrence. What are the implications of basing defense of one's civilization against nuclear war on a theory that assumes a high degree of rationality in order to work and then at a critical juncture recommends irrationality to solve a tactical problem? What is even more ominous is that, at least in Berlin, such irrationality seems to have worked. This suggests that, if one state in a crisis is not deterred by Type I deterrence, it is logically possible and probably only a matter of time before both states are not deterred.

If the claim that the USSR never threatened nuclear war is correct, then it should be corroborated in the diplomatic record of the United States. Memoirs and government documents should reveal that the United States has used deterrence not to prevent nuclear war, but for other purposes. If this is the case, then this would not only provide evidence for the absence of a serious immediate threat of nuclear war, but also add another point against the deterrence myth — namely, that deterrence can not be said to have prevented nuclear war if the U.S. has not used deterrence for that purpose.

DETERRENCE AS CONTAINMENT STRATEGY

Of course, deterrence may have other purposes. Indeed, until recently, no one seriously advanced the notion that deterrence has been used primarily to prevent nuclear war. A close reading of George and Smoke's (1974) classic study reveals that deterrence was used mainly as

a politico-military strategy to implement the containment of the Soviet
Union (see also Betts, 1987). They often judge the success of deterrence
by its ability to prevent the Soviet Union from initiating any offensive
action, such as the Berlin blockade, or even such nebulous acts as the
Soviet penetration of the Middle East (George and Smoke, 1974:119-24,
134-36, 313-25, 357-58; see also pp. 25, 27, 33, 506-8).

Nuclear weapons were used in two different ways to implement containment. Under Eisenhower's doctrine of massive retaliation, nuclear
weapons were employed primarily as a bullying weapon. Under Kennedy
and even the late Eisenhower administration, the rise in Soviet capability
made this less feasible and nuclear weapons were used to play coercive
games of chicken.

In the Eisenhower administration, allegedly the first serious consideration given to threatening massive retaliation was the effort to end the
Korean war. Similar threats were considered in the Taiwan Strait crisis.
Although the administration later claimed these as successes for the new
policy, it is not clear the extent to which the *nuclear* aspect of American
threats was communicated and understood in Korea and the first Taiwan
Strait crisis (compare the different interpretations of George and Smoke,
1974:235-41, 291-92, and Gaddis, 1987b:125-29, 136-40, 144-46; on Korea
see Dingham, 1988/89:79-91, and Foot, 1989:101-7, 110-12). In these
cases, the threat to bring devastating conventional military force to the
mainland of China may have been the major factor at work. It seems
reasonable to assume, from what is known about Chinese actions, that
in 1953, 1954-55, and 1958, they did not want to become involved in a
military confrontation with the United States that would have involved
the massive (conventional) bombing and/or shelling of Chinese bases and
cities. This conventional threat alone probably would have worked, but
in each case, the threat to attack the mainland came with the implication
that nuclear weapons might be used if necessary, i.e., that their use was
not being ruled out. This was done as part of the doctrine of missive
retaliation, which saw the existence of nuclear weapons as a financially
less costly alternative to maintaining a large conventional force. Even
though the nuclear aspect of the threat may not have been necessary, it
should· be clear that nuclear weapons were being used by the United
States primarily as a bullying weapon, and not as a way of preventing
nuclear war.

By the time of the Kennedy administration, the Soviet Union was
sufficiently powerful that alternatives to massive retaliation were being
openly discussed. Now, the use of nuclear threats brought the United
States to the brink of nuclear war, although less so in Berlin than in
Cuba (and probably not to the actual brink but sufficiently close to sober
leaders in both states). The logic of deterrence was being used by the
United States to coerce the Soviet Union to stop initiating specific foreign
actions the U.S. found threatening. To achieve its ends, the United States
used the nuclear threat to play a chicken game whereby it was able to

manipulate its advantageous geographic situation and the timing of the crisis so that the Soviet Union would be put in a position of either backing down or setting off a military confrontation that might very likely lead to a U.S. nuclear strike. Using the logic of deterrence for this purpose is, of course, an exercise in nuclear coercion, not an exercise in the prevention of nuclear war. In reality, nuclear coercion proved too frightening and risky and gave rise to efforts at accommodation, not only after Cuba, but during the Cuban missile crisis itself.[6]

It seems on closer examination that the U.S. did not face an immediate threat of nuclear war; the danger of nuclear war always was a result of an American threat to use nuclear weapons. When the U.S. employed deterrence, it did so not to prevent nuclear war, but as a means to attain other ends. Since the Soviet Union did not consciously threaten nuclear war and the U.S. did not consciously use deterrence to prevent nuclear war, it cannot be logically concluded that the United States has deterred the Soviet Union from launching a nuclear war. The absence of nuclear war must be due to other reasons.

If this fundamental logical point were not enough, further examination shows that, as both a prescriptive and empirical theory, deterrence has major flaws. From the studies available of American behavior, it is clear that American policymakers have not followed the prescriptions of deterrence theorists. They do not always couch their demands and commitments the way they should according to deterrence theory (George and Smoke, 1974:130-31, 141-42, 162-72, 200-201, 216-22, 403-9, 421-24, 507). Moreover, other studies (of both conventional[7] and nuclear deterrence) show that some of the behavior states engage in during a deterrent situation is unexpected from the perspective of deterrence theory (Lebow, 1985:203-4, 211; George and Smoke, 1974:505; Garthoff, 1987:110). Sometimes states are more cautious than expected, while at other times they are more prone to risk-taking and lashing out than anticipated (Jervis, 1985:6). In addition, statistical analyses of situations of extended deterrence show that non-nuclear states are not deterred from attacking the proteges of nuclear states even when there is an overt threat by the defender to use nuclear weapons (Huth, 1988:428, 435; cf. Huth and Russett, 1988:38; Kugler, 1984: 476-82). The possession of nuclear weapons appears irrelevant; whereas local conventional military capability, particularly the ability to deny the attacker an easy and quick victory, is statistically significant (Huth, 1988: 435-38; see also Kugler, 1984:479). Finally, as a prescriptive doctrine, deterrence seems to fall short. It frequently offers incomplete guidance, leaving decision makers to improvise (George and Smoke, 1974:504-5); and at other times it requires a degree of rationality that collectivities cannot easily achieve.

As an empirical theory, deterrence theory is even more flawed. If deterrence theory cannot accurately describe and predict the actions of American decision makers, then it is unlikely that it would be able to predict how those with a different culture and/or belief system (like the

Russians or Chinese) might react in a nuclear confrontation. Yet it is precisely this information that must be accurate if deterrence is to prevent a nuclear war. This is the case because, if one's opponent does not react according to theory, then one cannot expect them to back away from the brink when they should. The result could very well be nuclear war.[8]

THE (IL)LOGIC OF DETERRENCE THEORY

Let us now examine whether the actions that are supposed to prevent nuclear war according to the logic of Mutual Assured Destruction are the kinds of actions that would be expected to deter war. The logic of MAD appears impeccable, but this may very well be because of its familiarity and internal consistency rather than its strict logical validity. Deterrence theory appears persuasive because it assumes that war is a rational calculation to gain an end. A state will not attack if it finds the likely outcome of a war unacceptable. War will not be initiated if the costs are too high and the political ends which the war is supposed to attain have little chance of being achieved. This kind of argument seems most convincing for nuclear war, because it is so clear that there could be no victors in an all-out nuclear war.

Part of the persuasiveness of deterrence theory stems from its affinity with realism and power politics. Its view of reality is one in which power is the key factor. States do things to seek power, and they can be prevented from actions by the power of other states. This view of the world has dominated Western thinking, so deterrent actions are naturally seen as the kinds of actions that would work. Yet despite the dominance of the realist paradigm, extensive scientific testing of its hypotheses has produced little support for its claims (Vasquez, 1983). Many of its basic concepts and assumptions, like power, national interest, the balance of power, and states as rational unitary actors have been found deficient.[9] For these reasons, among others, the realist approach has been severely criticized in recent years (Burton, 1979, 1982; Kegley, 1988; Mansbach and Vasquez, 1981; Cox, 1981).

The deficiency of realism can be illustrated by examining the axiom that a state will not attack if it is clear it will lose the war. The entire edifice of deterrence logic is based on this axiom, yet there are instances, like the 1973 Egyptian attack on Israel, where states violate it (Jervis, 1985:20; Stein, 1985). More generally, the axiom clearly overestimates the extent to which states actually rationally calculate costs and benefits before war and the extent to which such calculations may be correct. World War I, Hitler's invasion of the Soviet Union, Japan's attack on Pearl Harbor, and U.S. intervention in Vietnam are all instances of wars that did not turn out the way the initiators had "rationally calculated." Furthermore, it is a mistake to assume that all wars are initiated for rational Clausewitzian reasons, or that they will remain that way once the fighting begins (Mansbach and Vasquez, 1981:313-28). Likewise, the axiom underestimates the extent to which wars occur that neither side wanted or really anticipated. Usually, this occurs through intervention in an ongoing war, like the war between China and the U.S. in Korea. Given these problems, one should not be too quick to assume the effectiveness of power and capability to deter (Garthoff, 1987:112-13; Kugler and Zagare, 1990).

Whatever the outcome of the debate over the role of capability, it is highly unlikely, from what is known about wars in general, that any single factor causes or prevents wars. Nuclear war may have been prevented not because of deterrence, but because those factors pushing the U.S. and the USSR toward war have not been sufficiently great to override the risks and costs of total war.

In this sense, Gaddis (1987b:230) is correct to see nuclear weapons as instilling a greater sense of caution within the two superpowers, but one should not disregard the fact that the experience of total war has also instilled a sense of caution. The experience of modern total war has done much to shift fundamentally the aristocratic Western conception of war as heroic, glorious, just, and useful to one of war as self-defeating, immoral, and a waste (Fussell, 1975; Johnson, 1984:107-9, 127; Mueller, 1988b:57, 66, 68, 75-76). In many ways, early fears about the horror of nuclear war can be seen as projections of fears of what a third world war would be like. It would be a mistake to underestimate the "deterrent" effect the experience of the two world wars had on the actions of both the U.S. and the Soviet Union. Neither the Soviet Union nor the United States was prepared to risk another total war in the immediate postwar period. Given the devastation the Soviet Union suffered in the Second World War and its dependence on lend-lease, the threat of a third world war, even without nuclear weapons, would have made Stalin cautious. Indeed, the record shows that he was cautious, as was the United States, which did not face a nuclear threat.

RAISING THE PROVOCATION THRESHOLD

It has been argued that one of the main effects of nuclear weapons is to raise the provocation threshold; that is, actions which would have produced war in the past now do not (Lebow, 1981:277; Jervis, 1988:83-84; for some evidence that this is the case, see Kugler, 1984:479, 482). What has been left unnoticed is that modern total war first produced this effect.[10] In fact, it may be the case that, even without nuclear weapons, the Cold War would not have escalated to an all-out fight to the finish. If one looks at the factors associated with total wars like World War I and World War II, one finds that either they have not been present, or remarkably, American and Soviet leaders have been able to defuse them.

The raising of the provocation threshold by modern total war was probably enough of an inducement to make the leaders cautious and willing to try to defuse factors that seem explosive. The further raising of the provocation threshold by nuclear weapons probably provided more than ample insurance that total war would be avoided.[11] At the same time, the fear and horror induced by the world wars tended to make each side exaggerate the threat posed by the other.

One of the factors that in the past has usually overridden the existing provocation threshold has been the presence of a highly salient territorial dispute, usually involving territory contiguous to one of the disputants. The absence of this factor in Soviet-American relations probably played a crucial role in preventing war. Most wars between major states involve territorial claims. Paul Diehl (1985), for example, finds that among enduring rivalries between major states from 1816-1980, militarized disputes that involve land contiguous to one of the disputants are much more apt to escalate to war than those that involve other stakes. About one-fourth of these 50 disputes escalated to war, whereas only 1 of 54 noncontiguous disputes (2 percent) escalated.[12] Of the 13 wars in Diehl's sample, 12 started with a dispute that was contiguous to one or both of the parties. Additional evidence on the relationship between territorial contiguity and escalation of disputes is presented by Gochman and Leng (1983; see also Most and Starr, 1980).

For a variety of reasons — perhaps even going back to a fundamental human predisposition — territory has been regarded within the global political culture as a vital issue for which the use of force is considered legitimate and usually worth the costs. States will fight over territory when they will not fight over other things. The absence of a direct territorial dispute between the United States and the Soviet Union is probably the main irenic factor that has prevented war. The lack of geographical proximity, other than Alaska, is also probably the main reason why Tsarist Russia and the United States never fought a war (see Gaddis, 1987b:4-5, 223).

The absence of such a strong war-promoting factor raises serious questions about the role deterrence has played in preventing a war. Nuclear deterrence has worked in a highly favorable environment; it has worked with the absence of a territorial dispute. Would it work as well in a rivalry, like that between Israel and the Arabs, India and Pakistan, or Iran and Iraq, where contiguous territory is the main focus of contention? In this kind of situation, deterrence is unlikely to prevent a general conventional war from occurring, and the question would be whether both sides could prevent the war from escalating to the nuclear level. It has been the stated American policy that in such a war in Europe, the U.S. would use nuclear weapons to prevent the Soviet Union from gaining an overwhelming advantage. Recent developments in Israeli nuclear doctrine suggest that the Israelis would use nuclear weapons in extreme circumstances. Such declarations indicate that while nuclear weapons may raise the provocation threshold, they do not make nuclear weapons either unthinkable or unusable in the right circumstances.

Some sense of what these circumstances might be can be ascertained by looking at the two instances in which the world has come closest to nuclear war. Significantly, it has been when one superpower has felt that the other illegitimately used territory contiguous to the frontiers of its "world" — Berlin and Cuba (Betts, 1987:98, 116-22). Just as two individual states who are neighbors will, over their history, often use violence to establish and maintain a border, so the leaders of the Cold War blocs have skirmished at the frontiers (see Blachman and Puchala: Chapter 8). This is not surprising. What is surprising is that Berlin and Cuba — comparatively tiny pieces of territory owned by neither state and which were important only for their symbolic value rather than their intrinsic worth — could actually bring the two states to the brink of war. If the U.S. would risk nuclear war for so little, what would Israel, Pakistan, or South Africa do for their survival? The Berlin and Cuban crises underline the ominous power of territorial disputes to bring about war, and the weakness of deterrence to prevent it.

The absence of a territorial dispute raises the question of what, exactly, has been at issue in the Cold War. Despite the ideological fervor of the Cold War, both sides have generally avoided challenging the real tangible stakes of the other. Wars are often associated with a feeling that, given the issues at stake and the intransigence of the other side, violence is the only way out (Holsti, 1972a:150-68; Barringer, 1972:105). Many wars are motivated by attempts to change the status quo and occur when at least one side can no longer accept the status quo, and believes that violence is the only way to bring about change. What is significant about the Cold War is that neither side has felt so choked and frustrated that it would rather risk losing a total war (conventional or nuclear) than go on with the status quo.

There have been two reasons for this. First, the status quo was not that bad for each side. The Soviet Union secured its eastern borders, and the United States has seen most of the world welcome its investment and accept capitalist arrangements for the world economy. Second, there have been ways to change the status quo without risking total war. Here Gaddis' (1987b:239-43) emphasis on rules is the most important part of his analysis. Informal rules that have served to regulate the relationship have emerged. These rules have been established tacitly, rather than formally, through diplomatic discussion. Probes and resistance in Berlin, Korea, Hungary, and elsewhere were important in defining for each side and its domestic constituents what could and could not be challenged without a fight.[13] Each side learned what was most important to the other and the limits of its own capabilities. More significant, there evolved ways of competing and even fighting whereby each side was prepared to accept the outcome on the basis of the rules of the particular game at hand. Each side was prepared to lose, rather than trying to win by switching (usually through escalation) to another game.

CREATING NEW GAMES

Of the various games the two states developed, limited war was the most important. Beginning with Korea, the precedent was established that if one state committed itself to full combat, then the other would not become involved in the combat with its own troops. This unspoken rule has prevented the territorial wars of the divided nations and revolutions of the poor from escalating to direct wars between the two major states. The informal rules have also limited wars by establishing boundaries of competition, confining the war to a specific geographical area and to conventional weapons.[14]

Limited war is only one game by which the United States and the USSR have learned to compete and interact with each other. Foreign aid, covert action, outside intervention, coercive diplomacy, arms control negotiation, and détente are others. Indeed the cold war itself (in the narrow sense of not talking, trading, or recognizing areas of the other as a way of expressing one's moral repugnance) is a kind of game. Games are important because they provide an arena for the conduct of politics, including the resolution of issues. If war is regarded as a way of making authoritative decisions in the absence of government, then informal games can be seen as attempts by major states to create a substitute (or functional equivalent) to war. Not all games work equally well, but if the status quo and the change being sought are not intolerable, they can go a long way toward preventing the conditions that spawn war.[15]

Evidence that agreement on rules of the game is associated with peace is provided by several studies. Peter Wallensteen (1984) shows that the periods between 1816-1976 that have no wars between major states and few militarized disputes are those in which the major states have followed policies that are consistent with certain rules of the game that have been established to guide behavior (what he calls "universalist policies"). When common rules have not been developed and major states follow "particularist policies" based on unilateral actions, wars break out and militarized disputes increase twofold (Wallensteen, 1984:246, especially Table 2).

In a set of articles that are more operationally precise, Kegley and Raymond (1982, 1984, 1986) find that peace is associated with periods in which alliance norms are considered binding and the unilateral abrogation of commitments and treaties illegitimate. The rules imposed by the global political culture in these periods result in fewer militarized disputes and wars between major states. In addition, the wars that occur are kept at lower levels of severity, magnitude, and duration, i.e., they are limited wars.

Finally, Väyrynen (1983) also finds war less frequent among major states when the system of "political management" of interstate relations restrains unilateral actions. When alliances and institutionalized norms are restraining, as in a system managed by a concert of states or institutionalized regional or global organizations, then wars among major states are less frequent. When the system is unrestrained, as in a balance-of-power system in which management is based solely on calculations of distribution of power, war is more frequent. Of the nine wars he examines, only two — the Crimean War and the Korean War — occur when the political management of the system has been restraining. All the others occur in unrestraining periods. Although Väyrynen's (1983:403) measurement of this variable is *post hoc* and his analysis is concerned primarily with the role of economic cycles, his political management variable implies that the ability of a political system to restrain allies and adversaries by setting up norms and rules to resolve disputes is an important factor in reducing the probability of war.

THE ROLE OF CRISIS DIPLOMACY

These analyses suggest that one of the keys to peace is to get major states to control their unilateral actions in favor of some set of rules that will allow them to contend over certain issues, while leaving other more highly salient (and less resolvable) issues off the political agenda. When major states have been unable or unwilling to institutionalize such rules, they have had to rely on their own unilateral actions, which in the modern global political system means they have relied on the practices of power politics to gain their ends — military buildups, alliance making, Machiavellian stratagems, the balancing of power, coercion, and so forth (Vasquez, 1983:216). Elsewhere (Vasquez, 1987; Vasquez, forthcoming), I have argued that power politics behavior is a series of steps to war, rather than a path to peace. It is significant that the Cold War began with unilateral actions and reached its most dangerous peak during the Khrushchev-Kennedy era when the power politics behavior of the two sides was at its height.

One of the reasons war did not occur over Berlin and Cuba was that the two sides found crisis diplomacy an inadequate game to resolve their disputes. Both sides have done fairly well in managing crises, each trying to prevent escalation, each giving the other enough room (contrast this with the feelings and behavior of major states in 1914; see Holsti, 1972b; see also McClelland, 1972). In more recent times, the Soviet Union and the United States have moved from concerns about crisis management to crisis prevention (George, 1988; Garthoff, 1987:107-8, 127; George, et al., 1983).

This is significant because many wars grow out of crises, and recent evidence has shown that it is exceedingly difficult to avoid war when there is a pattern of repeated crises. In a study of major states from 1816-1976, Peter Wallensteen (1981:74-75, 84) found that 75 percent (12 of 16) of the pairs of major states that had repeated confrontations also experienced war (see also Houweling and Siccama, 1981:147-87). Some of the reasons for this are delineated by Russell Leng (1983), who finds that among evenly matched states involved in at least three successive crises there is a definite learning pattern. The loser in the previous crisis, on the basis of realpolitik reasoning, attributes its loss to a failure to demonstrate resolve, and hence is more hostile in the second crisis. In addition, the loser is apt to initiate the second crisis. Consequently, both participants escalate the level of coercion as they move from one crisis to the next (a finding that held in 17 of his 24 cases), with war becoming increasingly likely by the third crisis, if it has not already occurred. This suggests that the use of realpolitik tactics in successive crises between equals encourages war. Such coercive strategies lead to war, because they are unable to resolve the underlying issue. What is significant about Soviet-American relations is that during crisis bargaining over Berlin and Cuba the escalatory spiral abated (McClelland, 1972; Holsti, North, and Brody, 1968; Holsti, Brody, and North, 1964). This paved the way for a *modus vivendi* that relied not on realpolitik tactics but on the traditional techniques of conflict resolution, thereby ending the deadly pattern of successive crises resulting in war (Leng, 1983). This was an important turning point, because it has long been recognized that at best deterrence could only buy time — it could not serve as a means of resolving the underlying issues of a rivalry (George and Smoke, 1974:508; Maoz, 1990: Chapter 3).

The ability of Soviet and American leaders to control escalation, both vertical (intensifying conflict by raising the force employed) and horizontal (enlarging the conflict by bringing in other issues or other areas of the world) has also been significant in avoiding nuclear war. Both Kennedy and Khrushchev were successful in avoiding horizontal escalation in the Cuban missile crisis. If Khrushchev had made a move on Berlin during the Cuban missile crisis, as Kennedy feared (Betts, 1987:115), then the probability of war, which was already high, would have increased dramatically.

Another factor associated with the escalation of a crisis to war that has not been discussed is the role of arms races. Arms races do not always result in war, but when they are associated with crises they often do. Michael Wallace (1982:46) has found that in 15 militarized disputes having arms races, 11 escalated to war, and only 4 did not; in contrast, among the 65 militarized disputes where there was no ongoing arms race, only 2 escalated to war.[16] This is important evidence that arms races are a crucial factor in the escalation of crises to war.

To the extent that deterrence has had beneficial consequences, it may be because the acceptance of mutual assured destruction has served as a basis for moderating arms races and institutionalizing arms control.

When both sides are content to accept mutual assured destruction, this reduces the threat each poses of a potential first strike. Without arms control, any arms race can become a race for a first strike. Arms control has provided a floor of stability that has made the nuclear arms race less threatening than some of the conventional arms races of the past. In addition, early arms control *talks* made it clear that both sides did share some mutual interests, namely the avoidance of nuclear war, even if they disagreed on most issues. Subsequent agreements and negotiations have shown that the U.S. and the Soviet Union can have a working relationship within a rivalry to achieve specific gains, like the elimination of fallout due to atmospheric nuclear testing.

CONCLUSION

Each of these factors — the absence of territorial disputes, tolerance of the status quo, the raising of the provocation threshold by the experience of the two world wars, the creation of rules of the game, crisis management, and arms control — have probably been very important in establishing the long peace. Although our knowledge is not sufficient to determine the precise role each plays, their roles should not be minimized in favor of an explanation relying on the success of nuclear deterrence. It is difficult to see how nuclear deterrence could have prevented nuclear war when: 1) the Soviet Union did not threaten nuclear war, 2) the U.S. was not deterred by Soviet Type I deterrence, and 3) the U.S. used deterrence primarily as a coercive strategy rather than as a means to prevent nuclear war.

Even if deterrence has had an effect, it has worked *with* these six other irenic factors, not against them. If one or more of these factors had not been working with deterrence, deterrence may not have "succeeded." Indeed, the experiences of Berlin and Cuba suggest how fragile deterrence can be if just one of these factors is put in jeopardy. Could it work if all these other factors were pushing toward war? Even if it could work once or twice, could it work time after time, ad infinitum? One failure in infinity, those are the odds.

That is the reality the myth must confront.

All of this suggests that humanity should not rely on nuclear deterrence as a way of avoiding nuclear war.[17] The strategy has always been highly risky, since it would take only one failure to end Western civilization. The fact of the matter is that the strategy may have provided no insurance at all. The lessons of the Cold War are that nuclear war can be prevented by removing those factors which produce a war-prone environment, namely — territorial disputes, successive crises, unilateral actions, and arms races. If these factors are present and a war-prone environment exists, then nuclear war can still be avoided by rules limiting war to conventional means, greater tolerance, crisis management, and arms control.

How and why the Soviet Union and the United States have avoided nuclear war are questions that must be addressed on the basis of the best historical and scientific evidence available, and not on a myth. The answers scholars and policymakers give to these questions will provide important precedents for other states and will constitute the lessons of the first nuclear rivalry.

A number of states that, in recent years, have moved or sought to move toward a nuclear capability — for example, Israel, India, Pakistan, Iraq — are involved in rivalries that lack one or more of the irenic factors present in the Soviet-American rivalry, especially the absence of territorial disputes. If the analysis presented in this chapter is at all correct, reliance by these states on nuclear deterrence as a way of avoiding nuclear war with their rivals could be disastrous.

ENDNOTES

My thanks to Marie T. Henehan, Jack Levy, Patrick Morgan, Bikash Roy, Frank Zagare, and the contributors to this volume for useful comments and suggestions. As in any scholarly exchange, valuable discussion does not usually come out of agreement, so I am solely responsible for the points made here.

1. See George and Smoke (1974:24, 32-33, 46-53) on the evolution of American leaders' thinking about the use of nuclear weapons to prevent the Soviet Union from launching an all-out war against the United States; for greater detail see Freedman (1981).

2. Of course, facts are neither as obvious nor as free of interpretation as the early advocates of science supposed. Nevertheless, a distinction can be made between the symbols and statements made to interpret the world (or construct a reality) and the evidence used to support the accuracy (or adequacy) of the interpretation. Strategic theorists themselves, being modernists, have had little difficulty in accepting standard scientific criteria of knowledge. Therefore, the application of such criteria of evaluation and appraisal in this chapter cannot be seen as the imposition of criteria that the discourse itself does not accept.

3. See Gaddis (1987b:132) for some documentary support for this position. On American perceptions of the nature of the Soviet threat, see Gaddis (1987b:25, 44, 62, 64, 114, 143, 145).

4. The same can be said of Soviet attempts to extend its nuclear umbrella over China. As Gáddis (1987b:145) points out, the first explicit Soviet threat to employ nuclear weapons against the U.S. occurred in the 1958 Taiwan Strait crisis when Khrushchev warned the U.S. that nuclear weapons could not be used against China without the Soviet Union responding with the same means. This reflects a response to perceived American bullying and not necessarily a serious threat to attack the United States.

5. Although beyond the scope of this essay, it should not be assumed that the effort to use deterrence to prevent Soviet domination of Western Europe has been successful, simply because that domination has not occurred. The success

of this use of deterrence, which Kahn (1960:138-44) called Type II deterrence and which today is called *extended deterrence*, is also open to question, because it is not clear that, other than in Berlin (Betts, 1987:11), the Soviet Union has had any serious foreign policy objectives in Western Europe for which it was willing to use extensive military force. It is one thing for Stalin and his successors to hope that the French or Italian Communist parties might come to power in the late forties or seventies through election; it is another to be willing to expend scarce resources and use troops to gain these ends. There is no explicit evidence that the Soviet Union has had such foreign policy objectives. Indeed, given the wartime recovery problems Stalin faced, such objectives seem far-fetched. Brodie (1966:71-72) and Kennan (1987:888-89), both of whom are cited in Mueller (1988b:60), have questioned the seriousness of the Soviet threat to Western Europe.

6. Indeed, the notion that the Cuban missile crisis is an example of successful coercion (George, Hall, and Simons, 1971) is also a myth. As more information about that crisis becomes available, it is clearer that the crisis was ended not so much through pure coercion, but by a bargain which involved concessions by both sides (Jervis, 1988:80; Blight, Nye, and Welch, 1987; Blight and Welch, 1990).

7. Although studies of conventional deterrence are often used to generalize about nuclear deterrence, I have tried to avoid this procedure. The very notion of conventional deterrence often involves reading into the past a popular contemporary policy and way of viewing the world that did not have much influence prior to 1946. It is unlikely that leaders in the prenuclear era thought in terms of "deterring," and thus one is in the position of imputing the ideas and perceptions of the present to the past. Analysis of "conventional deterrence" after 1946 involves a different and more subtle kind of distortion. Political scientists often use the concept of deterrence to describe the behavior of states the way diplomatic historians use the concepts of balance of power and power vacuums. In both instances, the utility of these concepts is assumed rather than examined critically. It may be that thinking of the world in terms of deterrence is such a fundamental misconception that it will lead to a failure to understand how and why states behave the way they do (Burton, 1982:50-56). It is unlikely that states or nonstate actors can be deterred for long periods from pursuing highly salient objectives. At any rate, it is unlikely that the logic of deterrence, which was developed to explain and elucidate how atomic weapons revolutionized traditional balance-of-power thinking, could work in a non-nuclear situation. If this is the case, one would expect that states that rely on conventional deterrence, as Israel appears to do at times, would experience policy failures.

8. One of the indicators that the Soviets do not think in terms of the logic of the deterrence doctrine is the absence of an equivalent Russian term. According to Geoffrey Jukes (cited in Betts, 1987:5), the Soviets, prior to the 1970s, used the term *ustrasheniye* (which is similar to the English meaning of intimidation) for Western deterrence directed at them.

9. See Vasquez (1983: Chapter 8); on national interest, see Wolfers (1952); on the balance of power, see Haas (1953); on states as unitary actors, see Allison and Halperin (1972).

10. One can get a sense of how high this threshold can be raised, especially when coupled with war-weariness, by looking at what Chamberlain, France, and the U.S. were willing to tolerate before getting involved in a war with Hitler.

11. In this sense, while Jervis (1988:83-84) is correct in arguing that nuclear weapons have qualitatively different effects which Mueller's (1988b) general argument about world war misses, Jervis and most analysts do not give sufficient credence to the role that the threat of conventional total war has played in moderating Soviet and Chinese behavior in the specific instances that were most apt to escalate to war (especially the Berlin and Taiwan Strait crises).

12. The first figure is based on my recalculation of Diehl's (1985) Table 1. Interestingly, the only noncontiguous dispute to escalate is one that began in 1940 between the U.S. and Japan.

13. Establishing rules tacitly rather than through formal negotiation is probably more effective and easier for three reasons. First, it permits each side to avoid taking positions on questions on which they disagree, thereby breaking a cycle whereby persistent disagreement provokes hostility. Second, and perhaps most important, tacit agreements allow leaders to avoid gaining the formal approval of bureaucratic and domestic factions that might oppose such rules or use that opposition for undercutting the leadership. Finally, tacit agreements are unwritten and hold only as long as they are in the mutual interest of each side. They therefore do not provoke the disagreements that written agreements, particularly those containing face-saving devices, do; nor can they easily be used by domestic critics as a way of criticizing a leader for dealing with the enemy or having been duped by the enemy.

14. For other interpretations of this rule see, in addition to Gaddis (1987b:239-40), George (1988:583-85) and Carnesale, Nye, and Allison (1985:238).

15. I present a fuller conceptualization of games and a discussion of how they relate to the Cold War in Mansbach and Vasquez (1981: Chapter 8).

16. Wallace drew this sample from a set of 99 serious disputes between major states from 1816 to 1965 (Wallace, 1979), as a response to critics who argued for the need to eliminate multiple cases that resulted in a simultaneous entry into the same war (see Weede, 1980; Diehl, 1983; see also Houweling and Siccama, 1981).

17. For other analyses that question the role of nuclear deterrence in preventing an American-Soviet nuclear war, see Organski and Kugler (1980), Modelski and Morgan (1985), and Kugler and Zagare (forthcoming). Their respective rationales, however, are based on an explanation of war which differs from the one I employ.

CHAPTER TEN

Do Preparations for War Increase or Decrease International Security?

Robert C. Johansen

Perhaps no idea has been voiced more consistently by students of war and peace throughout the ages than the maxim: "If you want peace, prepare for war."[1] A familiar, current formulation of this idea is that the best way to prevent war is to be ready to win it.[2] Yet this widely held belief has little scientific foundation.[3]

The purpose of this chapter is to explore some empirical and logical grounds for questioning the utility of preparations for war, despite widespread faith in their necessity. This exploration focuses on three themes. First, the claim that U.S. preparations for war have kept the peace is based on an assumption that the United States and Soviet Union would have fought a major war in the absence of such preparations.[4] Yet the historical evidence does not support the notion that either of the two superpowers intended deliberate, large-scale military aggression.[5] Thus, one cannot demonstrate that high levels of U.S. (or Soviet) military preparedness prevented it.

Second, although many people believe that preparations for war — especially nuclear war — increase U.S. security by exerting a generally pacifying, stabilizing effect in international relations,[6] it is difficult to find sustained positive consequences flowing from continuous military preparations.[7] To be sure, policymakers feel their own preparations, unlike those of their rivals, discourage would-be aggressors. But these calculations seem heavily weighted toward short-term considerations. They also are insensitive to the overall impact of preparations for war on arms control, on the international code of conduct more broadly, and on the evolving, global political culture.

Third, despite many uncertainties in discerning the specific relationship between preparations for war and the likelihood of war, a plausible case can be made that chronic military buildups decrease international security because they underpin and legitimize an obsolescent, war-prone international system.

THE IMPACT OF PREPARATIONS FOR WAR ON THE U.S.-SOVIET PEACE

Our perceptions of two profound historical experiences have reinforced the belief that U.S. preparations for war produce peace. First, many national security experts believe that the military weakness of the countries opposed to Adolf Hitler's aggressive policies and the willingness of other governments to appease Hitler at the Munich meetings in 1938 contributed to the coming of World War II. Second, many observers believe that the high level of U.S. military preparedness, in particular the strategy of nuclear deterrence, has contributed mightily to U.S.-Soviet peace since World War II.

These beliefs, although deeply held, rest on a narrow view of diplomatic possibilities, murky evidence, and a disinclination to search for alternative explanations of how peace might have been achieved in both instances. With regard to the Munich analogy, there can be no assurance that additional military preparations against Hitler's fanaticism would have produced a more durable peace than would have a quite different set of cooperative international economic and diplomatic policies in the interwar period. The latter might well have prevented Hitler's rise to power in the first place, or at least might have limited his subsequent ability to bring the German people along on his destructive journey. Hitler's political success, after all, grew out of an extreme preparation-for-war mentality.

One can easily conclude that marshalling more troops against Hitler in the1930s would have deterred him a bit longer. But one cannot safely conclude that more intense preparations for war in the 1920s and 1930s would have been the most powerful means to avert World War II. More intense preparations to ensure peace through peaceful means during the same period might have prevented the Second World War altogether.

In considering the role of nuclear weapons, John Vasquez has shown in the preceding pages that there is no logical or empirical foundation for the belief that nuclear deterrence has prevented nuclear war. His analysis, as well as recent work of others,[8] shows, in effect, that the central element of U.S. preparations for war throughout four decades, nuclear deterrence, may have had little to do with nullifying the main perceived threat to U.S. security.

To be sure, many other security consequences flow from the nuclear arsenal. It is possible that the nuclear deterrent and the fear of escalation from conventional to nuclear conflict have inhibited the two superpowers from engaging in conventional war. In addition, the non-nuclear preparations for war, which consume roughly four-fifths of the military budget, are themselves a powerful factor in both leaderships' calculations about whether to make war.

Yet one cannot make a compelling case for the idea that U.S. preparations for war have produced U.S.-Soviet peace unless one can show strong evidence that war between them would have been almost certain in the absence of those preparations, or that war was a natural outcome of post-1945 international politics. But the evidence is inconclusive. On the one hand, some historians, such as John Gaddis (1987b:217, 231), believe that the period of peace between the United States and the Soviet Union is historically extraordinary. "How," he asks, "does one explain why the great [military] conflict between the United States and the Soviet Union, which by all past standards of historical experience should have developed by now, has not in fact done so?" After considerable analysis, he concludes that, amidst many factors, nuclear weapons have played the most important role in averting a third world war: "It seems inescapable that what has really made the difference in inducing this unaccustomed caution [about world war] has been the workings of the nuclear deterrent."

Yet, is a long peace between Moscow and Washington something which "by all past standards of historical experience" could not be expected to occur? These two countries have lived in peace not only in the age of nuclear deterrence, but throughout all of history. They have never fought each other, with one exception which occurred during the Russian civil war as the Bolsheviks were consolidating their revolution at the end of World War I. Although Moscow and Washington have had severe conflicts over political and economic ideology and organization, the two societies are not natural enemies in the traditional sense. They have no common border conflicts, no irredentist ethnic minorities, no severe disputes over natural resources, no crusading religious or racial antagonisms. Moreover, they are geographically distant, except in the Bering Strait.

The available evidence shows no determined Soviet intention to attack Western Europe or the United States at any time since 1945.[9] The eminent historian George Kennan (1987:888-89), for example, has written that the Soviet leaders never saw it in their interests to overrun Western Europe militarily. Moreover, he has "never believed that . . . they would have launched an attack on that region generally even if the so-called nuclear deterrent had not existed". Mueller's recent work (1989) draws the same conclusion.

The disputes that Washington has had with Moscow can be reduced to two: the Soviet government's treatment of its own citizens internally, and its projection of power abroad. The first of these, however cruel, is hardly a sufficient cause for launching a war that, even without nuclear combat, would be extremely costly.[10] The second grievance has not produced war because the Soviet Union's capability to extend its power directly beyond its sphere of influence in Eastern Europe was either relatively limited in the early years or its motivation to expand seemed modest later on.

To the extent that Soviet efforts to bully West Europeans did occur, they were more pronounced soon after World War II, when the United

States wielded an overwhelming nuclear superiority, than they were later on when Moscow was militarily stronger and U.S. threats to retaliate against Soviet misdeeds were less plausible. Soviet intimidation, to the extent that it did exist in events like the Berlin crisis and the construction of the Berlin Wall, was apparently dampened more by changes in Soviet leadership, by a deeper sense of Soviet security, and by the development of friendlier economic and political relations between Eastern and Western Europe, than by overwhelming U.S. military power.

To be sure, the U.S. nuclear and conventional capability may have diminished any Soviet appetite for expansion. Similarly, the Soviet nuclear arsenal may have added to the United States' reluctance to roll back communism during the Hungarian uprising in 1956. Yet to acknowledge such influences on decision making does not establish that preparations for war were the only or even the most effective means of war prevention.[11] Nor does it confirm that the precise nature and continuation of the U.S.-Soviet military buildup played a central role in war avoidance. There is ample evidence that international security was not enhanced by U.S. decisions to move far beyond a minimum nuclear deterrent or to develop a forward-based, deep-strike conventional arsenal and strategic doctrine (Boston Study Group, 1982; Johansen, 1980:38-125; 1983).

Even Moscow's efforts to stock Soviet arsenals with far more weapons than necessary for what is now called "reasonable sufficiency" does not show that the Soviet Union was actually preparing for a surprise attack on the West. Instead, the excess deployments seem to be an almost habitual accumulation of weapons, prompted by the simple idea that more military power is better than less, and that peace can best be maintained through preparations for war. Insofar as the U.S. arms buildup reinforced a belief in the utility of preparations for war, it discouraged Soviet leaders from abandoning their military habit. If no Soviet attacks on the West were in fact likely, then the expensive, habit-creating U.S. preparations for war may have added more to U.S. and European insecurity than to their security.[12]

Beyond the particularities of U.S.-Soviet relations, empirical studies of relations between empires (see Chapter 8 by Blachman and Puchala in this volume) and by long-cycle theorists (see, for example, Modelski and Morgan, 1985) cast doubt on the conventional wisdom that the long peace since 1945 is an exceptional event or that it demonstrates the utility of preparations for war in achieving long-term war prevention. Long-cycle studies suggest that the nearly five decades of U.S.-Soviet peace since World War II may be only a temporarily peaceful segment of a much longer cycle, of a century or more in length, that will include another world war if the cycle is not interrupted.[13]

A typical long cycle in international relations may be understood as a period of dominance by one great power — the United States in the present period — and by efforts of rivals to undermine its hegemony. The major challenge to the global leader and the transfer of power from one leader to another does not usually occur within a period as short as has existed since 1945, but has often been as long as a century.[14] When seen from this perspective, intense systemic violence is not equally likely at any time. It results periodically from a serious attempt to displace the dominant power.

The last such change of leadership occurred when Germany challenged Britain's nineteenth- and early-twentieth-century dominance of the international system. This challenge led to both world wars. Within the perspective of a long cycle of many decades, these wars may be seen as two segments of a single global upheaval from which the United States emerged as the new dominant power. According to this view, the international stability that the global system has experienced since 1945 is not an aberrant historical event but the normal peaceful phase that usually follows a period of global war and major readjustment.

After a new state rises to a hegemonic position, international relations among major powers are, for several reasons, relatively stable. The new dominant power is somewhat magnanimous (e.g., U.S. reconstruction of Japan and Germany, the Marshall Plan). That power consolidates a new world order that other governments like or are forced to accept (e.g., establishment of the United Nations and Bretton Wood institutions, forced demilitarization of Japan and Germany). Its potential challengers are either exhausted from the last war or not yet strong enough to threaten the leading power (e.g., Soviet economic weakness and the unreliability of Warsaw Pact allies, the Japanese tendency to eschew military strength, German dismemberment). The strains of world military leadership have not yet begun to exhaust the economic means, imagination, and psychological energies of the dominant power. Such strains appeared to be growing in the 1970s and 1980s when, despite great military strength, the relative power position of Washington slipped and the United States suddenly fell from being the largest creditor to being the largest debtor nation in the world.

For our purposes here, it is not important that one agrees with the details of long-cycle thinking in international relations. It is sufficient to acknowledge that long-term changes in world leadership do indeed occur, that they are punctuated with large-scale wars, that long periods of peace at first accompany the order established by the new world leader, and that major challenges to the world's leading power often do not occur in spans as short as the period from 1945 to the present. Such an acknowledgment would suggest that U.S. preparations for war since 1945 have played a much smaller role in maintaining superpower peace than is commonly assumed. Avoidance of global war would have occurred anyway, given reasonably good diplomacy.[15]

Plausibly, the stability of the international system, following the 1914-1945 upheaval, has made nuclear deterrence safe; nuclear weapons have not made the international system safe. The preparations for war have not brought the peace; peace has made the military buildup tolerable. But as the world moves into a less stable phase, war prevention will prove more difficult. Assuming that past fluctuations of the balance of power are not interrupted, global shifts in power, wealth, dynamism, and dissatisfaction will increase the difficulties attending war prevention despite a vast array of U.S. weapons. Indeed, Paul Kennedy (1987) provides historical evidence that the effort to accumulate more and more weapons saps the economic strength of the leading great power until it eventually falls. The United States' current decline as a world economic and political leader, at a time when it has poured unprecedented resources into preparations for war, lends plausibility to Kennedy's conclusion. Prior to Kennedy's account, Robert Gilpin (1981:232) observed that a "disequilibrium" has developed "between the existing governance of the international system and the underlying distribution of power in the system." The United States remains the dominant state in the system, yet it no longer has "the power to 'govern' the system as it did in the past."

The preceding analysis suggests that a continual preoccupation with large-scale preparations for war, from this point on, will not add to U.S. security; instead, such an overemphasis on military power will assure a more rapid and certain U.S. demise. This is especially likely when such preparations are accompanied by a disregard for multilateral diplomacy, international law, and the UN system such as characterized the policies of the Reagan and early Bush administrations. In contrast, multilateral norms and procedures can serve as system stabilizers and ease worldwide geo-political and economic adjustments during this era of transition.

THE IMPACT OF PREPARATIONS FOR WAR ON U.S. SECURITY POLICY

The preceding paragraphs suggest that there has been a tendency to overestimate both the likelihood of Soviet attack and the pacifying effect of nuclear weapons and of U.S. preparations for war as explanations for why Moscow did not interrupt the peace. Preparations for war may receive too much credit for keeping the peace; the utility of "nonpreparation for war" may receive too little. The obvious tendency is for people in one country to feel that their military preparedness leads to peace and arms reductions, while an adversary's preparations engender war. From a national perspective one's own preparations for war easily appear to have a positive utility that, from a global perspective, they appear to lack.

Nationally biased decisions made amidst chronic preparations for war often have little to do with careful calculations about the conditions under which the entire symbiotic process of accumulating military power may undermine rather than guarantee peace. For example, U.S. officials chose to deploy multiple independently targetable reentry vehicles (MIRVs) at a time when the Soviet Union had none but would have entertained proposals to ban them completely. U.S. officials rationalized their deployments at the time with arguments that these preparations for war would help prevent war (Johansen, 1980:44-105). After it was too late, mainstream U.S. security analysts acknowledged that the deployment of MIRVs had made deterrence less stable and the United States less secure.[16]

Although chronic military buildups are understandable from the standpoint of preparing for battle, they are hardly sensible from the standpoint of preparing for peace because each increase in U.S. military capability is usually only the prelude to an increase in counterthreats to U.S. security. From a global perspective, almost all preparations for war make someone nervous. One exception is preparedness that is strictly defensive (Fischer, 1984), such as practiced by the Swiss Confederation. But the preparations of most nations increase tensions, stimulate counter-armaments, facilitate the use of force, and waste resources needed to alleviate conditions that give rise to violence. Empirical studies of war fail to confirm the ancient maxim counseling those who want peace to prepare for war. On the contrary, competitive arms buildups by states in conflict lead more frequently to war than to peace (Wallace, 1982).

Intense military preparations are more ominous than modest ones.[17] Yet, seemingly modest preparations for war, even in democratic societies governed by intelligent leaders, may make war more likely. The fascination of U.S. officials with counter-insurgency warfare early in the Kennedy administration, for example, encouraged the United States to become embroiled in war in Southeast Asia. Without the preparations for counter-insurgency warfare and a previously developed naval and air capability designed to project military power thousands of miles from home, the United States would have avoided the Indochinese chapter in its military history, and without any apparent harm to its security.

The most recent manifestation of an uncritical acceptance of military preparations is the belief that the Reagan administration's vast military expenditures and its attitude toward arms control have exerted a positive influence on world peace and U.S. security.[18] The chairman of the Joint Chiefs of Staff, Admiral William J. Crowe (1989), for example, argues that the increase in U.S. global military strength during the Reagan years "is paying high dividends." The dividends he attributes to the U.S. arms buildup include Soviet interest in arms reduction, Moscow's withdrawal of Soviet forces from Afghanistan, and the willingness of Vietnam and Angola to make political compromises. The U.S. policy of " 'peace through strength' has been instrumental in producing these developments and will most likely play a critical role in shaping future Soviet actions. It would make no sense to abandon this policy, just as it is beginning to bear fruit." This view overlooks the economic and political conditions in Soviet society that no doubt did far more than U.S. military power to bring new Soviet thinking.

Gaddis has also applied some of his carefully reasoned arguments from *The Long Peace* to recent changes in Soviet policies. In an article entitled "Hanging Tough Paid Off," Gaddis (1989:11) notes that "Ronald Reagan has presided over the most dramatic improvement in U.S.-Soviet relations — and the most solid progress in arms control — since the Cold War began." He attributes this success to the toughness of the Reagan administration's policies.

But the judgment that Reagan's toughness led to arms control success can be considered compelling only if we forget where the arms control agenda stood when Reagan took office, only if we forget how his policies moved the center of judgment over arms control toward a highly militarized, unilateralist foreign policy, and only if we forget how Reagan's positions deliberately blocked many arms control possibilities. The Reagan administration sabotaged negotiations already far advanced, refused to ratify treaties already signed, and then from the rubble that remained finally agreed to a treaty banning intermediate-range nuclear arms.

For example, one set of negotiations that Reagan derailed was that leading toward a comprehensive nuclear test ban. By the time Reagan took office, the United States, Great Britain, and the Soviet Union had agreed on all of the most important points for a test ban, including the possibility of on-site inspection (Goldblat and Cox, 1988:14-15). But the Reagan administration suspended negotiations, reversed the policies of all previous presidents since Eisenhower, and flatly rejected an opportunity to achieve a total ban on nuclear weapons tests, regardless of its verifiability.[19]

Moscow continued to call for a ban. To communicate its seriousness, for a year and a half the Soviet government unilaterally stopped its nuclear testing, and repeatedly invited the United States to reciprocate. Because of official U.S. opposition to Soviet overtures for strengthening verification of testing prohibitions, Moscow also invited private U.S. scientists to the Soviet Union to calibrate seismographic equipment.

It is easy for proponents of preparations for war to forget that to reject a test ban was not an inconsequential matter. Most independent weapons experts agree that under a test ban "further nuclear weapon development would be rendered largely impossible" (Goldblat and Cox, 1988:37). Among other benefits, the race for qualitative improvement of nuclear weapons would have been dampened. Because of the danger of unpredictable breakthroughs, this race constitutes one of the most destabilizing aspects of the present military competition. Even an INF agreement to eliminate approximately 3 percent of the U.S.-Soviet nuclear arsenal could not equal the benefits that would have accrued from a comprehensive test ban that a more positive Reagan stance easily could have achieved.

The Reagan administration also could have achieved approximately a 50 percent reduction in strategic nuclear weapons if it simply had been willing to affirm that it would not violate the Anti-Ballistic Missile (ABM) treaty, which Washington had previously signed and ratified. But the Reagan administration refused, because the treaty stood in the way of developing space weapons for the Strategic Defense Initiative (SDI). Seen in this light, it seems surrealistic to view SDI "as the successful bargaining chip it turned out to be" (Gaddis, 1989:13).

Many observers have noted that Reagan's arms policies, especially testing components for SDI, would perniciously terminate the ABM treaty or gut it by reinterpreting its major provisions. Because abandoning a limit on defensive antimissile forces would stimulate a new offensive missile buildup, the Reagan efforts, if not stopped, would have unraveled the entire structure of arms control. The Reagan administration's announced testing policies meant that, in the words of Ambassador Gerard Smith, former director of the Arms Control and Disarmament Agency, "We are already in an anticipatory breach of contract" (Smith, 1984). Senator Sam Nunn noted that support did not exist in either the House or the Senate "for the United States to breach the ABM Treaty" (Nunn, 1988). After conducting a detailed study, the Senate Committee on Foreign Relations concluded that "the Reagan administration's 'reinterpretation' of the ABM Treaty constitutes the most flagrant abuse of the Constitution's treaty power in 200 years of American history" (U.S. Senate Committee on Foreign Relations, 1987:66).

The Reagan administration also refused to ratify the SALT II treaty on strategic nuclear arms that had been negotiated before Reagan took office. U.S. officials deliberately decided to violate those treaty limits as a way of terminating the moral obligation to live within them. Yet there was no militarily significant reason to do so (Warnke, Smith, McNamara, and Keeny, 1986). The Reagan administration also rejected proposals to prohibit weapons from space and to ban submarine-launched cruise missiles. It insisted on testing antisatellite weapons with technology which could well be considered a further encroachment on the prohibitions of the ABM treaty.

Reagan's preparation for war undermined U.S. security sufficiently that Congress, for the first time in history, formally and repeatedly constrained the U.S. president from spending appropriated funds in a manner inconsistent with international obligations. Congress required that the administration not test space weapons in violation of the ABM treaty; that it not reinterpret the ABM treaty so as to destroy its central provision banning ABM systems; that it not move farther outside the SALT II ceilings even after it deliberately did exceed them; and that it not spend nearly as much on Star Wars weapons as it wanted.

One of the more surprising developments of this period was Gorbachev's persistence in seeking arms control despite Reagan's obstructions of word and deed. But this does not mean that the true source of Soviet initiatives sprang from Washington's anti-Soviet rhetoric and policies. On the contrary, Gorbachev's own priorities, coupled with

Congressionally imposed constraints on the Reagan administration's military buildup, kept diplomatic prospects alive despite the administration's policy of "hanging tough."

Private conversations with Soviet officials indicate that the Reagan posture impeded arms control and that Reagan's hurdles would have been too high for any Soviet leader who lacked Gorbachev's boldness.[20] His unusual willingness to compromise probably yielded more success in arms control than Reagan's policies otherwise would have,[21] or than occurred during earlier periods of U.S. toughness. Almost certainly, more far-reaching arms control could have occurred without the anti-Soviet toughness than did occur with it.

Seasoned arms control experts, including Gerard Smith and Paul Warnke, who respectively negotiated the ABM and SALT II agreements, believe that the Reagan administration's arms policies were recklessly designed in ways that, whether intentional or not, dangerously stimulated the arms race and in fact closed off important opportunities for arms control (Warnke, Smith, McNamara, and Keeny, 1986). This view was shared by six former secretaries of defense, three Republican and three Democratic, who together publicly opposed the Reagan effort to dismantle the centerpiece of the current arms control regime, the ABM treaty.[22]

Finally, to the extent that the administration did achieve arms control successes — and indeed the INF agreement is a positive achievement — these were probably due less to "hanging tough" than to the Reagan administration's willingness to move away from such policies after a lackluster foreign policy record and a tarnished image, caused by the Iran-Contra scandal, began to make the First Family worry about the president's place in history. Only when Reagan and his advisers began to be less confrontational did the prospect of an agreement move into view. So even if the Reagan administration is judged to have achieved a great success, it is simplistic, if not inaccurate, to attribute the success to "hanging tough."

Chronic preparations for war produce expectations that high levels of military preparedness constitute an acceptable, even a desirable, norm. Such expectations lead officials to misperceive and underrate the utility of less militaristic diplomatic options. "Selective inattention"[23] to inconvenient evidence causes observers to overlook evidence which calls into question the arms control utility of the tough Reagan approach. The partial historical record that remains may appear, erroneously, to demonstrate that a tough stance, rather than other factors, "did lead to negotiations" and "did eventually pay off" in arms control (Gaddis, 1989:14).

When scholars and officials accept preparations for war uncritically, this collective acceptance inadvertently shapes intellectual and diplomatic agendas. For example, it may be historically less surprising, intellectually less innovative, and diplomatically less useful to note that the

United States and the Soviet Union have lived in peace since 1945 than to note that France and Germany have behaved peacefully toward each other since 1945, after many decades of war and preparations for war against each other. The U.S.-Soviet peace has been riddled with tensions and threats; there is nothing systemically new in it. On the other hand, the peace between France and Germany, unlike the more widely acclaimed U.S.-Soviet peace, no longer contains any expectation of war between them.

Aspects of the German-French metamorphosis, and the ability of the Nordic countries[24] to take war completely off their political agendas with each other, are relevant to domesticating East-West and U.S.-Soviet relations.[25] But to examine these demilitarizing successes draws one away from what is widely considered to be more important, more "realistic" study that usually justifies the open-ended preparations for war which we have become accustomed to believe are essential for security.

PREPARATIONS FOR WAR AND THE EVOLUTION OF THE INTERNATIONAL SYSTEM

Two mutually reinforcing beliefs — an exaggerated sense of the likelihood of Soviet attack, and an overemphasis on the importance of U.S. armaments in keeping the peace and in achieving arms control — lead in turn to an underestimation of the real dangers of war that are inherent in the balance-of-power system over the long run. This view of national security underemphasizes war-prone conditions that are outside of a single government's control. It expresses overconfidence about the ability of U.S. officials to maintain peace through military buildups, because the main security problem is incorrectly perceived to be the Soviet Union (or another adversary) rather than the unreliable system of international relations itself — a system whose instabilities are exacerbated by preparations for war.

The balance of military power as a world security system never has and presumably never will be completely successful in eliminating major war, regardless of how large the U.S. arsenal may be. Yet because global war, even once a century, is no longer tolerable, neither is the current balance-of-power system. As Inis Claude noted nearly three decades ago, "the suitability of the world for the operation of the balance-of-power system has been steadily diminishing for well over a century." He concluded that "all the most fundamental tendencies affecting the political realm in recent generations run counter to the requirements of a workable system of balance of power" (Claude, 1962:92).[26]

Modern technology at work within this system renders the possibility of massive destruction easy, swift, and impossible to defend against. As a result, today's security problems are more systemic than adversarial: Washington can destroy any adversary but cannot stabilize or pacify the system. System-wide constraints on violence and inducements to non-violence are necessary to have an effective defense against the threat of attack, whether from people armed with a nuclear arsenal or a suitcase bomb.

As a result, U.S. military preparations aimed at the traditional mode of defense against adversaries do not meet the need to change the global security system. On the contrary, the systemic consequences of these old-fashioned, chronic military preparations are likely to impede the pacification of the international system, even if they do not inflame bilateral security relations with an adversary.

If we seek to enhance U.S. security, our acknowledged inability to discern the precise relationship between preparations for war and the likelihood of war between two actors or alliances should be given less weight than our ability to see clearly that military competition in the highly decentralized balance-of-power system needs to be curtailed and the system modified. Without transformation, this competition and the existing system together are a permissive cause of war, if not always a sufficient one (Independent Commission on Disarmament and Security Issues, 1982:3-9).

Despite ambiguity about the impact of preparations for war on discrete conflicts (see Kegley and Raymond in this volume; Huth and Russett, 1984; Wallace, 1982; Levy, 1981; Singer and Small, 1968; Small and Singer, 1979; Wright, 1965), negative systemic consequences seem clear (Independent Commission on Disarmament and Security Issues, 1982). Preparations for war have continued to legitimize a militarized code of international conduct and to ensure a prominent role for military power in international relations while eroding normative constraints on the use of force. They exacerbate adversarial relations and stimulate counter-military preparations. They build economic-technological-scientific-bureaucratic vested interests pressing for expanded arsenals, often with noxious side effects for democratic processes. And they habituate dependence on military instruments while inhibiting the growth of nonmilitary means for conflict management throughout the international system. Economically, they divert resources from human needs, which if unmet often exacerbate conflict and perpetuate higher rates of population growth. Environmentally, they threaten the collapse of life support systems. Each of these three areas deserves brief elaboration.

Security Costs

Throughout this century, and especially since World War II, military competition, stimulated by chronically high levels of military preparedness in the United States and Soviet Union, have militarized international political relations in virtually every corner of the globe. Since 1945 the world has devoted far more productive skills and energies to military purposes than before either the First or Second World War. The real value of resources poured into armaments has, on the average, been more than 10 times larger in the 1980s than from 1925 to 1938. World military expenditures have risen steadily for nearly three decades with the current amount, in constant dollars, 2.5 times the level of 1960 (Sivard, 1987:6, 8). In 1913, after several years of a competitive arms race among the great powers, the world spent 3 to 3.5 percent of output on military uses. In the early 1930s, the percentage was approximately the same. But the average from 1950 to 1970 was 7 to 8 percent, more than twice the 1913 figure. It now remains about 6 percent of gross world product, an amount greater than the total income of the poorest half of the world's people.[27]

Since the early 1980s, real world military spending has grown an average of 3 percent per year, up from an average growth rate of 2 percent from 1975 to 1980 (Tullberg, 1986b:229). Although developing countries now spend about 18 percent of total world military expenditures, compared to 6 percent as recently as 1965, NATO and Warsaw Pact countries together spend roughly 75 percent of the world total (Tullberg, 1986b:231).

The threatening potential of the large standing military forces sustained by the $16 trillion in expenditures since 1960[28] is expanded by the bureaucratic, industrial, and research infrastructures devoted to the procurement, design, and production of weapons. The secretary of defense and his functional equivalent in every land actively pursue ways to justify their militaries' demands for increased resources by calling attention to, if not exaggerating, external military threats. The military sector also has a great advantage over the civilian sector of the global economy because it claims a near monopoly on information that serves as the basis on which the threat can be assessed.

Often the pace of militarization bears little connection to actual security threats. Preparations for war are self-propelled: As soon as the United States developed cruise missiles, for example, officials assumed that a defense would be attempted against them, so work began immediately on an advanced cruise missile that would be able to penetrate defenses that have yet to be developed, let alone deployed (Blackaby, 1986:219).

According to Frank Blackaby, former director of the Stockholm International Peace Research Institute, today's worldwide concentration of resources and energies on military purposes in peacetime "increases the risk of the use of force in international relations." The mere presence of large military establishments puts military options on the policymaking table that otherwise could not be there. In addition, "the development of new weapon systems is almost always destabilizing" (Blackaby, 1986:217). Because military innovations rarely occur at precisely the same moment or with symmetrical consequences between adversaries (Kennedy, 1987:xv), they produce fear which is a precursor to diplomatic tensions and war. Indeed, "it is difficult to think of any significant number of weapon developments in history which can be regarded in any sense as stabilizing in the long run" (Blackaby, 1986:218). Such a judgment deserves at least as much weight as the idea that the development of new bargaining chips, to be used in arms control negotiations, has paid off.

Chronic preparation for war also has a corrosive effect on basic values like openness and honesty in government, human decency, and reciprocity in international relations. Arms competition stimulates some kinds of intelligence activity in peacetime that would otherwise only be undertaken if war occurred. Intelligence services thus already feel at war and conduct activities that deepen suspicion and distrust. The use of espionage to discover military secrets of the other side reinforces the idea that one's rival is an inevitable adversary in war. Further, because the activities are covert, the officials engaged in them often do not believe they need to honor domestic law or international norms in this domain. Preparations for war thus erode respect for democratic government at home and become a powerful source of distrust abroad.

The militarization of world society is the most pervasive consequence of unrelenting preparation for war. Certainly in U.S.-Soviet relations military competition has dominated diplomacy for 40 years and taken attention away from initiatives to demilitarize international life. For Washington officials, the two central drives have been to avoid appearing militarily inferior to Moscow and to demonstrate resolve or willingness to use the U.S. armed forces at any time. Even after the reduction of any Soviet threat because of Mikhail Gorbachev's impressive initiatives in arms control and the successful anti-autocracy movements that swept Warsaw Pact nations in 1989, U.S. military expenditures have remained relatively high. This indicates the extent to which military spending is not closely related to a rational appraisal of security needs and benefits. Former Secretary of Defense Robert S. McNamara and Lawrence J. Korb, assistant secretary of defense in the Reagan administration, for example, testified before the Senate Budget Committee that the $300 billion annual Pentagon budget could be safely cut by 50 percent over the next decade (Rosenbaum, 1989:1).

While the U.S. and Soviet governments have been busily attempting to enhance their security through military preparedness, they have acquiesced in the spread of dangerous technology around the world. Israel, India, South Africa, and Pakistan have now apparently joined the ranks of the nuclear powers. Israel may even have developed H-bomb capabilities and integrated nuclear weapons into its military planning (Spector, 1988:3). Argentina and Brazil have secretly pursued a nuclear weapons capability, and Iran, Libya, Taiwan, and South Korea have taken steps to acquire technology useful for producing nuclear weapons, although the latter have not advanced far toward this goal.

Even though the spread of nuclear weapons capabilities could vastly increase the human costs of future conflicts in some of the planet's most volatile regions, it has occurred with "surprisingly few diplomatic costs" (Spector, 1988:4) to those acquiring nuclear capability. The U.S. and Soviet preoccupation with their own military preparedness leads them to treat proliferating countries as strategically important. As a result, the superpowers have refrained from imposing tough nonproliferation measures on potential nuclear powers for fear of injuring underlying relations. With the exception of South Africa, which is isolated because of its racial — not its nuclear — policies, all the new nuclear-weapons countries continue to receive substantial economic and military aid from their allies (Spector, 1988:4). Moreover, the superpowers have set a dangerous precedent in treating nuclear weapons as key symbols of power and prestige, to which other rising powers are likely to aspire. Washington and Moscow have failed to remove political incentives for others to acquire the bomb.

In addition to nuclear proliferation, the technology for producing aircraft and missiles has been spreading ominously. The world's six most advanced newcomers to nuclear weapons technology — Israel, India, Pakistan, South Africa, Brazil, and Argentina — possess advanced aircraft and are in the process of developing a missile delivery capability, if they do not already have it. Israel has proven missile technology. Recently India successfully tested an intermediate-range ballistic missile with a range of 2,500 kilometers. China has sold a number of its missiles, with a range of 2,200 kilometers, to Saudi Arabia. More than 20 Third World countries currently possess ballistic missiles or are making serious efforts to develop them (Karp, 1988).

The potential dangers to global security from the further spread of these military technologies are profound (Spector, 1988:34). Their spread to regionally hegemonic countries exacerbates the problem of uneven growth of power among states, which some theorists long ago concluded is the most fundamental problem of international relations in the contemporary world (Gilpin, 1981:230). The fear that Israel could target Baghdad with missiles, for example, may have contributed to Iraq's decision to modify its Scud-B missiles to extend their range to over 500 miles. The prospect of stopping the further spread of technology capable of delivering conventional explosives, chemical weapons, or nuclear warheads is dim indeed unless serious steps are taken to achieve a universal ban on testing ballistic missiles. Yet such a ban cannot occur, nor can the spread of other advanced military technology be halted, as long as the superpowers insist on their own preparations for war.

The heavy emphasis on military preparedness, which of course embraces weapons of mass destruction, also has stunted the growth of an international code of conduct that could gradually reduce the role of military power in international relations. This emphasis keeps military force at the top of options on diplomatic agendas and at the forefront of decision makers' minds. It scorns the importance of World Court decisions and erodes respect for legal settlement, while making efforts to move disputes from the battlefield to the courtroom or to the negotiating table appear soft-headed. It denigrates nuclear-free zones and the policies of allies like New Zealand who seek security through non-nuclear alignment. It adds pressure to deploy threatening weapons in new environments such as space and the territories of the least militarized countries on earth. It contributes to disrespect for norms aiming to delegitimize bombing of cities, to protect noncombatants, and to ban poison gas and other weapons of mass destruction. It undermines hard-headed efforts to broaden and deepen the application of Nuremberg principles designed to constrain political leaders against the aggressive use of force and to hold nations responsible for their destructive conduct.

Economic Costs

Studies of the rise and fall of great powers demonstrate that substantial military preparations usually end in war or economic exhaustion (Kupchan, 1989; Kennedy, 1987; Kaldor, 1981; Wright, 1965:71-72, 166-68, 396, 428-29). U.S. and Soviet economic growth has slowed and their shares of global production and wealth have shrunk dramatically while they have been busily arming. True security may elude these military giants because economic power is essential to maintaining a leadership position over time, and they have, by their own military decisions, been sapping their economic and industrial strength.

The redistribution of power away from a bipolar world to a multipolar system is well under way. Japan, which was forced to give up preparations for war after 1945, has had an impressive economic growth record since then, and recently overtook the Soviet Union in total GNP. It has surpassed the United States as a creditor nation. Kennedy's study (1987:xxii-xxiii) shows a "causal relationship between the shifts which have occurred over time in the general economic and productive balances and the position occupied by individual powers in the international system." He substantiates this point by noting that Great Britain today has far more wealth and military power than it had in its mid-Victorian prime, but its absolute power matters far less than the relative shrinkage of its share of the world product from 25 percent to 3 percent. The United States is now following the tendency of great powers in decline "instinctively [to] respond by spending more on 'security,' and thereby [to] divert potential resources from 'investment' and compound their long-term dilemma."

Military spending has drawn skilled personnel out of the civilian sector, diverted capital into unproductive military activities, and encouraged wasteful management practices both inside and outside the military sector (Oden, 1988).[29] There is also growing evidence, although still disputed by some economists, that military spending contributes to inflationary pressures;[30] creates significantly less employment than would an equal amount of nonmilitary spending by government or private consumers;[31] leads to lower levels of investment;[32] destroys an economically healthy composition of the investment that does occur;[33] and is an inefficient way to stimulate technical change.[34] In the developing world, military expenditures often produce disastrous effects on development.[35]

Ecological Costs

Preparations for war also consume vast resources and produce persistent pollutants that strain the environment's capacity to provide a sustainable life of dignity for all people. When competitive arms races breed insecurities among nations, governments misdirect scarce resources. As military spending, in constant prices, has jumped sevenfold among Third World governments since the early 1960s (Sivard, 1987:5), they have become less able to combat mass poverty, inequity, and environmental degradation, thus adding further to insecurity and the conditions that give rise to violence. As military abundance has spread, deserts expand, rain forests fall, ozone density thins, protein harvests from the seas decline, and population growth continues — all exacerbated by insufficient funds to take corrective action. The number of scientific personnel working on weapons research exceeds the combined number working on finding new energy sources, improving human health and family planning, raising agricultural productivity, and controlling pollution (World Commission on Environment and Development, 1987:298). The UN Action Plan for Desertification, for example, which needs $4.5 billion a year, amounts to less than two days of world military spending. Yet it lacks the funds to carry on its work.

CONCLUSION

Despite abundant evidence, which the preceding analysis has only begun to tap, epistemological impediments pose large problems for scientific conclusions regarding the causes of the long peace since 1945. Yet, a common-sense examination of historical events demonstrates that when preparations for war are examined to discern their impact on U.S.-Soviet peace and on making wise U.S. arms control and national security policies in general, the evidence fails to show, on balance, that the high levels of military preparedness have been constructive. The scales tip decidedly against preparations for war if one seeks not merely to deter a given war but also to pacify international relations and to transform the balance of military power eventually into a balance of legally constituted political power.[36] If all preparations for war were dampened, tensions arising from competitive arms buildups would decrease, international rules to reduce arsenals capable of large-scale aggression, if they became enforceable, would eliminate global wars, and resources could be husbanded to advance human and environmental well-being.

U.S. preparations for war have targeted the wrong enemy. They probably have done less to deter attacks on the United States by the Soviet Union than to deter ourselves, together with our opponents, from sensible efforts to change the international system. Yet such efforts appear to be the most important security need today.

Because of insensitivity to the systemic consequences of its behavior as the world's leading military power, the United States has continued, even stimulated, the military patterns that now appear so harmful. Given the security threats attending global militarization, economic dislocation, and ecological decay, it may not be an exaggeration to say that the consequences of U.S. military preparations have brought a greater threat to the future of U.S. security than has any adversary since 1945.

Whether the long peace continues will depend on the extent to which the United States, the Soviet Union, and other countries redirect their policies and institutions toward a deliberate multilateral diplomatic program aimed at ending chronic preparations for war and establishing stronger world institutions capable of presiding over peaceful change and enforcing a less war-prone code of international conduct.

ENDNOTES

I would like to thank Charles W. Kegley and the other contributors to this volume for their helpful comments and criticisms. In addition, I am grateful to Cris Toffolo, John W. Chambers, and Kenneth Brown for substantive comments and editorial advice. I want to thank the John D. and Catherine T. McArthur Foundation and the Institute for International Peace Studies, University of Notre Dame, for support of the research and writing of this essay.

1. As George Washington (1790) put it in his first annual address to both houses of Congress, "To be prepared for war is one of the most effectual means of preserving peace." Of course, this was a time-honored idea many centuries before Washington spoke.

2. Gilpin (1981:216) reports Hedley Bull's historical assessment of the use of force: "The more potentially destructive a war seemed to be, the less the probability of its occurring." Also see Robert Jervis' (1984:11-12) discussion of U.S. national security experts who argue that "the best way to deter wars and aggression is to be prepared to fight. . . ."

3. Wallace (1982) and Kegley (1988) discuss the failure of systematic studies to substantiate this maxim.

4. Edward L. Warner discusses typical arguments for the case that Moscow pursued an expansionist foreign policy (in Kaufman, McKitrick, and Leney, 1985:42-50). For a view by a leading U.S. Air Force general that Moscow held Europe hostage, that the United States needed to prepare for war even more intensely than it did, and that Washington could best keep the peace by opposing the Soviet Union more forcefully than possible within the relatively static concept of containment, see Twining (1966).

5. A vast literature exists on this subject. Raymond Garthoff (1962; 1966; 1985) and George Kennan (1982) are especially helpful. Mueller (1989) provides a recent statement that the Soviet Union had a distaste for large-scale conflict of any kind and did not have a need to conquer any part of the West because of relative contentment with the post–World War II status quo. McGeorge Bundy (1988) expresses general agreement. Kenneth Waltz (1979) has concluded that "the United States, and the Soviet Union as well, have more reason to be satisfied with the status quo than most earlier great powers had." See also Nye (1987), Wolfe (1984), and Sabin (1989).

6. Typical arguments are contained in Robert J. Art and Kenneth Waltz (1983). Other recent literature making this point is discussed in Mueller (1988b). In his critique of Mueller, Jervis (1988) concludes that nuclear weapons have added to the deterring quality of conventional arms.

7. For a discussion of the literature assessing the impact of nuclear weapons on postwar stability, see Mueller (1988b; 1989). Wallace (1982) assesses arms-race consequences.

8. This literature is examined by Mueller (1988b; 1989).

9. Some authors, of course, disagree. Michael Mandelbaum (1989), for example, believes that "the threat of Soviet aggression against Western Europe was credible precisely because it had already occurred — and indeed continues to this day — in Eastern Europe."

10. It also would have been foolish to fight a war that would actually have targeted for destruction the Soviet people whose human rights the United States would have been attempting to uphold.

11. For historical and empirical studies on this point, see Wright (1965), Singer and Small (1968), Small and Singer (1979), Levy (1981), Wallace (1982), and Huth and Russett (1984).

12. This point is documented at length by Mary Kaldor (1981). One of the particularly dangerous consequences of U.S.-Soviet military competition, nuclear proliferation, is discussed by Spector (1988).

13. The clearest expression of this idea is Modelski (1978; 1983; 1987b), Modelski and Morgan (1985), Modelski and Thompson (1988), and Thompson (1983a; 1983b; 1988).

14. Data collected by Modelski (1978; 1983; 1987a), Modelski and Thompson (1988), and Modelski and Morgan (1985), for example, indicate five long cycles in the period of the modern nation-state. The global power with a preponderant capacity for power projection dominated each cycle, especially its early phase:

Cycle	Formative Conflict	Dominant World Power	Duration of the Cycle	Principal Challenger
1.	Italian wars, 1494-1516	Portugal	1517-1608	Spain
2.	Spanish wars, 1581-1609	The Netherlands	1609-1713	France
3.	Wars of Louis XIV, 1688-1713	Britain I	1714-1815	France
4.	Revolutionary and Napoleonic wars, 1792-1815	Britain II	1816-1945	Germany
5.	World Wars I & II	United States	1946-	USSR

15. On this point, one of the keenest early analysts of nuclear deterrence has recently commented: "I have thought the likelihood of war sufficiently small during the entire period since the 1970s that I am not inclined to attribute much of the success in avoiding nuclear war to any particular measures that were taken or not taken" (Schelling, 1989:29). During much of the period before 1970, of course, the Soviet Union was hardly in a position to attack the United States and its allies because Moscow was preoccupied with recovering from World War II, strengthening its industrial base, and holding its own allies in line.

16. This position was publicly acknowledged and consolidated in the Scowcroft Commission Report, excerpted in the *New York Times*, April 12, 1983, p. A18.

17. Germany, for example, roughly doubled its military spending each year during the period from 1932 through 1938 (Richardson, 1960:115).

18. A typical example of this thinking is Powell (1989).

19. President Reagan said, "A nuclear test ban is not in the security interests of the United States, our friends or our allies" (Gordon, 1986).

20. Conducted by the author with officials in the Soviet Permanent Mission to the United Nations, January, 1987–June, 1988.

21. In addition to terminating ongoing negotiations in progress from the Carter administration, the Reagan administration did not offer its own meager arms control policies until 18 months after it entered office. Even these were in part a political response to the expression of public dissatisfaction with its hostility toward arms control.

22. See the statement of Harold Brown, Clark Clifford, Melvin Laird, Robert McNamara, Elliot Richardson, and James Schlesinger (R. Jeffrey Smith, 1987).

23. As Ralph White (1984:154) explains, selective inattention is "the tendency to push certain things out of one's mind." It is "a *process* whereby subconscious motives influence a person's thought process and consequently influence the person's entire picture of the world he lives in."

24. Historically they of course exhibited familiar prejudice and hatred against one another, and they sought through force to dominate one another. Yet the fact that Sweden is neutral, Norway and Denmark are members of NATO, and Finland has been careful not to offend the Soviet Union has not led them to develop any expectations of war against one another.

25. The relevant nonmilitary evidence is as varied as the Rush-Bagot agreement of 1817 that permanently demilitarized the border between the then revolutionary former British colonists of the United States and the remaining British colony of Canada, the pacification of Nordic international relations, the growth of comity between France and Germany, and the theoretical work of Karl Deutsch and others on the growth of security communities (Deutsch, et al., 1957).

26. Although he recently (1989) acknowledged that the balance-of-power system has a bit more stability than earlier indicated, the fundamental tendencies to which he referred in his earlier study remain.

27. See World Commission on Environment and Development (1987:297) and Tullberg (1985; 1986a; 1986b:229).

28. Sivard (1987:6) reports that $15.2 trillion, measured in 1984 dollars, was spent by 1987.

29. For analysis of the Soviet equivalent of the U.S. military-industrial complex, see Holloway (1981).

30. See Oden (1988:37) and Dumas (1986a; 1986b). The Bureau of Economic Analysis reports that overall U.S. inflation was 123 percent from 1972 to 1984, but in the military sector it rose by 147 percent (Oden, 1988:37).

31. See, for example, Anderson, Frisch, and Oden (1986), Oden (1988:38-39), Bezdek (1975), and Dumas (1986a).

32. A respected study of 14 industrial democracies demonstrates that for the group as a whole and for the United States estimated separately, investment has declined when military spending increased (Smith, 1977, 1978, 1980; DeGrasse, 1983; Oden, 1988).

33. The composition of investment and the emphasis of research and development are militarized. The United States spends roughly the same share of its GNP on R & D as its main competitors, Japan and West Germany. But approximately 35 to 40 percent is used for military purposes in the United States, while only 4 percent goes to a similar purpose in West Germany and 1 percent in Japan (Lichtenburg, 1986).

34. See, for example, Oden (1988:37) and Dumas (1986a; 1986b).

35. See, for example, Brzoska and Ohlson (1986), Ball (1988), Deger (1986), and Deger and West (1987).

36. For early discussion of the need for and benefits of international systemic change, see Mendlovitz (1975), Falk (1975), and Galtung (1980).

PART FIVE

Inhibiting War: The Uncertain Contribution of Some Alleged Constraints

CHAPTER ELEVEN

Arms Control, Disarmament, and the Stability of the Postwar Era

Joseph Kruzel

The most significant fact about international politics in the half-century following World War II is that two ideologically hostile, ambitious, and expansive world powers managed to avoid direct conflict despite being armed to the teeth with the most devastating weapons ever invented. How the United States and Soviet Union accomplished this feat is an interesting and important question for students of international relations.

One widely held explanation is that arms control and disarmament maintained the long peace. Such efforts codified a U.S.-Soviet *modus vivendi* and established rules of the game that moderated superpower conflict and contributed significantly to the maintenance of peace. Despite periodic death knells sounding the end of arms control, condemning it as an obsolete remnant of a naive and misguided approach to superpower relations, the process is alive and well in the 1990s, with George Bush eagerly pursuing the agenda of Ronald Reagan, a late but enthusiastic convert to arms control.

To someone from another planet the crucial role ascribed to arms control and disarmament in postwar U.S.-Soviet history might seem surprising. After all, there has been no U.S.-Soviet disarmament, as that term is properly understood, and on those few occasions when disarmament was discussed, superpower dialogue produced more ill will than good feelings. There have been a number of arms control agreements and confidence-building measures (CBMs) concluded in the postwar era (shown in Table 11.1), but the substantive impact of such accords has always been open to debate. In any case, negotiations on strategic nuclear weapons did not begin until late 1969, leaving the world's deliverance through the first quarter-century of the long peace to be explained by some phenomenon other than arms control. Still, the belief that arms control and disarmament activity played a key role in the maintenance of U.S.-Soviet peace is deeply held and widely accepted, yet the idea is so seldom analyzed that it is appropriate to put the question to a serious nonpolemical test.

**TABLE 11.1 U.S.-Soviet Arms Agreements in the
Post–World War II Era**

1963	Limited Test Ban Treaty	Banned nuclear weapons testing in atmosphere, outer space, and underwater
1967	Outer Space Treaty	Banned weapons of mass destruction from space
1968	Non-Proliferation Treaty	Intended to prevent spread of nuclear weapons to "have not" states
1971	Seabed Treaty	Banned weapons of mass destruction from seabed
1971	Hot Line Modernization	Established satellite link
1971	Accident Measures Agreement	Prevention and notification of accidental launch
1972	Biological Weapons Convention	Banned bacteriological and toxin weapons
1972	Incidents at Sea Agreement	Agreement on the prevention of incidents on the high seas
1972	ABM Treaty (SALT I)	Limited antiballistic missiles systems to two sites
1972	Interim Agreement (SALT I)	Set temporary limits on strategic offensive forces
1972	"Basic Principles" Agreement	Accord on basic principles of relations
1973	Preventing Nuclear War Agreement	Accord on principles of conduct to reduce the risk of nuclear war
1974	ABM Protocol	Reduced permitted ABMs to one site
1976	Peaceful Nuclear Explosions Treaty*	Limited detonations other than weapons tests
1979	SALT II*	Limits on strategic offensive nuclear weapons
1986	Confidence-Building Measures	Notification and observation of conventional military exercises in Europe
1987	Nuclear Risk Reduction Centers	Established facilities in each national capital
1987	INF Treaty	Banned intermediate-range nuclear forces with ranges of 300-3,500 miles

*Signed but not ratified

This chapter evaluates the proposition that arms control and disarmament have played a pivotal role in creating, or at least in preserving, the long peace. The first step will be to define the relevant terms — arms control and disarmament — and also to consider what it means to characterize the postwar U.S.-Soviet relationship as one of "peace." The following section will sketch the record of superpower arms control and disarmament efforts, and analyze the various theories and hypotheses, explicit and implicit, put forward about the effect of arms control and disarmament activity on the evolving superpower relationship.

ARMS CONTROL, DISARMAMENT, AND "PEACE"

The terms *arms control* and *disarmament* are often used as if they were synonymous, or at least complementary, pursuits. Arms control is usually portrayed as a more modest version of disarmament, or as the first step on the long road to a weapons-free world. In the U.S. government, the Arms Control and Disarmament Agency is nominally responsible for both endeavors, and most people instinctively think of the two as closely related activities. However, it may be more useful to think of arms control and disarmament as quite different pursuits rather than as variations on a common theme.

In its most general conception, arms control is any type of restraint on the use of arms, any form of military cooperation between adversaries. Arms control can be implicit or explicit, formal or informal, and unilateral, bilateral, or multilateral (Schelling and Halperin, 1961; Lamb, 1988: Chapter 2). It is a process of jointly managing the weapons acquisition processes of the participant states in the hope of reducing the risk of war. For our purposes, we may include in the category of arms control a variety of confidence-building measures intended to reduce the risk of accidental, unauthorized, or catalytic war. Examples include the "hot line" communication channel between Washington and Moscow, the 1972 Incidents at Sea Agreement signed by the United States and Soviet Union in an effort to avert potentially dangerous encounters between their navies, and the 1986 agreement allowing NATO and Warsaw Pact observers to monitor the military exercises of the other side. While arms control is a versatile instrument, and certainly not limited to the product of formal superpower negotiations, too broad a conception can encompass the entire spectrum of U.S.-Soviet relations. In this chapter arms control will be used in a narrower sense to refer to formal agreements imposing significant restrictions or limitations on the weapons or security policies of the signatories.

Disarmament rests on a fundamentally different philosophical premise than arms control. It envisions the drastic reduction or elimination of all weapons, looking toward the eradication of war itself. Disarmament is based on the notion that if there were no more weapons there would be no more war. This is a compelling proposition, with enough truth to give it a very long life in the history of thought about war and peace. Arms control, on the other hand, accepts the existence of weapons and the possibility of conflict. Contrary to popular impression, it is not necessarily about reducing arms levels. Arms control attempts to stabilize the status quo and to manage conflict, to encourage peaceful resolution of disputes and limit the resort to military force. Although many visceral opponents would be shocked at the thought, arms control is fundamentally a conservative enterprise. Disarmament, by contrast, is a radical one. Disarmament seeks to overturn the status quo; arms control works to perpetuate it (Freedman, 1983: Chapter 13; Myrdal, 1977). Disarmament is an end in itself, the creation of a world in which force and the threat of force play no role. Arms control is an instrument, not an end in itself, a tool for managing the weapons and their threatened use.

Arms control and disarmament are thus competing ideas, not complementary ones. Properly understood, arms control is not a path to disarmament, with partial measures leading eventually to the withering away of weapons. It is an alternative to disarmament.

Finally there is the notion of "peace" as that term has commonly been applied to U.S.-Soviet postwar relations. Peace has many meanings and interpretations in any language; in Russian, peace is a homonym for "world." Even when used by scholars of international relations, peace can describe an enormous range of relationships from absolute accord to unbridled hostility just short of war. For example, peace could be used to describe both U.S.-Soviet and U.S.-Canadian relations, although the two relationships have few features in common. In the Cold War era, the United States and Soviet Union enjoyed a narrow type of peace that did not prevent either side from challenging the other's interests by force of arms, usually through subversion or the use of surrogate forces. The two superpowers have never been formally at war with each other (not even when the United States sent troops to Siberia during the Russian civil war, an intervention the Soviets have never forgotten). But during the long postwar peace there have been numerous clashes of important national interests that led to military conflict, often involving large numbers of U.S. and Soviet troops, in Korea, Vietnam, the Middle East, Central America, and Afghanistan.

To label the U.S.-Soviet postwar relationship one of peace stretches the word to its semantic limit. What we call the long peace has in fact been a durable and often violent conflict that has managed to observe two crucially important rules of international behavior:[1]

Rule #1: No use of nuclear weapons — anywhere, anytime. Neither combatant has ever used nuclear weapons against the other, or against any other state;

Rule #2: No direct U.S.-Soviet military conflict. With a few isolated, sometimes tragic but generally unintended exceptions, no American soldier has killed a Soviet soldier, and no Russian has ever killed an American GI.[2]

The maintenance of these two rules for nearly a half-century is no small achievement, but hardly what Kant had in mind in describing *Perceptual Peace*.

Having defined the relevant terms, it is now possible to pose the issues to be examined in this chapter. There are four basic questions: To what extent has the disarmament dialogue (for there has been no real superpower disarmament) helped to establish or maintain rule #1? To what extent has it influenced rule #2? The same questions may be asked of arms control, but in this arena there is a substantial record of concluded agreements as well as negotiations. We may therefore also ask what effect arms control negotiations and the resulting agreements have had on the maintenance of rules #1 and #2.

EFFORTS AT NUCLEAR DISARMAMENT

The record of superpower disarmament negotiations is slim, and even that meager history is largely taken up with theatrics and political posturing. Shortly after the end of World War II, the United States came forward with the Baruch Plan, a proposal for abolishing all nuclear weapons and creating a United Nations agency that would control nuclear energy and research around the world. The Soviets would have nothing to do with the Baruch Plan, seeing in it a scheme for perpetuating the American monopoly of nuclear weapons. Moscow responded with its own plan for the abolition of nuclear weapons, a proposal with many conditions which the Soviets knew the United States would find unacceptable. The real problem with the two proposals was not in the technical details of control or inspection but the fact that both were really schemes for limited world government. As Moscow and Washington were quick to realize but loathe to admit, such plans could not possibly succeed in the world lacking a basic consensus on values, ideology, and law.

The abortive postwar attempt at nuclear disarmament set an unfortunate precedent for U.S.-Soviet arms negotiations. It suggested that arms control was not a serious business, that negotiations were more likely to be exchanges of propaganda than serious efforts at understanding and compromise. For the next decade the United States and the Soviet Union conducted what might be called "parallel monologues." Each side was more interested in justifying its position to world opinion than in negotiating seriously with the other.

The disarmament dialogue continued intermittently through the 1950s and early 1960s, with each side ensuring that it had on the table a defensible proposition for general and complete disarmament. It was not until the late 1980s, in a quite unexpected manner, that the two superpowers returned to the question of nuclear disarmament.

At the November 1986 summit meeting in Reykjavik, Iceland, General Secretary Mikhail Gorbachev proposed the elimination of all strategic nuclear weapons over a ten-year period (a "quicker, cheaper way" to achieve nuclear disarmament, Gorbachev said, than the U.S. Strategic Defense Initiative). President Reagan seemed interested in the notion, but negotiations foundered on the question of whether there should be an associated limitation on strategic defensive systems.

The Reykjavik summit raised many questions about the role of nuclear weapons in international security. To some, Reykjavik revived the possibility of genuine nuclear disarmament, suggesting that deep cuts might be possible and that a world ultimately rid of nuclear weapons might be something other than a rhetorical flight of fancy. To others Reykjavik revealed the hazards of a disarmament dialogue and brought home the dismaying thought that reducing nuclear forces could actually threaten the crisis stability that arms control had striven to enhance.

This meager record suggests that the two rules of the long peace — no use of nuclear weapons and no direct superpower military conflict — owe little or nothing to U.S.-Soviet disarmament activity in the postwar era.

THE FOUNDATIONS OF ARMS CONTROL

The intellectual foundations of nuclear arms control were established in the late 1950s and early 1960s, more than 15 years after Hiroshima and Nagasaki, and a decade after the Soviets had made nuclear strategy a bipolar game. Early nuclear strategists such as Bernard Brodie and Albert Wohlstetter had little to say about arms control. They believed nuclear weapons themselves provided the deterrent, and nothing further was needed. This was the connotation implied in Brodie's (1946) use of the term *absolute weapon*. For these believers in "existential deterrence," formal arms control could do little to reinforce the horror of prospective nuclear holocaust (Wieseltier, 1983). Strategic stalemate was inevitable, but it was also inevitably stable. Arms control could do nothing to alter the fate which technology was certain to impose. Nuclear weapons imposed a certain lethal symmetry on the two nations that overwhelmed any differences in doctrine or ideology. If arms control had any function at all, it was to refine and confirm the condition of mutual deterrence that already existed, imposed on the United States and the Soviet Union by the nature of the weapons themselves.

The *annus mirabilis* of arms control was 1961, when at least seven important books were published on the subject (Bechhoeffer, 1961; Brennan, 1961; Bull, 1961; Frisch, 1961; Hadley, 1961; Henkin, 1961; Schelling and Halperin, 1961). Two themes emerge from a survey of this early literature. First is the importance attached to enhancing stability and reducing vulnerability to surprise attack. "The first priority of arms control is to reduce the extreme vulnerability of the United States' strategic nuclear deterrent," wrote Arthur Hadley (1961:62-63). The most important objective is the "development of strategic weapons that are invulnerable" (Bull, 1961:208) and the abandonment of those that are not.

A second theme was the avoidance of accidental war. Hedley Bull (1961:207) declared that "the danger of accident is more serious than that of deliberate and premeditated attack." This danger could be reduced by improving communication between the two superpowers, a favorite theme of Thomas Schelling and Morton Halperin (1961: Chapter 1), perhaps by "some form of emergency communication link" (Hadley, 1961:90), such as a hot line between Washington and Moscow.

The early theorists were not starry-eyed visionaries out to remake the world by limiting armaments. They demonstrated a keen appreciation for the limits of arms control, and stressed the difference between arms control and disarmament: "Arms control does not try to alter human nature and usher in perpetual peace. Its interest is in avoiding war by increasing stability between nations" (Hadley, 1961:208).

Arms control was also distinguished from arms reduction. "There is nothing in the concept of arms control to prevent the increase of certain types of armament," wrote Donald Brennan (1961:31). Several authors warned that limits on strategic nuclear arms might well require an increase in conventional forces. Others worried about the impact of arms control on extended deterrence. Several foresaw the danger of a "tranquilizing effect" on U.S. will — not just from agreements but from negotiations as well (Schelling and Halperin, 1961:131). As a whole, these early writings presented arms control as a modest but useful process, carrying with it the potential for benefits but also the possibility of abuse.

THE PRACTICE OF ARMS CONTROL

Whether by coincidence or design, the development of arms control theory was soon followed by the first serious practical steps toward agreement. The two superpowers shifted from the exchange of non-negotiable proposals for general and complete disarmament to the advancement of practical and limited steps to restrain the nuclear competition. In 1963 the Limited Test Ban Treaty was signed. This accord prohibited the testing of nuclear weapons in the atmosphere, underwater and in outer space — everywhere except underground. The Limited Test Ban Treaty, open to all nations, was followed by other partial agreements such as the Outer Space Treaty which banned weapons of mass destruction from earth orbit and from placement on the moon and other planets. Agreements such as these were important, but they were still corollary or confidence-building measures. Ahead was the more critical and difficult task of negotiating an agreement on the most destructive nuclear weapons. By the late 1960s the stage was set, and Strategic Arms Limitation Talks (SALT) began in the fall of 1969.

When SALT commenced, the United States had already completed its ballistic missile deployment program on land and at sea and was turning to qualitative improvements in the form of multiple independently targetable reentry vehicles (MIRVs) which could expand the number of deliverable nuclear weapons without increasing the number of launchers. Construction had begun on the nation's first Anti-Ballistic Missile (ABM) complex, called Safeguard, but there was also a vigorous national debate underway about the technical reliability of ballistic missile defense and about its impact on nuclear deterrence. The Soviet Union, on the other hand, had far fewer operational nuclear delivery vehicles than the United States, but it had a vigorous missile building program underway. It had also deployed an operational ABM complex around Moscow and maintained a dynamic program of defensive research and development.

After two and a half years of negotiation, the SALT process produced two agreements, the ABM Treaty and the Interim Agreement on strategic offensive arms. The first limited each side to two ABM complexes, and was later amended to restrict each side to the one site it already had in existence: the U.S. system in North Dakota and the Soviet complex around Moscow.

The Interim Agreement froze for five years the number of strategic offensive missile launchers for each side. During this freeze a more comprehensive agreement was to be negotiated. To some observers at the time (and to many since), the Interim Agreement looked unfair because it froze the United States at a lower number of launchers than were permitted the Soviet Union. Congress approved the agreement by a vote of 88-2, but also passed the Jackson Amendment, which required that any future agreement not mandate American inferiority in levels of strategic forces.

SALT I also created the Standing Consultative Commission (SCC), a U.S.-Soviet working group to deal with questions of treaty compliance and implementation. The SCC has met regularly since 1972, even during periods when formal arms negotiations were suspended. Washington and Moscow have seen the benefit of maintaining a forum for considering technical questions related to the control of strategic arms even when relations between the two countries were not at their best.

The task of converting the interim freeze of SALT I into a treaty on offensive forces took seven years, much longer than anyone expected, and was finally concluded in 1979. The SALT II Treaty set a ceiling on the total number of strategic nuclear delivery vehicles, and under that ceiling imposed a number of important sub-limits — on the number of missiles with multiple warheads, for example, and on the number of warheads that each missile type could carry. SALT II was a disappointment to many arms control advocates who had hoped for more. To some, the treaty seemed to be little more than stapling together the strategic programs of the two sides. Hardliners registered even greater dissatisfaction, claiming that the treaty gave the Soviets a permanent advantage in the number of heavy ICBMs and an exploitable loophole by not counting the Soviet Backfire bomber as a strategic weapon.

Even these shortcomings might have been acceptable at another time, but by late 1979 the U.S.-Soviet political relationship had deteriorated so much that SALT II had no chance of winning ratification in the Senate. When the Soviets invaded Afghanistan in December, 1979, President Carter quietly withdrew the treaty from consideration by the Senate.

Even though it was never ratified, the SALT II Treaty was generally observed by both the United States and the Soviet Union through 1986.

President Reagan, who before assuming office criticized the treaty as being "fatally flawed," adopted a policy as president of doing nothing to undercut the treaty. The principal military leaders of the United States, the Joint Chiefs of Staff, consistently supported SALT II as a set of "modest but useful" constraints on the Soviet arsenal of strategic forces.

On another arms control front, the United States and the Soviet Union began negotiations in 1981 on limiting intermediate-range nuclear forces (INF) in Europe. Progress on this agreement was slow until Gorbachev's rise to power in 1985 and shifts in the posture of the Reagan administration toward arms control in general provided renewed impetus toward agreement. After the Reagan-Gorbachev summit in Reykjavik in 1986, a treaty to eliminate this entire class of weapons was successfully negotiated and signed by the two leaders in Washington in 1987.

The INF Treaty broke new ground in verification. The treaty included a Memorandum of Understanding that provided a concise description of the number and location of all facilities, launchers, and missiles subject to control under the terms of the treaty, a measure of openness that was unprecedented in the history of postwar arms control activities. An additional protocol spelled out procedures for on-site inspection, including highly intrusive short-notice inspections of all facilities mentioned in the treaty — except missile-production facilities — for thirteen years from the time of ratification. The treaty also held the promise of serving as a model for other arms control agreements, at least in this most crucial area of verification.

While public attention and most official effort was focused on U.S.-Soviet strategic arms control, other multilateral arms negotiations went on, some of which produced significant and enduring results. The Non-Proliferation Treaty (NPT) concluded in the late 1960s may ultimately have as much impact on international relations as the superpowers' bilateral efforts to limit their own nuclear arsenals. Since the NPT was really the brainchild of the United States and the Soviet Union, it also revealed the superpowers' common interest in having a world with as few other nuclear weapon states as possible.

The NPT obliged its signatories without nuclear weapons not to produce or acquire any nuclear weapons and to submit their peaceful nuclear facilities to international inspection. For their part, the nuclear "haves" promised not to transfer nuclear weapons and to provide the fullest possible exchange of nuclear technology so that the "have-nots" will be able to share in the benefits of peaceful nuclear technology.

By the late 1980s, the NPT had well over 130 signatories, and in its first decade and a half of existence had done much to quell nuclear anxieties in many parts of the world. However, several states with the capability and the perceived need to acquire nuclear weapons have not yet ratified the treaty. Among the most significant holdouts are Pakistan, India, Brazil, Argentina, and Israel.

Several states, both signatories and holdouts alike, criticized the NPT as blatantly discriminatory. The treaty divided the world into two classes of states, and while requiring that the have-nots renounce their right to the most powerful weapons ever conceived, asked almost nothing in return from the favored few who possessed nuclear weapons. Many complained that unless the superpowers did something meaningful to restrain their own vertical proliferation, the non-nuclear weapon states would not feel bound to refrain from horizontal proliferation.

Despite these complaints and criticisms, the NPT must be judged one of the most successful postwar arms control agreements. It served to reinforce and give legal weight to the global consensus that nuclear proliferation is dangerous and destabilizing. Since the NPT's entry into force, only one nation — India in 1974 — is known to have detonated a nuclear device. There has been speculation that South Africa tested a nuclear device in 1979, but that remains conjecture. A generation ago almost no expert would have predicted so slow a pace of nuclear acquisition, and the NPT deserves a significant measure of credit for retarding the spread of nuclear weapons.

Several other multilateral arms control agreements have also been concluded. The Antarctic Treaty of 1959 prohibited the permanent stationing of military forces on that continent. In 1967 a number of Latin American nations signed the Treaty of Tlatelolco, which prohibited the deployment of nuclear weapons in Latin America. The Biological Weapons Convention of 1972 not only outlawed germ warfare, but also prohibited the production and stockpiling of such weapons.

Some of these treaties have probably been violated. There have been numerous allegations about chemical and biological weapons, such as the Iraqi use of chemical agents against Iran, and the Soviet use of chemical weapons to produce the yellow rain of Southeast Asia. But even honor in the breach illustrates the residual value of arms control, which establishes an international norm and standard of behavior against which to measure actual conduct.

Efforts at conventional arms control since World War II took longer to yield results. In 1986, the multinational Conference on Disarmament in Europe reached agreement on a number of confidence-building measures, such as prior notification of troop movements and exercises; but the Mutual and Balanced Force Reductions (MBFR) talks of the 1970s and 1980s aimed at limiting conventional force deployments in Central Europe made little progress toward agreement. In the aftermath of the INF agreement, however, the issue of conventional arms control received greater attention, and new negotiations on conventional forces in Europe began in Vienna in March of 1989.

In the postwar era there have been some strides in the areas of arms control and confidence-building measures (CBMs). The United States and the Soviet Union have concluded three agreements on strategic nuclear arms, with a fourth nearing conclusion at the time of this writing. Numerous CBMs, such as the hot line, the accidents agreement, the agreement on prior notification of military exercises, the creation of a nuclear risk reduction center, and others, all speak of a continuing dialogue between the superpowers, although the concrete results of that dialogue remain unclear. And, of course, efforts at disarmament simply failed.

THE OBJECTIVES OF ARMS CONTROL

It used to be said that arms control had three objectives: (1) to make war less likely, (2) to lessen the destructiveness of war if it should occur, and (3) to reduce the cost of armaments. While cost control and reducing the risk of conflict have remained important goals of arms control in the nuclear age, concern with the second objective has all but disappeared, at least as an arms control *desideratum.* If arms control were really concerned with this objective, civil defense shelters and active defenses against enemy missiles and bombers would be welcomed as prudent arms control moves. But in fact most arms control advocates oppose such steps. They believe that on the nuclear level at least, deterring war is far more important than reducing the amount of damage that might result if war should occur. Some might even suggest that the real objective of contemporary arms control should be to increase the amount of destruction if war should occur, in the expectation that more massive damage would serve as an even greater deterrent.

The most generally accepted notion of contemporary arms control is consistent with that conservative view. The primary function of arms control is to promote stability, especially in a crisis. Crisis stability is achieved by reducing as much as possible the incentive for either side to launch a preemptive attack. Perfect crisis stability is a situation in which there is no difference between going first with a preemptive strike and going second in retaliation. If preemption and retaliation can inflict the same level of damage on an adversary, then there is no incentive in a crisis for either side to go first: better to keep talking and hope for a peaceful settlement of differences.

Crisis instability results when there is a great difference between going first and going second, between preemptive and retaliatory capability. The greater the difference, the greater the incentive to go first. In a political crisis, if giving diplomacy a chance means the difference between survival and devastation, a nation that finds itself in such a situation will be sorely tempted to strike first. Crisis stability is enhanced by prohibiting or eliminating weapons that are primarily for use in a first strike and by encouraging the deployment of weapons that are less vulnerable to preemptive attack. In essence, crisis stability is enhanced when conditions of Mutual Assured Destruction (MAD) prevail — when each side has a survivable capacity to inflict unacceptable damage on the other.

Arms Reductions Versus Arms Limitations

It may sound heretical, but nuclear arms control is not necessarily about reducing the number of existing weapons. The popular image of arms control undoubtedly gives reductions the highest priority, and governments have actively encouraged this misconception. The Reagan administration changed the name of the U.S.-Soviet negotiations from SALT (Strategic Arms Limitation Talks) to START (for STrategic Arms Reductions Talks) to emphasize the importance of moving beyond simple limitations to actual reductions. In the mid-1980s both the United States and the Soviet Union gave great rhetorical emphasis to radical reductions in the size of nuclear arsenals.

Popular interest in reductions stemmed not only from the widely held belief that nuclear arsenals had grown too large, but also from the conviction that dramatic reductions would save money and reduce the risk of war. There is some truth to the notion that ever-increasing inventories of weapons may encourage plans for war fighting; but nuclear weapons account for only a small fraction of the defense budget (less than 10 percent of the U.S. defense budget, for example). Any economic savings to be derived from reducing the nuclear stockpile would likely be minimal. Some types of reductions could actually increase the danger of war, particularly if such cuts degraded crisis stability. A reduction by half in the number of strategic nuclear launchers, for example, could be dangerously destabilizing if it put no corresponding limit on the size and number of warheads. Reductions of the wrong kind could reduce crisis or arms race stability, thus increasing the danger of preemptive attack.

PROPOSITIONS ABOUT ARMS CONTROL

Over the years, three general propositions about the nature and implications of arms control have been developed:

1. *The conventional wisdom.* While not living up to its full potential, arms control has been a modest but useful factor in moderating U.S.-Soviet strategic instability.
2. *The optimists' view.* Arms control can be a major force for transforming U.S.-Soviet relations, but so far it has been generally misused and subverted to perpetuate the arms race.
3. *The pessimists' view.* Arms control, whatever its theoretical appeal, has been a practical failure. It has lulled the West into a false sense of security and therefore heightened the danger of war.

Underlying these three very different interpretations of the arms control record and its potential as a mechanism for system transformation is one implicit point of accord: whether arms control is good, bad, or a squandered opportunity, adherents to all three views agree that it is an important enterprise. A fourth interpretation of arms control should also be considered, and that might be labeled (4) *the indifferent view*. This sees arms control as basically irrelevant to U.S.-Soviet relations and the stability of the postwar international order. Arms control is occasionally interesting, often mystifying, but almost always a side show. It is, if anything, an effect rather than a cause of systemic change, but mostly it is pointless, fiddling with marginal limitations on weapons while ignoring the true sources of conflict and crisis.

Which of these propositions most nearly approaches the truth is largely an empirical question. But history is not a tidy laboratory. We cannot rerun experiments. There are too many independent variables, and our efforts to isolate these forces and analyze them separately blind us to the critical interactions among the variables as history marches on. We are also drawn to the highly visible and easily identifiable and away from factors that we know are important yet do not lend themselves to easy definition or comprehension. Yet conclusions *must* be drawn or paralysis will stunt the decision-making process.

Arms Control and the Risk of Nuclear War

Reducing the risk of war is not so much an objective as a hope. Our understanding of what causes war, and hence what can be done to reduce its likelihood, is pathetically rudimentary. No problem has occupied scholars of international relations more in the past 50 years, but the massive intellectual effort has yielded little in the way of practical results. Most authors who tackle this subject end up assembling lists of factors that might make war more likely. Do arms races cause war? Sometimes they do, but more often arms races seem to fizzle out short of conflict. Occasionally an arms race might even reduce the risk of war, particularly if it prevents one side from achieving an overwhelming military superiority. The dictum of *si vis pacem, para bellum* (if you want peace, prepare for war) has been proven correct at least as often as it has been wrong.

Since we have so little understanding of what causes war, if we say that arms control is concerned with reducing the risk of war, we have declared the result we are after but have said nothing about how the job is to be done.

Every American president from Nixon to Bush has committed the United States to maintaining strategic parity (or sufficiency or essential equivalence) with the Soviet Union. The Bush administration's margin of safety depends more on keeping a lead in technology than on achieving demonstrable quantitative superiority. Maintaining parity does not depend on arms control; the United States is committed to keeping pace with the Soviet Union even in an unconstrained environment. But arms control gives the strategic future some structure and predictability. It makes planning easier. In the best of circumstances it permits the two sides to maintain parity at marginally lower rather than higher levels. The result may be substantial economic savings and a modest reduction in tensions. This is not much, and certainly not the end of the arms race, but it is something.

To the extent that there is any consensus on what might reduce the risk of war, it has centered on the notion of crisis stability. Reducing the risk of nuclear war, which neither side wants anyway, means reducing the incentive to strike first. The ABM Treaty made a critical contribution to this notion of stability by reducing the "reciprocal fear of surprise attack."

Impact on Military Forces

In the United States at least, the military services have often been the most enthusiastic supporters of arms control within the government. Harold Brown and Lynn Davis (1984) put the military case for arms control in the following terms:

> [Agreements] can provide greater confidence as to the future character-istics and size of the nuclear force postures of each side than would exist in the absence of any agreements. . . . They can constrain modernization, either overall or of the most destabilizing kinds of threats, e.g., accurate intercontinental ballistic missiles, which can destroy missile silos in a preemptive strike.

Despite these optimistic claims for the potential of arms control, arms agreements have not resulted in any wholesale reduction of deployed armaments. The weapons levels achieved in most arms control agree-ments might well have been substantially the same if there had been no limitation at all. The forces which gave rise to the negotiated settlement would very likely have worked to achieve a *de facto* limitation on the forces in question.

Those who hoped that the SALT era would stop the growth of stra-tegic nuclear arsenals have been profoundly disappointed. From 1969, the beginning of the SALT dialogue, until 1988 the number of strategic nuclear weapons deployed by the Soviet Union increased by over 500 percent. The increase for the United States was almost 300 percent.[3] Of course the true test of the impact of SALT agreements was whether the rate of growth might have been even higher in the absence of constraints.

This question can only be answered speculatively, but it is plausible that force levels might have been marginally higher without arms control.

This does not mean that arms control is meaningless. The impact of an agreement may be substantial, even if it does nothing more than ratify each side's existing plans for deployment of the limited systems. If an arms "limitation" amounted to nothing more than stapling together the defense plans of the signatories — a common criticism of the SALT II accord — it could still have important long-term consequences for weapons acquisition.

Opposition to the deployment of new military weapon systems is usually weak, loosely organized, and short term. Effective opposition is difficult to sustain over long periods of time. An arms control agreement confers legitimacy and a sense of permanence on such opposition by helping to break the momentum of support for further deployment of the system in question. An agreement is also useful because it sets in motion various pressures for compliance with the provisions of the accord.

Even if they do not have a significant direct effect, most arms control agreements do have an important indirect impact on the weapon systems they limit. Arms agreements almost invariably diminish interest in the limited system. The Limited Test Ban Treaty practically killed any serious interest in nuclear testing in the three proscribed environments, and the ABM Treaty substantially diminished interest in ballistic missile defense for a number of years — again, for about a decade — but on the offensive side the net effect of strategic arms negotiations was to create a greater awareness of, and interest in, the relative force levels of the United States and the Soviet Union.

Frequently an arms control agreement will rechannel defense efforts, turning the competition into new areas unrestricted by the accord. The Limited Test Ban Treaty resulted in a substantial increase in underground nuclear testing, the only type of testing permitted by the agreement. SALT I shifted strategic arms competition from quantitative into qualitative fields, and enhanced the attractiveness of nonlimited systems. Secretary of Defense Melvin Laird saw the ABM Treaty and the Interim Agreement as two parts of a "triple play for peace," the third part being a major boost to the cruise missile program not limited by the SALT accords. Many believe that President Carter would not have approved the MX missile had it not been pledged to the joint chiefs as compensation for their support of SALT II.

In addition to the effects discussed above, arms control agreements often have an important secondary effect in framing a military relationship. Strategic parity, or essential equivalence between strategic forces, depends on a number of factors, not all of them amenable to limitation. But when a treaty which mandates certain limits and ratios is signed, those limits and ratios tend to become the new military reality (Fairbanks and Shulsky, 1987:71).

Impact on Political Relationships

The original Nixon-Kissinger conception of détente saw arms control as the centerpiece of the U.S.-Soviet relationship that would advance on all fronts. By giving the Soviets something positive to fear losing, arms control would add a carrot to the stick of American military power. This implied a linkage between U.S.-Soviet arms control and political competition around the world. Because the Soviets would not care to undermine the arms control regime, they would be increasingly reluctant to challenge U.S. actions and interests in the Third World.

Arms control induced no such timidity on the part of the Soviets. The Basic Principles of Agreement signed in 1972 were so general and ambiguous that they had no effect on Soviet or U.S. behavior. Subsequent efforts to begin a dialogue on regional issues have yielded little benefit, and neither side has ever altered its own policies on such issues (Poland, Afghanistan, the Middle East, Central America) for arms control reasons.

There is a widespread belief that arms control agreements improve diplomatic relations between the signatories. This happy assumption deserves challenge for reasons mentioned earlier. Many other events affect relations between partners in an arms agreement, and it is impossible to know how relations between the parties would have developed in the absence of an agreement. Since history does not provide the luxury of controlled experiments, there is no way of assessing in any precise fashion the impact of arms accords.

Arms agreements and CBMs that are negotiated at relatively tense moments in a diplomatic relationship — such agreements are rare events in themselves — may have an important effect simply by proving that some area of agreement exists between two contentious nations. Certainly the Limited Test Ban, Outer Space, and SALT I treaties all had important symbolic implications by demonstrating that negotiation and agreement could occur between rivals. As the first arms accord of the nuclear age, the LTBT had a particularly strong impact in symbolizing the shift in superpower conduct toward accommodation.

The SALT I agreements were negotiated in a period of reasonably tense Soviet-American relations, the popular recollection of détente notwithstanding. It is possible that the SALT negotiations provided a sort of centrifugal force that kept U.S.-Soviet relations reasonably stable through such perturbations as the Nixon opening to China, the Indo-Pakistan war, and the mining of Hanoi and Haiphong. In the longer run, however, the negotiations may even have had an adverse impact on U.S.-Soviet relations. SALT was the centerpiece of détente, the beginning of a new era in superpower diplomacy. When the benefits of détente failed to measure up to initial expectations, disillusionment with the entire process of strategic arms control began to set in.

The ongoing dialogue between the parties to an arms negotiation may itself contribute to political stability, even if no actual agreement is concluded. The negotiation may give each side a better understanding of what is bothering the other and in some modest way serve to reduce the level of tension. The benefit of such a dialogue should not be exaggerated, but there may be some value in keeping open a channel of communication between adversaries. As Winston Churchill said, better to "jaw, jaw than war, war."

Some modest accords have enjoyed quiet but enduring success. The 1972 Incidents at Sea Agreement established a series of regular bilateral meetings to develop specific guidelines and to implement the accord. The result over time has been a reduction in risk and cost to the U.S. and Soviet navies (Lynn-Jones, 1985).

Finally, some have expressed the hope that arms control could be the mechanism for transcending sovereignty (McCain, 1989). This is a hope hardly justified by the postwar experience to date, which if anything has tended to confirm the legitimacy of the two superpowers and the bipolar conception of the international system (Falk, 1975a:40).

THE RISKS OF ARMS CONTROL

To say that arms control has both attendant costs and benefits may be trivial, but in practice proponents have tended to ignore the risks and opponents have tended to ignore the costs. Any serious assessment of the process must be cognizant of both.

Too often in the past arms control initiatives were undertaken without any evident appreciation of the implicit costs involved merely in taking a seat at the negotiating table. At least three potential costs must be assessed before agreeing to talk.

First, to what extent will the talks themselves create problems for force design, defense strategy, and alliance politics? Any serious arms control negotiation simplifies and compartmentalizes military reality. Any negotiation narrower than a world disarmament conference covering all the military forces of all the nations in the world has to set some limits on participants and agenda. Some nations will participate, others will be excluded. Some weapons, modes of employment, or geographical regions will be discussed; others will not. Such simplifying conditions are necessary to reduce the problem of arms control to manageable proportions, but they are also a distortion of military reality, which is more a seamless web of interactions than a neat matrix of weapons and nations.

This is a particularly troublesome fact of life for the United States, which relies heavily on the "seamlessness" of its military doctrine — the indivisibility of NATO, the risk of escalation to nuclear weapons — for the success of its defense strategy. Any negotiation that isolates one type of weapon (strategic nuclear weapons, as in START) or a geographical region (as in the Carter administration's Indian Ocean talks), imposes strains on doctrines and alliances. These strains cannot be entirely overcome with reassurances and consultations. Some distortions of military reality may be acceptable in the higher interest of securing a useful agreement, but they should not be ignored.

Arms control negotiations also complicate a nation's internal defense decision making. Bargaining chips are an indispensable commodity for any negotiator, but they also provide a convenient rationale for new weapons systems, even those with no discernible military merit. In fact, such systems may make ideal bargaining chips because they will not be missed if they are given up in negotiations.

It is also possible for a nation to use arms control as a means of blunting pressures for unilateral force reductions and for rallying domestic support for new defense expenditures. The MBFR negotiations were in part an effort by the Nixon administration to head off Senate pressures for a reduction in the number of U.S. troops deployed in Europe. In this case, the instrument of arms control was used to protect existing force levels. The 1979 NATO decision to proceed with the development of long-range theater nuclear forces while simultaneously exploring the possibility of limitations on such forces was as much an effort to secure consensus within the alliance as a serious offer to negotiate with the Soviets. In this case, arms control was used as a mechanism for forging alliance solidarity.

An additional potential cost is the danger of illusions fostered by arms control. One is well known and generally appreciated: the sense that nations that are negotiating won't start fighting. There is an understandable tendency to assume that so long as the parties are talking, problems are manageable and on the way to resolution. Many critics and some supporters of SALT II feared that the ratification of a new treaty would tranquilize the American people and cause them to lose interest in necessary defense modernization. But this tranquilizing effect operates even while negotiations are going on. The muted public reaction in the United States to the tremendous expansion of Soviet strategic forces in the early 1970s was in part a function of the ongoing SALT negotiations.

There is another illusion, less often appreciated, that arms control may generate, and that is the idea that negotiations promote détente and have other useful political consequences even if the talks produce no formal agreement. Implicit in this argument is the assumption that there is no harm in trying, that a nation takes on no risk in entering a negotiation, that the process may be as beneficial as the product. In fact, failure to reach agreement can jeopardize many other elements of a diplomatic relationship. If negotiations generate more acrimony than accord, the result might well be a deterioration in bilateral affairs. Arms control therefore risks exaggerating the fluctuations that seem to typify American foreign policy. If the United States takes too much goodwill into negotiations, as is often alleged, it may also react too harshly to the failure of negotiations.

There is a final danger in the arms control process, that of false expectations. Throughout the years of U.S.-Soviet arms control negotiations, undoubtedly opportunities were lost for more meaningful agreements, and political pressures deflected the negotiations from results they might otherwise have achieved. But the real failure of arms control was not in the process; it was in the fundamental and widespread public misunderstanding of what arms control was capable of producing. This public misperception was aided and abetted in the United States by every president from John Kennedy to Jimmy Carter, who was eager to tout the virtues of agreements that his administration had negotiated.

Arms control became the strategic Holy Grail. It was advertised as offering the triple benefits of slowing the arms race, improving U.S.-Soviet relations, and saving money. But arms control could not possibly deliver on this promise; and as the gap widened between promise and reality, so did disappointment with the process.

NUCLEAR LEARNING

One explanation for the long U.S.-Soviet peace indirectly related to arms control is what Joseph Nye (1987) has called "nuclear learning." Through experience and the acquisition of new information the two states have developed a shared knowledge base about nuclear issues. They have learned the destructive power of nuclear weapons, the value of secure and redundant command and control systems, the value of arms control negotiations, and most important, the inadmissibility of nuclear threats in a crisis.

This was not a lesson that came naturally or easily. After all, nuclear weapons were invented to be used, as indeed they were in the closing days of World War II. Few people could have imagined, in the early days of the nuclear era, that Hiroshima and Nagasaki might well be the end as well as the beginning of the history of the use of nuclear weapons. The United States seriously considered using nuclear weapons at several times during the 1950s (in Korea, to help the French at Dien Bien Phu, and in the Quemoy-Matsu crisis), and President Kennedy reckoned the odds on nuclear war in the Cuban missile crisis as one in three. But since the 1962 missile crisis there has been no evidence of serious discussion at the highest level of government of the use of nuclear weapons, and other than the U.S. raising of its defense alert during the 1973 Yom Kippur War virtually no overt attempts at coercive nuclear diplomacy. In the various crises of the 1970s and 1980s Washington and Moscow have eschewed nuclear threats, and in so doing they have expanded the class of conflicts for which nuclear use is inadmissible.

THE BALANCE SHEET

Arms control does have problems and shortcomings, but its limitations should not obscure the very real benefits that it has produced and may continue to offer in the future. Arms control can provide regularity and predictability to arms competition so that each party can look to the future with more confidence and less uncertainty. By committing the signatories to various limitations and restrictions, arms control can reduce the impulse toward worst-case planning. The U.S. military establishment has consistently supported strategic arms control because such accords can limit the number and type of strategic nuclear forces the Soviet Union can deploy. This makes it easier for American planners to design U.S. strategic forces and may free up money to be spent on other military functions.

Arms control can fence off dangerous and destabilizing areas of military competition. The Antarctic Treaty, the Outer Space Treaty, the Seabed Treaty, and the Biological Weapons Convention all prohibited various military activities in certain environments. Even the process of arms negotiation can enhance transparency and communications between adversaries, thus reducing fear and increasing understanding.

Arms control is a primary mechanism for building a stable U.S.-Soviet security regime. It establishes rules and institutions that obligate the two sides, channel competition into mutually acceptable arenas, and encourage the two sides to put long-term mutual interests above short-range self-interests.

Arms control is much more than two teams of negotiators glaring at each other across a bargaining table. It is primarily a way of thinking about outputs, about the consequences of weapons and doctrines on the military environment. It is an effort to give some coherence and structure to an interstate relationship that involves the risk of war.

Arms control is an attempt, in an imperfect world, to establish guidelines for behavior and rules of engagement between adversary nations. Occasionally this effort involves formal negotiations aimed at producing treaties, but more generally it is an intellectual effort to anticipate and avoid the most dangerous aspects of a military competition.

Arms control is a flexible and varied enterprise. In the future it need not take the form nor play the role it did in earlier years. Arms control can never be isolated from other elements of military policy; nor can it bear the full weight of a political relationship between the signatories. It is a modest but useful way of reducing the uncertainties that invariably beset sovereign states as they seek security in an international system whose dominant features are anarchy and insecurity.

But just because arms control did not produce the millennium is no reason to abandon the process and the modest but useful results it may produce. Measured against more realistic expectations, the accomplishments of arms control have actually been significant. The SALT treaties have helped to keep strategic weapons levels and expenditures lower than they might otherwise have been. The ABM Treaty itself may have averted a costly competition in ballistic missile defense, and the communication channel established between the two superpowers through arms control has added a valuable element of political stability.

Conclusion

It is surprising, looking back, at how much controversy surrounded the whole enterprise of arms control for much of the postwar era. Before the late 1950s, even the basic notion that arms agreements might contribute to national security was a novel one; at that time the conventional wisdom held that arms talks served only a utopian or propaganda purpose (Halperin 1989:31-32). By the end of the 1960s, the United States and Soviet Union had begun SALT negotiations, and the intellectual battle over arms control raged between those who saw it as the last best hope of mankind and those who thought it signaled disaster for the United States. By the end of the 1980s, arms control in principle had come to be accepted as an integral part of the East-West security relationship. The old refrains of great promise and dire threat could still be heard, but arms control was generally acknowledged to be a modest but nonetheless useful instrument.

Arms control by itself has not kept the nuclear peace. War between the nuclear superpowers would be irrational, counterproductive, and at least since the mid-1960s, mutually suicidal. But irrational, counterproductive, and even suicidal wars have been waged in the past, and arms control can contribute in a small way to demonstrating that elemental truth.

The two nuclear superpowers are caught in a dilemma about the use and non-use of nuclear weapons. Their leaders have said repeatedly that "a nuclear war cannot be won and must never be fought,"[4] a pronouncement reflected in the various crises of the Cold War era involving the possible use of nuclear weapons. But deterrence depends on the possibility that nuclear weapons might be used. Without such a possibility, the weapons would lose their deterrent value, and paradoxically, the likelihood of use would increase (Nye, 1986).

Arms control is a good way of getting the most out of both halves of the nuclear dilemma. It provides protective cover for nuclear ambivalence. By its very existence the process of arms control reminds all concerned that nuclear use is a real danger. Unless there were some threat of use, there would be no need for arms control. At the same time the talks themselves and the accords that occasionally result provide a sense of restraint and moderation, tangible evidence of commitment to the idea that nuclear weapons must never be used.

Anarchy and distrust are the chief characteristics of international politics today. In a world such as this, each nation has two means of protecting its security. It can build arms, competing with other states that pose a military threat; or it can pursue arms control agreements that try to constrain the threat. The history of the postwar era proves that arms control, if pursued wisely and properly, can reduce the threat; it can never eliminate the risk of war altogether. Arms control is not a substitute for weapons but a complement to them. Arms and arms control, one by creating the means to inflict unacceptable damage on a potential enemy and the other by protecting that capability from enemy attack, are both necessary for national security. A defense policy that fails to pursue the two together, that emphasizes one approach to the exclusion of the other, is dangerous and incomplete.

Nuclear weapons concentrate the mind, but not always in a constructive manner. To many the choices are stark and absolute: either disarmament or Armageddon. Disarmament may be a reasonable goal for the long-term future, but its achievement depends on a fundamental alteration of international politics not evident in the foreseeable future, and not obtainable through the practice of arms control. Premature disarmament may actually raise the risk of war.

It is not true that holocaust is our inevitable fate if we fail to move to disarmament. The United States and the Soviet Union have lived without war for over a generation, no small achievement for such ambitious and ideologically hostile nations. History reveals many long periods of international peace, of antagonistic neighbors living together in peaceful coexistence, if not outright harmony. Ten years ago the question of who started the Cold War could be guaranteed to provoke a lively academic debate, but now the Cold War is studied as a good example of crisis management — how two global superpowers, heavily armed with nuclear weapons, managed to avoid a nuclear war. The ultimate task is to realize that true international security depends not as much on arms or arms control as on reducing as much as possible the sources of conflict in international relations and on finding effective nonviolent means of resolving the conflicts that remain. This is the daunting but vitally important challenge of the future.

History reveals arms control to be a modest enterprise. This realization, slow to sink in during the decade of the 1970s, created great disillusionment among many early advocates who saw superpower arms control as the path to a new world order. In fact, as this chapter has argued, arms control is basically cautious, conservative, and oriented to the status quo. It can help stabilize a military balance, but cannot bring about the abolition of weapons. Modest agreements with modest objectives negotiated by conservative states oriented to preserving the status quo have the best prospect of being accepted, and of enduring. After a quarter-century of arms control experience, the United States and the Soviet Union seemed to have reached a common appreciation of the value of arms control, as well as the limitations inherent in the process.

ENDNOTES

1. There have been a number of attempts to apply the concept of regime theory and rule observance to U.S.-Soviet relations. See Nye (1987), Rice (1988), and Caldwell (1981).

2. In 1950 a few Soviet pilots flew MIGs in the Korean War, and in 1989 Soviet Lt. Gen. Anatoly Sidorov revealed that Soviet soldiers often manned the SA-2 surface-to-air missile systems directed against U.S. bombing missions over North Vietnam (see *The Philadelphia Inquirer*, October 13, 1989, p. 17D). The 1985 killing of Major Arthur Nicholson, a military liaison officer assigned to duty in East Germany, was a mistake for which the Soviet Union belatedly apologized.

3. Data derived from *The Military Balance*, vols. 1969-1970 and 1988-1989, published by the International Institute for Strategic Studies, London.

4. This phrase became President Reagan's favorite dictum on nuclear weapons and was accepted by the Soviets in the communiqué issued after the first Reagan-Gorbachev summit in Geneva in November, 1985.

CHAPTER TWELVE

Alliances and the Preservation of the Postwar Peace: Weighing the Contribution

Charles W. Kegley, Jr.
Gregory A. Raymond

Upon returning to Washington from the first Big Three summit conference in Teheran, President Franklin D. Roosevelt told a national radio audience: "I got along fine with Marshall Stalin. . . . I believe that we are going to get along very well with him and the Russian people — very well indeed" (*Public Papers and Addresses of Franklin D. Roosevelt*, 1943:558). At the Yalta conference fourteen months later, Joseph Stalin echoed Roosevelt's optimism. According to James F. Byrnes, director of the Office of War Mobilization, Stalin had been lavish in his praise of the United States; in fact, "Joe was the life of the party" (Yergin, 1977:67).

Yet the party was almost over. The period between the Teheran (1943) and Yalta (1945) summit conferences marked the apogee of Soviet-American relations. With their armies sweeping toward the Oder and the Rhine rivers, mutual suspicions in Moscow and Washington hardened into policy disagreements over the future of the postwar world. The day before his suicide, Adolph Hitler predicted that the "laws of both history and geography" would compel the Soviet Union and the United States to engage in "a trial of strength" (Bullock, 1962:772-73).

As allied collaboration plummeted in a downward spiral of charges and countercharges, it seemed as if the ominous prediction voiced deep within the bowels of the Reich Chancellery would come to pass. On the one hand, Stalin (1946) insisted that the defeat of Germany did not eliminate the danger of foreign aggression, and his heir-apparent, Andrei Zhdanov (1947), identified American expansionism as the major threat to world peace. On the other hand, W. Averell Harriman, United States ambassador to the Soviet Union, warned of a "barbarian invasion of Europe" (Truman, 1955:71), and George F. Kennan, his chief assistant, asserted that the Soviet leadership sought to destroy "our traditional way of life" (*Foreign Relations of the United States*, 1946:706). Lacking the glue of a common external threat, the Grand Alliance of World War II unraveled amidst distrust, apprehension, and bitter recriminations.

But war has yet to erupt between the Soviet Union and the United States. Despite nearly five decades of intense rivalry and numerous serious disputes, the superpowers have avoided a trial of military strength. How do we explain this rather surprising pattern of prolonged — though hostile — peace? Definitive answers are elusive, and any attempt to find them must confront a number of analytic obstacles. Not only are the sources of the so-called long peace rooted in a web of interdependent factors, but it is exceedingly difficult to disentangle their relative importance. Nevertheless we have powerful incentives to try, for knowledge about the factors that have contributed to the long postwar peace may assist future efforts to avoid war.

Alliances are among the many factors that have been cited to explain the long peace. Following the Second World War, policymakers constructed them to augment defense capabilities, deter aggression, and increase national security. The wisdom of this strategy, however, has been challenged by the growth of unilateralism in the latter stages of this century. Superpowers and smaller states alike have begun to opt for going it alone (Kegley and Raymond, 1989), a strategy that raises the further question of whether dismantling the elaborate network of alliances built in the wake of World War II will strengthen or erode the foundations on which the long peace has rested.

To begin our analysis of the contribution that alliances have made to the long peace, we shall describe various theoretical propositions that have been advanced about the nature of alliances and summarize findings on the relationship between alliances and war. This review of the perceived advantages and disadvantages of alliances will set the stage for an examination of the uses to which the superpowers have put alliances in the post–World War II era. We shall then evaluate the ways that alliances may have preserved the great-power peace since 1945, and finally, we shall project the implications of our evaluation for the future of the international system.

ALLIANCES IN THEORY AND PRACTICE

Alliances are formal agreements among sovereign states "for the putative purpose of coordinating their behavior in the event of certain specified contingencies of a military nature" (Bueno de Mesquita and Singer, 1973:241).[1] These agreements are a byproduct of the "security dilemma" confronting states in a decentralized, self-help system. They may be designed to deter aggressors, to defend oneself in the event of war, or to initiate military action against some opponent. As Grace E. Iusi Scarborough and Bruce Bueno de Mesquita (1988:87) note, "Alignment and dealignment are the main short-term strategies for increasing

security. . . ." When confronted with an external threat, a strategic choice
is presented by the options of "[1] adding or expanding relations with
nations that can provide immediate increases in one's security, and [2]
eliminating or curtailing relations with nations that are a drain on security." To make informed choices about these options, statesmen must
weigh the advantages of an alliance against its costs and risks. This has
seldom proven easy, for it requires that they assess a host of uncertainties, ranging from the military strength and credibility of potential partners, to the goals, motivations, and capabilities of adversaries.

The Calculus of Alliance Partner Choice

Explanations of why states join alliances are often couched in terms
of gaining "coldly calculated advantages" (Jordan and Taylor, 1984:474).
In the first place, they provide a mechanism for aggregating military
capabilities. Second, they can help reduce the costs associated with offensive or defensive action by spreading them among several partners. Third,
they furnish a medium for exerting leverage to mobilize or restrain a
partner, to neutralize those who might otherwise interfere with some
foreign policy undertaking, or to preempt an adversary by bonding with
a strategically important third party. Finally, alliances may help a state
acquire benefits that it could not have attained by acting unilaterally.
Aside from the common benefit of security which accrues as a "public
good" to all members, alliances bestow private benefits on certain states.
For example, a relatively weak state can gain access to additional
resources, obtain a steady supply of sophisticated weaponry, or receive
instruction on the use of new technology. Even a powerful state may
enhance its position through alliance membership by acquiring overseas
bases and support facilities from which it may project its power. Thus
states form alliances for diverse reasons, despite the restrictions that
these alliances impose.

Decisions to ally are often made with caution and some reluctance.
Generally, it is assumed that the opportunity to form an alliance is likely
to be seized only when (1) the perceived benefits exceed the costs, and
(2) the costs are politically sustainable. To put this assumption another
way, many observers assert that regardless of the risk-taking propensity
of a nation's leadership, alliances will be shunned if leaders believe that
their country "is strong enough to hold its own unaided or that the burden
of commitment resulting from the alliance is likely to outweigh the advantages" (Morgenthau, 1973:181). Moreover, this assertion is backed by historical evidence showing that "potential alliances which fail to increase both
partners' security levels almost never form" (Altfeld, 1984:538).

The preeminent risk inhibiting the decision to ally resides in the
chance that an alliance treaty will bind one's state to a commitment
which later ceases to remain in its interest. Ever mindful of this risk,

statesmen tend to be wary about entrusting their security to the pledges of others. They know that by doing so, they allow their future foreign policies to be held hostage by the chains of previous commitments. Reflecting on this basic inhibition, George F. Kennan summarized the decision calculus of most policymakers with respect to alliances in the following manner:

> The relations among nations, in this imperfect world, constitute a fluid substance, always in motion, changing subtly from day to day in ways that are difficult to detect from the myopia of the passing moment, and even difficult to discern from the perspective of the future one. The situation at one particular time is never quite the same as the situation of five years later — indeed it is sometimes very significantly different, even though the stages by which this change came about are seldom visible at the given moment. This is why wise and experienced statesmen usually shy away from commitments likely to constitute limitations on a government's behavior at unknown dates in the future in the face of unpredictable situations. This is also a reason why agreements long in process of negotiation, particularly when negotiated in great secrecy, run the risk of being somewhat out of date before they are ever completed. (Kennan, 1984:238)

Despite this compelling logic, states frequently have overcome their inhibition to form alliances. Without the risk of a promise, there is little prospect for assistance. There is only solitary self-help. To avoid this dreaded circumstance, states have warily forged alliances. As Arnold Wolfers (1968:269) points out, "Whenever in recorded history a system of multiple sovereignty has existed, some of the sovereign units when involved in conflicts with others have entered into alliances." The incentives to ally for defensive purposes have often proven irresistible when two or more states have faced a common threat. In fact, they can be so strong that states have even found it attractive to make common cause with partners they otherwise find morally repugnant.

Necessity, not ideological affinity, is thus conventionally regarded as the primary cement of most alliance bonds. To acknowledge that "nearly *all* alliances are formed in anticipation of *some* probability of war" (Levy, 1981:611) is to highlight the seriousness of the commitments that are made. The seriousness stems from three sources. First, an agreement to join forces reduces a state's freedom of maneuver by requiring it to conform with certain treaty obligations. Second, the agreement also makes the state dependent on each ally's compliance with those responsibilities. Third, enforcing an agreement is often more difficult than bargaining over its terms. Disputes about duties may be expected to arise as new circumstances provoke controversies about the meaning of any alliance; therefore states have found it necessary to invest considerable effort in the management of alliance relationships in order to ensure compliance with commitments.

Even as alliance treaties are signed, the reliability of the parties may be shrouded in suspicion. Though inertia may lengthen the life of an alliance, suspicion will grow when the common threat recedes. There are, as one foreign policymaker has noted, distinct seasons to the life of every alliance:

> Almost by definition alliances have a limited life cycle..... National objectives change, the threat which made it worthwhile to subordinate some national interests to the evolution of a collaborative policy changes also, and the strains of alliance become too great to bear. For though alliance has been an essential device of international politics for nearly three thousand years, it is bound to develop internal strains once the period of clear and present danger is past, since it must involve a relationship between strong and less strong powers, restricting the freedom of both without giving either a decisive influence upon the policy of the other. (Buchan, 1965:295)

To be sure, many leaders place a positive value on preserving alliances despite the erosion of their utility over time. But if the costs of honoring the commitment are thought to be increasing due to incompatibility of interests, the temptation to rescind one's promises will become powerful, even if the decision to defect is not easy.

States seldom assume a fixed policy toward their obligations. Instead, they have historically demonstrated a preference to reserve the right to abandon an agreement if and when the costs of adherence become too burdensome. Because future conditions can never be known at the time that the provisions of an agreement are negotiated, all states respect the concept of *raison d'etat*, a classic "escape clause" by which policy reversals can be justified by citing the exigencies of a particular situation. Many national leaders have claimed that such clauses "are tacitly annexed to every covenant" (Garner, 1927:509), and examples abound of states that have tried to escape from alliance agreements by using the justification that national security interests override international obligations.

The provisions of most treaties are drafted loosely in order to leave each ally room to interpret the nature of the commitment. According to advocates of *realpolitik*, prudent statesmen should put more trust in their own power than in the goodwill of others. Yet by writing a treaty with elastic language to diminish the chance of becoming entangled in a partner's problems, the prospects of being betrayed by that partner at a subsequent point in time are increased. Simply put, the risks of entrapment and abandonment "tend to vary inversely: reducing one tends to increase the other" (Snyder, 1984:467).

Upon what do all these elements of alliance decision making converge? In short, that "alliances are typically against, and only derivatively for someone or something" (Liska, 1962:12). They inspire both hopes and fears because, by their very nature, they provide opportunities and entail obligations. Whether they actually increase or decrease the likelihood of war is a subject of considerable scholarly debate. Let us outline the parameters of this debate as an introduction to the question of whether alliances have contributed to the long great-power peace experienced since 1945.

The Uncertain Relationship Between Alliances and War

Are alliances bulwarks of security or conduits along which conflict may flow? Both opinions are generally voiced with passion and eloquence. Those who contend that alliances promote global stability draw inspiration from the famous maxim: *si vis pacem, para bellum* (if you want peace, prepare for war). Presumably, alliances enhance preparedness in two ways. First, they may make a state sufficiently strong to deter an attack. Second, they may foster vigilance and thus encourage states to marshal countervailing power whenever it is necessary to parry the expansionist thrusts of aggressors. Speaking before the National Press Club on October 27, 1988, Colin L. Powell, assistant to the president for national security affairs, exemplified this point of view when he declared: "A side that sees an easy victory will go after it."

In contrast to this "peace-through-preparedness" school of thought, those who believe that alliances contribute to global instability contend that the number of allies possessed by a state may not deter an aggressor, particularly when the coalition is composed of minor powers. Wars, they insist, could still occur under a variety of conditions: an irrational leader might strike because of his utter contempt for the opposing alliance's capabilities and resolve; a desperate leader might see preemption as the only solution to a costly, protracted conflict; or a risk-acceptant leader might use surprise as a force multiplier to create a *fait accompli* before the victims could mobilize and deploy their military forces.

But even if a state possesses military partners of considerable strength, there are several reasons why critics of alliance-building consider it destabilizing. First, alliances look menacing; hence it is likely that they will cause others to scramble for allies of their own, and therein raise tensions to a new, more dangerous, level. Second, alliances are entangling; they can drag members into conflicts which do not affect their vital interests. Finally, alliances are sanguineous; their very existence means that even if a nation's armies are beaten and its leaders can see that resources are inadequate to sustain further combat, it would be encouraged to continue fighting by the hope of aid from its allies. In sum, whereas some theorists and statesmen advance the proposition that alliances sustain peace, others echo Sir John Frederick Maurice's lament that "if you prepare thoroughly for war you will get it."

Despite the significance of this debate over the consequences of alliance formation, until J. David Singer and Melvin Small (1968) pioneered the effort to bring the scientific method to bear on the possible connection between alliances and war, virtually all of the arguments made by both sides hinged on historical anecdotes and personal impressions. Yet, rather than resolving the debate, the research undertaken by Singer and Small actually aroused further controversy by revealing that alliance aggregation and the onset of war were positively related in the twentieth century but negatively related in the nineteenth. This unanticipated finding inspired numerous replication studies based on different data sets, measurement techniques, domain assumptions, and statistical tests. Although the results from these studies have not yielded a single set of conclusions, various clues have been discovered about the puzzling relationship between alliances and war. In light of these clues, it appears that whereas alliances by themselves may not cause war or preserve peace (Levy, 1981; Thompson, et al., 1980; Ostrom and Hoole, 1978), they may be indirectly linked to the onset of war and directly associated with the expansion and enlargement of war once it occurs (Vasquez, 1987:119).

The indirect link between alliance aggregation and the onset of war lies in the stimulation of arms races. Alliances have been found to be related to subsequent increases in arms expenditures (Wallace, 1972:65), and serious disputes that take place during an arms race historically have tended to escalate into wars (Wallace, 1979; 1982).

Beyond this indirect linkage with the onset of war, there is further evidence that alliances are directly associated with an increase in the number and types of belligerents who subsequently enter a war after it has begun (Siverson and King, 1979). Alliance aggregation spreads hostilities and engenders larger, more complex conflicts, particularly when the war in question began as a major-minor power confrontation (Sabrosky, 1985) or involved the key ally of some larger country (Midlarsky, 1986). Specifically, alliances decrease the number of interaction opportunities available to states (Most, et al., 1990) and may stimulate intense competition over the acquisition of additional partners (Beer, 1981:230). Given that high levels of alliance polarization have been found to be war-prone (Wayman, 1985; Wallace, 1973), and given that war rarely occurs during periods of decreasing tightness (Bueno de Mesquita, 1978), should competition for new allies result in the creation of extremely rigid blocs, the magnitude and severity of any war that is fought will be high, especially if these blocs possess relatively equal capabilities.

Alliances thus have a dual personality: they both derive from and may contribute to global insecurity. Tying the existing evidence together, it would seem that peace is best preserved when alliance commitments are made judiciously and not left open-ended. When applying this evidence to the post–World War II era, we shall see that answering the question "What contributions have alliances made to the long peace?" requires us to distinguish between those alliances that are carefully crafted around areas of vital concern versus those that have led commitments to exceed capabilities, entrapping the superpowers in disputes where their primary interests were not at stake. To explore this thesis further, let us examine the purposes to which great-powers have put alliances in the postwar era, the commitment norms they have supported, and the consequences which have resulted from these practices and norms. A review of the post–World War II history of alliances can assist us in evaluating the contribution of alliances to the long peace.

ALLIANCE POLITICS IN THE COLD WAR

The post–World War II era of alliance politics can be divided into two phases. One phase was fathered by what Hans J. Morgenthau (1970:98) called a Cold War of *Position*; the other, by a Cold War of *Movement*. The former entailed efforts by Washington and Moscow to limit external influence over geographic regions that each considered of vital interest. The latter involved vigorous searches for new partners that could be enlisted by either superpower against its rival. One way to approach the question of whether alliances have been a supporting pillar of the edifice of the post–World War II peace is to differentiate between those alliances that were associated with the Cold War of Position and those that were associated with the Cold War of Movement. Although combat did not erupt between the superpowers during either period, each phase in the post-1945 evolution of alliance-building had different consequences for national security and international stability.

Alliances in the Cold War of Position

Despite the promise of universalism that was embodied within the Atlantic Charter (1941) and the Declaration of the United Nations (1942), the early postwar era witnessed a novel version of the principle *cujus regio, ejus religio* (whose the region, his the religion) applied to those territories that were liberated from Axis control. "Whoever occupies a territory," declared Stalin, "imposes on it his own social system . . . as far as his army can reach" (cited in Djilas, 1961:114). Both Washington and Moscow used alliances to consolidate what their armies had reached. Far from being flexible coalitions of fairly equal members, these alliances developed into blocs (Russett, 1974:321). That is to say, they became groups of secondary powers clustered around one of the two superpowers.

Driven by an American desire to contain Russian expansionism and an equally strong Soviet desire to build a buffer zone that would preclude another invasion of the USSR, the alliance blocs of the immediate postwar period took on the characteristics of a war of position. For the United States, a line of political entrenchment was constructed by means of the

Inter-American Treaty of Reciprocal Assistance (1947), the North Atlantic Treaty Organization (1949), the ANZUS Pact (1951), and a number of bilateral alliances designed to reinforce U.S. geopolitical interests as well as to protect noncommunist centers of world industrial capacity (e.g., Japan [1951], the Philippines [1951], and Spain [1953]). For the Soviet Union, a more secure frontier was established through a series of agreements that were reached between 1945 and 1948 with various Eastern European countries, agreements that were later institutionalized under the auspices of the Warsaw Treaty Organization (1955). When combined with previous arrangements with the Mongolian People's Republic (1936), a new treaty with Finland (1948), and ties with the People's Republic of China (1950), the alliances with Moscow's western neighbors produced a belt of friendly states around much of its border.

Alliances in the Cold War of Movement

In addition to the alliances that were used to delineate specific spheres of interest, both nations also engaged in an intense, almost predatory competition for new allies outside of the main strategic theater. Beginning with the efforts of Secretary of State John Foster Dulles and First Secretary Nikita Khrushchev, the U.S. and USSR began to woo states from the periphery of the world system. Globalization of the superpower alliance race during this period of "pactomania" resulted in a welter of alliances with Third World states. The Southeast Asia Treaty Organization (1955), the Central Treaty Organization (1959),[2] and the Soviet alliance with Cuba (1961) exemplified the attempts emanating from Washington and Moscow to outflank each other. The Cold War was no longer a setpiece encounter between deadlocked giants; it had become a contest of improvisation and maneuver.

Underpinning the search for new allies was a belief that nations tend to gravitate toward the powerful; hence irresolution on the part of either superpower would weaken its ability to attract and maintain allies. As President John F. Kennedy put it, "If the United States were to falter, the whole world would inevitably move toward the Communist bloc" (cited in Brown, 1968:217). Similarly, the Kremlin interpreted the ebb and flow of its influence over other countries as a product of the "correlation of forces." Both sides implicitly assumed that alliance formation was governed by bandwagoning. In President Lyndon Johnson's words, there were "a hundred little nations" watching how the United States and the Soviet Union responded to international challenges, nations that presumably would make decisions to align or dealign based on what they observed.

Since the mid-1970s, leaders in the White House and the Kremlin have included what might be called "proto-alliances" in their flanking maneuvers. Rather than forging defense treaties of the sort that the U.S.

signed with South Korea (1953) and the USSR concluded with North Korea (1961), they began to make less obtrusive agreements pledging more modest commitments. The proto-alliances designed during the Carter and Reagan administrations have been described by Terry L. Deibel (1987:114) as highly discrete arrangements based on a mix of *ad hoc* diplomatic contact, arms transfers, economic aid, facilities construction, and basing access. Like the earlier Dulles alliance system, the geographic scope of these new security arrangements has been diffuse, embracing such countries as Morocco, Saudi Arabia, Oman, Honduras, Pakistan, and Thailand. Similarly, the proto-alliances nourished by General Secretary Leonid Brezhnev and his successors have been far-reaching. Buttressed by treaties of friendship and cooperation that promise consultation on issues of common defense and cooperation in the event of threats to peace, this new form of security arrangement has been made by the Soviets with Vietnam, Iraq, Yemen, Angola, Mozambique, and several other Third World countries.

THE PROBLEMATIC CONTRIBUTION OF ALLIANCES TO THE LONG PEACE

To recapitulate our argument thus far, a review of the long postwar peace suggests the presence of two overlapping phases of alliance formation: in the first, alliances were used to draw demarcation lines around areas of perceived vital interest along the western and northeastern Eurasian strategic fronts; in the second, a more geographically extensive system of alliances was built in the hope of cultivating allies to the rear of the rival superpower. Threats to peace were frequent throughout both phases, yet none of the many superpower disputes escalated to war. Moreover, peace prevailed even when some of these alliances began to unravel and were replaced by new combinations of informal proto-alliances.

At first glance it thus would seem that alliances have been unrelated to the preservation of the long superpower peace. War occurred neither during the period of rapid alliance formation nor during the following period of alliance dissolution. Yet a second, more careful examination is needed, for it is not the magnitude of alliance aggregation that matters, but the kinds of alliances and supporting commitment norms that most affect the prospects for continued peace.

Alliances and Extended Immediate Deterrence

The conventional wisdom of the peace-through-preparedness school of thought holds that alliances help preserve peace by enabling a state to deter an attack upon itself or upon some client by providing the means either to deny the potential aggressor its immediate battlefield objectives, or to punish it through military retaliation. Conversely, the findings from scientific research on the alliance/war relationship indicate that changes in the level of alliance aggregation are not directly linked with historical fluctuations in the onset of war. If the long peace deviates from this general pattern by being a product of deterrence through alliance-building, then we should find evidence that alliances prevented a superpower attack in one or more situations that were ripe for war.

But a perusal of Soviet-American relations since 1945 does not yield such evidence. The alliances that were erected at the beginning of the Cold War were conceived at a time when neither side was willing to risk a major armed conflict. Following the Japanese surrender on August 14, 1945, national leaders in Washington felt mounting public pressure to demobilize; those in Moscow faced the enormous task of reconstruction. Kremlin officials estimated that 20 million Soviet citizens had perished in the maelstrom of the Second World War; additionally, the country had suffered half of the total material destruction in Europe, amounting to one-quarter of the USSR's reproducible wealth. By 1948, the United States had cut back from a wartime peak of approximately 8 million troops to roughly 1.4 million, while the Soviet Union reduced the number of people in uniform from 12 million to somewhere between 2.5 and 4 million (Wolfe, 1970:10-11).

Despite a hesitancy to engage the rival superpower on the battlefield, the exigencies of several situations propelled both Moscow and Washington in that very direction. The Azerbaijan incident, the coup in Czechoslovakia, the Berlin blockade, and, most important, the Korean War led both sides to revamp their security policies. The United States instituted sweeping organizational changes under the National Security Act of 1947, adopted new policies toward military (the Truman Doctrine) and economic assistance (the Marshall Plan), and undertook a complete reassessment of its strategic situation (National Security Council Memorandum No. 68). At the same time, the Soviet Union began a full-scale drive to produce an atomic bomb, reorganize its defenses, and launch a major military modernization program.

Though alliances were a key component of such security policy innovations, it is unlikely that they deterred the superpowers from fighting over the future direction of the postwar world. According to the results from several data-based studies, formal military alliances are not statistically associated with deterrence success (see Russett, 1963; Huth and Russett, 1984).[3] Peace during the early years of the Cold War would thus seem to owe more to the twin constraints of demobilization and reconstruction, plus a complex mix of American nuclear superiority, Soviet preponderance in theater conventional forces, and the web of economic and political ties between the superpowers and their proteges. Whereas the U.S. could threaten nuclear punishment if its homeland was attacked and could be expected to defend those third parties with whom it had important and direct material interests, the decisive Soviet advantage in conventional combined-arms forces allowed the USSR to hold Western Europe hostage for American restraint. In view of historical evidence that extended deterrence is bolstered by local conventional superiority and ties of trade, investment, and assistance (see Organski and Kugler, 1980:176-79; Kugler, 1984; Huth and Russett, 1988), there are reasonable grounds for arguing that alliances did not make a direct, independent contribution to preventing the Cold War from becoming hot.

It would be wrong, however, to infer that alliances have made no contribution to the long postwar peace. It is our thesis that their impact has been contingent upon the kind of commitment that was made: those alliances associated with the Cold War of Position have tended to advance the cause of peace by fostering tacitly coordinated problem-solving, whereas those associated with the Cold War of Movement have been counterproductive, fostering overcommitment, confusion, and global instability.

Alliances and the Coordination of Expectations

The rivalry between the Soviet Union and the United States can be conceptualized as a geographically diverse group of "mixed-motive games," each containing elements of mutual dependence and conflict, partnership and competition (Schelling, 1960:89). As Alexander L. George (1986:251) has pointed out, many of these games have different structures and somewhat different implications for conflict management. Two types of game structures lend themselves to the development of normative rules that allow contestants to coordinate their expectations: those in which both superpowers recognize that they have strong interests (e.g., Berlin), and those in which both recognize that one side has strong interests (e.g., Eastern Europe for the Soviet Union and Latin America for the United States). Game structures where both sides have modest, disputed, or uncertain interests are less likely to engender rulemaking.

The alliances formed as part of the Cold War of Position were located in arenas where game structures were conducive to the creation of ground rules. To be sure, these norms lacked symmetry and elegance, and they underwent slow, sporadic, and uneven growth following the failure of planned rule-making at the 1945 United Nations Conference in San Francisco. Nevertheless, they helped regulate competition, and thereby added a modicum of order and predictability to the superpower rivalry.[4]

Foremost among these tacit "rules of the game" were those that pertained to delineating spheres of influence and avoiding direct military confrontation. Like the Tordesillas regime between Spain and Portugal in the fifteenth century and the various nineteenth century agreements over respective European interests in Africa and Asia, the alliances born of the Cold War Position clarified the political landscape. They provided a "focal point solution" to pressing questions about the architecture of the bipolar system that was to be built on the ashes of the old Eurocentric balance of power (Weede, 1975:55; Schelling, 1966:137-38). The lines of demarcation drawn by NATO, the Warsaw Pact, and the other alliances of the Cold War of Position were simple, recognizable, conspicuous, and unambiguous. In contrast to the nebulous, ephemeral configurations produced by such grandiose alliances as CENTO and SEATO, they contributed to the long peace in at least two ways.

First, clear lines of demarcation helped prevent potential disputes over areas of vital interest from accumulating in crises of accelerating frequency. Historically, such patterns have proven to be dangerous (Midlarsky, 1984). One source of danger is the tendency of national leaders to use more coercive bargaining techniques in each subsequent encounter (Leng, 1983), a tendency that has been found to be associated with the escalation of crises into wars (Gochman and Leng, 1983; Leng and Wheeler, 1979). Another source of danger is that during a series of disputes, numerous distinct political stakes become linked into a single over-arching issue which increases the intractability of the conflict and lessens the prospects for an amicable settlement (Mansbach and Vasquez, 1981). Where superpower spheres of influence have been clear, neither side has mounted a significant challenge to its rival;[5] where they have been unclear (as in the case of South Korea after Secretary of State Dean Acheson's "defensive perimeter" speech) or in decay (as in the case of Cuba following the Bay of Pigs invasion), recklessness and opportunism have overcome prudence and caution.

Second, as qualitatively prominent focal points for the coordination of reciprocal expectations, the lines of demarcation drawn by the alliances of the Cold War of Position provided a framework for subsequent rule-making. Take, for instance, A. W. DePorte's example of Europe, where the superpowers not only used alliances to define their own mutual relations,

> but in the process, and as a by-product of it, also established a system of relationships with and among the countries of Europe, their own allies and dependents, and those of the other. They thereby provided a solution, inadvertently, to the problem which the countries of Europe had faced and failed to master since 1890: the place of a too-powerful Germany in a European system which could not of itself preserve the independence of its members in the face of German strength. (DePorte, 1979:116)

As described by Lord Ismay, first secretary general of NATO, the purpose of the Atlantic Alliance was "to keep the Russians out, the Americans in, and the Germans down." Not only did this help allay the fears of those Western Europeans who were concerned about future German rearmament, but it furnished some of the political scaffolding that was later used to construct such agreements as the Austrian State Treaty (1955) and the Helsinki Accord (1975).[6]

If alliances are to coordinate expectations, it is advantageous for them to remain stable over time, since alliances of long duration produce a greater clarity in the system than alliances that must be repeatedly restored (Midlarsky, 1988:167). Whether alliances become lasting linkages depends upon their reliability, which has been found to be a function of the type of commitment that is made, the nature of the relationship between the signatory parties, and the prevailing normative climate of opinion regarding the sanctity of promissory obligations. Specifically, defense pacts and ententes tend to be honored more often than nonaggression agreements; alliances composed of politically compatible states possessing roughly equivalent power are upheld more frequently than those with a major power linked to one or more minor powers (Sabrosky, 1980); and a restrictive international normative order that supports binding agreements is more conducive to alliance reliability than a permissive order that allows the unilateral abrogation of commitments (Kegley and Raymond, 1990).

Whether alliances will contribute to peace in the next century depends upon their stability. Unfortunately, few military partnerships nowadays fit the above profile of reliability, a troublesome pattern that is compounded by signs that normative support for the sanctity of promissory obligations is declining. Historically, in diplomatic cultures of mistrust, where states have been permitted unrestrained freedom to renounce their alliance agreements, four results have occurred: the incidence of serious disputes among nations has climbed, the percentage of major powers involved in these disputes has risen, a greater number of disputes escalated into wars, and the magnitude and severity of those wars which erupted have increased (Kegley and Raymond, 1982; 1984). In view of the dangers inherent in these trends, let us conclude with a projection of the implications of our analysis for the immediate future.

THE TWILIGHT OF THE COLD WAR ALLIANCES

In the aftermath of World War II, the superpowers strongly endorsed alliances as instruments for security. Neutrality was chastised, the nonaligned movement had not yet gathered momentum, and the needs of the colonial states awaiting independence were not taken into account. The overriding need was for collective defense pacts resting on assured compliance with treaty agreements. But beginning in the mid-1960s, the perceived costs of alliances began to receive increased critical attention. With the dispersion of military capabilities, the advent of multiple centers of autonomous political decision, and the emergence of détente, the first tears in the web of Cold War alliances became visible. Nations have always been acutely aware of the risks involved with tying their fate to others, but by the late 1970s those fears rose to new heights. Behind all the pious rhetoric about friendship and the merits of collective defense, statesmen openly began to ask whether changing international conditions had made the security interests of many allies incompatible.

The accelerating pace of global change had heightened the risks of permanent alignments and concomitantly reduced the perceived utility of standing agreements. Furthermore, the emergence of conditions of complex interdependence had placed unprecedented burdens on commitments to alliance obligations, expanding both the number of issues dividing nations and the linkages among them. Distinguishing between friend and foe became increasingly difficult. The title of a book by a policymaker in the Reagan administration captured this new sentiment: *The Treaty Trap* (Beilenson, 1969).

In many respects the end of the 1960s represented a transition in alliance politics. Conflicting interests arose from deep structural changes in the international system, and policy opinion began to swing toward a dual emphasis on the dangers of entangling alliances and the right of states to unilaterally renounce the promises contained in treaties of alliance. Three sets of indicators speak to this trend: (1) the changing normative temper of international law, (2) state practices generally, and (3) the policies and conduct of the United States.

International Treaty Law

At the conclusion of World War II, a treaty regime emerged that stressed the inviolability of promissory obligations in accordance with the norm *pacta sunt servanda* (treaties are binding). Approximately one quarter of a century later, support for the legal doctrine of *rebus sic stantibus* (by reason of changed conditions) began to mount. By allowing a state to terminate an agreement unilaterally if a fundamental change occurs in those circumstances that existed at the signing of the agreement, *rebus sic stantibus* facilitates rapid realignment and a fluid system of opportunistic partnerships.

The first hints of support for a more flexible interpretation of promissory obligations arose in 1966, when the International Law Commission ruled that although the obligation to abide by agreements was valid, "evidence of the acceptance of the doctrine [*rebus sic stantibus*] is so considerable that it seems to indicate a recognition of a need for this safety-valve in the law of treaties" (Weinstein, 1969:43). Further signs were seen in the Vienna Conference on the Law of Treaties, which concluded its deliberations and issued a final report in 1969. Although a comparison of Articles 26 and 62 of the Draft Treaty shows that *pacta sunt servanda* remained the dominant commitment norm in international law, its force in legal discourse was mitigated by the renewed attention given to *rebus sic stantibus*. Hence the Vienna negotiations opened the door for a more relaxed definition of one's duty to adhere to promissory obligations. States acquired greater freedom to shed undesired or obsolete commitments which no longer seemed to serve the original purposes for which those alliances were designed (Carty, 1986:67-68).

State Practices

International law tends to codify changes in customary state practice. Since the late 1960s, that practice has reflected the growing reluctance of states to enter into formal alliances and has reinforced the movement toward what Inis Claude (1981) calls "casual commitment." A catalyst in this process was the shift of the international system away from tight bipolarity. With the advent of détente, the horizontal and vertical proliferation of military capabilities, and the diffusion of economic power, the need for rigid, cohesive bloc structures receded. Both the policies of states and the commitment norms they supported underwent modification. The American severance of its formal promise to protect Taiwan in 1980, and the "strategic divorce" in 1986 between the United States and New Zealand over the issue of the harboring of U.S. nuclear ships, are representative of this trend. Strained and broken relations between present or former alliance partners (the U.S. with Iran and Nicaragua; the USSR with its Warsaw Pact satellites, the People's Republic of China, Ethiopia, and Egypt) attested to the fragility of alliances whose permanence was assumed when they were forged. As Terry L. Deibel (1987:113-14) notes, entire alliance systems had dissolved, with the only remembrances of some of these schemes being "pale, proxy alliances like ASEAN, the Gulf Cooperation Council, or the Organization of Eastern Caribbean States, which enjoy only U.S. support, not direct American commitment."

Another example of this trend toward a preference for prudent noncommitment was seen in the observable (but vehemently denied) decline in NATO cohesion during the 1980s. General Secretary Mikhail Gorbachev's advocacy of arms reductions, his theme of a common "European Home," and the end of Communist party rule in Poland, Czechoslovakia, Hungary, and Romania eroded the perception of a clear and present danger from the East. At the same time, the rise of Euroneutralism, the increasing pace of Western European economic and political integration, and calls for a "defensive defense" and a nuclear-free European theatre raised the prospect of a new security system, one based on decoupling Europe from the United States. Indeed, the disarray within the Western Alliance was so deeply rooted that in many respects NATO resembled "a phantom alliance" (Draper, 1988) whose main continuity had become a "continuity of discord" (Jackson, 1985). Unless Atlantic relations were fundamentally reordered, observers warned, the alliance could collapse amid bitter recriminations (Layne, 1987:22).

Nor did this metamorphosis unfold only in the Western Alliance. Eastern European nations requested the withdrawal of Soviet forces from their territories, requests that were facilitated by the Soviet Union itself, where Mikhail Gorbachev's emphasis on *glasnost* (plain-speaking), *perestroika* (restructuring), and "new thinking" loosened Moscow's grip on the Warsaw Pact. In addition, a comparison of treatises authored by Soviet publicists from Kozhevnikov to Levin to Tunkin revealed a gradual acceptance of the *clausula rebus sic stantibus*. According to Gyorgy Haraszti (1975:31), "The headway that the clause [was] making in the Soviet literature on international law [influenced] Soviet diplomatic practice." As in the West, acceptance of a more elastic definition of commitment enabled bloc members to sever their allegiance to the bloc leader.

"Global unilateralism" is the current code word for the effort of states to detach themselves from existing treaty obligations. It "implies withdrawal from any and all alliances," but "more properly and soberly understood, it means little more than a partial disengagement from many of the extravagant . . . commitments that were embodied in truly 'entangling alliances' " (Kristol, 1986:23). This lack of confidence in the capacity of alliances to increase security has been reinforced by the previously mentioned growth in support for flexible commitment norms. There is irony (and, perhaps, danger) in the fact that trust in promissory obligations within the realm of "high politics" has declined at precisely the same time that the scope of international obligations on matters of "low politics" has expanded to unprecedented proportions (Brewin, 1988). Few leaders in today's interdependent, pluralistic world recommend isolation. Few doubt their countries' inescapable entanglement in the economic affairs and security concerns of other states. But few today express faith in the agreements necessary to manage this level of collaboration among allies.

American Foreign Policy and Norm Revision

The alliance policies and code of conduct that prevail at any given time within the international system have always been influenced by the behavior practiced and rules supported by the system's most powerful member. Yet the Reagan administration's erratic behavior with respect to the over forty treaty commitments that the United States has made in the postwar period undermined the image of alliances and reduced confidence in their capacity to protect peace. The American record across a broad spectrum of cases showed a clear intent to shed perceived treaty encumbrances, bypass multinational institutions, and avoid international legal strictures. Its rejection of the Law of the Sea Treaty, withdrawal from UNESCO, reinterpretation of the ABM Treaty, and position on compulsory jurisdiction by the International Court of Justice exemplified the effort to loosen international legal restrictions on unilateral state action (Malawer, 1988). In short, the United States adopted the same preference for acting alone without prior consultation that it previously found so objectionable when practiced by its allies.

With the gradual decline in the power and authority of the United States throughout the 1970s and 1980s, normative backing for binding commitments deteriorated and portions of the vast network of American alliances slowly dissolved into a kaleidoscope of ambiguous proto-alliances. Washington failed to heed the principle of the conservation of commitments.

The task now facing the United States is to arrest the decay of commitment norms and steer a path between the twin dangers of pactophobia and pactomania. True leadership in world affairs does not reside in the unilateralism of going it alone. Nor does it lie in forging more alliances of maneuver. Leadership entails building support for those rules that will strengthen global stability, as well as encouraging other states to act in concert with those rules.

ALLIANCES AND PEACE IN THE "POST-POSTWAR" ERA

The international system is presently moving through a period of fundamental readjustment. Profound shifts in the European political landscape presage the end of the containment doctrine that has underpinned American geostrategic thinking for more than four decades. "The multipolar world into which we are moving," observed Deputy Secretary of State Lawrence Eagleburger, "is not necessarily going to be a safer place." Greater vision will be required than in the simpler bipolar era, especially throughout the difficult transition from bipolarity to multipolarity.

The Bush administration recognized the importance of making this transition as smooth as possible, and toward that end sought a new architecture for what Secretary of State James Baker optimistically termed a "post-postwar" era. Through a series of public statements, President Bush alleviated fears that the United States would, in a fit of isolationist withdrawal, disengage itself from Europe and abandon its allies. Yet his attempt to safeguard the long peace by restoring confidence in American commitments may be undermined by other elements in the administration's architectural design. Specifically, the proclaimed goal of easing the Soviet army out of Eastern Europe while simultaneously attempting to bring a united Germany into a reconstituted Atlantic Alliance could breed the very instability that the president sought to prevent. Such a possibility would deprive Moscow of its most strategic ally (East Germany) and reinvigorate NATO at the same time that the Warsaw Pact disintegrated. This, the Soviets repeatedly stressed in 1989, was unreasonable and unacceptable. As West German Foreign Minister Hans-Dietrich Genscher agreed in February, 1990, it was unrealistic to push the integrated NATO defense forward to the Polish border.

The fate of Germany may not be the "central problem of the universe," as General de Gaulle once quipped, but it is central to Soviet security concerns. Any architectural arrangement that fails to take their security interests into account will be structurally unstable and will lack the means to anchor new rules of the game through which the great powers will be able to regulate their competition in an emerging multipolar environment. The prospects for a continuation of the longest period of great-power peace in modern history will be jeopardized if one of the postwar alliances of Position decays while the other reconsolidates and grows. Prudence thus recommends conducting the negotiations over German reunification with an eye toward building a new alliance structure that will be sensitive to the Soviet Union's security interests and conducive to establishing rules that guide superpower behavior in the post-postwar era. For such a structure to take root, prevailing norms must be supportive of binding commitments. During the turbulent, uncertain times spawned by the collapse of the Warsaw Pact and the reunification of Germany, confidence in security pledges will be needed more than ever.

Steadfast adherence to commitments may not guarantee a continuation of the long peace. But foreign policy derives from "states of mind," and in the absence of the expectation that agreements will be observed, the ground rules that delineate areas of interest and legitimate modes of engagement in a world untethered by the bonds of bipolarity are less likely to coordinate the behavior of the great powers. For peace to persist, confidence in these rules is imperative. A diplomatic culture that condones breaking those security pledges that buttress these rules is a culture condemned to a shattered peace.

ENDNOTES

1. The degree of coordination may differ according to the nature of the commitment that is formalized by an alliance treaty. One way to classify these commitments is to differentiate between *wartime alliances*, whose members join together to fight some third party, and three types of alliances that typically are formed in peacetime: (1) *defense pacts*, where the signatory parties agree to intervene militarily in the event of an attack on one of their numbers; (2) *non-aggression agreements*, in which the parties pledge to remain neutral should one of them become involved in a war; and (3) *ententes*, which merely require consultations if one of the signatories is attacked (Singer and Small, 1966).

2. Strictly speaking, the United States was a tacit partner in the Central Treaty Organization (CENTO). Although the U.S. did not formally join CENTO, it sent an observer delegation to CENTO Council meetings and sat on the Military Committee and the Economic Committee.

3. This finding, however, must be regarded as tentative since the research design used in assessing whether preexisting military alliances contribute to deterrence success may contain a biased selection of cases. For a discussion of this methodological problem, see Levy (1988:507-10).

4. Much of the traditional balance-of-power thinking suggests that durable alliances of position are destabilizing because they reduce systemic flexibility. In

contrast to this view, we contend that the fluid, ad hoc alliances advocated by many balance-of-power theorists increase the probability of international conflict by retarding the development of a code of conduct that would set limits on competition and enable states to establish fiduciary relationships in pursuit of mutual goals.

5. In addition, Erich Weede (1983) has demonstrated that war among *allies* of the superpowers also became less likely, a pattern that he attributes to the propensity of Washington and Moscow to function as substitutes for the superordinate authority lacking in an anarchic international system.

6. For a Soviet perspective on postwar lines of demarcation as a focal point solution to the problem of European security, see Soviet Committee for Security and Cooperation in Europe (1985).

CHAPTER THIRTEEN

International Norms and the Regulation of War

James Turner Johnson

THE NATURE AND SOURCES OF INTERNATIONAL NORMS ON WAR AND PEACE

The concept of international norms is problematic almost by definition within the context of the realist perspective that has informed mainstream analysis of international relations since World War II. For doctrinaire realism, international norms are a projection of idealistic imagination, and a nation that allows itself to be seduced into attempting to honor such norms is thereby betraying the legitimate base on which its policies and decisions should be founded, the national interest. Such norms may be observed, of course, if doing so serves the national interest, and in turn an appropriate expression of national interest may be to contribute to the establishment of international norms that serve such interests and to convince other nations collectively to ratify and observe these norms. Thus, a discussion of the contribution of international norms to the prevention of war within this realist perspective must be skewed from the outset: the realist is convinced in advance that such norms cannot have mattered much, except in the ability of one or another power to manipulate international behavior through them.

Yet realism has never been particularly good at showing how to distinguish the national interest from the realm of norms and the values underlying those norms, whether domestically or internationally. What are perceived to be interests rests in fact on the normative value system of the perceiver. This is obvious in the case of conflicting ideologies, where opponents regularly expose and discount claims based on ideologically defined values and perceptions. It is less obvious, but nonetheless real, within the tradition of value of one's own nation, where the value base of the cultural system is simply taken for granted and serves unreflectively as a basis for judgments, decisions, and policies. A historical example of this is the concept of natural law, which functioned to provide a base reference point in Western political thought throughout the Middle Ages and into the modern period, until experience of non-Western cultures with differing conceptions of the natural made it impossible to sustain the West's conception as the only real one (see Johnson, 1981:85-118). Contemporary examples include such concepts as "aggression" (as evidenced in the long postwar United Nations debates over this concept) and "human rights" (as evidenced in the contemporary debates over exactly what content to put into this term; see Falk, 1981; Hoffmann, 1981:95-140; Stackhouse, 1984).

The importance of recognizing a relationship between normative concepts and perceptions of the "real" national interest can also be illustrated through an example from international law on war. As recently as two decades ago some international lawyers were using the term "principle of civilization" to denote the rationale for provisions in Hague and Geneva law aimed at reducing the destructiveness of war, especially through limits on "uncivilized" means of war and "uncivilized" treatment of POWs and enemy civilians (Schwarzenberger, 1967: Chapter 1). This terminology directly reflected a consensus among the Western powers on what was "civilized," and a conception of international law as reaching out from them to draw other nations into the sphere of Western civilization. Today the term "principle of humanity" has consensually replaced "principle of civilization." More significant, international lawyers now employ the positive content of Hague and Geneva law to define the meaning of the "principle of humanity" rather than the other way around (McDougal and Feliciano, 1961: Chapter 6). Nonetheless, except for some elaboration and extrapolation, the content within Hague and Geneva law remains the same as before the shift in terminology, and the same cultural norms that were once called by the term "civilization" remain at their root.

The international legal effort to limit recourse to war in the settlement of international disputes has its deep roots in the "perpetual peace" theories of the seventeenth and eighteenth centuries and their romantic transformation in the nineteenth. Broadly, these theories began with a judgment that war, taken in itself, represents a grave evil and should be abolished in relations among states. The question was how to do this, and the main line of argument was that it could be accomplished through the creation of an international parliament or league of nations. States would give up national armies, instead contributing to the maintenance of an international armed body as a kind of police force to keep the peace and protect the league against attacks from nonmember nations (though these too would eventually become part of the compact). Member states would agree to settle their disputes by arbitration and would renounce the resort to force for settling disputes (Best, 1980:31-70; Johnson, 1987:176-98).

Two competing answers to the "how" question also deserve mention. Rousseau (1920) exemplifies those theorists who conceived the end of international war to be in the paring down of states' size and interests to a level of self-sufficient prosperity with minimal interaction across the boundaries with other states. Perhaps the best practical example of this conception was for Rousseau and remains today the Swiss Confederation, neutralist and secure in its own borders — though hardly self-sufficient any longer. Isolationism in its contemporary form, as in Lawrence Beilenson's (1980) *Survival and Peace in the Nuclear Age*, also exemplifies this approach to securing international peace.

The other competing answer to the question of how to ensure the abolition of war for all time is dramatically exemplified in the attitude and arguments of Prince Andrei in Tolstoy's (1957: Book 3, Part 2, Chapter 25) *War and Peace:* the way to convince nations to give up war is to make war so horrible that no one in his right senses would ever think it could produce a balance of good over evil. For Prince Andrei this was simply to "let war be war," not restrict its prosecution with niceties about protection of noncombatants, mercy toward prisoners of war, and so on. Such a view has affinities with Clausewitz on "absolute war," but more deeply it expresses the conviction that the very essence of war is evil, that war always is disproportionate and beyond human moral control, and that the only way to avoid the destruction of values that war brings is not ever to resort to war in the first place.

There is an ironic similarity of logic in this argument and in the argument for nuclear deterrence, which British analyst Oliver O'Donovan (1988:37-47) has noted. Both Andrei's argument and the logic of deterrence assume that if war is made destructive enough, then no political leader or people will ever engage in it. Critics of both positions argue instead for a conception of war as a necessary tool of statecraft, neither good nor evil in itself, but able to be shaped by human moral control; and they argue that such control must include consideration of the rights of noncombatants and a conscious effort to keep the harm done by war in proportion to the values served by it (Johnson, 1984:1-29; O'Brien, 1981:1-36).

International law on the resort to war has followed the main line of "perpetual peace" theory toward the establishment of international peace through international order, and it has, without expressly outlawing nuclear deterrence, developed its law of armed conflicts around the assumption that war can and should be prosecuted within the framework of restraint as to the targets and the methods of war. Here, as already noted, the principal focus will be on the former aspect of international law. Isolationism has not been a major factor in the behavior of the powers that have kept "the long postwar peace." That leaves the third approach, that exemplified by Prince Andrei and the logic of that approach to peace-keeping (or war-avoiding), within the rationale for nuclear deterrence.

Historically, then, the thrust of the international-law approach to avoiding war is distinct from that of deterrence theory; thematically and in the logic of the two positions they are in important tension with one another. Deterrence theory, like realism, assumes international anarchy and a kind of rationality of irrationality; international law assumes and depends upon at least a floor of consensus and orderly behavior among nations, and it seeks to raise the level of that floor and extend it under all nations. It further assumes the rationality of nations, or rather that of the leadership of nations. International agreements like SALT I and II and the ABM treaty, products of the mutual deterrence relationship between the United States and the USSR, significantly differ from the benchmark documents in international law defining what was classically called the *jus ad bellum* — the right to go to war. These benchmarks, which will be discussed further below, are the League of Nations Covenant, the Pact of Paris, and the United Nations Charter.

While the focus of this chapter is on those international norms having to do with restraining or limiting the decision to wage war, it is also worth noting that the above deterrence-shaped treaties also point in a fundamentally different direction from the historical main line of international normative restraints on the conduct of war (*jus in bello*), found in the historical just war tradition and expressed in the international law of armed conflicts. (See Schindler and Toman, 1973, for the contents of this law.) In either form, this *jus in bello* centers on two principles, proportion and discrimination. The principle of proportion is exemplified by bans on weapons deemed to cause unnecessary suffering and on means of war that are disproportionately destructive relative to the good ends they achieve; the principle of discrimination is exemplified by conventions defining protection of various sorts of noncombatants. The SALT agreements had the ironic effect of encouraging as a putative means to avoid war weapons that would be disproportionate if used in war; the ABM treaty had the equally ironic effect of banning defenses that might protect noncombatants because of the destabilization that such protection would exert on deterrence.

In short, the approach to war-avoidance through deterrence is historically, thematically, and logically different from the international normative tradition having to do either with avoidance of war through creation of greater international order or the restraint of war's destructive impact through limits on the means and targets of war. A preference for the one approach carries with it a necessary suspicion of the other. The following discussion outlines the case for the normative traditions.

For purposes of this analysis, international norms may be divided into two sorts: those expressed in positive fashion as international law, denoting the presence of binding commitments by states concerning their relations with other states; and those falling in the broad area of normative cultural traditions, customary international law, and *lex ferenda* (that which is posited as desirable to be made into positive law). The relations of states to these two types of international norms differ considerably, and the relations of particular states to specific examples of each type of international norms may also vary greatly.

International Norms, Normative Substructures, and Viewing Norms Through Behavior

Positive International Law

A discussion of the full range of international legal instruments relating to the keeping of the peace between the United States and the Soviet Union during the post–World War II period, the subject of this book as a whole, would encompass far more than it is possible to treat in the space of this chapter: the international law of armed conflicts; international legal restrictions on the right to resort to war; the Helsinki Declaration on human rights; specific Soviet-American treaties, especially those on arms control; a large amount of material generated by actions of the United Nations; and more besides. All could easily merit discussion.

For the purposes of this chapter, though, we shall focus on that portion of international law aimed at restricting the right of recourse to war. Specifically, this is found in those three major benchmark documents already identified in the previous section: the League of Nations Covenant, the Pact of Paris, and the United Nations Charter.

The first international legal effort to limit the right to resort to war was the Covenant of the League of Nations in 1919 (text in International Intermediary Institute, 1922), which (1) attempted to substitute arbitration for war as a means of settling international disputes, (2) defined an international judicial body for the purpose of such arbitration, (3) attempted to guarantee safety against aggression to members of the League, and (4) provided for sanctions against any nations resorting to war in violation of the provisions of the Covenant.

The 1928 General Treaty for the Renunciation of War, also known as the Pact of Paris and the Kellogg-Briand Pact (text in U.S. Department of State, 1928), went a step beyond the provisions of the Covenant to the absolute renunciation of war. The three articles of this agreement bind its signatories to "condemn recourse to war for the solution of international controversies, and renounce it as an instrument of international policy in their relations with one another," to seek resolution of disputes among themselves by peaceful means, and to keep the treaty open for additional signatories "as long as may be necessary for adherence by all the other powers of the world." The principals made clear that they did not understand this agreement as in any way inhibiting the right of self-defense by military means, though the nature of this right was left to customary understanding.

The next important stage in the development of international legal instruments to effect "perpetual peace" through an enhanced world order and mutual renunciation of war was the Charter of the United Nations (text in United Nations, n.d.; see Articles 2 and 51), whose provisions regarding resort to war define the stance of postwar international law on the legitimacy of the use of force between states.

Neither the League of Nations Covenant nor the Pact of Paris seems, by empirical standards, to have had much influence on restraining resort to war. It is of course a truism about international law that it binds only those nations that want to appear bound by it, and not others. In the case of the Covenant, examples of peace among most of the members of the League of Nations and between them and nonmember states does not, for critics, count for as much as the gross failure of the League in the case of Italy's making war on Ethiopia: the renunciations and the promises to arbitrate disputes were not able to prevent Italy's aggression, nor were the sanctions fitfully imposed by other league members able to secure Italy's withdrawal. Again, neither the Covenant nor the Pact was able to prevent the Spanish Civil War, which was an internal conflict, albeit one as fierce as many international wars; and neither international agreement was able to prevent the aggressive acts of Hitler which led to the beginning of World War II in Europe, the Japanese invasion of Manchuria and of China proper, or the attacks against American, British, and Dutch territories that began the war in the Pacific.

This pre–World War II background has given critics reason to be skeptical about the influence of the United Nations Charter on the postwar peace between the superpowers that has existed for over forty years. Let us examine the Charter's provisions a bit more closely, focusing on Articles 2 and 51, those most immediately relevant to the question at hand.

Article 2 represents a carrying forward of the provisions of the Covenant and Pact, prohibiting member states from "the threat or use of force against the territorial integrity or political independence of any state" and empowering the Security Council to preserve international peace (without specifying how it should do so). The assumptions of the "perpetual peace" movement are clearly visible here as elsewhere in the Charter: war is bad in itself and is to be avoided; the route to avoidance is through renunciation of force, acceptance of arbitration, and the establishment of a parliament of nations through which disputes can be avoided or arbitrated; and threats to the peace can be deterred or suppressed by an international peace-keeping force under the authority of this parliamentary body. Exactly what was to be read out of the terms "territorial integrity" and "political independence" remained to be debated, and no consensus has yet been reached as to their extent. What is clearly present, though, is the assumption of the validity of the state system and the need to protect and preserve existing states both as geographic territories and as political entities.

Article 51 makes national integrity and the right of self-defense explicit — as it had not been, for example, in the Pact of Paris. But the permitted defense is defense against "armed attack," not other forms of aggression that might be employed by one state against another. This provision is thus, on *prima facie* reading, a reinforcement of the concept that war is to be avoided by renunciation of force. Debate has, however, established a case for the continued existence of the older consensus within customary international law accepting an extended right of defense, including the right to strike preemptively to ward off an imminent invasion (modern case: the Israeli actions against Syrian and Egyptian forces at the start of the Six-Day War) and the right to recover territory wrongly seized (modern case: the British response to Argentina's taking the Falklands) or to protect or recover endangered nationals (modern cases: Entebbe, Grenada). It is also generally presumed that the right of self-defense against armed attack extends to the right to retaliate against such attack (as would be the case in a nuclear strike-counterstrike scenario). (On the debate over "armed attack" as meaning "first use of force" see Kaplan and Katzenbach, 1966, and Meyrowitz, 1970:144-48; on the permissibility of retaliation as a means of defense, see Freedman, 1983:34-44, and Mandelbaum, 1979:41-68.)

The status of the *jus ad bellum* (the law relating to the decision to make war) in international law as defined by the Charter is, on the whole, somewhat ambivalent. The Charter prohibits "the threat or use of force" by states against the "territorial integrity or political independence of any state"; it sanctions defense by individual states or regional alliances against "armed attack" but not threats, though the consensually accepted concept of defense is somewhat broader; it sets up enforcement mechanisms including negative sanctions and international peace-keeping forces, but does not challenge the principle of national sovereignty. It represents a compromise between the idealism of the "perpetual peace" approach to international order at its extreme and the realism of the anarchic conception of international relations at its extreme. The truth is that the *jus ad bellum* of international law, as stated most definitively in the United Nations Charter, is quite fragile in itself and is much less than a general prohibition of the use of force among states.

Nor has there ever been any clear, definitive reconciliation of this doctrine on resort to war with the provisions of the law of armed conflicts (*jus in bello*) setting limits on the prosecution of the war. Indeed, there is a tension between the effort to limit resort to war and that to restrain the conduct of war: if an aggressor (by the terms of Article 2) can be opposed effectively only by means counter to provisions of the law of armed conflicts, then the provision for self-defense in Article 51 either is meaningless or else the law of armed conflicts is abrogated by necessity in cases of defense against armed attack.

It is easy to make the case that the superpowers, as well as numerous lesser states and nonstate entities, have operated over the last forty years so as to use the lack of clarity and tensions within positive international law for their own purposes. Under the umbrella of an international renunciation of aggressive force between states, the Soviet Union developed an extensive network of support for "wars of national liberation" within states. Under the umbrella of a peace-keeping force sanctioned by the United Nations, the United States and an allied force fought a war in Korea whose purpose was to contain communist expansion. Regional self-defense has provided the rationale for military involvements by both the United States and the Soviet Union. Avoidance of formal declarations of war and the use of clients have provided mechanisms for the use of military force to serve national interests without the stigma attached to the initiation of a legal state of war.

Yet it is also true that the state of peace between the superpowers has endured despite such activity. It is further the case that the declarative policy of both the Soviet Union and the United States affirms the rule of international law on resort to force as defined in the Charter. While it is possible to dismiss this as mere lip service, it is also possible that such declarative policy represents the substantive position of the two superpowers after all, and the incidents cited in the previous paragraph are the result of a positive law that is at once ambiguous and inadequately extended.

It is impossible to test either possibility empirically, but they may be tested theoretically by examination of the role of international law in relation to the behavior of states as compared to the role of domestic law in relation to the behavior of citizens. The two are not the same, and the role of positive law in particular is quite different. In order to undertake this theoretical testing, it is first necessary to look briefly at the underpinnings of positive international law on war, the normative components that have fed it and are resident in it, the broader concept of customary international law, and the notion of *lex ferenda* (a kind of bridge between what is normatively defined as desirable and that which is provided for in positive international agreements).

Normative Traditions, Customary International Law, and *Lex Ferenda*

The major normative traditions that have fed into the production of positive international law relating to war are those of the "perpetual peace" ideal of world order, which today finds expression in the *jus ad bellum* of international law as preeminently stated in the United Nations Charter, and the just war tradition, which finds expression in the *jus in bello* of positive international law, the law of armed conflicts as defined in agreements aimed at protecting noncombatants and at restricting the means of war to make it less destructive. These two traditions are historically and thematically different, and so are the two branches of contemporary positive international law, as already noted. The just war tradition accepts the use of armed force among political entities as a fact of history. The decision to use armed force, whether in first place or in response to first use, is "premoral" for this tradition — that is, it is neither good nor evil in itself, but it becomes good or evil according to the circumstances surrounding it: whether it was for a justifying cause, whether it was undertaken on proper political authority, whether it serves the ends of peacefulness and order, whether it observes appropriate restraints of proportionality and consideration of the rights of persons in the way of war, and so on. At bottom, just war tradition favors the establishment of justice, through armed force if necessary, as a prior requirement for the establishment of peace and order among nations. The "perpetual peace" tradition, by contrast, regards the use of armed force by states as an evil, and as one that can be eradicated from history by the creation of a superior form of political ordering that removes from states the right and power to use armed force. The peace that results from this new orderliness without war is, on this tradition, an essential prerequisite to the establishment of justice within and among nations.

Where are these traditions found? One place, of course, is in the writings of the various theorists that have contributed to each one: authors like Augustine, Aquinas, Vitoria, Grotius, and (in the contemporary era) Paul Ramsey and Michael Walzer in the case of just war tradition (Johnson, 1975; 1981); authors like Cruce, St.-Pierre, Bentham, Kant, and (in the contemporary era) Richard Falk in the case of the "perpetual peace" tradition (Johnson, 1987). Yet to identify these moral traditions only with formal theoretical writings is to understand their meaning and significance far too narrowly; it is also necessary to recognize their presence in various forms of social behavior through history. For the context of this chapter, this need directly implies an examination of customary international law as an expression of behavior.

The term *customary international law* signifies nothing more or less than the rules that can be inferred from the patterns of action and interaction among states over time. Long before the positive law of the Geneva conventions, for example, there was in Western culture, observable in the practice of belligerents, a customary law of protection of civilians and soldiers rendered *hors de combat* by wounds or taken prisoner. The writings of theoreticians like Grotius (1925), Vattel (1916), and, in the United States at the time of the Civil War, Lieber (United States War Department, 1863), all testify to such customary rules of behavior and incorporate such rules into their juridical attempts to define the uses and limits of war. Indeed, the earliest formal agreements establishing positive laws of war could never have been reached without such a broad consensus having already been reached, and the same can be said for subsequent statements of the positive law (Nardin, 1983; Barkun, 1968).

Positive law thus should be understood as a concrete expression of an agreement already existing. It is one of the ironies of the relationship between these two forms of law that where the customary consensus is strongest, positive law is redundant, and where it is weakest, positive law either will not come into existence or will be ineffective in determining the conduct of subjects of the law. The most important role of positive law, that is, may be in the region between these extremes, where it may help to crystallize a further consensus as to appropriate behavior. At the same time, a decline of consensus can withdraw support from positive law and limit its effectiveness as a control on actors. The growth of a consensus during World War II that strategic bombing is a morally allowable form of war undermined the earlier consensus against direct, intentional attacks on noncombatants (Freedman, 1983:3-21; Johnson, 1984:129-36). While the Geneva conventions remain as bulwarks to the maltreatment of noncombatants in the specific cases they define, deterrence doctrine remains as a symbol of the broader moral ground lost to the acceptance of strategic targeting as a proper means of war. (On the moral case against deterrence, see Finnis, Boyle, and Grisez, 1987, and O'Donovan, 1988.)

The above argument on the nature of law follows and extrapolates the lines of Lon L. Fuller's thought (1964). Fuller developed his position, arguing against the positivism of H. L. A. Hart, for the case of domestic law. Yet his concepts are all the more applicable to international law, where no single governing body exists to lay down binding regulations for behavior among states or to enforce conformity to existing positive law. Positive law, in Fuller's view and the view that I am maintaining here, is an expression of an underlying and broader set of "laws" defining appropriate behavior within a community — whether a community of individuals or of affinity groups, or a community of nation-states. Where positive law diverges from such underlying consensus, it loses its force — as, for example, exemplified by the failure of national prohibition in the United States in the 1930s.

Moving one step further, moral attitudes can be read through customary behavior, though the two are not identical. The moral values expressed in such attitudes are the motivational factors behind customary behavior; thus the moral attitudes and values of a nation can be inferred from the way it acts in the world, and specifically from the laws it enacts and is able to enforce. This is not the whole story; moral values and attitudes are complicated realities and are not always easy to read, or read accurately, through a study of behavior. But for our purposes, it is enough simply to note and catalogue the relationship between moral values and attitudes, customary "laws" of behavior, and positive law.

Lex ferenda, the last form of international law to be taken into account, thus can be represented as the intermediate stage between the customary and positive forms of law. It draws its power as what "should" become positively binding from its fundamental rooting in the moral values and attitudes underlying all the forms of law.

The Problem of Normative Pluralism

Normative pluralism among nations, rooted in differing historical experiences and cultural inheritances, poses a serious problem, both theoretically and practically, for international norms in the period since 1945. Georg Schwarzenberger (1962: Chapter 1) has defined three sorts of international law: the "law of power," based on the domination of one or more groups by another, which imposes its own norms on the behavior of all; "community law" or the "law of coordination," in which units sharing a consensus as to norms establish rules coordinating their behavior toward the support of those norms; and the "law of reciprocity," where the groups establishing the law do not share common normative assumptions but no one is powerful enough to dominate the others. Rules of reciprocity, in this third type of relationship, serve to provide maximal service and protection of the normative values of all the groups, though such rules do not protect and serve all the norms of all the groups equally.

International law originated as an expression of the "community law" of Western culture, and the normative traditions of that culture, as noted above, can still be read out of the major benchmarks of positive international law on warfare. The extension of this international law over non-Western nations and peoples by the global hegemony of the West in the period prior to World War II exemplifies the "law of power" or domination. Yet since 1945 this hegemony has broken down, and rules for international behavior can accordingly no longer be based reliably on this earlier historical situation. Without community and without hegemony, an international law based in reciprocity seems, on Schwarzenberger's analysis, to be the only remaining possibility.

On this model rules of international behavior can still be established, and indeed they may remain formally the same as before. Yet the underlying consensus necessary to support such rules now depends on individual decisions by the various actors, despite their division by lines of normative pluralism, such that their own values are served and protected by the rules in question. In such a context, formal treaties take on a special importance as the concrete expression of such decisions.

For the particular case of United States-Soviet relations over the period since 1945, the above analytical model shows how meaningful, effective international norms may exist even across strongly defined lines of cultural and political separation. It is not necessary for such norms to be based in community of normative value; nor is it necessary for one actor to dominate the other. All that is needed is for the two actors to determine that their mutual normative priorities (interests) are served and protected by mutually agreed-upon rules of the relationship, however different the normative bases of each actor underlying their separate judgments. Thus, for the particular case of the interaction between the two superpowers, assessment of the role of international norms in keeping "the long peace" should be aided by close examination of the degree to which tacit and expressed "rules of the game" have in fact served the two actors' respective value systems (Gaddis, 1987b:238-43). At the same time, it may well be that such an examination would uncover causes for tension in inadequate forms of reciprocity, in which the rules of interaction favor one or the other party on one or another issue.

INTERNATIONAL NORMS AND THE CREATION AND SUSTAINING OF PEACE

The burden of the above analysis has been to invert the usual form of the question of the relation between international norms and the avoidance of war or, in other words, the creation and sustaining of a condition of international peace. The question, as recognized early in this chapter, is usually put in such a way as to balance the answer toward the position of the skeptics. Where there are norms inhibiting resort to war and yet war begins, the skeptic can argue that this empirically demonstrates the ineffectiveness or irrelevance of such norms to keeping the peace. The problem is that such cases prove nothing of the sort. Such an argument, though ostensibly empirical, is worthless as a scientific claim, as the cases are too few and too varied for such a simple argument to have any meaning at all. A genuinely empirical test would have to be far more sophisticated and would accordingly be far harder to carry out, if it could be carried out at all. For such an approach would also have to take account of instances where the norms were in effect and war did not occur — which amounts to the great majority of the duration of history. It would also have to depend on nonempirically determined choices of what counts as ingredients of cases to be studied. There are other problems as well. Empirical reasoning simply cannot answer the question of the influence of norms on the avoidance of war.

My approach in this chapter has been to take a different tack entirely, to examine the issues theoretically rather than empirically. This has required inverting the question of the relation of norms to war-avoidance so that the focus is on the production of the norms themselves and the underlying values supportive of war-avoidance that such norms express. This has been, because of the space available, only a sketch of such an approach; yet on its basis it is possible to make some concluding general observations.

First, the very existence of norms having to do with restraining or avoiding war and sustaining peace is *prima facie* evidence of a predisposition toward achieving these ends. This connection must of course be tested by exploring the degree to which the actors in fact subscribe to the norms in question, through demonstrating convergence or lack of convergence between the norms present on the international level and the various actors' individual normative priorities. This is why positive international law is important as an expression of international normative restrains on war: for positive international law comes into being by a process of value-centered debate and interaction and by the formal acceptance of the results of this process in a treaty, agreement, convention, or some other form of international instrument. Of course, nations enter such agreements for their own reasons — this is what reciprocity, after all, is about — but so long as the behavior of one or more of the parties does not void an agreement, it is reasonable to take it as expressing the common area of values shared by the signatories.

Second, where international norms substantively reflect the normative value priorities and relationships of a particular culture or cultural tradition, the stress points where the effectiveness of such norms should be expected to break down are found at the boundaries between that culture and others. This follows from the nature and sources of normative value structures, and it is exemplified by a wealth of historical evidence. Put simply, the most unrestrained wars are most likely to take place across major cultural boundaries, whether these be set by secular ideology, religion, historical links with particular geographic territories, linguistic traditions, or any of the other traits commonly used to define cultures.

Returning to Schwarzenberger's modeling of the three types of international law, "community law" or the "law of coordination" is notably freer of stress points than either of the other two forms: the "law of power," which a dominant culture imposes on others, and the "law of reciprocity," in which no single culture is shared by all the participants and none is able to dominate the rest. The point of the reciprocity is, of course, to identify or carve out areas of community of value on which all the participants can agree. Such a relationship is inherently unstable, and it can be expected, over time, to break down and be transformed into one of the other forms of relation: dominance or community. In the worst case, the breakdown of reciprocity leads to war, from which a dominant culture may emerge (or, alternatively, a new relationship of reciprocity will be restored among nations too weak to dominate). In the best case, the minimal area of initial agreement carved out by reciprocal interaction will expand gradually the area of community so as to tend toward a new "law of coordination." Reciprocity is no end in itself, and recognizing that it has been the basis of international normative structures in the period since 1945 should be no cause for relief. The question is what will follow.

In this context, it becomes even more significant that the superpowers during this period have avoided a major, direct struggle between themselves and have, in significant ways, established mutually agreed-upon rules of the game, whether tacitly expressed in behavior or formally incorporated in international agreements. In so doing they have gradually identified and expanded an area of common normative value between them, and joining them and their allies. This is not yet a "community," and the rules of the game are not yet a "law of coordination"; yet it is evidence that the interactions of reciprocity are not, as they might under other circumstances, degenerating toward war.

So far as weaker nations are concerned, this is a case of their having to accept the world as the superpowers define it; the convergence of interest joining the superpowers establishes a "law of power" over the rest, not by the domination of one but by a condominium of the superpowers. The most prominent example of this may be the nuclear Non-Proliferation Treaty and a shared resolve among the nuclear powers (including the superpowers) to prevent others from acquiring nuclear weapons. But an international order expressed in a "law of domination" — even if by a condominium — can be very stable, as the *pax Romana* shows.

The prospects for continued expansion of the area of commonality remain uncertain, even in the era of *glasnost*. Yet the historical momentum has been in that direction rather than the other way, and this in itself is cause for a certain optimism about the long run.

A third and final general observation about the relevance of international norms to international war-avoidance and the sustaining of peace is that norms are but one element in a mix of factors affecting the restraint or avoidance of war and the promotion of a stable and enduring peace. Not only are norms themselves extremely complicated structures, with multiple roots and expressions, complex priority relationships, and connections to one or another cultural tradition that may not be shared by all to whom the norm ostensibly applies; not only do norms break down at significant cultural boundaries between nations; the existence of norms is, in fact, only part of the story. The outbreak of war (or the maintenance of peace) ought not to be connected to international norms unidimensionally; wars begin or peace is maintained for a host of contributing reasons. Yet norms are nonetheless an important part of the story. Contemporary social-scientific study of the causes of war examines the other factors in the mix and attempts to correlate their presence or absence, in greater or lesser degree, with the outbreak of war or the maintenance of peace. International norms are rightly a part of this mix as well, and while their effect is difficult to measure empirically, consideration of that effect rightly belongs alongside examination of the effect of economic, political, and other factors which historically correlate with war and peace.

PART SIX

The Problematic Future: Projections and Scenarios

CHAPTER FOURTEEN

Interdependence and the Simultaneity Puzzle: Notes on the Outbreak of Peace

James N. Rosenau

Comprehending the causes of war is, relatively speaking, much easier than explaining the prolongation of peace. War has a finite beginning — a decision, a declaration, an attack — and from this (normally) unquestioned reality inquiry can proceed to peel off the layers of causation that culminated in the onset of combat. In the case of peace, however, there are no self-evident historical junctures around which to organize analysis. Leaders, publics, and societies do not opt for peace in ways that are comparable to deciding to wage war. They simply continue conducting themselves in ways that do not result in violent conflict with adversaries.

Unlike students of war, therefore, those who explain peace prolongation must focus on conditions rather than choice points, on evolving orientations rather than decisive actions, on disparate developments rather than coordinated efforts. In short, there are no clear-cut layers of causation that, starting with the perceptions of the chief of state and moving back through governmental, societal, and systemic variables, can logically be peeled off to reveal the full panoply of interacting dynamics which give rise to specific outcomes.

To be sure, periods of prolonged peace are not lacking in historic moments. Crises do occur that render the peace precarious as adversaries find themselves eyeball-to-eyeball. And there are also occasions when agreements are signed which strengthen the underpinnings of nonviolent conflict. Such junctures are well illustrated by, respectively, the Cuban missile crisis and the INF Treaty. Yet, while insights into the dynamics sustaining the peace can surely be developed out of these junctures when war was averted or peace solidified, the Cuban missile crisis, the INF Treaty, and other historic moments remain but single events in a much larger and longer sequence. Focusing on them does not position the analyst to scan longer historical processes and locate each event in a series that contributes to the cumulation of the orientations and institutions through which prolonged peace is maintained as a normal condition rather than as an aberration. An event focus does not incline one to trace the learning, the habit formation, wherein each event builds on the predispositions acquired through its predecessors. It averts one's analytic eyes away from the deeper social, economic, and political soil wherein the prolongation of peace is treated as a presumption rather than a delicate challenge.

OBSTACLES TO THE STUDY OF PROLONGED PEACE

As we are not accustomed to prolonged periods of peace, in other words, so are we not accustomed to thinking about how to study them. In the field of world politics the available conceptual equipment is designed largely to unravel the dynamics of conflict and war. Through inexperience and unfamiliarity (as distinguished from avoidance and misperception) we have not evolved a storehouse of conceptual tools, much less theoretical frameworks, with which to sort out and explain all the factors that can underlie long periods of peace. Under what conditions, for example, does the elapse of considerable time transform adversarial into cooperative relations? Does the persistence of peace across generations reinforce the inclinations to stay at peace, or are new generations for whom prior wars are experienced only through textbooks free to yield to adversarial impulses? Is peace best conceived as a series of decisions not to go to war, or is it more appropriate to think of it as a set of circumstances in which such decision points never occur? Or is it both, with each nonwar decision enriching the underlying conditions in such a way that the occasion for future nonwar decisions is enhanced? Is peace a process that requires continuous attention, or does it consist of structural arrangements that obviate the need for conscious management? Can top public officials develop strategies of peace — contingent plans, capability estimates, and game theoretical scenarios — comparable to the war strategies that they formulate? What kinds of civic orientations and loyalties are conducive to publics that resist leaders who foment war hysteria?

Perplexity over questions such as these — and many more could be posed — reveals the weakness of our theoretical foundations for explaining prolonged periods of peace. And they also highlight the large extent to which the dynamics that foster peace prolongation are not the obverse of those that conduce to war. One cannot use the same layering scheme to peel off the causes of peace that one employs in comprehending the causes of war. At each causal level the key variables relevant to the perpetuation of peace are likely to be different in scope, direction, and intensity from those around which the outbreak of war is centered.

The emphasis here is on prolonged periods. There is no lack of theoretical and empirical work on specific types of immediate situations that have peaceful outcomes. A rich literature, for example, has evolved on the practices and premises of nuclear and conventional deterrence (e.g., Huth, 1988; Quester, 1987; Russett, 1989) and hardly less voluminous is the literature on alliances (Walt, 1987), cold wars (Larson, 1985), and game theoretical calculations (Schelling, 1960). Lately, too, a provocative literature on the role of hegemons (Huntington, 1988/89; Russett, 1985; Strange, 1987) and the dynamics of cooperation (Axelrod, 1984; Oye, 1986) has begun to cumulate. Impressive and valuable as the progress along these lines has been, however, none of these literatures systematically addresses the convergence of underlying social conditions that foster the prolongation of peace. All of them are concerned with short-term considerations, and thus do not focus on the long-term learnings and orientations through which publics come to tacitly encourage — rather than inhibit — the readiness of their leaders to back away from decisions that might result in war.

Perhaps a qualification is in order. Theorizing about long-term processes has come to occupy a place in the literature on world politics; but the focus tends to be on the prolonged buildup of dynamics that culminate in war rather than on those that preserve peace. Most notable in this regard are the long-cycle theories, many of which are impressive in the extensive time periods they span and the kinds of empirical data they offer (Goldstein, 1988; Kennedy, 1987; Modelski, 1987b), but none of which asks the questions that need to be explored to comprehend the processes of peace prolongation. Indeed, since their analyses focus on the capabilities of states, hegemons, and shifting power relationships at the macro level, none is concerned with how learning and orientations at the micro level interact with dynamics operative at macro levels to fashion the underpinnings of peace across long stretches of time. Put differently, while long-cycle theories that predict the outbreak of war have become available, comparable formulations that anticipate — or at least allow for — possible breaks in the war cycles have not been developed.

How, then, to proceed? If periods of peace that extend across four or more decades are lacking in clear-cut choice points wherein their initiation or renewal is decided, around what empirical materials can analysts organize their inquiry? And if the extant literature on how to explain such periods is scant, on what theoretical premises can the inquiry be founded?

This is obviously not the occasion to develop a full response to these queries. The other chapters in this book, taken together, offer the bases for beginning to evolve such a theory of peace prolongation, and hopefully they will provoke readers to undertake such a task. What does seem feasible, however, is to undertake a two-part probe into some of the deeper foundations on which prolonged periods of peace rest. The other chapters address mostly the immediate and intermediate factors that have conduced to prevent the onset of global war, but clearly these are in turn rooted in the more encompassing context of a world that has undergone, since 1945, a profound transformation to a postindustrial order in which local and national communities are ever more interdependent. The technologies underlying this transformation are proving to be so dynamic that the constraints and configurations of present-day global interdependence cannot be ignored as fundamental sources from which the inclinations appropriate to the prolongation of peace derive.

Although the ensuing two-part response to the how-to-proceed dilemma is admittedly makeshift, it does seem to offer opportunities for subsequent refinement that could become the basis for a systematic research strategy. The first part consists of four theoretical propositions that spring from the premise that as more and more time elapses without the onset of major war in a period of explosive technologies and ever greater interdependence, the more deeply do the roots of peace get implanted in the social and political soil of nations. The second phase of the inquiry seizes upon an unusual set of empirical circumstances to begin to explore the incisiveness of the four propositions.

A THEORETICAL PERSPECTIVE

Obvious as it may seem, there are hidden and yet crucial implications that stem from an initial presumption that time is itself a variable in the dynamics that sustain prolonged periods of peace. Most notably, it implies that the composite of dynamics which conduce to peace at any stage of such a period are altered as a consequence of the prior success that kept the peace intact. To be a high official pondering the conduct of foreign affairs in 1989, in other words, is not the same as occupying such a role in 1979, 1969, 1959, or 1949. With each decade — indeed, with each month and year — the social, economic, and political atmosphere in which the clouds of war evolve or dissolve changes as precedents, habits, orientations, and structures cumulate in response both to the previous decades and to the anticipated projection of the past patterns into the future.

Periods of prolonged peace, in other words, ought not be conceived in static terms. Common patterns may mark the onset and fighting of wars, but this does not mean that the world lurches from war to war unchanged and that the time separating them can be held constant. Just as the wars involved different weaponries, strategies, and alliance arrangements as a consequence of technological dynamics, so do peace periods undergo variation as the same dynamics foster new domestic relationships and foreign commitments.

Stated in another way, despite the blockages to change interposed by the habitual loyalties of publics and the inherent inertia of bureaucracies, people and their institutions are learning entities. They react to experience and cumulatively adjust their processes of perception and reasoning to the shifting stimuli to which they are subjected. Such adaptive reactions may not be immediate; they may occur in only the smallest of increments; and they may not even be recognized until well after they have begun; but their cumulative impact across time can surely be substantial and, thus, they cannot be discounted as a critical variable as the practices of peace build up across extended periods of time.

From the initial premise that time is a variable during periods of peace, two main propositions as to how it operates can readily be derived:

I.   The more time passes, the more do the causes of prolonged peace expand outward across systemic boundaries from individual public officials to active publics to societal norms to international relationships;

II. The more time passes without decisions to wage war, the less do historic antagonisms serve as the bases of habitual responses and the more can processes of learning cumulate and take root in political cultures;

    a. As consecutive years and decades without war cumulate, the more do habitual responses to world affairs that value non-violent accommodation spread through all systemic levels;

    b. The more time passes, the less are citizens accustomed to having their lives interrupted by the deprivations of war;

    c. As consecutive years and decades without war cumulate, the more do public officials get constrained by bureaucratic, political, and societal expectations that they must avoid international circumstances that can lead to war.

But there is another prime parameter that must be considered besides learning processes expressed through the passage of time. It consists of all the dynamics inherent in a persistent spread of interdependence among communities and nations. The learning processes depicted in propositions I and II can evolve slowly or rapidly through time, depending upon the era and the extent to which its communications systems, transportational facilities, and other sources of complex sociopolitical relations remain constant. In periods when movement toward greater interdependence occurs gradually, the predispositions toward new learnings are minimal and the prolongation of peace is especially vulnerable to the misperceptions of officials and/or the breakdown of alliances. But the present, longest-of-all period of peace is of a different order. As indicated, it has been marked by explosive communications and transportational technologies that have greatly intensified the density, complexity, and dynamism of world politics. The microelectronic revolution has made possible the rapid circulation of ideas, pictures, and information on a global scale, and the jet plane has facilitated the rapid movement of people around the world. As a result, the period has been distinguished by increasing numbers of relevant individual and collective actors (the density), each of which has evolved a greater number and variety of relationships with counterparts and adversaries elsewhere in the world (the complexity), and all of which have both the incentives and the competence to engage in a broad range of diverse behaviors (the dynamism) as they seek to protect and advance their interests in the face of increasingly unfamiliar and interdependent circumstances.

Among the many consequences of this extraordinary interdependence that is presently continuing to expand through a fifth decade — what I have described elsewhere as a period of global turbulence (Rosenau, 1990) — three are perhaps particularly relevant to the prolongation of peace. One is that citizens and officials everywhere, being better educated and being as close to developments elsewhere in the world as they are to a television screen, are expanding their analytic skills and their sense of where they fit in the course of events and how the causal chains of world politics link them into what happens in distant places. These greater capacities at the micro level have resulted in people being increasingly ready to question and challenge whole-system authority and to turn to subsystem affiliations for the satisfaction of their needs and wants.

Second, operating both as sources and consequences of increasingly skillful citizenries, macro collectivities and relationships in all parts of the world have been subjected to powerful decentralizing tendencies as the densities, complexities, and dynamism of modern-day interdependence continue to unfold. Sometimes planned as the goal of privatization policies, but more often evolving uncontrollably out of sociopolitical disarray and upheaval, these decentralizing dynamics have weakened states, rendered national governments less effective, enhanced the role of subnational groups, and fostered the emergence of a multicentric system to rival the state system as a mechanism for managing global order (Rosenau, 1988).

Third, even as global structures become more decentralized, so is the spread of interdependence also fostering centralizing tendencies that add to and intensify the density, complexity, and dynamism of world politics. Most notably, recent years have witnessed the emergence of new political issues on the global agenda that are distinguished by their transnational scope. Currency crises, terrorism, atmospheric pollution, the drug trade, refugee flows, and AIDS are the most conspicuous of the these new interdependence-induced issues, and they are all transnational in the sense that they originate and unfold in diverse parts of the world and can only be effectively managed through the centralizing dynamics of transnational cooperation. The tensions between these centralizing tendencies and those tending toward decentralization noted above seem bound to be major features of the world scene well into the twenty-first century.

Given an endless clash between centralizing and decentralizing dynamics, it might be wondered, are not the probabilities of major war increased? If the global system is undergoing bifurcation, with the authority of states challenged by new transnational issues and the privileged position of elites undermined by decentralizing tendencies, are not strong incentives building to restore the status quo and prevent the deepening of interdependence even if this means resort to war? No, quite to the

contrary, the decentralizing tendencies at work within virtually all international organizations, alliance systems, polities, and communities
encompass several processes which mitigate reliance on large-scale military action. One is that as the world's growing complexity leads elites
to evolve multiple, overlapping, and transnational relationships, so does
it confound their readiness to draw the line clearly between their "fellow
citizens" and "foreigners." Today's "enemy" is not so much another country that can be targeted for military action as it is subnational rivals or
competitors who have to be challenged through greater efficiency and/or
legal protection.

Much the same can be said for nonelites: having moved widely around
the world either through direct travels or television cameras, and having
a greater capacity to recognize how their welfare is crucially linked to
trends abroad, people are not likely to be responsive to appeals to support
extensive military commitments. Their appreciation that the world has
shrunk, that its complexity does not lend itself to the simple solutions
that military combat implies, is no less acute than their leaders' recognition of the many untoward consequences that attend and follow the
fighting of wars.

Second, and related, the decentralized foundations of today's interdependence have diffused authority structures and obfuscated the locus
of effective war-making decisions. The continuing debate in the United
States over the meaning of the War Powers Act is illustrative of the
growing difficulties that face top leaders everywhere who may wish to
undertake decisive military action. Just as citizens are increasingly likely
to resist being mobilized for war, so are national leaders likely to encounter greater problems in conducting themselves as mobilizers.

Third, and no less important, the tendencies toward centralization
and cooperation inherent in the new interdependence issues foster a sense
of "shared fate" that undermines the readiness of leaders and publics to
define the we-and-they dichotomy in terms of countries. Increasingly,
that is, the "they" is unlikely to have a national identity and to refer
instead to bankers who manipulate currencies, to polluters who damage
the environment, to terrorists who hijack airplanes, or to crime syndicates
that traffic in drugs. Or consider how the maintenance of human rights
has lately evolved as a universal norm, as part of a global culture that
says, in effect, there are limits to national sovereignty and that the world
is morally justified in intervening wherever violations of such rights are
uncovered and publicized.

Increasingly, in other words, the tides of opinion are not confined to
national shores. The changes may still be marginal and occur in small
increments, but increasingly the fault lines of global conflict are vulnerable to a sharing and emulation of worldwide practices that affirm nonviolent means of managing bitter animosities.

In sum, it is no accident that the long peace since World War II
unfolded precisely at the time when the dynamics of global interdepend-

ence accelerated at an exponential rate. Indeed, by placing learning processes in the context of a rapidly expanding global interdependence, two more overall propositions can usefully be framed:

III. The more the world becomes interdependent, with events in one part of the globe having consequences elsewhere, the denser and more elaborate do transnational networks become and the less are national officials able to mobilize publics to go to war;
   a. The more complex global interdependence becomes through time, the less do problems lend themselves to military solutions and the more attractive do innovative but nonviolent policy solutions become;
IV. The more the world becomes interdependent, the more swiftly can a momentum toward peace catch on and spread.

An Empirical Exploration: The Simultaneity Puzzle

As previously noted, periods of prolonged peace do not have finite beginnings that are determinative of all the accommodations that mark ensuing decades. While the study of war can benefit from an intense inquiry into a particular event such as the outbreak of World War I or the Cuban missile crisis, empirical explorations of the dynamics of peace prolongation cannot ordinarily be so temporally focused. If there are specific turning points during prolonged periods of peace, normally they are discernible only years later when the passage of time allows for retrospective inquiry. Occasionally a successful revolution or a technological innovation may be so clear in its implications for diminished conflict as to acquire immediate status as a major historical juncture, but usually the course of world affairs is too complex for such sharp delineations at the time of its occurrence. The twelfth to last year of the present millennium, however, would seem to be an exception in this regard: a series of events in 1988, each explicable by itself, cumulated to what some called a "peace epidemic," what many regarded as the year the Cold War ended, and what most seem to agree constituted a historical juncture even before the year ended (Barnet, 1988; Hoffmann, 1988; Markham, 1988).

Whatever the most appropriate characterization of the significance of these events, when considered together they pose an extraordinary opportunity to explore the soundness of the foregoing theoretical perspective. The similarity of the direction of these events, the simultaneity of their occurrence, and the diversity of their locales — serious steps to terminate six international wars initiated or completed within weeks of each other — suggest that 1988 may prove to be an unprecedented occasion in modern history when the balance between international cooperation and conflict shifted sharply in favor of the former, a singular moment when it could fairly be said that the world was being rewarded for having muddled through some four decades without a war among its great powers by having peace break out on a global scale.

It is precisely the simultaneity and singularity of these events that is so theoretically challenging. One can readily cite unique circumstances that led to the Soviet withdrawal from Afghanistan, the accession to a ceasefire by Iraq and Iran, the truce and ceasefire in Nicaragua, the meeting of the parties to the war in Cambodia, the start of peace talks in Angola, and the agreement to end the 13-year-old war over the Western Sahara between Morocco and the Polisaro Front guerrillas. But how to account for the fact that all six of these war-terminating processes began or culminated within relatively few weeks of each other? Certainly there is no obvious explanation of this simultaneity. The wars did not commence in the same time period; they were fought on four different continents; they were waged over different issues; they varied widely in their strategic circumstances; and they differed extensively in their intensity and scope.

Nor is the simultaneity limited to combat situations. If the analytic focus is expanded to include intense nonviolent-but-always-on-a-military-alert situations as well as those involving outright war, this period has also been witness to reversals of course in four additional international conflicts: those between the two Koreas, between Taiwan and Mainland China, between Greece and Turkey, and in the nuclear arms race between the United States and the Soviet Union. Given their histories of deep-seated animosity, it is hardly less remarkable that these long-standing situations also underwent significant steps toward amelioration in roughly the same time frame. So the question bears repeating: How to account for the simultaneity of so much effort at accommodation?

And if the initiation of conflict-terminating processes in ten international situations is construed as part of a larger trend toward redressing balances and away from authoritarian, power-based solutions to which domestic conflicts may also contribute, then a number of additions can be made to the 1988 sample of cases wherein publics acquired more scope for their needs and wants. Poland, Burma, the West Bank and Gaza, Algeria, Soviet Armenia, Yugoslavia, and Chile all witnessed mass uprisings that exerted effective pressure for new, more equitable domestic arrangements.[1] In some of these instances, violence accompanied the upheaval, but they nevertheless can be viewed as part of the outbreak of peace in the sense that they forced a readiness to accommodate upon previously resistant regimes. Once again, in short, the initial question can be enlarged and posed anew: How to account for the simultaneity in the righting of so much imbalance?

The question is as puzzling as the reality is encouraging. No, it is more than puzzling; it is also inhibiting. It reminds us of how fully our theories of the international system are oriented toward explaining the

onset and persistence of conflict and how little they anticipate the outbreak and spread of cooperation. It confronts us with our own pessimism
as we begin to appreciate that our grasp of international affairs is profoundly unidirectional, that it allows us to probe a conflict-ridden world
but denies us the conceptual equipment with which to explore a more
benign (if not a cooperation-ridden) world. Yet, at the same time, the
question also begins to alert us to the possibility that 1988 may have
been witness to the first surfacing of the long-term learning processes
noted above as inherent in the accelerated interdependence that accompanied the advent of a postindustrial order.

Some Caveats

To be sure, caveats are in order. The outbreak of peace may be only
a transitory development. The habits of conflict and the values from
which they spring may require many more than four decades to attenu-
ate. Enmities serve psychological and sociopolitical needs, and only under
unusual circumstances do they get relaxed and reversed. So it is certainly
possible that any or all of the ten sets of conflict-terminating negotiations
and the several cases of domestic redirection will founder or collapse and
return each situation to even greater levels of distrust and conflict. But
this very likelihood makes the simultaneity of their 1988 reversals all
the more extraordinary and provocative. Whatever may be their future
course, and however intense the enmity inherent in these situations may
yet become, history has recorded a brief moment in time when the improbable occurred, when global tendencies toward peaceful accommodation
became unmistakably manifest and when comparable signs of domestic
justice surfaced with unremitting clarity.

Nor is this to suggest that the outbreak of peace is universal. The
Middle East remains locked into deadly conflicts[2] and the racial tensions
of southern Africa persist even as reforms have commenced. All in all, it
has been estimated, some nineteen situations in 1988 ran counter to the
mushrooming pattern of cooperation and were marked by the persistence
of violent conflict (Reston, 1988).[3] Domestically, too, countertrends can
be cited, with the most notable perhaps being the reacquisition of control
by power-based, authoritarian regimes in Burma and Haiti along with
the extension of such controls by a similar regime in Singapore. Again,
however, the very pervasiveness of violence makes the onset of ameliorative
processes in ten major international situations all the more remarkable.

Still another caveat must be recorded at the outset. To derive encour-
agement from the several signs of spreading cooperation is not to say, or
even to imply, that the lot of people is improving. Poverty, famine, and
disease continue unabated as global scourges, and the plight of most
countries in the Third World evidences no indication of turning for the
better. Nor is it immediately clear that the outbreak of peace in several

parts of the world will lead to an improvement in the world's standard of living. Political accommodation can result in economic gains if swords get turned into ploughshares, but such a transformation is far from automatic. It may well be that with their swords sheathed, people and communities will turn to nonproductive pursuits and economic rivalries. Our theories of cooperation are too rudimentary to make reasonable estimates as to the likelihood that a more equitable distribution of wealth will become a hallmark of a more militarily benign world. Certainly one can readily imagine circumstances in which both the politics of peace and the economics of poverty coexist and intensify.

Yet, despite these caveats, 1988 remains a landmark (that arguably set the stage for the revolutionary changes that followed in Eastern Europe in 1989). Even if subsequent events obfuscate its significance for historians, 1988 will long remain an intriguing challenge for theoreticians. Simultaneity across diverse political systems and international relationships is too rare a happening not to explore whether it is an indication that the deeper structures of world politics are moving in the direction anticipated by the foregoing analysis of how interdependence-induced dynamics may alter the underpinnings of global life.

Types of Simultaneity

Two broad lines of inquiry might be pursued to come to terms with this remarkable simultaneity. One treats it as mere coincidence and the other presumes that it results from systemic dynamics which, interactively or otherwise, give rise to the same responses within the same time frame. Designated, respectively, as **coincidental** and **systemic** simultaneity, the former type is here judged as too improbable to be explored at length. A more extensive analysis of the latter type, on the other hand, facilitates a conclusion in which a combination of five systemic variables is considered to offer the basis for a cogent, multivariate solution of the simultaneity puzzle.

More specifically, as the summary in Table 14.1 anticipates, the analysis assesses shifts in the values of none of the variables as alone sufficient for the onset of the ten conflict-terminating processes. Nor does it treat all of them as necessary to each situation. Considered as an interactive whole, however, the five sets of variables are suggestive of how it is possible for peace to break out on a global scale.

The improbability of coincidental simultaneity derives from the fact that it is founded on an idiographic perspective in which every historical sequence is seen as deriving from unique circumstances. Viewed in this way, the simultaneity of the ten conflict-terminating processes is a non-development, a mere coincidence that is not even noteworthy inasmuch as the several situations cannot, by definition, be systematically linked to the same sources.

TABLE 14.1 The Simultaneity Puzzle: Summary of Possible Sources of Ten Conflict-Terminating Processes Initiated or Completed in 1988

	Iran-Iraq War	Afghanistan	Angola	Western Sahara	Cambodia	Nicaragua	Taiwan and Mainland China	North and South Korea	Greece and Turkey	U.S.-Soviet arms control
Coincidental Simultaneity										
Idiographic Factors	+[1]	–	–	–	–	–	+[2]	–	–	+[3]
Systemic Simultaneity										
Fatigue Factors	+	+	+	+	+	+	–	–	–	–
Obsolescence of Force	+	+	+	+	+	–	–	–	–	–
Post-Industrial Factors	+	+	+	+	+	+	+	+	+	+
Lowering of Superpower Tensions	–	+	+	–	+	+	+	+	+	+
Contagion Factors	+	+	+	+	+	+	+	+	+	–

+ probably present as a source of the 1988 developments
– probably not relevant as a source of the 1988 developments

[1] The reference here is to the Ayatollah's failing health.
[2] The reference here is to the passing of Chiang Kai-shek's generation with the early 1988 death of his son as President of the Republic of China.
[3] The reference here is to the consolidation of Gorbachev's authority and to President Reagan's desire to secure a place in history as his Administration came to an end.

On the other hand, the presence of idiographic factors cannot be entirely dismissed if one adopts, as the following discussion does, a nomothetic perspective which presumes the presence of systematic factors that infused the ten situations with common systemic antecedents or with interactive causal dynamics. Nomothetic inquiry employs probabilistic analysis to identify central tendencies, but in so doing it does not deny the possibility of idiographic factors accounting for some of the variance. Indeed, it even allows for the extreme case in which no central tendencies are operative, for disparate situations evolving and playing out as a result of disparate and unrelated causal factors. It is not beyond the realm of possibility, therefore, that the close juxtaposition of the various conflict-terminating processes was an historical anomaly: it just so happened, the probabilist could argue, that for no systematic, interconnected reasons the particular circumstances at work in the several situations independently converged at the same time upon bases for reversing course. Indeed, given the diverse goals sought in each case, not to mention the wide social and geographic spaces dividing them, they might just as easily have been separated by years and decades as by weeks and months. That they occurred close upon each other may make it seem as if systematic factors were at work, such an argument would stress, but it stretches analysis beyond both empirical and logical limits to presume that such dissimilar situations could all be tied into the same systemic dynamics.

While probabilistic analysis does not permit rejection of this null hypothesis, it hardly seems plausible. The simultaneity of the ten conflict-terminating processes is too conspicuous to treat as mere coincidence. Important idiographic factors may have been relevant in some of the cases (as noted in the footnotes of Table 14.1), but the probability of ten major international conflicts all turning in cooperative directions within the same time frame for no underlying systematic reasons appears so remarkably low as to warrant exploring whether certain common dynamics operated to bring about the juxtaposition of the several situations. At the very least such an exploration can help in refining the conceptual tools needed to apply a theoretical perspective which accords a central place to learning processes in a postindustrial order of rapidly expanding interdependence.

Contextual, Causal, and Systemwide Variables

In order to resolve the simultaneity puzzle, it is important to distinguish among the values of three sets of variables: those that conduce to conflict-terminating processes by virtue of shifts in the systemic structures or contexts of conflict situations; those that foster these processes as a result of direct, causal stimuli to action; and those that precipitate stimuli to action on a systemwide or global scale. Henceforth these three sets shall be referred to, respectively, as **contextual**, **causal**, and **systemwide** variables.

Contextual variables involve those aspects of conflicts, their histories, structures, and resource distributions, that can undergo a shift in values such that the participants find themselves in new circumstances that enable them to ponder or seek an end to their hostilities. That is, if the values of key variables that underlie the onset and persistence of international conflict undergo change in directions that are conducive to the diminution of violence, the background conditions for the outbreak of peace will have been established. Being only a setting for action — rather than actions themselves — these contextual variables cannot in themselves trigger a reversal of course toward peace; but without their evolution as part of the setting within which conflicts are waged, there is little likelihood of peace overtures being offered or seized by the participants. Various systemic dimensions, in other words, are necessary to the onset of conflict-terminating processes, but their contextual nature is such that they can never be sufficient to initiate these processes in any conflict, much less in many conflicts at the same time.

For conditions favorable to conflict-termination to be transformed into actual processes of tension reduction, contextual variables must be supplemented by causal variables. The latter consist of actions and interactions that alter opportunities and constraints and thereby have impacts on perceptions and motives. Once such actions and interactions shift in directions conducive to the reduction of tensions and violence, they become causal in their impact. As such, as direct stimuli to action, they are different from those indirect contextual conditions which facilitate conflict-terminating responses.

But a further distinction must be drawn if simultaneous signs of peace in ten situations are to be explained. Some causal variables may be more situation-specific than systemic in their scope, with the result that their shifts in conflict-terminating directions may occur at various times. In addition, the dynamics of systems are such that the fluctuations of causal variables may vary widely, with some shifting slower and less erratically than others. Thus it is possible for the global system to become more benign without giving rise to the circumstances of simultaneity. As will be seen, however, a few variables are reflective of systemwide developments that result in similar impacts upon diverse situations at the same moment in time. In the case of the 1988 peace outbreak, two such systemwide variables have been identified as evolving values that may have fostered causal simultaneity.

Fatigue as a Contextual Variable

Either wars end through conquest and surrender or they grind to a halt and terminate with negotiated settlements. When the latter pattern occurs, it tends to result from a sense of fatigue on all sides bolstered by an appreciation that military victory is not possible. This fatigue factor is a contextual and not a causal variable in the sense that it does not determine when the turn toward peace will occur. Armies and publics can be exhausted for a long while before they abandon the goal of military triumph or otherwise decide that the descent into conflict is best reversed. Without the presence of considerable fatigue, such a turn is unlikely to occur, but the onset of fatigue does not necessarily predict when peace negotiations begin to loom as attractive and worthy of undertaking.

Since all the conflicts involved in the 1988 peace outbreak were of long duration, it can readily be argued that each of them had persisted long enough to create the contextual conditions of fatigue — the sociopolitical breakdown of institutions and publics as well as military exhaustion on the battlefield — on which peace negotiations thrive.[4] While this reasoning is tautological in the sense that by definition fatigue is operative in wars that do not end with an outright victory by one side, and while it is also faulty because it does not embrace any systemic processes that might explain why exhaustion should set in at exactly the same time in all the conflicts, it does call attention to one piece of the puzzle. The fact that all of the conflicts had been in progress for years means that the energy and capability levels of the combatants had moved from zeal and confidence toward doubt and hesitation, a mental condition that may have thus readied all concerned for accommodation when shifts in the values of other variables (noted below) altered the prevailing circumstances on which the conflicts had rested. To repeat, fatigue was surely not a sufficient condition for the simultaneity of the policy reversals, but it may well be regarded as one of several necessary conditions.

The Obsolescence of Force as a Contextual Variable

Related to the exhaustion factor is another contextual variable that may have facilitated decisions to seek an end to long-standing conflicts, namely, an emergent appreciation in national capitals that world affairs have become so complex as to reduce the likelihood that force can be used as an effective instrument of foreign policy, that in effect the costs of large-scale, prolonged military actions normally outweigh the benefits. Faced with a continuing depletion of their resources and a deepening erosion of public morale, confronted with so many other situations in which the military conflicts dragged on at great cost to the opposing sides, and ever conscious that local conflicts run the risk of nuclear escalation, leaders in the six war-terminating situations had good reasons to conclude that they were banking on an ineffective and obsolete tool of statecraft and that a reversal of course was in order. Force has proved useful as a deterrent; demonstrating its presence in navies and combat-ready troops may sometimes inhibit potential adversaries, and quick air strikes have been shown to produce desired outcomes. But modern history records that whenever a prolonged commitment to military action is undertaken, stalemate and exhaustion follow.

That a number of considerations have converged to render interstate war obsolete is evident in the statistics for the wars that continued in 1988 as well as those that moved toward termination. As previously indicated, at the outset of 1988, twenty-five wars of all kinds — situations in which at least two sides contested each other with organized violence — were in progress. Of these, six were essentially interstate wars involving weaponry and/or soldiers supplied by two or more states, and the remainder were internal wars among rival ethnic, religious, and ideological groups (Reston, 1988). All of the latter were still underway as this chapter went to press, whereas all of the former constituted the situations in which conflict-terminating processes were initiated.

The reasons why interstate wars have become obsolete are too numerous to detail here. Suffice it to take note of two observations that summarize lengthy analyses of the evolving systemwide predisposition to close out or avoid international war. One is by a political scientist, John Mueller, who traces "a substantial historical process in which major war — war among developed countries — has gradually moved, like dueling and slavery, toward terminal disrepute because of its perceived repulsiveness and futility" (Mueller, 1988b). Similarly, a military historian, Michael Howard, has concisely noted

> that the state apparat is likely to become isolated from the rest of the body politic, a severed head conducting its intercourse with other severed heads according to its own laws. War, in short, has once more been denationalized. It has become, as it was in the eighteenth century, an affair of states and no longer of peoples. The identification of the community with the state, brought to its highest point in the era of the two World Wars, can no longer be assumed as natural or, militarily speaking, necessary. No Third World War is likely to be fought by armies embodying the manpower of the Nation while the rest of the population work to keep them armed and fed. (Howard, 1979)

Again, of course, it would be absurd to argue that leaders in the six 1988 situations of interstate war independently, and within the same time frame, came to the identical conclusion that their efforts to realize their goals through organized force were founded on an obsolete instrument of persuasion. Rather, as with the fatigue variable, it can only be said that they shared a growing appreciation of how changes in the nature of global politics had undermined the utility of sustained military action and that this understanding also contributed to their readiness to accommodate to peace overtures when they arose. The force-obsolescence variable, in short, is a contextual and not a causal source of simultaneity and, as such, it can also be regarded as a necessary but not a sufficient condition for the outbreak of peace.

Postindustrial Order as a Contextual Variable

A third contextual variable that is global in its repercussions and that, as such, may have also facilitated the outbreak of peace concerns the aforenoted dynamic transformation inherent in the world's evolution from an industrial civilization based on manufacturing industries to a postindustrial order organized around information services. As stressed earlier, among the many ramifications of this transformation are the global tendencies toward decentralized authority and influence that postindustrialism has unleashed. For all the fears that modern communications and computer technologies would result in centralized systems exercising authoritarian controls over people, quite the opposite has unfolded in recent years. States have become increasingly less effective, national governments have devolved many of their responsibilities either upon the marketplace or upon less encompassing political entities, subgroups have proliferated and flourished as the ineffectiveness of whole systems has become manifest, and individuals have become more analytically skillful. While these consequences of the microelectronic and communications revolutions can be easily exaggerated, surely they are powerful enough to operate as contextual conditions of present-day conflict-terminating processes in the sense of facilitating a worldwide recognition that authority and legitimacy evoked on behalf of war efforts can be subject to review and revision, that publics can tire of war and other intense long-standing conflicts, that they can thus be effectively mobilized to undermine and oppose them, and that value conflicts have economic and social aspects which need not lead to resolution through military means.

The postindustrial era, in short, has solidified the isolation of the state apparatus to which Howard refers and, in so doing, it has fostered social and political structures that are unreceptive to the waging of interstate wars and the maintenance of intense, nonviolent-but-always-on-a-military-alert interstate conflicts. The reactions of the American and Soviet publics to their countries' wars in Vietnam and Afghanistan, the restlessness of the European peace movement, the mass protests in South Korea on behalf of reconciliation with their northern compatriots, and the signs of disquiet among Iranians over their war with Iraq exemplify the way in which postindustrial circumstances are altering the calculus through which interstate conflicts are waged.

The Lowering of Superpower Tensions

A less general and more concrete source of the converging of several peace processes, one that has elements of all three types of variables, involves the conduct of the superpowers, the relationship between them, and the decline in their capabilities relative to the rest of the world. The fact that both the Soviet Union and the United States, each for their own reasons, began to appreciate that their arms race was counterproductive and moved toward accommodation in the military realm — a movement which, in turn, facilitated cooperation on a number of other issues and the fostering of a generalized atmosphere of global harmony — surely contributed to a momentum that spread to other interstate conflicts and provided a context for considering their termination. Even as the two superpowers long served as exemplars of conflict behavior, in other words, so did their commanding positions enable them to assume a contrary role model in which their cooperative endeavors were deemed worthy of emulation.

In all probability, moreover, the weaknesses of the superpowers revealed by their efforts to accommodate to each other also operated as a contextual consideration. Once the Soviets exhibited the need to transfer resources away from the arms race, and once the U.S. sought to cope with its huge budget deficits by cutting back on defense spending, leaders in the various interstate wars may well have more acutely discerned the limits inherent in their own military commitments. Furthermore, with the superpowers moving into a period of accommodation, the leaders could reason, the opportunities for turning to one or another of them for help in the military pursuit of their own wars were bound to diminish, thus casting their military calculations in a far different light than had been the case when they undertook to do battle.

And the same might be said about the diplomatic and economic calculations made in some of the nonviolent-but-always-on-a-military-alert conflicts that underwent a reversal of course during the same period. Most notably, the regimes in Taiwan and South Korea may well have factored in the moderating systemic environment prior to relaxing their authoritarian controls over their domestic scenes and making gestures toward reconciliation with their counterparts on the Chinese mainland and in North Korea. Or at least it is plausible that contextual variables were operative in the sense that both the South Korean and Taiwanese leaderships could anticipate that an ameliorating Soviet-American relationship would lead to a less harsh international scene in which their isolated authoritarian rule would be more conspicuous and, thus, more vulnerable. Even more plausibly, the superpower accommodation also pointed to the probability of a diminished readiness on the part of the United States to back them in their conflicts with opposition groups at home and adversaries abroad. Doubtless, too, memories of the recent U.S. reversal of course in the Philippines contributed to heightened readiness to resolve long-standing domestic conflicts.

Nor did the dynamics of lowered tension between the superpowers function only as contextual variables. There is substantial evidence that the "new thinking" of Mikhail Gorbachev led the Soviets to cut back on their support for allies in several of the wars, a policy change that occurred within the same time frame and manifestly operated as a causal variable (as did the concurrent change represented by the U.S. Congress's refusal to provide continuing support for the Contras in Nicaragua). Indeed, it might be said that the outbreak of peace began with the Soviet indication of a readiness to withdraw troops from Afghanistan, a decision that reinforced the global atmosphere of accommodation even as it was also a concrete reversal of course that was quickly followed by an apparent reduction of support for the Vietnamese in Cambodia, the Sandinistas in Nicaragua, and the Cubans in Angola.

Yet, it cannot be concluded that the lessening of superpower confrontation and the advent of new policies in the Kremlin are a sufficient as well as a necessary explanation of the outbreak of peace in 1988. It is doubtful whether any of the war-terminating processes would have begun if the superpowers had maintained their high levels of support for surrogates abroad, but the diminution of this support occurred in only four of the six war-terminating situations. As such, they operated as causal dynamics that fell two short of being systemwide in scope. They accounted neither for the end of the Iran-Iraq war nor for the agreement to terminate the war in the Western Sahara. To be sure, by 1988 both the U.S. and the Soviets were pressing for a truce in the Iran-Iraq war, but this is hardly a sufficient explanation inasmuch as neither of the combatants had previously demonstrated a readiness to yield to outside pressures. It seems likely, rather, that the aforenoted systemic contexts — the fatigue factor, the obsolescence of war, the advent of a postindustrial order, and the specter of superpower accommodation — were particularly relevant to the onset of a peace process in those situations where the superpowers could not exercise leverage by withdrawing support from their surrogates. Such an interpretation helps to account for the shift of direction in the Greek-Turkish conflict as well as the Iran-Iraq war.

A Contagion Effect

There may have been one set of systemwide variables operative in all ten conflict situations that underlies their simultaneity and that goes a long way toward infusing theoretical unity into the diverse considerations outlined above. It involves the communications technology inherent in the postindustrial order. While the advent of this order fostered a number of contextual conditions that facilitated the simultaneous convergence of conflict-terminating processes in far-flung parts of the world, its communications dynamics seem likely to have operated as a direct precipitant of the simultaneity. The war fatigue of postindustrial publics, not to mention their intensified readiness to challenge the legitimacy of those leading the war efforts, developed prior to 1988 and might have just as easily been activated at earlier or later stages in one or the other of the conflict-terminating processes; but the existence of a vast global network of electronic channels for the flow of information — computer hookups, television satellites, video cassettes, radio tapes, etc. — meant that mechanisms were available for direct links among the several conflict situations. Where word of developments in one part of the world once traveled in months and years via stagecoach and sailing ship, only seconds and minutes elapse before such information spreads in the postindustrial era. For the first time in human history, therefore, an event in one part of the global system can be *instantaneously* an event for the whole system, and the motives and strategies underlying any outcome can thus be a stimulus or model for actions elsewhere in the world. Just as financial markets have been globalized to the extent that a rise or fall on the Tokyo market has immediate consequences for the level of prices in New York and Zurich, so can the politics of struggle and war in the Middle East have ramifications for comparable contests in Southeast Asia, southern Africa, and Central America. Stated more generally, the microelectronic revolution has created the means for rapid transformations of the global system's political environment, quickly undermining a conflictful context and infusing it with an atmosphere in which accommodative actions seem plausible and acceptable.

Simultaneity, in short, is built into the current structure of world politics. It is not a mysterious wind that, like a wildfire, cascades ideas and issues across continents and over legal and political barriers; rather, the cascades take concrete form in televised scenes, taped speeches, recorded deliberations, written appeals, and smuggled cassettes which, legitimately or otherwise,[5] leap from one national capital or revolutionary stronghold to another and, in so doing, foster the occurrence of similar events in diverse places within the same time frame.

Put somewhat differently, it is now possible to speak of a contagion factor — of specific emulative and learning processes — in world politics wherein public protests and policy decisions spread in traceable patterns across the full breadth of the global system. Indeed, it can be said that the system is now global precisely because a simultaneity of events can give rise to a shift in the tone of the international environment which then serves as the basis of political reality.

It follows that systemic simultaneity may have been at work in the 1988 outbreak of peace through the contagion factor. Most notably, and as previously suggested, the negotiations of a Soviet withdrawal from Afghanistan early in the year may have cascaded in important ways into the waging of the other five wars, if not through conscious comparisons, then in the subconscious form of legitimating thought about the alternative of agreeing to a ceasefire or a truce proposal. If the Soviets can consider backtracking in Afghanistan, leaders in the other situations might have reasoned, can we afford to do otherwise in our conflict? And as a peace process thus got initiated in the six situations, so might have each step in the negotiations of one situation cascaded as reinforcing information for those who undertook conflict-terminating actions elsewhere.

A THEORETICAL PERSPECTIVE REINFORCED?

To conclude that a number of variables underlay the converging events of 1988, all of them necessary but none alone sufficient as a basis for the simultaneity, is to highlight the density, complexity, and dynamism of the cooperation-ridden world that seems to be evolving out of the long period of great-power peace. While the accuracy of the foregoing analysis may be wanting, it does appear consistent with the theoretical perspective and four propositions set forth at the outset. Or, if it does not fully reinforce that perspective, at least it is an approach to the simultaneity puzzle that calls attention to the need for an understanding of world politics which takes into account the extraordinary degrees of interdependence among the issues that crowd the global agenda and which allows for swift-moving developments that transform the issues into a coherent and structured web of relationships. If such a conception can be refined, then the simultaneity puzzle will no longer seem puzzling. What once appeared to be separate situations marked by simultaneity will emerge, instead, as a singular process unfolding on a global scale.

If this is so, it suggests that the amelioration of violence and the channeling of its energies into nonviolent forms of conflict may be emerging as a global way of life, that learning across more than four decades may be fostering and cumulating expectations, inclinations, and mechanisms that are increasingly conducive to sustaining the prolonged peace. Indeed, if it is the case that the deepening of global interdependence involves densities, complexities, and dynamics that inhibit large-scale military undertakings, then the probabilities of great-power peace being perpetuated are further heightened in proportion to the continuing increases in the density, complexity, and dynamism of world politics.

All of this is not to contend, of course, that the dynamics of interdependence have insured the preservation of great-power peace and that the present generation can begin to walk off into the sunset secure in the knowledge that the missiles of war have been permanently silenced. After more than four decades, the dynamics of peace prolongation do seem to be on a more secure footing, to be caught up in the complex webs of global interdependence, but such webs are still being woven and are thus still subject to unraveling.

In short, the foregoing analysis refers not to wholesale changes that are so thoroughgoing as to never be undone, but to marginal changes that remain fragile even as they are also discernible and encouraging.

The idea that the world's increasing interdependence has improved the likelihood of enduring peace — that the early postwar years of muddling through from crisis to crisis has given way to a density, complexity, and dynamism that facilitates the cascading of cooperative inclinations from situation to situation — needs to be viewed as a hypothesis subject to endless testing rather than as an assumption to be taken for granted.

ENDNOTES

1. If the time frame is expanded to include the previous three years, still others could be added to the sample, most notably Taiwan, South Korea, the Philippines, Sri Lanka, Tibet, and the European peace movement. Even more impressive, if the time frame is expanded ahead one year to embrace 1989, the sample would include the dismantling of the Berlin Wall and the transformation of dictatorial regimes in Bulgaria, Czechoslovakia, East Germany, Hungary, Romania, and (momentarily) China.

2. But even here the very end of 1988 was marked by faint signs of accommodation as the United States agreed to enter into discussions with the PLO after the latter agreed to abandon its long-standing opposition to the existence of Israel.

3. This estimate includes the six wars treated here as moving away from violence and toward ameliorative resolutions. For another assessment that enumerated the existence of "36 full-scale conflicts, involving 40 nations and five million solders," see Markham (1988).

4. The situation in Nicaragua was the most recent of the conflicts (with U.S.-assisted Contra raids having begun in 1981), followed by the Iran-Iraq war (1980), the Soviet invasion of Afghanistan (1979), the Vietnamese invasion of Cambodia (1978), the Portuguese departure from Angola (1975), and the onset of hostilities between Polisario Front guerrillas and Morocco over the Western Sahara (1975). Three of the remaining four conflicts had their origins decades earlier with the onset of the Cold War in the late 1940s, while the start of Greek-Turkish tensions cannot be easily located at a fixed point in time.

5. It is noteworthy that Khomeini's vision of the future expressed in tapes smuggled into prerevolutionary Iran has been credited as a crucial factor in the success of the Iranian revolution, just as videotapes of Aquino's assassination smuggled into the Philippines are considered central to the subsequent downfall of the Marcos regime.

CHAPTER FIFTEEN

Threats to Protracted Peace: World Politics According to Murphy

James Lee Ray

This chapter serves a purpose both for its author and this anthology.[1] As Charles Kegley's introductory remarks suggest, this volume is meant to emphasize the positive. It focuses on the causes of peace rather than the causes of war, much as medical researchers might investigate the effects of positive behaviors that promote good health rather than those factors which lead to heart attacks or other health problems. A recent article by Ray (1989), inspired in part by the work of Gaddis (1987b) on the long peace, argues that international war, like slavery before it, may be on the verge of disappearing. That article, like this volume, certainly emphasizes the optimistic and the positive. A book which concentrates on the sources of peace and is inspired by the hope that international war will disappear from the face of the earth because of the impact of moral progress is clearly in need of the balanced perspective that a determinedly pessimistic analysis might provide. Such perspective is the purpose of the following discussion.

We will begin with a couple of questions: Has the post–Second World War period of major-power peace really been as unusual as the theme of this volume suggests? If not, what are the implications for its prolongation? Then we will turn to an analysis of some of the allegedly important underpinnings of this period of peace, with a view toward emphasizing their fragility. The concluding remarks will assess briefly the possible relevance of such an exercise for future research and policy.

How Long Is Long?

According to a useful rule of thumb, any attempt to explain ought to be based on a clear definition of the phenomenon to be explained. A notion clearly exists that the post–Second World War period is unusual, even unique, with respect to the length of time that has passed without a war between the great powers. Holsti (1986:369), for example, asserts that "by historical standards a forty-one-year period without an intra–Great-Power war is unprecedented." More recently, Jervis (1988:80) declares that "the most striking characteristic of the postwar world is just that — it can be called 'post-war' because the major powers have not fought each other since 1945. Such a lengthy period of peace among the most powerful states is unprecedented."

But whether the long peace is really unusual depends on what is meant by *long* and by *peace*, not to mention *great power*. Both Levy (1983) and Small and Singer (1982) categorize the conflict between China and the United States in Korea (which ended in 1953) as a great-power war. That makes the current era of great-power peace shorter, for example, than the 38 years of peace that followed the Napoleonic Wars ending in 1815. It is also shorter (if we categorize the Russo-Japanese war in 1904-1905 as a non–great-power war)[2] than the hiatus in great-power conflict between the Franco-Prussian war in 1870-1871, and the beginning of the First World War in 1914.

In short, the long peace which serves as the focus of this volume is not, upon inspection, so extraordinary and unprecedented. It has been surpassed in length twice in the last 175 years. This suggests, in a general way, that the forces producing it are also probably not so unusual, and it is therefore reasonable to suspect they will soon be overwhelmed by one or more of the destabilizing factors that we will discuss below.

Even if one insists on a different resolution of the definitional issues at hand, and concludes that the contemporary period is unusual, there are ominous historical precedents one ought to keep in mind in interpreting the significance — as well as the durability — of the long peace. The prolonged period of great-power peace immediately preceding this one (after the Franco-Prussian War in 1871) culminated in what was the bloodiest great-power war in history up to that time. Also, Levy and Morgan (1984) have shown that there is a systematic tendency within the last 500 years for less frequent wars to be more serious. Thus, if the pattern holds, we have an empirical basis for anticipating that the longer the next major-power war is postponed, the more catastrophic it will be.

A prudent observer will also recall that such previous interludes have systematically provoked optimism about the "end of war." In 1853, encouraged in part by the long peace after the Napoleonic Wars, the *Manchester Examiner* asserted that "the principles of the Peace Society . . . have unquestionably gained ground among us; statesmen shrink from war now, not only on account of its risks, its cost, its possible unpopularity, but from a new-born sense of the tremendous moral responsibility which lies on those who . . . bring upon humanity this awful curse" (Hinsley, 1967:114). The period of major-power peace following the Franco-Prussian War, given a decade or two, spawned several works which forecast the demise and eventual disappearance of international war. One of the more ambitious was Jean de Bloch's (1899) suggestively titled *The Future of War in Its Technical, Economic, and Political Relations:*

Is War Now Impossible? The 1911 edition of the *Encyclopaedia Britannica* contained an article on peace written by an international law specialist, Thomas Barclay. "Three years before the beginning of the most calamitous war the world had known, Barclay confidently predicted the reign of brotherhood . . . Heartened by the growth of international conferences and agreements and by a surge of opinion calling for peace and working for peace, he prophesied that the causes of war would ultimately be eliminated" (Blainey, 1988:24). Perhaps the most famous work in this genre was *The Great Illusion* by Norman Angell, first published in 1910, and again in a new edition in 1913. Although Angell protested after the First World War, with some validity, that his argument in that book had been that war had become irrational on economic grounds, and not that it would not occur, there was in fact considerable optimism about the impact of the economic futility of war on its incidence.[3] Even in the relatively brief period of time between the world wars, such a distinguished military historian as J. F. C. Fuller (1933) foresaw the elimination of war in *The Dragon's Teeth*. It should not be surprising then, that the contemporary period of major-power peace is also evoking hopeful predictions of the end of international war. Werner Levi (1981:15), for example, in *The Coming End of War*, argues that "developed states are unlikely to engage in modern war with each other directly [because] . . . wars are too costly and . . . they need each other for the fulfillment of important interests which can be most adequately achieved by nonviolent methods."

Levi's argument is virtually identical to the thrust of Angell's thesis in *The Great Illusion*,[4] which in turn shared much in common with the arguments of the "Manchester liberals" in the nineteenth century who argued that nations "now grew richer through commerce than through conquest" (Blainey, 1988:18). And Levi will not necessarily turn out to be wrong, just because so many similar past predictions have experienced a sad fate. Surely, though, optimism about the demise of international war ought to be tempered with awareness that previous eras of peace have misled informed analysts of international politics into believing that international war is obsolete. It also behooves contemporary analysts to be conscious of the many things that could go wrong in today's international system, any one of which might bring the current long peace to a tragic, cataclysmic conclusion.

PEACE THROUGH NUCLEAR WEAPONS?

Perhaps the most prevalent idea about the prolonged peace between the United States and the Soviet Union asserts that nuclear weapons have been primarily responsible. This too, like forecasts of permanent peace, is a predictable consequence of peaceful interludes. "Those living in the three generations after Waterloo . . . wondered at the long peace and sought explanations in events that were happening simultaneously"

(Blainey, 1988:29). So, for example, Nogee and Spanier (1988:189) proclaim that "the principle impact of nuclear weapons for the last 40 years . . . has prevented a total war between the United States and the Soviet Union despite the scope and intensity of their rivalry."

John Gaddis, John Vasquez, and Robert Johansen, in Chapters 2, 9, and 10 of this volume, respectively, analyze in some detail the plausibility of such claims. Whatever one concludes about their past impact, nuclear weapons certainly do not guarantee that no international war will occur in the future, no matter how great their destructive potential. As Jack Levy (1976:552) notes, "history provides a number of optimistic forecasts of the end of war due to the development of the 'ultimate' weapon." Such arguments have been made about artillery, smokeless powder, dynamite, the submarine, and poison gas. They have all been wrong. "There is little evidence in history," Evan Luard (1986:396) concludes, "that the existence of supremely destructive weapons alone is capable of deterring war."

Nevertheless, such arguments stressing the destructive potential of nuclear weapons are undeniably impressive; they are almost certainly the most persuasive in the long line of admittedly similar arguments about preceding technological developments. Perhaps the most impressive to date stresses the possibility of nuclear winter. Wallace, Crissey, and Sennot (1986:25-26) declare that "most atmospheric scientists now believe that even if one side were to deal a strategically successful preemptive blow . . . the aggressor would be unable to escape devastation. . . ." This would mean, as Nogee and Spanier (1988:127) point out, that the power that struck first, even if it could prevent any retaliation, would win, but "only for a week or two!" Thus, the best-known proponent of this idea, Carl Sagan (1983/84:277) concludes that "a decision to launch a major first strike is now much less rational. . . ."

It is tempting to conclude that under these conditions, the long peace will endure. Unfortunately, though, Wallace, et al. (1986) may overstate their case when they assert that "most atmospheric scientists" believe in the nuclear winter theory. Atmospheric scientists Stanley Thompson and Steven Schneider (1986:483), for example, claim to show that "on scientific grounds the global apocalyptic conclusion of the . . . nuclear winter hypothesis can now be relegated to a vanishingly low level of probability." Even before that article appeared, Albert Wohlstetter (1985:963) claimed that Sagan and his coauthors had "greatly overstated the scientific consensus" in their original article on nuclear winter. More recently, Robert Jervis (1988:84), not exactly a scholar with a reputation for a Dr. Strangelove-like attitude about "the bomb," has declared, without qualification, that "a total 'nuclear winter' and the extermination of human life would not follow a nuclear war. . . ."

In addition, even if meteorologists, or nuclear deterrence specialists, were unanimously convinced by the nuclear winter theory, a nuclear war might still occur, by accident. As Wallace, et al. (1986:15, 17) observe, if either the United States or the Soviet Union should attack the other with

SLBMs (or, what may be even more crucial, if either side comes to *believe* that such an attack is underway), the target of such an attack would have 9 to 12 minutes to decide whether or not to launch a counterattack, or risk suffering a " 'C³I [that is, command, control, communication, and intelligence] disabling' opening salvo." Because, under these conditions, a lot of information must be processed in a very short time, the monitoring systems on both sides are very sensitive, responding even to subtle and ambiguous inputs. In 1980, a report to the Senate Armed Services Committee revealed that the nation's monitoring system had produced 147 false indications of Soviet missile attacks in the preceding year (Lackey, 1985:136-37). Between 1978 and 1983, there were at least six "serious" false alarms, and no less than 956 alarms of sufficiently grave character to trigger "Missile Display Conferences" to evaluate the incoming information (Wallace, et al., 1986:20). Such false alarms occur so frequently that there is a good chance that someday one will occur in the midst of a crisis in relations between the United States and the Soviet Union. "We may presume . . . that during a deep crisis there will be enormous pressure on the leadership of both superpowers to order a launch at the first indications that an enemy attack is under way" (Wallace, et al., 1986:19). In short, the speed and accuracy of contemporary delivery systems, combined with the ability of submarines to get close to their targets, as well as the possible vulnerability and complexity of C³I systems, make an accidental nuclear war a realistic possibility that should be taken into account in any attempt to evaluate the stability of the contemporary long peace.

Major-Power Peace Through Arms Control?

Even a pessimist, though, might wonder, since there are so many false alarms, whether any of them will ever be believed, no matter how tense the crisis might be. Perhaps the great number of such alarms will ultimately take its toll on the nerves of the participants in this process, and some day technicians will conclude that this last alarm *must* finally be valid. However, all such arguments have an air of unreality about them under current conditions. In the time of *perestroika, glasnost,* and the INF treaty, it seems unlikely that a "deep crisis" in the U.S.-Soviet relations will actually occur.

Unfortunately, however, there are several good reasons to suspect that the current era of good feelings between the superpowers will be short-lived. One reason is that such eras seem to come and go with predictable regularity, about once every decade or so. In the 1940s, the Americans and the Soviets were allies against the Nazis, and Americans learned to think of even such an unlikely character as Joseph Stalin as "Uncle Joe." In the 1950s, as dominated as they were by the Cold War, there was also the summit meeting in Geneva (1955), which created the "spirit of Geneva." At the meeting, Dwight Eisenhower, "bursting with good spirits," made his famous Open Skies proposal (recently revived in modified form by George Bush) to give each superpower the right and the capability to conduct aerial photography over its counterpart. "The Russians, for their part, seemed more relaxed than at any time since the war. Khrushchev assured his listeners that 'neither side wants war,' and back home *Pravda* and *Isvestia* were telling the Russian people the same thing" (Manchester, 1973:349). The 1960s were marked by the Cuban Missile Crisis and tension over the Vietnam War, as well as the Soviet invasion of Czechoslovakia. But even in the middle of that troubled decade, President Johnson met with Soviet Premier Kosygin in Hollybush, the home of the president of Glassboro State College in New Jersey, and emerged with the declaration that "it helps to reason together. That is why we went to Hollybush. Reasoning together was the spirit of Hollybush" (Manchester, 1973:1044). And, the most significant post–Second World War era of good feeling in U.S.-Soviet relations (at least, possibly, until the current one) involved the détente of the early 1970s. The point is that these eras come and go, usually within a fairly short time.

One of the factors that may jeopardize stable U.S.-Soviet relations, paradoxically enough, is arms control agreements. One of the problems with arms control agreements (as Joseph Kruzel suggests in Chapter 11) is that they encourage and evoke more rapid technological innovations. Prohibitions against existing weapons encourage the development of newer, often more expensive and deadlier replacements. This pattern is clearly visible in the history of strategic arms control efforts of the past two decades. "Limitations on the number of launchers encouraged the further development of MIRVs; limitations on 'conventional' missile defense systems using interceptors encouraged the development of laser defense systems; limitations on ballistic missiles encouraged the development of cruise missiles; and so on" (Berkowitz, 1987:29).

Another typical problem with arms control agreements and negotiations is that they create a need for "bargaining chips," that is, weapons systems that can be given up in order to get the other side to give up something in return. As Kruzel (1981:302) points out, "bargaining chips have a particularly insidious consequence. They provide a convenient rationale for new weapons systems, even those with no discernible military merit. In fact, such systems make ideal bargaining chips because they will not be missed if they are sacrificed in negotiations." (Kruzel reiterates this point in Chapter 11.) In 1985, for example, the Reagan administration made a successful effort to persuade Congress to keep the MX program alive. "The major argument used by administration officials during that debate was not based on the military utility of the MX but rather on its potential as a 'bargaining chip' in future arms control talks with the Soviets" (Ray, 1987:284).

The INF treaty is likely to solidify this tendency for the U.S. to accumulate bargaining chips. The Reagan administration pushed hard for the deployment of 572 new intermediate-range missiles in Western

Europe, against the vigorous opposition of demonstrators in Europe as well as the domestic nuclear freeze movement. From the viewpoint of the administration, it was only *after* those missiles were deployed and became available as bargaining chips that the Soviets could be persuaded to sign a treaty banning intermediate- and shorter-range missiles from Europe. Secretary of State George Shultz (1988:4) summarized the "lesson" of this experience that is likely to be carried over into the Bush administration in testimony to the Senate Foreign Relations Committee: "Opponents of our deployment have been proved dead wrong. If we had heeded the 'freeze movement' or the 'peace movement,' we would never have gotten this [INF] treaty."

In anticipation of bargaining over the limitations of strategic missiles, George Bush has so far refused to rule out the development of any new weapons systems, including the SDI, the MX, or the Midgetman missile. One of the earliest decisions of his administration was a "compromise" which called for the development of both the MX and the Midgetman, reportedly in part because he was impressed with the potential utility of both as bargaining chips. As Jack Ruina (1987:191) ruefully acknowledges, "An argument for a new ICBM is to add bargaining chips for arms control negotiations as quid pro quo for Soviet weapons. Unfortunately, and as much as we would like to see it otherwise, use of bargaining chips seems to be part and parcel of the arms control negotiating process."

If a 50 percent reduction in strategic launchers on both sides of the superpower confrontation is ever completed, it is easy to anticipate how that agreement will foster competitive efforts on both sides to develop more expensive and deadly weapons, in the manner historically typical of arms control agreements. Looking at the post-START agreement from the U.S. point of view, the Defense Department will want their 50 percent fewer missiles to be newer, better, perhaps bigger, and/or more mobile. One can also see an even more urgent need to develop SDI-type systems in order to protect the lower number of missiles that has been agreed upon. Stealth bombers might become a higher priority. The INF Treaty already has, and a possible START agreement would surely create pressure to modernize and improve conventional forces and weapons systems, thus making the superpower arms race more expensive.

Finally, the INF Treaty and a possible START agreement may well make the superpower military confrontation more dangerous in two other ways. First, there is the possibility that reducing by 50 percent the number of strategic missiles on each side will remove an important force for stability in the current situation. As Intriligator and Brito (1984:83-84) point out, an important virtue of the large number of missiles on both sides of the superpower arms race has been the protection they afford each side against technological breakthroughs. That is, the redundancy in missiles and weapons has provided a margin of safety for both sides, making it highly unlikely that any revolutionary technological breakthrough on one side or the other will make possible a disabling first strike. A START agreement reducing drastically the number of missiles on both sides at least flirts with the risk of compromising that margin of safety. Admittedly, reducing the number of missiles on *both* sides has countervailing effects in the direction of increasing stability, which might, however, be overwhelmed by a destabilizing impact if both sides compensate for the reduced number of launchers by putting more warheads on each launcher. (This would make each missile a more tempting target, since each would represent a larger proportion of the opponent's firepower.) Second, if both sides do decide that a reduction of their missile forces necessitates a beefing up or modernizing of the conventional capabilities, it might increase the possibility of a confrontation or conflict in which both sides would rely exclusively on their conventional capabilities. If one or both sides foresees this possibility, it might make both of them more willing to engage in military conflict, freed, in relative terms at least, from the fear that the conflict would become a nuclear one.

PEACE THROUGH INTERDEPENDENCE?

However, to repeat, in this era of good feeling between the United States and the Soviet Union, such confrontations seem unlikely, no matter how much the history of arms control agreements suggests otherwise. But arms control agreements, and their disagreeable side effects, are not the only kinds of danger that can be foreseen given the current drift of events. Another danger is that the relative independence of the superpowers from each other will be replaced by a less stable form of interdependence.

One of the more persuasive explanations of the long peace offered by Gaddis (1987b:225) stresses the fact that "the Russian-American relationship, to a remarkable degree ... has been one of mutual *in*dependence." He points out that at places where the Soviets and the Americans have come into direct contact, such as in Berlin and Korea, they have erected barriers like the Berlin Wall and the Korean demilitarized zone, in recognition of the idea that "good fences make good neighbors." Economically, the United States and the Soviet Union have avoided, so far at least, any important level of interdependence. "The relative invulnerability of Russians and Americans to one another in the economic sphere," Gaddis (1987b:225) concludes, "is probably fortunate, from the standpoint of international stability. . . ."

But *perestroika*, *glasnost*, and the contemporary era of good feeling between the United States and the Soviet Union, as well as the dismantling of the communist regimes in Eastern Europe, threaten to bring an end to that era of independence and mutual invulnerability between the superpowers. Cultural exchanges will be increased. International trade between the two, and international investment from the West in the Soviet Union and in Eastern Europe, will be greatly augmented. In general, the superpowers, as well as the Western European allies of the

United States and the Eastern European neighbors of the Soviets, will become more interdependent to an important and dangerous degree.

As Gaddis (1987b:224) notes, it is a tenet of the classical liberal faith that the higher the level of contact that takes place between nations, the greater are the chances for peace. War is unlikely in this view (as in the work of Angell and Levi discussed previously, for example) if nations have come to depend on one another economically. However, Gaddis also points out that "these are pleasant things to believe, but there is remarkably little historical evidence to validate them." He cites data from the Correlates of War project to support his claim that every one of the ten bloodiest interstate wars in the last century and a half grew out of conflicts between countries that were either contiguous and/or traded extensively with one another.[5] In short, in the opinion of Gaddis (1987b:226), "the extent to which the Soviet Union and the United States have been independent of one another rather than interdependent . . . has in itself constituted a structural support for stability in relations between the two countries." It may well be unfortunate, then, that that structural support is being eroded by the increasing interdependence between the two countries. This is especially regrettable because these eras of good feeling come and go. The current one is likely to go with a vengeance because of the serious, quite possibly insoluble internal problems facing both superpowers. And the problems facing the United States in particular are likely to exacerbate crises in both the industrialized West and the developing world. If the Soviet Union establishes closer contact with the United States, it will be more likely to be adversely affected by the crisis currently unfolding in the United States, the West, and the Third World.

PERESTROIKA, GLASNOST, AND THE FUTURE

The Soviet economy is in trouble. It grew about 5 percent a year in the 1960s, fell to about a 2 percent rate in the 1970s, and stopped growing altogether in the 1980s. The Soviet Union is the only industrialized country in the world where average life expectancy has *decreased* in recent years. Its technological backwardness is well known to the point of being legendary; the Soviets have yet to produce a personal computer which is available to the general public. In the words of Mikhail Gorbachev himself, "The economy is in a mess; we're behind in every area . . . the closer you look, the worse it is" (Allison, 1988:19-29).

For his efforts to deal with those problems, as well as his domestic political reforms and his diplomatic initiatives, Gorbachev is much appreciated in Western countries. *Time* named him Man of the Year in 1987 and Man of the Decade at the end of the 1980s. Public opinion polls in both the United States and Western Europe consistently find astonishingly high rates of approval for him (Allison, 1988:18).

However, at home it is not so clear that Gorbachev or his reforms are popular, or even tolerated. Goldman and Goldman (1987/88:561) note that "Soviet citizens have shown little spontaneous enthusiasm for the reforms." Well-known Sovietologist Marshall Shulman is not at all optimistic about Gorbachev's chances to succeed in his reform efforts. He points out that it is likely to be a decade or more before the benefits of *perestroika* will be visible. In the short run, the reform effort will mostly just threaten the jobs, privileges, and power of strong bureaucratic interest groups. The "modernizers," in contrast, are small in number. That small group will have to deal with "stubborn resistance to reforms from strong elements of the party and KGB bureaucracies, habituated to ruthless and arbitrary exercise of police controls" (Shulman, 1987/88:496-99).

That Shulman is correct about the delay in the beneficial impact of *perestroika* has become obvious. The Soviets are experiencing central government budget deficits that are about twice as great as those plaguing the Americans, as a proportion of the GNP, and they threaten to result in an economic "Great Crash" (Shelton, 1988). The *New York Times* reports that currently the economic problems facing the Soviet Union are "staggering . . . The factories are not equipped for the computer age and worse, neither is the workforce. Then there is the food system that is a mess at each step from farm to grocer's shelf. Then there are the crumbling roads and railroads and a phone system that is barely fit for human exchange, let alone data transmission" (Keller, 1988:1). As a result of these shortcomings, and because *perestroika* has so far increased purchasing power more rapidly than production, shortages are now worse than before the reform effort began. "Soviet products that have often been in short supply, like meat and butter, are scarcer than ever [in 1989]. . . . Everyday items like good shoes and toilet paper [were] also missing from the shelves. Shoppers in Moscow [were] queuing for laundry detergent, and . . . the capital was virtually bereft of gasoline." Overall, things are so bad that a Soviet economist recently reported in a Russian journal that "the people of the Soviet Union today have a worse diet than the Russians under Czar Nicholas II in 1913" (Doerner, 1989:33-36).

And to compound Gorbachev's problems, *glasnost* and *perestroika* have combined to produce, first, the demise of communism in Eastern Europe, and serious unrest among many of the various ethnic groups in the different republics of the Soviet Union. The Soviet empire in Eastern Europe is no more. In its wake will arise, it seems, a set of independent, perhaps ultranationalistic regimes, some, such as Romania and Hungary, with serious quarrels among themselves. Then, too, the possible reunification of Germany is full of potential for the creation of serious international conflicts. Within the Soviet Union itself, the Lithuanians are apparently bent on secession. If they go, the Latvians and the Estonians will surely not be far behind. The Azeris are likewise restless, and Azerbaijan constitutes a particularly dangerous (from the Soviet point of view) "Moslem domino," whose fall might provoke conflict with Iran. The Georgians are also mutinous, and the Moldavians are casting roving eyes in the direction of reformist Romania on their border. The Ukrainians have grievances going back decades. In short, the Soviet Union has begun to look like a seething cauldron of ethnic and nationalistic passions, providing fertile ground for civil conflicts with international repercussions. (The situation is vaguely and ominously reminiscent of the dissolution of the Austro-Hungarian empire that played such an important catalytic role in bringing about the First World War.) "Is not the inclination toward nationalism in the Caucasus, the Baltics, the Ukraine, and Central Asia a reaction to the bankruptcy of previously announced eternal truths? With 'perestroika,' Gorbachev has awakened hopes and material expectations. Either he succeeds quickly in fulfilling them, or the entire Soviet Union slides into a chaos of ungovernability and ethnic conflict" (*World Press Review*, 1989:10).[6]

The chances that he will succeed quickly, or at all, are just not very good. The problems are too formidable. There simply is no historical basis in the Soviet Union for the kind of sweeping political and economic changes that Gorbachev seems to have in mind, especially in the face of the kind of centrifugal forces that those changes will unleash in the republics and Eastern Europe. "Gorbachev is struggling against the consequences of five decades of misrule . . . and in some of his ambitions, against all Russian history as well" (Kaiser, 1988/89:101). That is the essential reason that reformist movements of the kind that Gorbachev is currently spearheading have such a miserable record in Russia.

> The reforms of Peter I and the expansionism of Catherine left the Empire in a backward status in the nineteenth century. The would-be reforms of Alexander I ended in the chauvinism and reaction of Nicholas I. The reforms of Alexander II succeeded only in the short run and could not prevent military defeat at the hands of Japan and the 1905 Revolution. The reforms of 1905-1907 were largely negated by the Stolypin reaction. The imperial regime imposed prohibition of vodka in 1914 but was unable to prevent its own demise. The reform efforts of Khrushchev in the 1950s and of Kosygin in the 1960s cannot be said to have been successful. (Reshetar, 1989:371)

In short, Gorbachev's efforts to reform the Soviet Union are not very likely to succeed, and the kind of Soviet Union that will emerge from his failed effort is not likely to be easy to deal with. Most of the simultaneous outbreaks of peace which James Rosenau notes in Chapter 14 can be traced to a greater or lesser degree to Gorbachev's initiatives and "new thinking" in Soviet policy. If Gorbachev is gone, such outbreaks will become much less likely. Also, the Soviets will ultimately have to depend on military force to keep their ethnic minorities (as in Azerbaijan) and Eastern European allies in line. By that time, the United States, as well as Western Europe, will have invested so much ideological energy (not to mention foreign aid and private capital) in the "liberation" of Eastern Europe (and perhaps even the Baltic states), that when the Soviet crackdown comes, all the current talk about the end of the Cold War will look foolish indeed. This will be especially true if the West, and in particular the United States, are going through their own time of troubles, putting them also in a prickly and belligerent mood.

THE LEGACY OF REAGANOMICS AND THE FUTURE OF THE WESTERN, NONCOMMUNIST WORLD

It is true at this writing that the U.S. economy is experiencing the longest peacetime period of economic growth in its history, without serious inflation, and with relatively low unemployment. But the Reagan years also brought consistent $150 billion dollar budget deficits and a near-tripling of the national debt, from about $1 trillion to almost $3 trillion. A succinct explanation of this phenomenon is offered by Gilpin (1987b:330): "A massive tax cut without a compensating reduction of the expenditures of the federal government [has] resulted in a huge and continuing budget deficit. . . ."

Rather than reduce expenditures, the Reagan administration dramatically increased defense spending. It believed that the expenditures were necessary to meet American military commitments all over the world, from the Far East to Western Europe to Central America. By the middle of the 1980s, the precarious nature of the American position in the world had become so obvious that a scholarly analysis focusing on it became a fixture on the *New York Times* bestseller list. Kennedy's (1987:515) *The Rise and Fall of Great Powers* explained that "the United States runs the risk, so familiar to historians of the rise and fall of previous Great Powers, of what might roughly be called 'imperial overstretch'; that is to say, decision makers in Washington must face the awkward and enduring fact that the sum total of the United States' global interests and obligations is nowadays far larger than the country's power to defend them simultaneously."

Or, to put it another way, the United States discovered by the late 1980s that it could no longer afford to perform the functions required of a hegemonic power to maintain the stability of the system. (See Levy's discussion of hegemonic stability theory in Chapter 7 of this book.) This began to be obvious in the 1970s, when President Nixon unhinged the dollar from gold, or "closed the gold window" (Gowa, 1983) in 1971. Then, the United States lost control of the world's oil market, and decline began in earnest. "In the oil area, the rules of the old regime were shattered between 1967 and 1977. . . . By 1977, the United States had apparently lost control of the regime for oil pricing and production to OPEC. . . ." (Keohane, 1980:154).

The 1980s brought an apparent halt to declining U.S. hegemony, but Gilpin (1987b:348) argues that this halt was more apparent than real.

"In the 1980s, the Reagan administration financed its massive military buildup and the remarkable economic recovery of the American economy mainly through foreign borrowing, especially with the financial assistance of the Japanese." The United States has become the largest debtor in the world, crucially dependent on the Japanese to finance its federal budget deficits, and owing the world in general something on the order of $500 billion. As the *Wall Street Journal* observed, "as a result of the rapid rise in overseas debt since 1981, the U.S. has ceded considerable control over its economy to foreign investors. They now hold the power to keep the U.S. economy growing, or to help plunge it into recession" (Murray, 1988:1).

The Japanese are sufficiently dependent on the American economy that they are not likely to have an incentive for plunging it into a recession in the near future. But it is not clear that the Japanese or anybody else can save the United States from a serious recession, or even a Great Depression. That, at least, is the contention of Ravi Batra (1987) in another harbinger of doom on the *New York Times* bestseller list as the 1990s approached, entitled *The Great Depression of 1990*. For the most part, this book was not taken seriously by professional economists.[7] But as Galbraith (1972:149-52) points out, a majority of distinguished professional economists failed to foresee the Great Crash of 1929.

And, while Batra is clearly in the minority, he is not the only economist of note who feels a depression may be on the way. Galbraith (1987), in "The 1929 Parallel," notes several discomforting similarities between the late 1920s and the late 1980s in the behavior of the stock market, financial speculations, and tax policies of the federal government, which clearly lead him to expect the worst. Perhaps, in light of Galbraith's liberal leanings and ties to the Democratic Party, this can be written off as "sour grapes." But Peter Peterson (1987:43), secretary of commerce for President Nixon and later chairman of an investment banking firm in New York City, has also argued that "America has let its infrastructure crumble, its foreign markets decline, its productivity dwindle, its savings evaporate, and its budget and borrowing burgeon. And now the day of reckoning is at hand."[8]

Even if a Great Depression does not occur, economic problems in the Western industrialized world may be quite serious in the 1990s. That world is showing disturbing signs of division. The recent U.S.-Canada trade agreement can be seen as an encouraging precedent in a trend toward freer trade. But it may also be a step in the direction of setting up a trading bloc in the Western Hemisphere, cut off to some extent from the rest of the world. The same can be said of plans by the European Community to create a unified internal market by 1992 (Greenhouse, 1988:1, 24). There is also a danger that the Western industrialized world could fall into serious wrangles over access to foreign oil in the not-too-distant future, especially since the United States is currently increasing its dependence on unstable sources of supply. "Imports have increased their share of America's oil consumption from a 1980s low of 32 percent to 42 percent now. By the mid-1990s, half of every American tankful will come from abroad. A rising proportion of each barrel is from the shaky Gulf" (*The Economist*, 1988:13-14). It does not take incredible foresight to anticipate the ominous possibility that a future increase in the price of oil (which might be precipitated by the current crisis in Azerbaijan) could throw the American economy into recession, with which its huge budget deficits and excessive dependence on foreign lenders will make it very difficult to deal.[9]

All of these problems in the Western industrialized world are bad enough; on top of those problems, interacting with them and making each other worse, are the dire economic straits of many developing countries. The World Bank reported in 1988 that "poverty in the developing countries is on the rise. . . . Since 1980, matters have turned from bad to worse. . . ." (World Bank, 1988:4). A root cause of this trend is the international debt problem of many large, important developing countries. By the late 1980s, Third World debt had passed the $1 trillion mark. "After 5 years of intense international effort, declining interest rates, and a falling U.S. dollar, the debt crisis not only has eluded solution, it has become chronic. . . . In some quarters the crisis is likened to the 1920s war debt and is considered a precursor to a worldwide depression" (Amuzegar, 1987:140).

Both a cause and an effect of the poverty in the Third World is war. In places like El Salvador, poverty and a tremendously unequal distribution of wealth, for example, fuel a rebellion which has continued for most of a decade. In Ethiopia, civil war combines with other problems, like drought, to create mass starvation. Although international wars among richer, larger countries, as this volume's theme suggests, have become a rarity, civil wars in poor countries definitely have not. Sivard (1987) reports that 22 wars were underway in 1987, but only one was truly international. All the rest were civil wars (as in Colombia, Guatemala, Indonesia, Lebanon, Nicaragua, Peru, the Philippines, South Africa, Sri Lanka, and the Sudan, for example), and in poor, underdeveloped countries. "The total death toll in these wars so far is at least 2,200,000. . . . Civil wars, representing power conflicts within nations, have increased sharply in the twentieth century, and are by now by far the major form of warfare" (Sivard, 1987:28).

Internal wars have a way of attracting intervention by the major powers, and particularly the superpowers, as the recent conflicts in Afghanistan and Nicaragua exemplify. And if civil wars do not drag in the major powers eventually, international wars involving middle-level powers and/or developing countries might. These promise to become the wave of the future. Between 1976 and 1984, for example, there were seven international wars, none between major powers.[10] The Iran-Iraq war dramatically demonstrated just how deadly such wars can be.

That war may also have given a preview of what is to come as more advanced military technology becomes available to a larger number of states. Iran and Iraq are thought to have fired some 500 ballistic missiles at each other during that war. India has a new ballistic missile (Agni) with the capability of hitting Pakistan, China, Iran, or Saudi Arabia. Saudi Arabia itself has acquired Chinese ballistic missiles capable of reaching Tel Aviv. Israel's Jericho-2 missiles could hit Soviet military bases on the Black Sea. Some 22 Third World countries have acquired ballistic missiles. "Missiles are expensive. . . . Using them merely to dump a little high explosive somewhere near their targets is like buying a Ferrari to collect groceries. But stick on nuclear or chemical warheads, and you become a first-rate military power" (*The Economist*, 1989:44).

Even if possible "high-tech" wars between middle-range powers do not attract major-power intervention, they could be extremely bloody. And chances are that such international wars, or one of the many civil wars likely to occur in the coming years, will ultimately embroil one or more of the major powers, particularly if the Western industrialized world sinks into economic depression, and at a time when the Soviet Union is entering a period of reaction and brutality after Gorbachev and his reforms have been banished.

CONCLUSION

This has been a determinedly pessimistic look at the future of world politics in general, and superpower relations in particular, based on the mythical "Murphy's Law" to the effect that anything that can go wrong will. Basing policy recommendations on this analysis would be imprudent, since it is not at all a balanced view of the future. Yet it may serve the useful purpose of reminding us that euphoria and complacency about the future of the long peace are uncalled for. Many things could "go wrong," and surely at least some of them will. Arms control agreements have historically had some disagreeable side effects. Interdependence is certainly no panacea. Reform in the Soviet Union is not guaranteed to be successful, and the United States, the entire industrialized world, as well as the Third World, face economic problems with the clear potential to produce catastrophes. Finally, the diffusion of more sophisticated military technologies around the world has the serious potential to exacerbate many conflicts between middle-range states. All these points might usefully be kept in mind when considering policy options in the area of arms control and other aspects of the U.S.-Soviet relationship, as well as the economic future of the Western, noncommunist world.

As for future research, perhaps this chapter will reduce the possibility that the post–Second World War era will be given too much importance as a "data point" in assessing the various theories about factors that produce peace. Nuclear weapons, arms control agreements, increased interdependence, as well as sustained economic growth in the United States, for example, may all have played a role in preserving protracted peace. But that peace is not necessarily as protracted as some contemporary analysts seem to believe, and its durability is certainly debatable.

ENDNOTES

1. Charles Kegley, Bruce Nichols, an anonymous graduate student in the political science department at Rutgers University, and participants in the conference on "The Long Peace" too numerous to mention all made helpful comments and suggestions regarding the first draft.

2. Levy (1983) categorizes it that way, but Small and Singer (1982) assert that it is a major-power war.

3. For example, at one point, Angell (1910:268-69) asserts that "not only is man fighting less, but he is using all forms of physical compulsion less . . . because accumulated evidence is pushing him more and more to the conclusion that he can accomplish more easily that which he strives for by other means."

4. If one can judge by the references he cites, one could conclude that Levi was unaware of Angell's ill-fated precursor to his (Levi's) work.

5. Another well-known historian and student of international war, Geoffrey Blainey (1988:30), makes precisely the same argument. "It is difficult to find evidence that closer contacts between nations promoted peace. Swift communications which drew nations together did not necessarily promote peace: it is indisputable that during the last three centuries most wars have been fought by neighboring countries — not countries which are far apart. The frequency of civil wars shatters the simple idea that people who have much in common will remain at peace."

6. Probably the most forcefully pessimistic analysis of this and other problems that Gorbachev faces can be found in Zbigniew Brzezinski (1990).

7. There are very few reviews of the book, and almost no citations of it in *The Social Sciences Citation Index*, even though Batra's other works are cited with some regularity. One of the reviews of it that does exist asserts that "every few years a book comes along that, much to the chagrin of experts . . . hits the best-seller list. . . . Now there is *The Great Depression of 1990*" (La Roe and Pool, 1988:63).

8. Peterson (1987:55) goes on to assert that "the 1980s and the 1990s may be remembered, with bitterness, as a turning point in America's fortunes — a period of transition when we took the British route to second-class economic status."

9. "Should we have the worst hard landing — a lengthy U.S. depression — let us simply be forewarned that our traditional policy responses would be of limited use. Hardship-bloated budget deficits would prevent us from applying more fiscal stimulus; a low and skittish dollar would defy our attempts to loosen monetary policy" (Peterson, 1987:54).

10. These were the Somali-Ethiopian (1977-1978), Ugandan-Tanzanian (1978-1979), Sino-Vietnamese (1979), Russo-Afghan (1979-1990), Iran-Iraqi, (1980-1988), Falkland Islands (1982), and Israeli-Syrian in Lebanon (1982). See Gochman and Maoz (1984:612-13).

About the Contributors

Morris J. Blachman earned his Ph.D. in political science from New York University in 1976. He holds the position of Associate Professor in the Department of Government and International Studies at the University of South Carolina, where he also is Associate Director of the Institute of International Studies. He is also a Senior Research Associate of the Bildner Center for Western Hemisphere Studies of the Graduate School of the City University of New York, and has taught at New York University, the Foreign Service Institute, and the Instituto Universitario de Pesquisas do Rio de Janeiro. His publications include *Confronting Revolution: Security Through Diplomacy in Central America* (1986); *Terms of Conflict: Ideology in Inter-American Politics* (1977); "Things Fall Apart: Trouble Ahead in El Salvador"; "Central American Traps: Challenging the Reagan Agenda"; and "Dedemocratizing American Foreign Policy: Dismantling the Post-Vietnam Formula." His current writing focuses on U.S. foreign policy toward Central America and on the impact of the "war on drugs" on U.S. foreign policy in Latin America as well as on constitutional democracy in the United States.

Michael Brecher was educated at McGill University and at Yale University, where he received his Ph.D. in international relations in 1953. He has been a member of the McGill faculty since 1952, and Professor of Political Science since 1963. He has also held visiting appointments at the University of Chicago, the University of California-Berkeley, Stanford University, and the Hebrew University of Jerusalem. The first phase of his research focused on the international relations and domestic politics of South Asia and found expression in half a dozen books including the prize-winning *Nehru: A Political Biography* (1959). This was followed by research on comparative foreign policy, reflected in *The Foreign Policy System of Israel* (1972) (winner of the APSA's Woodrow Wilson Award the following year) and *Decisions in Israel's Foreign Policy* (1975), which were made possible by fellowships from the Guggenheim and Rockefeller Foundations. Professor Brecher has also been the recipient of two Killam Awards from the Canada Council and is a Fellow of the Royal Society of Canada. Since the mid-1970s, Brecher has directed the International Crisis Behavior Project which explores the phenomena of crisis, conflict and war through in-depth studies of state behavior and aggregate analysis of more than 300 international crises. His most recent publications, in collaboration with Jonathan Wilkenfeld, are *Crises in the Twentieth Century* (2 volumes, 1988) and *Crisis, Conflict and Instability* (1989).

John Lewis Gaddis earned his Ph.D. in American diplomatic history from the University of Texas at Austin in 1968, and since 1969 has taught at Ohio University, where he is Distinguished Professor of History and Director of the Contemporary History Institute. He has also held visiting teaching appointments at the United States Naval War College, the University of Helsinki, and Princeton

University. His publications include *The United States and the Origins of the Cold War, 1941-1947* (1972); *Russia, the Soviet Union, and the United States: An Interpretive History* (1978, 2nd edition 1989); *Strategies of Containment: A Critical Appraisal of Postwar American National Security Policy* (1982); and *The Long Peace: Inquiries into the History of the Cold War* (1987). Professor Gaddis is now working on an interpretive history of United States foreign relations and on a biography of George F. Kennan.

Lloyd C. Gardner is the Charles and Mary Beard Professor of History at Rutgers University, where he has taught since 1963. Gardner received his Ph.D. from the University of Wisconsin in 1960. In addition to Rutgers, he has taught at Lake Forest College, and, as a Fulbright Professor, at the University of Birmingham (England) and Helsinki University. He also held a Guggenheim Fellowship during the 1973-74 academic year. He is the author of *Economic Aspects of New Deal Diplomacy* (1964); *Architects of Illusion: Men and Ideas in American Foreign Policy, 1941-1949* (1970); *Imperial America* (1976); *A Covenant With Power: America and World Order from Wilson to Reagan* (1983); *Safe for Democracy: The Anglo-American Response to Revolution, 1913-1923* (1984); and *Approaching Vietnam: From World War II Through Dienbienphu* (1988). His current projects are centered on the Anglo-American response to fascism in the 1930s, and the decline of presidential power in foreign affairs after Vietnam.

Robert C. Johansen earned his Ph.D. in international relations from Columbia University in 1968. He is a specialist in U.S. security policy, U.S.-Soviet arms control negotiations, and peace and world order studies. He has taught at Manchester College, Princeton University, and the University of Notre Dame. His book publications include *The National Interest and the Human Interest: An Analysis of U.S. Foreign Policy* (1980) and *Toward an Alternative Security System* (1983). Johansen is Director of Graduate Studies at the Institute for International Peace Studies at the University of Notre Dame, where he also serves as Professor in the Department of Government and International Studies. His current writing focuses on multilateral diplomacy, U.N. peacekeeping, and creative space in U.S.-Soviet relations. He is past president of the World Policy Institute, Contributing Editor to the *World Policy Journal*, and a member of the Boards of Directors of the Arms Control Association (Washington), the Institute for Defense and Disarmament Studies, and the World Order Models Project.

James Turner Johnson received his Ph.D. in religion from Princeton University in 1968. He is Professor of Religion and University Director of International Programs at Rutgers University. His scholarship focuses on the historical interaction between religious and nonreligious factors in the shaping of moral and legal doctrine on war, its justification, and its limitation. A former Guggenheim and Rockefeller Foundation fellow, his books include *Ideology, Reason, and the Limitation of War* (1975); *Just War Tradition and the Restraint of War* (1981); *Can Modern War Be Just?* (1984); and *The Quest for Peace: Three Moral Traditions in Western Cultural History* (1987). He has published over forty articles in American and European scholarly journals. His current research examines the relation between Western and Islamic religious and cultural traditions related to war, peace, and the conduct of statecraft.

Charles W. Kegley, Jr. earned his Ph.D. in international relations from Syracuse University in 1971. He holds the position of Pearce Professor of International Relations at the University of South Carolina, where he served as Chairman of the Department of Government and International Studies from 1981-1985 and Director of the Byrnes International Center from 1985 to 1988. He also taught at the Georgetown University School of Foreign Service and the University of Texas, as well as at Rutgers University as the Moses and Annuta Back Peace Scholar. Among his two dozen book publications, he has recently published *American Foreign Policy: Pattern and Process* (4th ed., 1991); *After the Cold War: Questioning the Morality of Nuclear Deterrence* (1991); *When Trust Breaks Down: Alliance Norms and World Politics* (1990); *International Terrorism: Characteristics, Causes, Controls* (1990); *The Nuclear Reader: Strategy, Weapons, War* (2nd ed., 1989); and *World Politics: Trend and Transformation* (3rd ed., 1989). His current writing focuses on the role of retaliation in international politics and the ethical implications of global problems.

Joseph Kruzel is a graduate of the U.S. Air Force Academy, and received his Masters of Public Administration and Ph.D. from Harvard University. He taught at Harvard, Duke, and the University of North Carolina before joining the faculty at the Ohio State University in 1983, where he is currently Acting Director of the Mershon Center and Associate Professor of Political Science. While on active duty in the Air Force, he served as current intelligence briefing officer for the Joint Chiefs of Staff and later as a member of the U.S. Delegation to the Strategic Arms Limitations Talks. His other government service includes assignments as defense and foreign policy advisor to Senator Edward Kennedy, and consulting work for the Arms Control and Disarmament Agency, the Department of Defense, and the National Security Council. Professor Kruzel has written extensively on defense policy and arms control, and serves as editor of the *American Defense Annual*, a yearly review and assessment of the major issues in U.S. security policy.

Jack S. Levy holds the position of Professor of Political Science at Rutgers University. He received his Ph.D. at the University of Wisconsin in 1976, and has previously taught at Tulane University, the University of Texas at Austin, Stanford University, and the University of Minnesota. Professor Levy's special interests include international relations, foreign policy decision making, and the causes of war, and his book publications include *War in the Modern Great Power System, 1495-1975* (1983). He has also published articles in numerous scholarly journals and edited volumes.

Manus I. Midlarsky received his Ph.D. from Northwestern University in 1969, and is the Moses and Annuta Back Professor of International Peace and Conflict Resolution at Rutgers University. He has taught previously at the University of Colorado, Boulder, where he was the Director of the Center for International Relations, and at the University of Florida. He has been President of the Conflict Processes Section of the American Political Science Association, Vice President of the International Studies Association, and President of the International Studies Association, West. Professor Midlarsky is the author of *The Onset of World War* (1988); *The Disintegration of Political Systems: War and Revolution in Comparative Perspective* (1986); *On War: Political Violence in the International*

System (1975); and editor of the *Handbook of War Studies* (1989) and *Inequality and Contemporary Revolutions* (1986). His articles have appeared in journals such as *The American Political Science Review*, *American Journal of Political Science*, *Journal of Conflict Resolution*, *International Studies Quarterly*, *International Interactions*, *Journal of Peace Research*, *Journal of Personality*, *Polity*, and *Mathematical Modelling*. Professor Midlarsky's research interests continue to center on the causes of war and peace; he is currently working on a book entitled *Warfare and the State: Equality in the Rise and Decline of Community*.

Donald J. Puchala earned his Ph.D. in international relations from Yale University in 1966. He holds the position of Charles L. Jacobson Professor of Public Affairs at the University of South Carolina, where he also serves as the Director of the Institute of International Studies. A specialist in the theory and history of international relations as well as a student of international organization and Western European affairs, he has taught at Yale University, Columbia University, and The State University of New York, Buffalo, and has held visiting appointments at Harvard University, the University of Pennsylvania and Carleton University in Ottawa. His book publications include *Western European Perspectives on International Affairs* (1969); *International Politics Today* (1971); *American Arms and a Changing Europe* (1973); *Global Food Interdependence* (1980); *Fiscal Harmonization in the European Communities* (1984); and *The State of the United Nations* (1988). His current research focuses on the United Nations and its functional agencies in the international environment of the 1990s.

James Lee Ray earned his Ph.D. in world politics from the University of Michigan in 1974, and he is presently Professor of Political Science at Florida State University, where he has served as Director of the International Affairs program since 1985. He is a specialist on the causes of war, various aspects of international political economy, and Inter-American relations, and has taught at the State University College at Fredonia (New York) and the University of New Mexico, where he served as chairman of the Department of Political Science from 1982 to 1984. His publications include articles in *International Interactions*, *International Organization*, *International Studies Quarterly*, and *The Journal of Conflict Resolution*; he is also author of *The Future of American-Israeli Relations* (1985) and *Global Politics* (1990). His current writing focuses on additional analyses of contending explanations of major power peace, with a special emphasis on the relevance of such explanations to an understanding of contemporary relationships involving the European Economic Community.

Gregory A. Raymond earned his Ph.D. in International Studies from the University of South Carolina in 1975. He is currently Professor of Political Science at Boise State University (Idaho), where he twice has been a recipient of the "Outstanding Teaching" award and currently serves as chairman of the Department of Political Science. Dr. Raymond has published numerous articles on foreign policy, international norms, and conflict resolution. His book publications include *The Other Western Europe: A Comparative Analysis of the Smaller Democracies* (1982); *Conflict Resolution and the Structure of the State System* (1980); *International Events and the Comparative Analysis of Foreign Policy* (1975); *Third World Policies of Industrialized Nations* (1983), which received an Outstanding Academic Book Award from the American Library Association; and *When Trust*

Breaks Down: Alliance Norms and World Politics (1990). His most recent research focuses on the role of retaliation in world politics.

James N. Rosenau is the Director of the Institute for Transnational Studies at the University of Southern California as well as Professor of Political Science and International Relations. He is a past president of the International Studies Association and previously has also been a faculty member of Rutgers—The State University of New Jersey and The Ohio State University. His research has focused on the analysis of foreign policy, global interdependence, and political adaptation. The holder of a Guggenheim Fellowship in 1987-1988, his most recent publications include authorship of *Turbulence in World Politics: A Theory of Change and Continuity* (1990); coauthorship of *American Leadership in World Affairs: Vietnam and the Breakdown of Consensus* (1984); and coeditorship of *Journeys Through World Politics: Autobiographical Reflections of Thirty-four Academic Travelers* (1989); *Global Changes and Theoretical Challenges: Approaches to World Politics for the 1990s* (1989); and *New Directions in the Study of Foreign Policy* (1987).

J. David Singer is Professor of Political Science and Coordinator of the World Politics Program at the University of Michigan. He obtained a B.A. from Duke University in 1946 and a Ph.D. from New York University in 1956. His academic career has included appointments at New York University and Vassar College, and he has served as a Visiting Fellow of Social Relations at Harvard University, a Visiting Professor at the U.S. Naval War College, and as a visiting scholar at the University of Oslo and the Graduate Institute of International Studies in Geneva. Dr. Singer is the author of numerous books, including *Financing International Organization: The United Nations Budget Process* (1961); *Deterrence, Arms Control, and Disarmament* (1962, 1984); *The Wages of War 1816-1965: A Statistical Handbook* (with Melvin Small, 1972); *Beyond Conjecture in International Politics: Abstracts of Data-Based Research* (with Susan Jones, 1972); *The Study of International Politics: A Guide to Sources for the Student, Teacher and Researcher* (with Dorothy LaBarr, 1976); *Resort to Arms: International and Civil War 1816-1980* (with Melvin Small, 1982); and the two-volume *Correlates of War* (1979 and 1980). Dr. Singer is also a contributor of numerous articles to professional journals, annuals, and anthologies, and serves on the editorial boards of several journals.

John A. Vasquez is Professor of Political Science at Rutgers University and is a specialist in international relations theory and in peace studies. He received his Ph.D. in political science from the Maxwell School at Syracuse University in 1974. His books include *In Search of Theory: A New Paradigm for Global Politics* (with Richard Mansbach, 1981); *The Power of Power Politics: A Critique* (1983); *Evaluating U.S. Foreign Policy* (1986); and *Classics of International Relations* (1986, 1990). He has published numerous scholarly articles, including publications in *World Politics, British Journal of Political Science, Journal of Politics, Western Political Quarterly, Journal of Peace Research, International Studies Quarterly,* and *International Organization,* among others. He is currently completing a book on foreign policy practices and war, *The War Puzzle,* to be published by Cambridge University Press.

Jonathan Wilkenfeld earned his Ph.D. in political science from Indiana University in 1969. He is Professor of Government and Politics and Director of the International Communications and Negotiations Simulations Project at the University of Maryland, where he serves as chairman of the Department of Politics. A specialist in foreign policy and international crisis, he has taught at the Hebrew University and the John Hopkins University School of Advanced International Studies. He is a past editor of *International Studies Quarterly*. His books include *Conflict Behavior and Linkage Politics* (1973); *Foreign Policy Behavior* (1980); *Crises in the Twentieth Century*, (2 volumes, 1988); and *Crisis, Conflict and Instability* (1989). His articles have appeared in *International Studies Quarterly*, *World Politics*, *Journal of Conflict Resolution*, and *International Interactions*.

References

Abshire, David M. 1988. *Preventing World War III: A Realistic Grand Strategy*. New York: Harper & Row.

Acheson, Dean. 1969. *Present at the Creation*. New York: Norton.

Albertini, Luigi. 1980. *The Origins of the War of 1914*. 3 vols. Trans. and ed. by Isabella M. Massey. Westport, CT: Greenwood Press.

Allison, Graham T. 1988. "Testing Gorbachev," *Foreign Affairs* 67 (Fall): 18-32.

Allison, Graham T., and Morton H. Halperin. 1972. "Bureaucratic Politics: A Paradigm and Some Policy Implications," *World Politics* 24 (Spring): 40-89.

Altfeld, Michael F. 1984. "The Decision to Ally: A Theory and Test," *Western Political Quarterly* 30 (March): 107-14.

Amuzegar, Jahangir. 1987. "Dealing with Debt," *Foreign Policy* 68 (Fall): 140-58.

Anderson, Marion, Michael Frisch, and Michael Oden. 1986. *The Empty Pork Barrel: The Employment Cost of the Military Buildup 1981-85*. Lansing, MI: Employment Research Associates.

Anderson, M. S. 1961. *Europe in the Eighteenth Century, 1713-1783*, 2nd ed. London: Longman.

Anderson, Paul A. 1987. "What Do Decision Makers Do When They Make a Foreign Policy Decision?" pp. 285-308 in Charles F. Hermann, Charles W. Kegley, Jr., and James N. Rosenau (eds.), *New Directions in the Study of Foreign Policy*. Boston: Allen & Unwin.

Angell, Norman. 1910. *The Great Illusion: A Study of the Relationship of Military Power in Nations to Their Economic and Social Advantage*. London: William Heinemann.

Aron, Raymond. 1967. *Peace and War: A Theory of International Relations*. London: Weidenfeld and Nicholson.

Art, Robert J., and Kenneth N. Waltz. 1983. "Technology, Strategy, and the Uses of Force," in Robert J. Art and Kenneth N. Waltz (eds.), *The Use of Force: International Politics and Foreign Policy*. Lanham, MD: University Press of America.

Atlas, James. 1989. "What Is Fukuyama Saying and To Whom Is He Saying It?" *New York Times Magazine* (October 22).

Avenhaus, Rudolf, Steven J. Brams, John Fichtner, and D. Marc Kilgour. 1989. "The Probability of Nuclear War," *Journal of Peace Research* 26 (February): 91-99.

Axelrod, Robert. 1984. *The Evolution of Cooperation*. New York: Basic Books.

Azar, Edward E., et al. 1977. "A System for Forecasting Strategic Crises: Findings and Speculations About Conflict in the Middle East," *International Interactions* 3 (No. 3): 193-222.

Ball, Nicole. 1988. *Security and Economy in the Third World*. Princeton: Princeton University Press.

Barkun, Michael. 1968. *Law Without Sanctions*. New Haven: Yale University Press.

Barnet, Richard J. 1988. "Looking to a Post-Cold War World," *Los Angeles Times* (June 6): II-7.

Barringer, Richard E. 1972. *Patterns of Conflict*. Cambridge, MA: MIT Press.

Batra, Ravi. 1987. *The Great Depression of 1990*. New York: Simon and Schuster.

Bechhoeffer, Bernard B. 1961. *Postwar Negotiations for Arms Control*. Washington, DC: The Brookings Institution.

Beer, Francis A. 1981. *Peace Against War*. San Francisco: W. H. Freeman.

Beilenson, Lawrence W. 1980. *Survival and Peace in the Nuclear Age*. Chicago: Regnery/Gateway.

Beilenson, Lawrence W. 1969. *The Treaty Trap*. Washington, DC: Public Affairs Press.

Berkowitz, Bruce. 1987. *Calculated Risks*. New York: Simon and Schuster.

Best, Geoffrey. 1980. *Humanity in Warfare*. New York: Columbia University Press.

Betts, Richard K. 1987. *Nuclear Blackmail and Nuclear Balance*. Washington, DC: The Brookings Institution.

Bezdek, Roger. 1975. "The Economic Impact — Regional and Occupational — of Compensated Shifts in Defense Spending," *Journal of Regional Science* 15 (No. 2): 183-98.

Bialer, Seweryn. 1986. *The Soviet Paradox: External Expansion, Internal Decline*. New York: Knopf.

Blachman, Morris J., William M. LeoGrande, and Kenneth Sharpe (eds.). 1986. *Confronting Revolution*. New York: Pantheon.

Blackaby, Frank. 1986. "On the Nature of SIPRI's Peace Research Studies," *Bulletin of Peace Proposals* 17 (No. 3-4): 217-28.

Blainey, Geoffrey. 1988. *The Causes of War*, 3rd ed. London: Macmillan.

Blight, James G., and David A. Welch. 1989. *On the Brink: Americans and Soviets Re-examine the Cuban Missile Crisis*. New York: Hill and Wang.

Blight, James G., Joseph S. Nye, Jr., and David A. Welch. 1987. "The Cuban Missile Crisis Revisited," *Foreign Affairs* 66 (Fall): 170-88.

Bloch, Ivan. 1898. *The Future of War*. New York: Doubleday & McClure.

Bloch, Jean de. 1899. *The Future of War in Its Technical, Economic and Political Relations: Is War Now Impossible?* Boston: Ginn and Co.

Borden, William S. 1984. *The Pacific Alliance: U.S. Foreign Policy and Japanese Trade Recovery, 1947-1955*. Madison: University of Wisconsin Press.

Boston Study Group. 1982. *Winding Down: The Price of Defense*. San Francisco: W. H. Freeman.

Boswell, John. 1989. *The Kindness of Strangers: The Abandonment of Children in Western Europe from Late Antiquity to the Renaissance*. New York: Pantheon.

Boulding, Kenneth E. 1978. *Stable Peace*. Austin: University of Texas Press.

Boyer, Paul. 1985. *By the Bomb's Early Light: American Thought and Culture at the Dawn of the Atomic Age*. New York: Pantheon.

Brecher, Michael, and Jonathan Wilkenfeld. 1989. *Crisis, Conflict, and Instability*. Oxford: Pergamon Press.

Brecher, Michael, Jonathan Wilkenfeld, and Sheila Moser. 1988. *Crises in the Twentieth Century, Vol. I: Handbook of International Crises*. Oxford: Pergamon Press.

Brecher, Michael, Patrick James, and Jonathan Wilkenfeld. 1990. "Polarity and Stability: New Concepts, Indicators and Evidence," *International Interactions* 16 (No. 1): 49-80.

Brecher, Michael, and Patrick James. 1986. *Crisis and Change in World Politics.* Boulder, CO: Westview Press.

Brennan, Donald G. (ed.). 1961. *Arms Control, Disarmament, and National Security.* New York: George Braziller.

Brewin, Christopher. 1988. "Liberal States and International Obligations," *Millennium* 17 (Summer): 321-38.

Bridge, F. R., and R. Bullen. 1980. *The Great Powers and the European States System: 1815-1914.* London: Longman.

Broder, David. 1983. "The Great Stabilizer," *Washington Post National Weekly Edition* (December 5).

Brodie, Bernard (ed.). 1966. *Escalation and the Nuclear Option.* Princeton: Princeton University Press.

Brodie, Bernard (ed.). 1946. *The Absolute Weapon.* New York: Harcourt, Brace.

Brown, Harold, and Lynn E. Davis. 1984. "Nuclear Arms Control: Where Do We Stand?" *Foreign Affairs* 62 (Summer): 1145-46.

Brown, Seyom. 1968. *The Faces of Power.* New York: Columbia University Press.

Brzezinski, Zbigniew. 1990. *The Grand Failure: The Birth and Death of Communism in the Twentieth Century.* New York: Charles Scribner's.

Brzoska, Michael, and Thomas Ohlson (eds.). 1986. *Arms Production in the Third World.* London: Taylor & Francis.

Buchan, Alastair. 1974. *Change Without War.* London: Chatto Windus.

Buchan, Alastair. 1965. "Problems of an Alliance Policy: An Essay in Hindsight," pp. 293-310 in Michael Howard (ed.), *The Theory and Practice of War.* Bloomington: Indiana University Press.

Bueno de Mesquita, Bruce. 1981. *The War Trap.* New Haven: Yale University Press.

Bueno de Mesquita, Bruce. 1980. "Theories of International Conflict: An Analysis and an Appraisal," pp. 361-98 in Ted Robert Gurr (ed.), *Handbook of Political Conflict.* New York: Free Press.

Bueno de Mesquita, Bruce. 1978. "Systemic Polarization and the Occurrence and Duration of War," *Journal of Conflict Resolution* 22 (June): 241-67.

Bueno de Mesquita, Bruce, and J. David Singer. 1973. "Alliances, Capabilities, and War: A Review of Synthesis," pp. 237-80 in Cornelius Cotter (ed.), *Political Science Annual*, Vol. IV. Indianapolis: Bobbs-Merrill.

Bull, Hedley. 1963. "Limitations in Strategic Nuclear War," *The Listener* 69: 147-49.

Bull, Hedley. 1961. *The Control of the Arms Race.* New York: Praeger.

Bullock, Alan. 1962. *Hitler: A Study in Tyranny.* New York: Harper & Row.

Bundy, McGeorge. 1989. "Revising the Bomb Thesis: Maybe War is Simply Gone," *Washington Post National Weekly Edition* (March 20-26): 36-37.

Bundy, McGeorge. 1988. *Danger and Survival: Choices About the Bomb in the First Fifty Years.* New York: Random House.

Bundy, McGeorge. 1952. *The Pattern of Responsibility.* Boston: Houghton-Mifflin.

Burton, John. 1982. *Dear Survivors.* London: Frances Pinter.

Burton, John. 1979. *Deviance, Terrorism and War.* New York: St. Martin's Press.

Butterfield, Herbert. 1981. *The Origins of History.* New York: Basic Books.

Buzan, Barry. 1984. "Economic Structure and International Security: The Limits of the Liberal Case," *International Organization* 38 (Autumn): 597-624.

Caldwell, Dan. 1981. *American-Soviet Relations: From 1947 to the Nixon-Kissinger Grand Design*. Westport, CT: Greenwood Press.

Calleo, David P. 1987. *Beyond American Hegemony: The Future of the Western Alliance*. New York: Basic Books.

Campbell, Jeremy. 1982. *Grammatical Man: Information, Entropy, Language and Life*. New York: Simon and Schuster.

Carnesale, Albert, Paul Doty, Stanley Hoffmann, Samuel P. Huntington, Joseph S. Nye, Jr., and Scott D. Sagan. 1989. "How Might Nuclear War Begin?" pp. 242-57 in Charles W. Kegley, Jr., and Eugene R. Wittkopf (eds.), *The Nuclear Reader*, 2nd ed. New York: St. Martin's Press.

Carnesale, Albert, Joseph S. Nye, Jr., and Graham T. Allison. 1985. "An Agenda for Action," pp. 223-46 in Graham T. Allison, Albert Carnesale, and Joseph S. Nye, Jr. (eds.), *Hawks, Doves, & Owls: An Agenda for Avoiding Nuclear War*. New York: W. W. Norton.

Carnesale, Albert, et al. 1983. *Living with Nuclear Weapons*. New York: Bantam.

Carr, Edward Hallett. 1961. *What is History?* New York: Vintage.

Carty, Anthony. 1986. *The Decay of International Law?* Manchester: Manchester University Press.

Chernus, Ira. 1987. *Dr. Strangegod: On the Symbolic Meaning of Nuclear Weapons*. Columbia: University of South Carolina Press.

Chomsky, Noam. 1957. *Syntactic Structures*. The Hague: Mouton.

Choucri, Nazli, and Robert C. North. 1975. *Nations in Conflict*. San Francisco: W. H. Freeman.

Clark, Ian. 1982. *Limited Nuclear War*. Princeton: Princeton University Press.

Claude, Inis L., Jr. 1989. "The Balance of Power Revisited," *Review of International Studies* 15 (April): 77-86.

Claude, Inis L., Jr. 1986. "The Common Defense and Great-Power Responsibilities," *Political Science Quarterly* 101 (December): 719-32.

Claude, Inis L., Jr. 1981. "Casual Commitment in International Relations," *Political Science Quarterly* 96 (Fall): 367-79.

Claude, Inis. 1962. *Power and International Relations*. New York: Random House.

Cox, Robert W. 1986. "Social Forces, States and World Orders: Beyond International Relations Theory," pp. 204-54 in Robert O. Keohane (ed.), *Neorealism and Its Critics*. New York: Columbia University Press.

Cox, Robert W. 1981. "Social Forces, States and World Orders: Beyond International Relations Theory," *Millennium* 10 (No. 2): 126-55.

Craig, Gordon A., and Alexander L. George. 1983. *Force and Statecraft: Diplomatic Problems of Our Time*. New York: Oxford University Press.

Crankshaw, Edward. 1981. *Bismarck*. New York: Viking.

Crowe, William J. 1989. "Don't Cut a Winner," *New York Times* (April 10): A19.

Cummings, Bruce. 1981. *The Origins of the Korean War*. Princeton: Princeton University Press.

Dahl, Robert A. 1970. *Modern Political Analysis*, 2nd ed. Englewood Cliffs, N.J.: Prentice-Hall.

Darnton, Robert. 1984. *The Great Cat Massacre and Other Episodes in French Cultural History*. New York: Basic Books.

Deger, Saadet. 1986. *Military Expenditures in Third World Countries: The Economic Effects*. New York: Routledge, Chapman, and Hall.

Deger, Saadet, and Robert West (eds.). 1987. *Defense, Security and Development*. New York: St. Martin's Press.

DeGrasse, Robert. 1983. *Military Expansion and Economic Decline*. New York: Council on Economic Priorities.

Deibel, Terry L. 1987. "Alliances for Containment," pp. 100-119 in Terry L. Deibel and John Lewis Gaddis (eds.), *Containing the Soviet Union*. Washington, DC: Pergamon-Brassy's.

DePorte, A. W. 1979. *Europe Between the Superpowers*. New Haven: Yale University Press.

Deutsch, Karl W., Sidney A. Burrell, Robert A. Kann, Maurice Lee, Martin Lichterman, Raymond Lindgren, Francis Loewenheim, and Richard W. Van Wagenen. 1957. *Political Community and the North Atlantic Area*. Princeton: Princeton University Press.

Deutscher, Isaac. 1966. *Stalin*. New York: Oxford University Press.

Diehl, Paul. 1985. "Contiguity and Military Escalation in Major Power Rivalries, 1816-1980," *Journal of Politics* 47 (No. 4): 1203-11.

Diehl, Paul. 1983. "Arms Races and Escalation: A Closer Look," *Journal of Peace Research* 20 (No. 3): 205-12.

Dingman, Roger. 1988/89. "Atomic Diplomacy During the Korean War," *International Security* 13 (No. 3): 50-91.

Djilas, Milovan. 1961. *Conversations with Stalin*. Trans. by Michael B. Petrovich. New York: Harcourt, Brace & World.

Doerner, William R. 1989. "Why the Bear's Cupboards Are Bare," *Time* (January 16): 33-37.

Doran, Charles F. 1983. "Power Cycle Theory and the Contemporary State System," pp. 165-82 in William R. Thompson (ed.), *Contending Approaches to World System Analysis*. Beverly Hills, CA: Sage Publications.

Doran, Charles F. 1971. *The Politics of Assimilation*. Baltimore: The Johns Hopkins University Press.

Doyle, Michael W. 1983a. "Kant, Liberal Legacies, and Foreign Affairs, Part I," *Philosophy and Public Affairs* 12 (Summer): 205-35.

Doyle, Michael W. 1983b. "Kant, Liberal Legacies, and Foreign Affairs, Part II," *Philosophy and Public Affairs* 12 (Fall): 323-53.

Draper, Theodore. 1988. "Coalition Dynamics: NATO, the Phantom Alliance," pp. 150-58 in Charles W. Kegley, Jr., and Eugene R. Wittkopf (eds.), *The Global Agenda*. New York: Random House.

Dukes, Paul. 1989. *The Last Great Game: USA Versus USSR, Events, Conjunctures, Structures*. London: Pinter.

Dumas, Lloyd J. 1986a. *The Overburdened Economy: Uncovering the Causes of Chronic Unemployment, Inflation, and National Decline*. Berkeley: University of California Press.

Dumas, Lloyd J. 1986b. "Military Burden on the Economy," *Bulletin of the Atomic Scientists* 42 (October): 22-26.

Eckhardt, William. 1989. "Civilian Deaths in Wartime," *Bulletin of Peace Proposals* 20 (March): 89-98.

The Economist. 1989. "Third-World Missiles: Look What I Found in My Backyard," *The Economist* (May 24): 44-45.

The Economist. 1988. "Tax Gas," *The Economist* (December 24): 13-14.

Fairbanks, Charles H., Jr., and Abram N. Shulsky. 1987. "From 'Arms Control' to Arms Reductions: The Historical Experience," *Washington Quarterly* 10 (Summer): 59-73.

Falk, Richard. 1989. "International Law: The Damaged U.S. Image," *Bulletin of the Atomic Scientists* 45 (January/February): 59-61.

Falk, Richard A. 1983. *The End of World Order*. New York: Holmes & Meier.

Falk, Richard A. 1981. *Human Rights and State Sovereignty*. New York: Holmes & Meier.

Falk, Richard. 1975a. "Arms Control, Foreign Policy, and Global Reform," *Daedalus* 104 (Summer): 35-52.

Falk, Richard. 1975b. *A Study of Future Worlds*. New York: Free Press.

Fay, Sidney B. 1928. *The Origins of the World War*. 2 vols. New York: Macmillan.

Finnis, John, Joseph M. Boyle, Jr., and Germain Grisez. 1987. *Nuclear Deterrence, Morality, and Realism*. Oxford: Clarendon Press.

Fischer, David Hackett. 1970. *Historians' Fallacies: Toward a Logic of Historical Thought*. New York: Harper & Row.

Fischer, Dietrich. 1984. *Preventing War in the Nuclear Age*. Totowa, NJ: Rowman & Allanheld.

Fischer, Fritz. 1974. *War of Illusions*. New York: W. W. Norton.

Fischer, Fritz. 1961. *Germany's Aims in the First World War*. New York: W. W. Norton.

Foot, Rosemary. 1988/89. "Nuclear Coercion and the Ending of the Korean Conflict," *International Security* 13 (No. 3): 92-112.

Foreign Relations of the United States. 1946. Vol. VI. Washington, DC: Government Printing Office.

Fox, Richard. 1985. *Reinhold Niebuhr: A Biography*. New York: Pantheon.

Francis, David R. 1989. "Soviets Eye Economic Institutions," *Christian Science Monitor* (October 24): 9.

Franck, Thomas M., and Edward Weisband. 1971. *Word Politics: Verbal Strategy Among the Superpowers*. New York: Oxford University Press.

Frederick, Suzanne Y. 1987. "The Instability of Free Trade," pp. 186-217 in George Modelski (ed.), *Exploring Long Cycles*. Boulder, CO: Lynne Reinner.

Freedman, Lawrence. 1983. *The Evolution of Nuclear Strategy*. New York: St. Martin's Press.

Frisch, David H. (ed.). 1961. *Arms Reduction: Program and Issues*. New York: The Twentieth Century Fund.

Fukuyama, Francis. 1989. "The End of History?" *The National Interest* 16 (Summer): 3-16.

Fuller, J. F. C. 1933. *The Dragon's Teeth*. London: Constable.

Fuller, Lon L. 1964. *The Morality of Law*. New Haven: Yale University Press.

Fussell, Paul. 1975. *The Great War and Modern Memory*. New York: Oxford University Press.

Gaddis, John Lewis. 1990. *Russia, the Soviet Union, and the United States: An Interpretative History*, 2nd ed. New York: McGraw-Hill.

Gaddis, John Lewis. 1989. "Hanging Tough Paid Off," *Bulletin of the Atomic Scientists* 45 (January/February): 11-14.

Gaddis, John Lewis. 1988. "The Evolution of U.S. Policy Goals Toward the USSR in the Postwar Era," pp. 303-46 in Seweryn Bialer and Michael Mandelbaum (eds.), *Gorbachev's Russia and American Foreign Policy*. Boulder, CO: Westview Press.

Gaddis, John Lewis. 1987a. "How the Cold War Might End," *The Atlantic Monthly* 260 (November): 88-100.

Gaddis, John Lewis. 1987b. *The Long Peace: Inquiries Into the History of the Cold War*. New York: Oxford University Press.

Gaddis, John Lewis. 1986. "The Long Peace: Elements of Stability in the Postwar International System," *International Security* 10 (Spring): 92-142.

Galbraith, John Kenneth. 1987. "The 1929 Parallel," *The Atlantic Monthly* (January): 62-66.

Galbraith, John Kenneth. 1972. *The Great Crash 1929*. Boston: Houghton-Mifflin.

Galtung, Johan. 1980. *The True Worlds: A Transnational Perspective*. New York: Free Press.

Gardner, Lloyd C. 1974. *American Foreign Policy: Present to Past*. New York: The Free Press.

Gardner, Lloyd C. 1964. *Economic Aspects of New Deal Diplomacy*. Madison: University of Wisconsin Press.

Garner, James W. 1927. "The Doctrine of Rebus Sic Stantibus and the Termination of Treaties," *American Journal of International Law* 21 (July): 509-16.

Garthoff, Raymond L. 1987. *Reflections on the Cuban Missile Crisis*. Washington, DC: The Brookings Institution.

Garthoff, Raymond. 1985. *Détente and Confrontation: American-Soviet Relations From Nixon to Reagan*. Washington, DC: The Brookings Institution.

Garthoff, Raymond. 1966. *Soviet Military Policy: A Historical Analysis*. New York: Praeger.

Garthoff, Raymond. 1962. *Soviet Strategy in the Nuclear Age*. New York: Praeger.

Gasiorowski, Mark J. 1986. "Economic Independence and International Conflict: Some Cross-National Evidence," *International Studies Quarterly* 30 (March): 23-38.

Gatlin, Lila L. 1972. *Information Theory and the Living System*. New York: Columbia University Press.

Geertz, Clifford. 1973. "Thick Description," pp. 3-30 in Clifford Geertz (ed.), *The Interpretation of Cultures*. New York: Basic Books.

George, Alexander. 1988. "U.S.-Soviet Efforts to Cooperate in Crisis Management and Crisis Avoidance," pp. 581-99 in Alexander L. George, Philip J. Farley, and Alexander Dallin (eds.), *U.S.-Soviet Security Cooperation*. New York: Oxford University Press.

George, Alexander L. 1986. "U.S.-Soviet Global Rivalry: Norms of Competition," *Journal of Peace Research* 23 (September): 247-62.

George, Alexander L. 1984. "Crisis Management: The Interaction of Political and Military Considerations," *Survival* 26 (September/October): 323-24.

George, Alexander L., et al. 1983. *Managing U.S.-Soviet Rivalry*. Boulder, CO: Westview Press.

George, Alexander L., Philip J. Farley, and Alexander Dallin (eds.). 1988. *U.S.-Soviet Security Cooperation: Achievements, Failures, Lessons*. New York: Oxford University Press.

George, Alexander L., David Kay Hall, and William E. Simons. 1971. *The Limits of Coercive Diplomacy*. Boston: Little, Brown.

George, Alexander L., and Richard Smoke. 1974. *Deterrence in American Foreign Policy: Theory and Practice*. New York: Columbia University Press.

Gilpin, Robert. 1987a. "American Policy in the Post-Reagan Era," *Daedalus* 116 (Summer): 33-67.

Gilpin, Robert. 1987b. *The Political Economy of International Relations*. Princeton: Princeton University Press.

Gilpin, Robert. 1981. *War and Change in World Politics*. Cambridge: Cambridge University Press.

Gilpin, Robert. 1975. *U.S. Power and the Multinational Corporation*. New York: Basic Books.

Gleick, James. 1987. *Chaos: Making a New Science*. New York: Viking.

Gochman, Charles S., and Russell J. Leng. 1988. "Militarized Disputes, Incidents and Crises: Identification and Classification," *International Interactions* 14 (No. 2): 157-63.

Gochman, Charles, and Russell J. Leng. 1983. "Realpolitik and the Road to War," *International Studies Quarterly* 27 (March): 97-120.

Gochman, Charles S., and Zeev Maoz. 1984. "Militarized Interstate Disputes 1816-1976," *Journal of Conflict Resolution* 28 (December): 585-616.

Goldblat, Jozef, and David Cox. 1988. *The Debate About Nuclear Weapon Tests*. Ottawa: Canadian Institute for International Peace and Security.

Goldman, Marshall I., and Merle Goldman. 1987/88. "Soviet and Chinese Economic Reforms," *Foreign Affairs* 66 (No. 3): 551-73.

Goldstein, Joshua S. 1989. "A War-Economy Theory of the Long Wave." Paper presented at the International Economic Association conference on Business Cycles, Copenhagen, Denmark, June.

Goldstein, Joshua A. 1988. *Long Cycles: Prosperity and War in the Modern Age*. New Haven: Yale University Press.

Gompert, David C., Michael Mandelbaum, Richard L. Garwin, and John H. Barton. 1977. *Nuclear Weapons and World Politics*. New York: McGraw-Hill.

Gorbachev, Mikhail S. 1987. *Perestroika: New Thinking for Our Country and for the World*. New York: Harper & Row.

Gordon, Michael. 1986. "U.S. Again Says It Won't Join Soviet Moratorium," *New York Times* (August 19).

Gould, Stephen Jay. 1987. *Time's Arrow, Time's Cycle: Myth and Metaphor in the Discovery of Geologic Time*. Cambridge, MA: Harvard University Press.

Gowa, Joanne. 1983. *Closing the Gold Window*. Ithaca, NY: Cornell University Press.

Green, Philip. 1966. *Deadly Logic: The Theory of Nuclear Deterrence*. Columbus: The Ohio State University Press.

Greenhouse, Steven. 1988. "The Growing Fear of Fortress Europe," *New York Times* (October 23): 3/1.

Grotius, Hugo. 1925. *De Jure Belli ac Pacis Libri Tres*. Oxford: Clarendon Press.

Haas, Ernst B. 1986. *Why We Still Need the United Nations: The Collective Management of International Conflict, 1945-1984*. Berkeley: Institute of International Studies, University of California.

Haas, Ernst B. 1953. "The Balance of Power: Prescription, Concept, or Propaganda?" *World Politics* 4 (July): 442-77.

Hadley, Arthur T. 1961. *The Nation's Safety and Arms Control*. New York: Viking.

Hall, John A. 1987. *Liberalism: Politics, Ideology and the Market*. Chapel Hill: University of North Carolina Press.

Hall, John A. 1985. *Powers and Liberties: The Causes and Consequences of the Rise of the West*. Berkeley: University of California Press.

Halle, Louis J. 1967. *The Cold War as History*. New York: Harper & Row.

Halperin, Morton H. 1989. "Has Arms Control Worked?" *Bulletin of the Atomic Scientists* 45 (May): 26-45.

Haraszti, Gyorgy. 1975. "Treaties and the Fundamental Change of Circumstances," *Recueil Des Cours* 146 (No. 3): 1-93.

Harding, Harry. 1987. *China's Second Revolution: Reform After Mao*. Washington, DC: The Brookings Institution.

The Harvard Nuclear Study Group. 1983. *Living with Nuclear Weapons*. Toronto: Bantam Books.

Heilbroner, Robert. 1989. "The Triumph of Capitalism," *New Yorker* 65 (January 23): 98-109.

Helprin, Mark. 1988. "War in Europe: Thinking the Unthinkable," *Wall Street Journal* (November 1): A28.

Henkin, Louis (ed.). 1961. *Arms Control: Issues for the Public*. Englewood Cliffs, NJ: Prentice Hall.

Hermann, Charles F. 1988. "Crisis Stability in Soviet-American Strategic Relations," pp. 211-28 in Joseph Kruzel (ed.), *American Defense Annual 1988-1989*. Lexington, MA: D. C. Heath.

Herz, John. 1951. *Political Realism and Political Idealism*. Chicago: University of Chicago Press.

Hinsley, F. H. 1967. *Power and the Pursuit of Peace*. Cambridge: Cambridge University Press.

Hixson, Walter. 1989. *George Kennan: Cold War Iconoclast*. New York: Columbia University Press.

Hoffmann, Stanley. 1989. "Do Nuclear Weapons Matter?" *The New York Review of Books* 36 (February 2): 28-31.

Hoffmann, Stanley. 1988. "Lessons of a Peace Epidemic," *New York Times* (September 6): 27.

Hoffmann, Stanley. 1981. *Duties Beyond Borders*. Syracuse, NY: Syracuse University Press.

Hoffmann, Stanley. 1971. "International Law and the Control of Force," pp. 34-66 in Karl W. Deutsch and Stanley Hoffmann (eds.), *The Relevance of International Law*. Garden City, NY: Doubleday-Anchor.

Hollins, Harry B., Averill L. Powers, and Mark Sommer. 1989. *The Conquest of War*. Boulder, CO: Westview.

Holloway, David. 1984. *The Soviet Union and the Arms Race*. New York: Yale University Press.

Holloway, David. 1981. *War, Militarism, and the Soviet State*. New York: Institute for World Order.

Holsti, K. J. 1987. *The Dividing Discipline: Hegemony and Diversity in International Theory*. Boston: Allen and Unwin.

Holsti, K. J. 1986. "The Horsemen of the Apocalypse: At the Gate, Detoured, or Retreating?" *International Studies Quarterly* 30 (December): 355-72.

Holsti, Ole R. 1989. "Models of International Relations and Foreign Policy," *Diplomatic History* 13 (Winter): 15-43.

Holsti, Ole R. 1972a. *Crisis Escalation War*. Montreal: McGill-Queen's University Press.

Holsti, Ole R. 1972b. "Time, Alternatives, and Communications: The 1914 and Cuban Crises," pp. 58-80 in Charles Hermann (ed.), *International Crises: Insights from Behavioral Research*. New York: Free Press.

Holsti, Ole R., Robert C. North, and Richard A. Brody. 1968. "Perception and Action in the 1914 Crisis," pp. 123-58 in J. David Singer (ed.), *Quantitative International Politics*. New York: Free Press.

Holsti, Ole R., Richard A. Brody, and Robert C. North. 1964. "Measuring Affect and Action in International Reaction Models: Empirical Materials from the 1962 Cuban Crisis," *Peace Research Society (International) Papers* 2: 170-90.

House, Karen Elliott. 1989. "As Power Is Dispersed Among Nations, Need for Leadership Grows," *Wall Street Journal* (February 21): A1, A10.

Houweling, Henk, and Jan G. Siccama. 1988. "Power Transitions as a Cause of War," *Journal of Conflict Resolution* 32 (March): 87-102.

Houweling, Henk W., and Jan Siccama. 1981. "The Arms Race–War Relationship: Why Serious Disputes Matter," *Arms Control* 2 (September): 157-97.

Howard, Michael. 1983. *The Causes of Wars*. Cambridge, MA: Harvard University Press.

Howard, Michael. 1979. "War and the Nation-State," *Daedalus* 108 (Fall): 101-10.

Howard, Michael. 1976. *War in European History*. Oxford: Oxford University Press.

Huntington, Samuel P. 1989. "No Exit: The Errors of Endism," *The National Interest* 17 (Fall): 3-11.

Huntington, Samuel P. 1988/89. "The U.S. — Decline or Renewal?" *Foreign Affairs* 67 (Winter): 76-96.

Huth, Paul. 1988a. "Extended Deterrence and the Outbreak of War," *American Political Science Review* 82 (June): 423-43.

Huth, Paul. 1988b. *Extended Deterrence and the Prevention of War*. New Haven: Yale University Press.

Huth, Paul, and Bruce Russett. 1988. "Deterrence Failure and Crisis Escalation," *International Studies Quarterly* 32 (March): 29-45.

Huth, Paul, and Bruce Russett. 1984. "What Makes Deterrence Work? Cases from 1900 to 1980," *World Politics* 36 (December): 496-526.

Ikenberry, G. John. 1989. "Rethinking the Origins of American Hegemony," *Political Science Quarterly* 190 (Fall): 4375-400.

Immerman, Richard H. 1982. *The CIA in Guatemala: The Foreign Policy of Intervention*. Austin: The University of Texas Press.

Independent Commission on Disarmament and Security Issues. 1982. *Common Security: A Blueprint for Survival*. New York: Simon and Schuster.

International Intermediary Institute, The Hague. 1922. *The Permanent Court of International Justice*. Leiden, The Netherlands: A. W. Sijthoff.

Intriligator, Michael D., and Dagobert L. Brito. 1984. "Can Arms Races Lead to the Outbreak of War?" *Journal of Conflict Resolution* 28 (March): 63-84.

Jackson, Robert J. 1985. *Continuity of Discord: Crises and Responses in the Atlantic Community*. New York: Praeger.

Jervis, Robert. 1989. *The Meaning of the Nuclear Revolution*. Ithaca, NY: Cornell University Press.

Jervis, Robert. 1988. "The Political Effects of Nuclear Weapons," *International Security* 13 (Fall): 80-90.

Jervis, Robert. 1985. "Perceiving and Coping with Threat," pp. 2-12 in Robert Jervis, Richard Ned Lebow, and Janice Stein (eds.), *Psychology and Deterrence*. Baltimore: The Johns Hopkins University Press.

Jervis, Robert. 1984. *The Illogic of American Nuclear Strategy*. Ithaca, NY: Cornell University Press.

Jervis, Robert. 1983. "Security Regimes," pp. 173-94 in Stephen D. Krasner (ed.), *International Regimes*. Ithaca, NY: Cornell University Press.

Jervis, Robert. 1982. "Security Regimes," *International Organization* 36 (Spring): 357-78.

Jervis, Robert. 1978. "Cooperation Under the Security Dilemma," *World Politics* 30 (January): 167-214.

Johansen, Robert. 1989. "Global Security Without Nuclear Deterrence," pp. 72-80 in Charles W. Kegley, Jr., and Eugene R. Wittkopf (eds.), *The Nuclear Reader*, 2nd ed. New York: St. Martin's Press.

Johansen, Robert C. 1986. "The Reagan Administration and the U.N.: The Costs of Unilateralism," *World Policy Journal* 3 (Fall): 601-41.

Johansen, Robert C. 1985. "The Future of Arms Control," *World Policy Journal* 2 (Spring): 193-227.

Johansen, Robert C. 1983. *Toward an Alternative Security System*. New York: World Policy Institute.

Johansen, Robert C. 1980. *The National Interest and the Human Interest: An Analysis of U.S. Foreign Policy*. Princeton: Princeton University Press.

Johnson, James Turner. 1987. *The Quest for Peace: Three Moral Traditions in Western Cultural History*. Princeton: Princeton University Press.

Johnson, James Turner. 1984. *Can Modern War Be Just?* New Haven: Yale University Press.

Johnson, James Turner. 1981. *Just War Tradition and the Restraint of War*. Princeton: Princeton University Press.

Johnson, James Turner. 1975. *Ideology, Reason, and the Limitation of War*. Princeton: Princeton University Press.

Joll, James. 1984. *The Origins of the First World War*. London: Longman.

Jönsson, Christer. 1982. "The Ideology of Foreign Policy," pp. 91-110 in Charles W. Kegley, Jr., and Pat McGowan (eds.), *Foreign Policy: USA/USSR*. Beverly Hills, CA: Sage Publications.

Jordan, Amos A., and William J. Taylor, Jr. 1984. *American National Security*. Baltimore: The Johns Hopkins University Press.

Joynt, Carey B., and Nicholas Rescher. 1961. "The Problem of Uniqueness in History," *History and Theory* 1: 150-62.

Kahn, Herman. 1960. *On Thermonuclear War*. Princeton: Princeton University Press.

Kaiser, Robert G. 1988/89. "The U.S.S.R. in Decline," *Foreign Affairs* 67 (Winter): 97-112.

Kaldor, Mary. 1981. *The Baroque Arsenal*. New York: Hill and Wang.

Kaplan, Morton A. 1957. *System and Process in International Politics*. New York: Wiley.

Kaplan, Morton A., and Nicholas de B. Katzenbach. 1966. "Resort to Force: War and Neutrality," pp. 276-306 in Richard A. Falk and Saul H. Mendlovitz (eds.), *The Strategy of World Order, Vol. II, International Law*. New York: World Law Fund.

Karp, Arron. 1988. "The Frantic Third World Quest for Ballistic Missiles," *Bulletin of the Atomic Scientists* 44 (June): 14-20.

Kattenburg, Paul M. 1985. "MAD Is the Moral Position," pp. 77-84 in Charles W. Kegley, Jr., and Eugene R. Wittkopf (eds.), *The Nuclear Reader*. New York: St. Martin's Press.

Katzenstein, Peter J. 1978. "Conclusion: Domestic Structures and Strategies of Foreign Economic Policy," in Peter J. Katzenstein (ed.), *Between Power and Plenty: Foreign Economic Policies of Advanced Industrial States*. Madison: University of Wisconsin Press.

Kaufman, Daniel J., Jeffrey S. McKitrick, and Thomas Leney (eds.). 1985. *U.S. National Security: A Framework for Analysis*. Washington, DC: Heath.

Kautsky, Karl. 1970. "Ultra-Imperialism," *New Left Review* 59 (January/February): 41-46.

Keesing's Contemporary Archives. 1980. (May 9): 30236.

Keesing's Contemporary Archives. 1958. (June 14-21): 16237.

Kegley, Charles W., Jr. 1988. "Neo-Idealism," *Ethics and International Affairs* 2: 173-97.

Kegley, Charles W., Jr. 1987. "Decision Regimes and the Comparative Study of Foreign Policy," pp. 247-68 in Charles F. Hermann, Charles W. Kegley, Jr., and James N. Rosenau (eds.), *New Directions in the Study of Foreign Policy*. Boston: Allen & Unwin.

Kegley, Charles W., Jr., and Patrick J. McGowan. 1979. "Environmental Change and the Future of American Foreign Policy," pp. 13-39 in Charles W. Kegley, Jr., and Patrick J. McGowan (eds.), *Challenges to America*. Beverly Hills: Sage Publications.

Kegley, Charles W., Jr., and Gregory A. Raymond. 1990. *When Trust Breaks Down: Alliance Norms and World Politics*. Columbia: University of South Carolina Press.

Kegley, Charles W., Jr., and Gregory A. Raymond. 1989. "Going It Alone: The Decay of Alliance Norms," *Harvard International Review* 12 (Fall): 39-43.

Kegley, Charles W., Jr., and Gregory A. Raymond. 1986. "Normative Contraints on the Use of Force Short of War," *Journal of Peace Research* 23 (No. 3): 213-27.

Kegley, Charles W., Jr., and Gregory A. Raymond. 1984. "Alliance Norms and the Management of Interstate Disputes," pp. 199-220 in J. David Singer and Richard J. Stoll (eds.), *Quantitative Indicators in World Politics*. New York: Praeger.

Kegley, Charles W., Jr., and Gregory A. Raymond. 1982. "Alliance Norms and War: A New Piece in an Old Puzzle," *International Studies Quarterly* 26 (December): 572-95.

Kegley, Charles W., Jr., and Kenneth L. Schwab (eds.). 1991. *After the Cold War: Questioning the Morality of Nuclear Deterrence*. Boulder, CO: Westview Press.

Kegley, Charles W., Jr., and Eugene R. Wittkopf. 1989. *World Politics: Trend and Transformation*, 3rd ed. New York: St. Martin's Press.

Keller, Bill. 1988. "The Consolidator: Why a Stronger Gorbachev Might Not Be Strong Enough," *New York Times* (October 9): 4/1.

Kennan, George F. 1987. "Containment Then and Now," *Foreign Affairs* 65 (Spring): 885-90.

Kennan, George F. 1984. *The Fateful Alliance: France, Russia and the Coming of the First World War*. New York: Pantheon.

Kennan, George F. 1982. *The Nuclear Delusion: Soviet-American Relations in the Atomic Age*. New York: Pantheon.

Kennan, George. 1967. *Memoirs, 1925-1950*. Boston: Little, Brown.

Kennedy, Paul. 1989. "Can the U.S. Remain Number One?" *New York Review of Books* 36 (March 16): 36-42.

Kennedy, Paul. 1988. "Why We Can't Give Up the Bomb," *Atlantic Monthly* 262 (August): 77-79.

Kennedy, Paul. 1987. *The Rise and Fall of the Great Powers: Economic Change and Military Conflict from 1500 to 2000*. New York: Random House.

Keohane, Robert O. 1989. *International Institutions and State Power: Essays in International Relations Theory*. Boulder, CO: Westview.

Keohane, Robert O. 1986. "Theory of World Politics: Structural Realism and Beyond," pp. 158-203 in Robert O. Keohane (ed.), *Neorealism and Its Critics*. New York: Columbia University Press.

Keohane, Robert O. 1984. *After Hegemony: Cooperation and Discord in the World Political Economy*. Princeton: Princeton University Press.

Keohane, Robert O. 1980. "The Theory of Hegemonic Stability and Changes in International Economic Regimes," pp. 131-62 in Ole R. Holsti, Randolph M. Siverson, and Alexander L. George (eds.), *Change in the International System*. Boulder, CO: Westview Press.

Keohane, Robert O., and Joseph S. Nye, Jr. 1989. *Power and Interdependence*, 2nd ed. Glenview, IL: Scott, Foresman/Little, Brown.

Keohane, Robert O., and Joseph S. Nye, Jr. 1977. *Power and Interdependence*. Boston: Little Brown.

Kern, Stephen. 1983. *The Culture of Time and Space, 1880-1914*. Cambridge, MA: Harvard University Press.

Kilgour, D. Marc, and Frank C. Zagare. 1989. "Credibility, Uncertainty, and Deterrence," mimeo.

Kim, Woosang, and James D. Morrow. 1990. "When Do Power Transitions Lead to War?" Paper presented at the Annual Meeting of the Midwest Political Science Association, Chicago, Illinois, April 5-7.

Kindleberger, Charles P. 1973. *The World in Depression, 1929-1939*. Berkeley: University of California Press.

Kissinger, Henry A. 1984. *Report of the National Bipartisan Commission on Central America*. Submitted to the President of the United States, January 10, 1984.

Kissinger, Henry A. 1957. *A World Restored: Matternich, Castlereagh and the Problems of Peace, 1812-1822*. Boston: Houston Mifflin.

Knorr, Klaus. 1966. *On the Utility of Military Power in the Nuclear Age*. Princeton: Princeton University Press.

Kochan, Lionel, and Richard Abraham. 1983. *The Making of Modern Russia*, 2nd ed. Hammondsworth, England: Penguin.

Koebner, Richard. 1965. *Empire*. New York: Grosset & Dunlap.

Krasner, Stephen D. (ed.). 1983. *International Regimes*. Ithaca, NY: Cornell University Press.

Krasner, Stephen D. 1976. "State Power and the Structure of International Trade," *World Politics* 28 (April): 317-47.

Kristol, Irving. 1986. " 'Global Unilateralism' and 'Entangling Alliances,' " *The Wall Street Journal* (February 3): 23.

Kruzel, Joseph. 1981. "Arms Control and American Defense Policy: New Alternatives and Old Realities," *Daedalus* 110 (Winter): 137-57.

Kugler, Jacek. 1984. "Terror Without Deterrence: Reassessing the Role of Nuclear Weapons," *Journal of Conflict Resolution* 28 (September): 470-506.

Kugler, Jacek, and A. F. K. Organski. 1989. "The Power Transition: A Retrospective and Prospective Evaluation," pp. 171-94 in Manus I. Midlarsky (ed.), *Handbook of War Studies*. Boston: Unwin Hyman.

Kugler, Jacek, and Frank C. Zagare. 1990. "The Long-term Stability of Deterrence," *International Interactions* 15 (Nos. 3-4): 255-78.

Kuhn, Thomas. 1970. *The Structure of Scientific Revolutions*, 2nd ed., enlarged. Chicago: University of Chicago Press.

Kuhn, Thomas S. 1962. *The Structure of Scientific Revolutions*. Chicago: University of Chicago Press.

Kupchan, Charles A. 1989. "Empire, Military Power, and Economic Decline," *International Security* 13 (Spring): 36-53.

Lackey, Douglas P. 1985. "Missiles and Morals: A Utilitarian Look at Nuclear Deterrence," pp. 109-51 in Charles R. Beitz, Marshall Cohen, Thomas Scanlon, and A. John Simmons (eds.), *International Ethics*. Princeton: Princeton University Press.

LaFeber, Walter. 1989. *The American Age: U.S. Foreign Policy at Home and Abroad, From 1750 to the Present*. New York: Norton.

LaFeber, Walter. 1971. *The Origins of the Cold War, 1941-1947*. New York: John Wiley & Sons.

Lamb, Christopher J. 1988. *How to Think About Arms Control, Disarmament, and Defense*. Englewood Cliffs, NJ: Prentice Hall.

LaRoe, Ross M., and John Charles Pool. 1988. "Mixing Economics with Mysticism," *Challenge* 31 (January/February): 63-65.

Larson, Deborah Welch. 1985. *The Origins of Containment: A Psychological Explanation*. Princeton: Princeton University Press.

Layne, Christopher. 1987. "Atlanticism Without NATO," *Foreign Policy* 67 (Summer): 22-45.

Lebow, Richard Ned. 1987a. "Is Crisis Management Always Possible?" *Political Science Quarterly* 102 (Summer): 181-92.

Lebow, Richard Ned. 1987b. *Nuclear Crisis Management: A Dangerous Illusion*. Ithaca, NY: Cornell University Press.

Lebow, Richard Ned. 1985. "Conclusions," pp. 203-32 in Robert Jervis, Richard Ned Lebow, and Janice Stein (eds.), *Psychology and Deterrence*. Baltimore: The Johns Hopkins University Press.

Lebow, Richard Ned. 1981. *Between Peace and War*. Baltimore: The Johns Hopkins University Press.

Leffler, Melvyn. 1988. "Strategic Dimensions of the Marshall Plan," *Diplomatic History* 12 (Summer): 279-306.

Leiken, Robert, and Barry Rubin (eds.). 1987. *The Central American Crisis Reader: The Essential Guide to the Most Controversial Foreign Policy Issue Today*. New York: Summit Books.

Leng, Russell J., and Hugh B. Wheeler. 1979. "Influence Strategies, Success and War," *Journal of Conflict Resolution* 23 (December): 655-84.

Leng, Russell J. 1983. "When Will They Ever Learn? Coercive Bargaining in Recurrent Crises," *Journal of Conflict Resolution* 27 (September): 379-419.

Levi, Werner. 1981. *The Coming End of War*. Beverly Hills: Sage Publications.

Levy, Jack S. 1991. "The Role of Crisis Mismanagement in the Outbreak of World War I," forthcoming in Alexander L. George (ed.), *Inadvertent War: Problems of Crisis Management*. Boulder, CO: Westview.

Levy, Jack S. 1990. "Big Wars, Little Wars, and Theory Construction," *International Interactions* 16: forthcoming.

Levy, Jack S. 1989a. "The Diversionary Theory of War," pp. 257-86 in Manus I. Midlarsky (ed.), *Handbook of War Studies*. Boston: Unwin Hyman.

Levy, Jack S. 1989b. "The Causes of War: A Theoretical Review," chapter 4 in Philip E. Tetlock, Jo L. Husbands, Robert Jervis, Paul C. Stern, and Charles Tilly (eds.), *Behavior, Society, and Nuclear War*, Vol. 1. New York: Oxford University Press.

Levy, Jack S. 1989c. Review of Joshua Goldstein, *Long Cycles*, in *Futures* 21 (April): 206-8.

Levy, Jack S. 1989d. "How Rare Is the Long Peace?" University of Minnesota, unpublished manuscript.

Levy, Jack S. 1988. "When Do Deterrent Threats Work?" *British Journal of Political Science* 18 (October): 485-512.

Levy, Jack S. 1987. "Declining Power and the Preventive Motivation for War," *World Politics* 40 (October): 82-107.

Levy, Jack S. 1985. "Theories of General War," *World Politics* 37 (April): 344-74.

Levy, Jack S. 1983. *War in the Modern Great Power System, 1495-1975*. Lexington: University Press of Kentucky.

Levy, Jack S. 1982. "Historical Trends in Great Power War," *International Studies Quarterly* 26 (June): 278-301.

Levy, Jack S. 1981. "Alliance Formation and War Behavior: An Analysis of the Great Powers, 1495-1975," *Journal of Conflict Resolution* 25 (December): 581-613.

Levy, Jack S. 1976. "Military Power, Alliances, Technology: An Analysis of Some Structural Determinants of War Among Great Powers," Ph.D. dissertation, University of Wisconsin.

Levy, Jack S., and T. Clifton Morgan. 1986. "The Structure of the International System and the Frequency and Seriousness of War," pp. 75-98 in Margaret P. Karns (ed.), *Persistent Patterns and Emergent Structures in a Waning Century*. New York: Praeger.

Levy, Jack S., and T. Clifton Morgan. 1984. "The Frequency and Seriousness of War," *Journal of Conflict Resolution* 28 (December): 731-49.

Lewis, John Wilson, and Xue Litai. 1988. *China Builds the Bomb*. Stanford: Stanford University Press.

Lichtenburg, Frank R. 1986. "Military R & D Depletes Economic Might," *Wall Street Journal* (August 22): 22.

Lilienthal, David E. 1964. *The Journals of David Lilienthal*, Vol. 2. New York: Harper & Row.

Lippman, Walter. 1932. "Ten Years: Retrospect and Prospect," *Foreign Affairs* 11 (October): 51-53.

Lipson, Charles. 1984. "International Cooperation in Economic and Security Affairs," *World Politics* 37 (October): 1-23.

Liska, George. 1967. *Imperial America: The International Politics of Primacy*. Baltimore: The Johns Hopkins University Press.

Liska, George. 1962. *Nations in Alliance: The Limits of Interdependence*. Baltimore: The Johns Hopkins University Press.

Lowenthal, Abraham F. 1971. "The United States and the Dominican Republic," pp. 99-114 in Steven L. Spiegel and Kenneth N. Waltz (eds.), *Conflict in World Politics*. Cambridge, MA: Winthrop.

Luard, Evan. 1986. *War in International Society*. London: I. B. Taurus.

Lundestad, Geir. 1986. "Empire by Invitation? The United States and Western Europe, 1945-1952," *Journal of Peace Research* 23 (No. 2): 263-77.

Lynn-Jones, Sean. 1985. "A Quiet Success for Arms Control: Preventing Incidents at Sea," *International Security* 9 (Spring): 154-84.

Malawer, Stuart S. 1988. "Reagan's Law and Foreign Policy, 1981-1987: The Reagan Corollary of International Law," *Harvard International Law Journal* 29 (Winter): 85-109.

Manchester, William. 1973. *The Glory and the Dream*. New York: Bantam Books.

Mandelbaum, Michael. 1989. "Ending Where It Began," *New York Times* (February 29): A19.

Mandelbaum, Michael. 1988. *The Fate of Nations: The Search for National Security in the Nineteenth and Twentieth Centuries*. Cambridge: Cambridge University Press.

Mandelbaum, Michael. 1981. *The Nuclear Revolution: International Politics Before and After Hiroshima*. Cambridge: Cambridge University Press.

Mandelbaum, Michael. 1979. *The Nuclear Question*. Cambridge: Cambridge University Press.

Mansbach, Richard W., and John A. Vasquez. 1981. *In Search of Theory: A New Paradigm for Global Politics*. New York: Columbia University Press.

Maoz, Zeev. 1990. *Paradoxes of War: On the Art of National Self-Entrapment*. Boston: Unwin Hyman.

Markham, James M. 1988. "Some Wars Are Failing the Cost-Benefits Test," *New York Times* (August 15): 4/1.

Mattingly, Garrett. 1964. *Renaissance Diplomacy*. Baltimore: Penguin.

May, Ernest. 1984. "The Cold War," pp. 209-30 in Joseph S. Nye, Jr. (ed.), *The Making of America's Soviet Policy*. New Haven: Yale University Press.

Mazour, Anatole G. 1962. *Russia: Tsarist and Communist*. Princeton: Van Nostrand.

McCain, Morris. 1989. *Understanding Arms Control*. New York: W.W. Norton.

McClelland, Charles A. 1972. "The Beginning, Duration, and Abatement of International Crises: Comparisons in Two Conflict Arenas," pp. 83-105 in Charles Hermann (ed.), *International Crises: Insights from Behavioral Research*. New York: Free Press.

McCloy, John J. 1969. *The Atlantic Alliance: Its Origin and Its Future*. New York: Columbia University Press.

McDougal, Myres S., and Florentino P. Feliciano. 1961. *Law and Minimum World Public Order*. New Haven: Yale University Press.

McNamara, Robert S. 1989. "The Military Role of Nuclear Weapons," pp. 174-85 in Charles W. Kegley, Jr., and Eugene R. Wittkopf (eds.), *The Nuclear Reader: Strategy, Weapons, War*, 2nd ed. New York: St. Martin's Press.

McNeill, William H. 1982. *The Pursuit of Power: Technology, Armed Force, and Society Since A.D. 1000*. Chicago: University of Chicago Press.

Mead, Walter Russell. 1987. *Mortal Splendor: The American Empire in Transition*. Boston: Houghton-Mifflin.

Mendlovitz, Saul M. (ed.). 1975. *On the Creation of a Just World Order: Preferred Worlds for the 1990s*. New York: Free Press.

Messer, Robert L. 1986. "World War II and the Coming of the Cold War," pp. 107-25 in John M. Carroll and George C. Herring (eds.), *Modern American Diplomacy*. Wilmington, DE: Scholarly Resources Inc.

Meyrowitz, Henri. 1970. *Le Principe de l'Egalite des Belligerents Devant le Droit de la Guerre*. Paris: A. Pedone.

Midlarsky, Manus I. 1988. *The Onset of World War*. Boston: Unwin Hyman.

Midlarsky, Manus I. 1986. "A Hierarchical Equilibrium Theory of Systemic War," *International Studies Quarterly* 30 (March): 77-105.

Midlarsky, Manus I. 1984. "Preventing Systemic War," *Journal of Conflict Resolution* 28 (December): 563-84.

Midlarsky, Manus I. 1984. "Political Stability of Two-Party and Multiparty Systems: Probabilistic Bases for the Comparison of Polarity Systems," *American Political Science Review* 78 (December): 929-51.

Midlarsky, Manus I. 1983. "Absence of Memory in the Nineteenth-Century Alliance System: Perspectives from Queuing Theory and Bivariate Probability Distributions," *American Journal of Political Science* 27 (November): 762-84.

Miller, J. D. B. 1986. *Norman Angell and the Futility of War: Peace and the Public Mind.* New York: St. Martin's Press.

Millis, Walter. 1956. *Arms and Men.* New York: Mentor Books.

Millis, Walter. 1951. *The Forrestal Diaries.* New York: Viking Press.

Modelski, George. 1987a. "A Global Politics Scenario for the Year 2016," pp. 218-48 in George Modelski (ed.), *Exploring Long Cycles.* Boulder, CO: Lynne Rienner Publishers.

Modelski, George (ed.). 1987b. *Exploring Long Cycles.* Boulder, CO: Lynne Rienner Publishers.

Modelski, George. 1987c. *Long Cycles in World Politics.* Seattle: University of Washington Press.

Modelski, George. 1983. "Qualifications for World Leadership," *Voice* (Japan) (October): 210-29.

Modelski, George. 1978. "The Long Cycle of Global Politics and the Nation-State," *Comparative Studies in Society and History* 20 (April): 214-35.

Modelski, George, and Patrick M. Morgan. 1985. "Understanding Global War," *Journal of Conflict Resolution* 29 (September): 391-417.

Modelski, George, and William R. Thompson. 1988. *Seapower in Global Politics, 1494-1993.* Seattle: University of Washington Press.

Morgan, Patrick M. 1983. *Deterrence: A Conceptual Analysis*, 2nd ed. Beverly Hills, CA: Sage.

Morgan, Patrick M. 1981. *Theories and Approaches to International Politics.* New Brunswick, NJ: Transaction Books.

Morgan, T. Clifton, and James Lee Ray. 1989. "The Impact of Nuclear Weapons on Crisis Bargaining: Implications of a Spatial Model," pp. 193-208 in Richard J. Stoll and Michael D. Ward (eds.), *Power in World Politics.* Boulder, CO: Lynn Rienner Publishers.

Morganthau, Hans J. 1973. *Politics Among Nations: The Struggle for Power and Peace*, 5th ed. New York: Alfred A. Knopf.

Morgenthau, Hans J. 1970. "The Origins of the Cold War," pp. 79-102 in J. Joseph Huthmacher and Warren I. Susman (eds.), *The Origins of the Cold War.* Waltham, MA: Ginn.

Morgenthau, Hans J. 1967. *Politics Among Nations*, 4th ed. New York: Knopf.

Most, Benjamin A., Philip Schrodt, Randolph M. Siverson, and Harvey Starr. 1990. "Border and Alliance Effects in the Diffusion of Major Power Conflict, 1815-1965," pp. 209-29 in Charles S. Gochman and Alan Ned Sabrosky (eds.), *Prisoners of War? Nation-States in the Modern Era.* Lexington, MA: D. C. Heath.

Most, Benjamin A., and Harvey Starr. 1989. *Inquiry, Logic and International Politics.* Columbia: University of South Carolina Press.

Most, Benjamin, and Harvey Starr. 1980. "Diffusion, Reinforcement, Geopolitics, and the Spread of War," *American Political Science Review* 74 (December): 932-46.

Mottahedah, Roy. 1985. *The Mantle of the Prophet: Religion and Politics in Iran*. New York: Pantheon.

Mueller, John. 1989. *Retreat from Doomsday: The Obsolescence of Major War*. New York: Basic Books.

Mueller, John. 1988a. "Dropping Out of the War System," *Los Angeles Times* (September 12): 5.

Mueller, John. 1988b. "The Essential Irrelevance of Nuclear Weapons: Stability in the Postwar World," *International Security* 13 (Fall): 55-79.

Murray, Alan. 1988. "Will Foreigners Shape Bush Policies?" *Wall Street Journal* (December 5): A1.

Myrdal, Alva. 1977. *The Game of Disarmament: How the United States and Russia Run the Arms Race*. New York: Pantheon.

Nagel, Ernest. 1961. *The Structure of Science: Problems in the Logic of Scientific Explanation*. New York: Harcourt, Brace & World.

Nance, R. Damian, with Thomas R. Worsley and Judith R. Moody. 1988. "The Supercontinent Cycle," *Scientific American* 219 (July): 72-79.

Nardin, Terry. 1983. *Law, Morality, and the Relations of States*. Princeton: Princeton University Press.

National Conference of Catholic Bishops. 1989. "Nuclear Strategy and the Challenge of Peace: The Moral Evaluation of Deterrence in Light of Policy Developments, 1983-1988," pp. 54-71 in Charles W. Kegley, Jr., and Eugene R. Wittkopf (eds.), *The Nuclear Reader: Strategy, Weapons, War*, 2nd ed. New York: St. Martin's Press.

National Conference of Catholic Bishops. 1983. *The Challenge of Peace: God's Promise and Our Response*. Washington, DC: United States Catholic Conference.

New York Times (Editorial). 1988. "Stirrings of Peace," *New York Times* (July 31): 24.

Newhouse, John. 1989. "Nuclear Hair Trigger Persists," *The Christian Science Monitor* (February 27): 19.

Nichols, Robert S. 1978. "Factors Influencing Perceptions of the US/USSR Military Balance," (May 30). Carlisle Barracks, PA: Strategic Studies Institute, U.S. Army War College.

Nogee, Joseph L., and John Spanier. 1988. *Peace Impossible — War Unlikely: The Cold War Between the United States and the Soviet Union*. Glenview, IL: Scott, Foresman/Little, Brown.

Nunn, Sam. 1988. "Arms Control in the Last Year of the Reagan Administration," *Arms Control Today* 18 (March): 3-7.

Nye, Joseph S., Jr. 1989. "The Long-Term Future of Deterrence," pp. 81-89 in Charles W. Kegley, Jr., and Eugene R. Wittkopf (eds.), *The Nuclear Reader: Strategy, Weapons, War*, 2nd ed. New York: St. Martin's Press.

Nye, Joseph S., Jr. 1988a. "Neorealism and Neoliberalism," *World Politics* 40 (January): 235-51.

Nye, Joseph S., Jr. 1988b. "Old Wars and Future Wars: Causation and Prevention," *Journal of Interdisciplinary History* 18 (Spring): 581-90.

Nye, Joseph S., Jr. 1987. "Nuclear Learning and U.S.-Soviet Security Regimes," *International Organization* 41 (Summer): 371-402.

Nye, Joseph S., Jr. 1986. *Nuclear Ethics*. New York: Free Press.

Nye, Joseph S., Jr., Graham T. Allison, and Albert Carnesale (eds.). 1988. *Fateful Visions: Avoiding Nuclear Catastrophe*. New York: Ballinger.

O'Brien, William V. 1981. *The Conduct of Just and Limited War*. New York: Praeger.

Oden, Michael Dee. 1988. "Military Spending Erodes Real National Security," *Bulletin of the Atomic Scientists* 45 (June): 36-42.

O'Donovan, Oliver. 1988. *Peace and Certainty*. Oxford: Oxford University Press.

Olson, Mancur. 1982. *The Rise and Decline of Nations: Economic Growth, Stagflation, and Social Rigidities*. New Haven: Yale University Press.

O'Neill, Barry. 1986. "International Escalation and the Dollar Auction," *Journal of Conflict Resolution* 30 (March): 33-50.

Oren, Nissan (ed.). 1984. *When Patterns Change: Turning Points in International Politics*. New York: St. Martin's Press.

Organski, A. F. K., and Jacek Kugler. 1980. *The War Ledger*. Chicago: University of Chicago Press.

Organski, A. F. K. 1968. *World Politics*, 2nd ed. New York: Knopf.

Ornstein, Donald S. 1973. *Ergodic Theory, Randomness and Dynamical Systems*. New Haven: Yale University Press.

Osgood, Robert E. 1967. "The Expansion of Force," pp. 41-120 in Robert E. Osgood and Robert W. Tucker (eds.), *Force, Order, and Justice*. Baltimore: The Johns Hopkins University Press.

Ostrom, Charles, Jr., and Francis W. Hoole. 1978. "Alliances and Wars Revisited," *International Studies Quarterly* 22 (June): 215-36.

Oye, Kenneth A. (ed.). 1986. *Cooperation Under Anarchy*. Princeton: Princeton University Press.

Pagels, Heinz R. 1988. *The Dreams of Reason: The Computer and the Rise of the Sciences of Complexity*. New York: Bantam Books.

Pagés, Georges. 1970. *The Thirty Years' War, 1618-1648*. Trans. by D. Maland and J. Hooper. New York: Harper.

Parker, Geoffrey. 1984. *The Thirty Years' War*. London: Routledge & Kegan Paul.

Pearson, Frederick S., and Robert A. Baumann. 1988. "International Military Interventions: Identification and Classification," *International Interactions* 14 (No. 2): 173-80.

Peterson, Peter G. 1987. "The Morning After," *The Atlantic Monthly* 260 (October): 43-69.

Phillips, Cabell. 1966. *The Truman Presidency*. New York: Macmillan.

Powaski, Ronald E. 1989. *March to Armageddon: The United States and the Nuclear Arms Race, 1939 to the Present*. New York: Oxford University Press.

Powell, Colin L. 1989. "Why History Will Honor Mr. Reagan," *New York Times* (January 15): 27.

Powell, Charles A., Helen E. Purkitt, and James W. Dyson. 1987. "Opening the Black Box: Cognitive Processing and Optimal Choice in Foreign Policy Decision Making," pp. 203-20 in Charles F. Hermann, Charles W. Kegley, Jr., and James N. Rosenau (eds.), *New Directions in the Study of Foreign Policy*. Boston: Allen & Unwin.

Princeton Seminar. 1953. Transcripts from the Harry S Truman Library, Independence, MO.

Pyne, Stephen J. 1986. *The Ice: A Journey to Antarctica*. New York: Ballantine Books.

Quester, George. 1987. *The Future of Nuclear Deterrence*. Lexington, MA: Lexington Books.

Rasler, Karen A., and W. R. Thompson. 1983. "Global Wars, Public Debts, and the Long Cycle," *World Politics* 35 (July): 485-516.

Ray, James Lee. 1989. "The Abolition of Slavery and the End of International War," *International Organization* 43 (Summer): 405-39.

Ray, James Lee. 1987. *Global Politics*, 3rd ed. Boston: Houghton-Mifflin.

Raymond, Gregory A., and Charles W. Kegley, Jr. 1987. "Long Cycles and Internationalized Civil War," *Journal of Politics* 49 (May): 481-99.

Record, Jeffrey. 1988. "The Nukes as Peacemakers," *The Sun* (Baltimore) (October 12): 5.

Reshetar, John S., Jr. 1989. *The Soviet Polity: Government and Politics in the USSR*, 3rd ed. New York: Harper & Row.

Reston, James. 1988. "25 Wars Are Still Going On," *New York Times* (June 3): 25.

Rhodes, Richard. 1986. *The Making of the Atomic Bomb*. New York: Simon and Schuster.

Rice, Condoleeza. 1988. "SALT as a Limited Security Regime," in Alexander George, Philip J. Farley, and Alexander Dallin (eds.), *U.S.-Soviet Cooperation: Achievements, Failures, Lessons*. New York: Oxford University Press.

Richardson, Lewis F. 1960. *Arms and Insecurity*. Pacific Grove, CA: Boxwood Press.

Ritch, John B. III, and James P. Rubin. 1988. "Arms Control — Now or Never," *Bulletin of the Atomic Scientists* 44 (December): 9-13.

Ritter, Gerhard. 1970. *The Sword and the Scepter, Vol. II: The European Powers and the Wilhelminian Empire, 1890-1914*. Trans. by Heins Norden. Coral Gables, FL: University of Miami Press.

Ritter, Gerhard. 1968. *Frederick the Great: A Historical Profile*. Trans. by Peter Paret. Berkeley, CA: University of California Press.

Rock, Stephen R. 1989. *Why Peace Breaks Out: Great Power Rapprochement in Historical Perspective*. Chapel Hill: University of North Carolina Press.

Roosevelt, Franklin D. 1943. *Public Papers and Addresses of Franklin D. Roosevelt*, Vol 12. Ed. by Samuel I. Roseman. New York: Macmillan.

Rosecrance, Richard. 1987. "Long Cycle Theory and International Relations," *International Organization* 41 (Spring): 283-301.

Rosecrance, Richard. 1986. *The Rise of the Trading State*. New York: Basic Books.

Rosecrance, Richard. 1963. *Action and Reaction in World Politics*. Boston: Little, Brown.

Rosenau, James N. 1990. *Turbulence in World Politics: Toward a Theory of Change and Continuity*. Princeton: Princeton University Press.

Rosenau, James N. 1988. "Patterned Chaos in Global Life: Structure and Process in the Two Worlds of World Politics," *International Political Science Review* 9 (October): 357-94.

Rosenau, James N. 1980. *The Study of Global Interdependence*. London: Pinter.

Rosenbaum, David E. 1989. "Pentagon Spending Could Be Cut in Half, Ex-Defense Officials Say," *New York Times* (December 13): 1, 16.

Rosenberg, David Alan. 1983. "The Origins of Overkill: Nuclear Weapons and American Strategy, 1945-1960," *International Security* 7 (Spring): 3-71.

Rostow, Walt W. 1988. "Beware of Historians Bearing False Analogies," *Foreign Affairs* 67 (Spring): 863-68.

Rothschild, Joseph. 1971. "The Soviet Union and Czechoslovakia," pp. 115-37 in Steven L. Spiegel and Kenneth N. Waltz (eds.), *Conflict in World Politics*. Cambridge, MA: Winthrop Publishers.

Rotter, Andrew. 1987. *The Path to Vietnam: Origins of the American Commitment to Southeast Asia*. Ithaca, NY: Cornell University Press.

Rousseau, Jean-Jacques. 1920. *L'Etat de Guerre and Projet de Paix Perpetuelle*. Introduction and notes by Shirley G. Patterson. New York: G. P. Putnam's Sons.

Ruggie, John Gerard. 1986. "Continuity and Transformation in the World Polity: Toward a Neorealist Synthesis," pp. 131-57 in Robert O. Keohane (ed.), *Neorealism and Its Critics*. New York: Columbia University Press.

Ruggie, John Gerard. 1982. "International Regimes, Transactions, and Change: Embedded Liberalism in the Postwar Economic Order," *International Organization* 36 (Spring): 379-415.

Ruggie, John Gerard. 1978. "Changing Frameworks of International Collective Behavior: On the Complementarity of Contradictory Tendencies," in Nazli Choucri and Thomas W. Robinson (eds.), *Forecasting in International Relations: Theory, Methods, Problems, Prospects*. San Francisco: W. H. Freeman.

Ruina, Jack. 1987. "More Is Not Better," *International Security* 12 (Fall): 187-92.

Russett, Bruce. 1989. "The Real Decline in Nuclear Hegemony," pp. 177-93 in Ernst-Otto Czempiel and James N. Rosenau (eds.), *Global Changes and Theoretical Challenges: Approaches to World Politics for the 1990s*. Lexington, MA: Lexington Books.

Russett, Bruce. 1985. "The Mysterious Case of Vanishing Hegemony: Or, Is Mark Twain Really Dead?" *International Organization* 39 (Spring): 207-31.

Russett, Bruce M. 1974. *Power and Community in World Politics*. San Francisco: W. H. Freeman.

Russett, Bruce M. 1963. "The Calculus of Deterrence," *Journal of Conflict Resolution* 7 (March): 97-109.

Sabin, Edward P. 1989. "Threat Inflation: U.S. Estimates of Soviet Military Capability," *Peace & Change* 14 (April): 191-202.

Sabrosky, Alan Ned. 1985. "Alliance Aggregation, Capability Distribution, and the Expansion of Interstate War," pp. 145-89 in Alan Ned Sabrosky (ed.), *Polarity and War*. Boulder, CO: Westview.

Sabrosky, Alan Ned. 1980. "Interstate Alliances: Their Reliability and the Expansion of War," pp. 161-98 in J. David Singer (ed.), *The Correlates of War II: Testing Some Realpolitik Models*. New York: Free Press.

Sagan, Carl. 1989. "Nuclear War and Climatic Catastrophe: A Nuclear Winter," pp. 320-35 in Charles W. Kegley, Jr., and Eugene R. Wittkopf (eds.), *The Nuclear Reader: Strategy, Weapons, War*. New York: St. Martin's Press.

Sagan, Carl. 1983/84. "Nuclear War and Climatic Catastrophe," *Foreign Affairs* 62 (Winter): 257-92.

Sanders, Jerry W. 1983. *Peddlers of Crisis: The Committee on the Present Danger and the Politics of Containment*. Boston: South End Press.

Scarborough, Grace E. Iusi, and Bruce Bueno de Mesquita. 1988. "Threat and Alignment," *International Interactions* 14 (No. 1): 85-93.

Schelling, Thomas C. 1989. "Has Arms Control Worked?" *Bulletin of the Atomic Scientists* 45 (May): 29-31.

Schelling, Thomas C. 1966. *Arms and Influence*. New Haven: Yale University Press.

Schelling, Thomas C. 1960. *The Strategy of Conflict*. New York: Oxford University Press.

Schelling, Thomas C., and Morton H. Halperin. 1961. *Strategy and Arms Control*. New York: The Twentieth Century Fund.

Schindler, Dietrich, and Jiri Toman (eds.). 1973. *The Laws of Armed Conflicts*. Leiden, The Netherlands: A. W. Sijthoff.

Schlesinger, Arthur S., Jr. 1967. "The Origins of the Cold War," *Foreign Affairs* 46 (October): 22-52.

Schwarzenberger, Georg. (ed.). 1967. *A Manual of International Law*, 5th ed. London: Stevens and Sons.

Schwarzenberger, Georg. 1962. *The Frontiers of International Law*. London: Stevens and Sons.

Shannon, Claude E., and Warren Weaver. 1949. *The Mathematical Theory of Communication*. Urbana: University of Illinois Press.

Shelton, Judy. 1988. *The Coming Soviet Crash*. New York: Free Press.

Sherry, Michael S. 1987. *The Rise of American Air Power: The Creation of Armageddon*. New Haven: Yale University Press.

Sherry, Michael S. 1977. *Preparing for the Next War: American Plans for Postwar Defense, 1941-1945*. New Haven: Yale University Press.

Shulman, Marshall. 1987/88. "The Superpowers: Dance of the Dinosaurs," *Foreign Affairs* 66 (No. 3): 494-515.

Shultz, George F. 1988. "The INF Treaty: Strengthening U.S. Security," *Current Policy* No. 1038, Washington, DC: Bureau of Public Affairs, Department of State.

Silberner, Edmund. 1946. *The Problem of War in Nineteenth Century Economic Thought*. Trans. by Alexander H. Krappe. Princeton: Princeton University Press.

Simes, Dimitri K. 1984. "Soviet Policy Toward the United States," pp. 291-322 in Joseph S. Nye, Jr. (ed.), *The Making of America's Soviet Policy*. New Haven: Yale University Press.

Sinai, Y. G. 1976. *Introduction to Ergodic Theory*. Trans. by V. Scheffer. Princeton: Princeton University Press.

Singer, J. David. 1986. "The Missiles of October — 1988," *Scandinavian Journal of Development Alternatives* 2 (No. 5): 5-13.

Singer, J. David. 1963. "The Return to Multilateral Diplomacy," *The Yale Review* 52: 36-48.

Singer, J. David. 1961. "The Level-of-Analysis Problem in International Relations," pp. 77-92 in Klaus Knorr and Sidney Verba (eds.), *The International System*. Princeton: Princeton University Press.

Singer, J. David, and Melvin Small. 1968. "Alliance Aggregation and the Onset of War: 1815-1945," pp. 247-86 in J. David Singer (ed.), *Quantitative International Politics: Insights and Evidence*. New York: Free Press.

Singer, J. David, and Melvin Small. 1966. "Formal Alliances, 1815-1939: A Quantitative Description," *Journal of Peace Research* 3 (January): 1-32.

Singer, J. David, and Richard J. Stoll (eds.). 1984. *Quantitative Indicators in World Politics: Timely Assurance and Early Warning*. New York: Praeger.

Singer, J. David, and Michael D. Wallace (eds.). 1979. *To Augur Well: Early Warning Indicators in World Politics*. Beverly Hills: Sage Publications.

Sivard, Ruth Leger. 1989. *World Military and Social Expenditures 1989*. Washington, DC: World Priorities.

Sivard, Ruth Leger. 1987. *World Military and Social Expenditures 1987-88*. Washington, DC: World Priorities.

Siverson, Randolph M., and Joel King. 1979. "Alliances and the Expansion of War," pp. 37-49 in J. David Singer and Michael D. Wallace (eds.), *To Anger Well*. Beverly Hills: Sage Publications.

Small, Melvin, and J. David Singer. 1982. *Resort to Arms*. Beverly Hills: Sage Publications.

Small, Melvin, and J. David Singer. 1979. "Conflict in the International System, 1816-1977: Historical Trends and Policy Futures," pp. 89-115 in Charles W. Kegley, Jr., and Patrick J. McGowan (eds.), *Challenges to America*. Beverly Hills: Sage Publications.

Smith, Gaddis. 1972. *Dean Acheson*. New York: Cooper Square.

Smith, R. Jeffrey. 1987. "Ex-Secretaries Urge Adherence to ABM Pact," *Washington Post* (March 10).

Smith, Ron P. 1980. "Military Expenditure and Investment in O.E.C.D. Countries 1954-1973," *Journal of Comparative Economics* 4 (March): 19-32.

Smith, Ron P. 1978. "Military Expenditure and Capitalism: A Reply," *Cambridge Journal of Economics* 2 (No. 3): 299-304.

Smith, Ron P. 1977. "Military Expenditure and Capitalism," *Cambridge Journal of Economics* 1 (No. 1): 61-76.

Smoke, Richard. 1984. *National Security and the Nuclear Dilemma*. Reading, MA: Addison-Wesley.

Snyder, Glenn H. 1984. "The Security Dilemma in Alliance Politics," *World Politics* 36 (July): 461-95.

Snyder, Jack. 1984. "Civil-Military Relations and the Cult of the Offensive, 1914- and 1984," *International Security* 9 (Summer): 108-46.

Soviet Committee for Security and Cooperation in Europe. 1985. *Helsinki: Ten Years Later*. Moscow: Progress Publishers.

Spanier, John. 1988. *American Foreign Policy Since World War II*, 11th ed. Washington, DC: Congressional Quarterly Press.

Spector, Leonard S. 1988. *The Undeclared Bomb*. Cambridge, MA: Ballinger.

Stackhouse, Max L. 1984. *Creeds, Society, and Human Rights*. Grand Rapids, MI: William B. Eerdmans.

Stalin, Joseph V. 1946. *Speech Delivered at a Meeting of Voters, February 9, 1946*. Washington, DC: Embassy of the U.S.S.R.

Starr, S. Frederick. 1988. "The Changing Nature of Change in the USSR," pp. 3-35 in Seweryn Bialer and Michael Mandelbaum (eds.), *Gorbachev's Russia and American Foreign Policy*. Boulder, CO: Westview Press.

Stein, Janice Gross. 1985. "Calculation, Miscalculation, and Conventional Deterrence I: The View from Cairo," pp. 34-59 in Robert Jervis, Richard Ned Lebow, and Janice Stein (eds.), *Psychology and Deterrence*. Baltimore: The Johns Hopkins University Press.

Stone, Lawrence. 1979. *The Family, Sex and Marriage in England, 1500-1800*. New York: Harper & Row.

Strange, Susan. 1987. "The Persistent Myth of Lost Hegemony," *International Organization* 41 (Fall): 551-74.

Strange, Susan. 1983. "Cave! Hic Dragones: A Critique of Regime Analysis," pp. 337-54 in Steven D. Krasner (ed.), *International Regimes*. Ithaca, NY: Cornell University Press.

Talbott, Strobe. 1988. *The Master of the Game: Paul Nitze and the Nuclear Peace*. New York: Knopf.

Taylor, A. J. P. 1971. *The Struggle for Mastery in Europe: 1848-1918*. Oxford: Oxford University Press.

Taylor, A. J. P. 1954. *The Struggle for Mastery in Europe: 1848-1918*. Oxford: Oxford University Press.

Thibaut, John W., and Harold H. Kelly. 1959. *The Social Psychology of Groups*. New York: Wiley.

Thompson, E. P. 1982. "Deterrence and 'Addiction,'" *The Yale Review* 72 (October): 1-18.

Thompson, Stanley L., and Stephen H. Schneider. 1986. "Nuclear Winter Reappraised," *Foreign Affairs* 64 (Summer): 981-1005.

Thompson, William R. 1988. *On Global War: Historical-Structural Approaches to World Politics*. Columbia: University of South Carolina Press.

Thompson, William R. 1983a. "Cycles, Capabilities and War: An Ecumenical View," in William R. Thompson (ed.), *Contending Approaches to World System Analysis*. Beverly Hills, CA: Sage Publications.

Thompson, William R. 1983b. "Succession Crises in the Global Political System: A Test of the Transition Model," in Albert Bergesen (ed.), *Crises in the World-System*. Beverly Hills, CA: Sage Publications.

Thompson, William R. 1983c. "Uneven Economic Growth, Systemic Challenges, and Global War," *International Studies Quarterly* 27 (September): 341-55.

Thompson, William R., and Karen A. Rasler. 1988. "War and Systemic Capability Reconstruction," *Journal of Conflict Resolution* 32 (June): 335-66.

Thompson, William R., Karen A. Rasler, and Richard P. Y. Li. 1980. "Systemic Interaction Opportunities and War Behavior," *International Interactions* 7 (No. 1): 57-85.

Thomson, David. 1966. *Europe Since Napoleon*, 2nd ed. New York: Knopf.

Thucydides. *The Peloponnesian War*. Trans. 1954 by R. Warner. New York: Penguin.

Tillema, Herbert K. 1989. "Foreign Overt Military Intervention in the Nuclear Age," *Journal of Peace Research* 26 (May): 179-95.

Tolstoy, Leo. 1957. *War and Peace*. Harmondsworth, Sussex: Penguin.

Toynbee, Arnold J. 1954. *A Study of History*. London: Oxford University Press.

Trooboff, Peter D. (ed.). 1975. *Law and Responsibility in Warfare*. Chapel Hill: The University of North Carolina Press.

Trudeau, Robert, and Lars Schoultz. 1986. "Guatemala," pp. 23-49 in Morris J. Blachman, William M. LeoGrande and Kenneth Sharpe (eds.), *Confronting Revolution: Security Through Diplomacy in Central America*. New York: Pantheon.

Truman, Harry S. 1955. *Memoirs*. Vol. I. Garden City, NY: Doubleday.

Tullberg, Ruth. 1986a. "World Military Expenditure," pp. 209-30 in *SIPRI Yearbook 1986*. Stockholm: Stockholm International Peace Research Institute.

Tullberg, Ruth. 1986b. "World Military Expenditure," *Bulletin of Peace Proposals* 17 (No. 3-4): 229-334.

Tullberg, Ruth. 1985. "World Military Expenditure," *SIPRI Yearbook 1985*. Stockholm: Stockholm International Peace Research Institute.

Twining, Nathan F. 1966. *Neither Liberty nor Safety: A Hard Look at U.S. Military Policy and Strategy*. New York: Holt, Rinehart, and Wilson.

United Nations. n.d. *Charter of the United Nations and Statute of the International Court of Justice*. New York: United Nations Press.

United States Department of State. 1928. *The General Pact for the Renunciation of War. Text of the Pact as Signed*. Washington, DC: U.S. Government Printing Office.

United States War Department. 1863. *Instructions for the Government of Armies of the United States in the Field*. New York: D. van Nostrand.

U.S. Senate Committee on Foreign Relations. 1987. *The ABM Treaty Interpretation Resolution*. Washington, DC: U.S. Government Printing Office.

Van Alstyne, Richard W. 1974. *The Rising American Empire*. New York: Norton.

Van Creveld, Martin. 1989. *Technology and War: From 2000 B.C. to the Present*. New York: Free Press.

Van Evera, Stephen. 1984. "The Cult of the Offensive and the Origins of the First World War," *International Security* 9 (Summer): 58-107.

Vasquez, John A. (Forthcoming). *The War Puzzle*. Cambridge: Cambridge University Press.

Vasquez, John A. 1987. "The Steps to War: Toward a Scientific Explanation of Correlates of War Findings," *World Politics* 40 (October): 108-45.

Vasquez, John A. 1983. *The Power of Power Politics: A Critique*. New Brunswick, NJ: Rutgers University Press.

Vattel, Emmerich de. 1916. *The Law of Nations; or, The Principles of Natural Law*. Washington, DC: Carnegie Institution.

Väyrynen, Raimo. 1983. "Economic Cycles, Power Transitions, Political Management and Wars Between Major Powers," *International Studies Quarterly* 27 (December): 389-418.

Vernadsky, G. 1953. *The Mongols and Russia*. London: Oxford University Press.

Wallace, Michael D. 1982. "Armaments and Escalation: Two Competing Hypotheses," *International Studies Quarterly* 26 (March): 37-51.

Wallace, Michael D. 1979. "Arms Races and Escalation: Some New Evidence," *Journal of Conflict Resolution* 23 (March): 3-16.

Wallace, Michael D. 1973. "Alliance Polarization, Cross-Cutting, and International War, 1815-1964," *Journal of Conflict Resolution* 17 (December): 83-111.

Wallace, Michael D. 1972. "Status, Formal Organization, and Arms Levels as Factors Leading to the Onset of War, 1820-1964," pp. 49-69 in Bruce M. Russett (ed.), *Peace, War, and Numbers*. Beverly Hills: Sage Publications.

Wallace, Michael D., Brian L. Crissey, and Linn I. Sennot. 1986. "Accidental Nuclear War: A Risk Assessment," *Journal of Peace Research* 23 (March): 9-27.

Wallensteen, Peter. 1984. "Universalism vs. Particularism: On the Limits of Major Power Order," *Journal of Peace Research* 21 (No. 3): 243-57.

Wallensteen, Peter. 1981. "Incompatibility, Confrontation, and War: Four Models and Three Historical Systems, 1816-1976," *Journal of Peace Research* 18 (No. 1): 57-90.

Wallersteen, Immanuel. 1984. *The Politics of the World Economy*. Cambridge: Cambridge University Press.

Walt, Stephen M. 1987. *The Origins of Alliances*. Ithaca, NY: Cornell University Press.

Waltz, Kenneth N. 1986. "Reflections on *Theory of International Politics:* A Response to My Critics," pp. 322-47 in Robert O. Keohane (ed.), *Neorealism and Its Critics*. New York: Columbia University Press.

Waltz, Kenneth N. 1981. *The Spread of Nuclear Weapons: More May Be Better*, Adelphi Papers, No. 171. London: International Institute of Strategic Studies.

Waltz, Kenneth N. 1979. *Theory of International Politics*. Reading, MA: Addison-Wesley.

Warner, Edward L., III, and David A. Ochmanek. 1989. *Next Moves: An Arms Control Agenda for the 1990s*. New York: Council on Foreign Relations.

Warnke, Paul C., Gerard C. Smith, Robert S. McNamara, and Spurgeon M. Keeny. 1986. "The Folly of Scrapping SALT," *Arms Control Today* 16 (May/June): 3-7.

Washington, George. 1790. "Annual State of the Union Address to Congress" (January 8), in Saxe Commins (ed.), *Basic Writings of George Washington*. New York: Random House.

Watkins, Frederick M. 1934. *The State as a Concept in Political Science*. New York: Harper and Bros.

Wayman, Frank. 1989. "Power Shifts and War, 1816-1980: An Empirical Analysis." Paper presented to the Annual Meeting of the International Studies Association, London, March 29-April 1.

Wayman, Frank. 1985. "Bipolarity, Multipolarity and the Threat of War," pp. 115-44 in Alan Ned Sabrosky (ed.), *Polarity and War*. Boulder, CO: Westview.

Weart, Spencer. 1988. *Nuclear Fear: A History of Images*. Cambridge, MA: Harvard University Press.

Weede, Erich. 1983. "Extended Deterrence by Superpower Alliance," *Journal of Conflict Resolution* 27 (June): 231-54.

Weede, Erich. 1980. "Arms Races and Escalation: Some Persisting Doubts," *Journal of Conflict Resolution* 24 (June): 285-87.

Weede, Erich. 1975. "World Order in the Fifties and Sixties: Dependence, Deterrence, and Limited Peace." *Papers* of the Peace Science Society (International), 24: 49-80.

Weinstein, Franklin B. 1969. "The Concept of Commitment in International Relations," *Journal of Conflict Resolution* 13 (March) 39-56.

Weltman, John J. 1974. "On the Obsolescence of War," *International Studies Quarterly* 18 (December): 395-416.

Wendt, Alexander E. 1987. "The Agent-Structure Problem in International Relations Theory," *International Organization* 41 (Summer): 335-70.

Westerfield, H. Bradford (ed.). 1959. *The Arms Race and Current Soviet Doctrine*. New Haven: Yale University Press.

Westing, Arthur. 1982. "War as a Human Endeavor: The High Fatality Wars of the Twentieth Century," *Journal of Peace Research* 19 (No. 3): 261-70.

White, Ralph K. 1984. *Fearful Warriors: A Psychological Profile of U.S.-Soviet Relations*. New York: Free Press.

Wieseltier, Leon. 1983. *Nuclear War, Nuclear Peace: The Sensible Argument About the Greatest Peril of Our Age*. New York: Holt, Rinehart.

Wildavsky, Aaron. 1989. "Serious Talk About the Nuclear Era," *Wall Street Journal* (March 16): A16.

Williams, Phil. 1976. *Crisis Management: Confrontation and Diplomacy in the Nuclear Age*. New York: Wiley.

Wohlstetter, Albert. 1985. "Between an Unfree World and None: Increasing Our Choices," *Foreign Affairs* 63 (Summer): 962-94.

Wolf, John B. 1968. *Louis XIV*. New York: W. W. Norton.

Wolfe, Alan. 1984. *The Rise and Fall of the Soviet Threat*. Boston: South End Press.

Wolfe, Thomas W. 1970. *Soviet Power and Europe, 1945-1970*. Baltimore: The Johns Hopkins Press.

Wolfers, Arnold. 1968. "Alliances," pp. 268-71 in David L. Sills (ed.), *International Encyclopedia of the Social Sciences*. New York: Macmillan.

Wolfers, Arnold. 1952. " 'National Security' as an Ambiguous Symbol," *Political Science Quarterly* 67 (December): 481-502.

World Bank. 1988. *World Development Report*. New York: Oxford University Press.

World Commission on Environment and Development. 1987. *Our Common Future*. New York: Oxford University Press.

World Press Review. 1989. "Viewpoints: The Soviet Republics," *World Press Review* (January 10).

Wright, Quincy. 1965. *A Study of War*, 2nd ed. Chicago: University of Chicago Press.

Yergin, Daniel. 1977. *Shattered Peace*. Boston: Houghton-Mifflin.

Zagare, Frank C. 1989. "Rationality and Deterrence," mimeo.

Zhdanov, Andrei. 1947. *The International Situation*. Moscow: Foreign Languages Publishing House.

Index